TIME ZONES

TEACHER'S BOOK | THIRD EDITION

CARMELLA LIESKE
NICHOLAS BEARE
IAN PURDON
TIM COLLINS
MARY JANE MAPLES
ANDREW BOON

Australia • Brazil • Mexico • Singapore • United Kingdom • United States

National Geographic Learning,
a Cengage Company

Time Zones Teacher's Book 1 Third Edition

Carmella Lieske, Nicholas Beare, Ian Purdon,
Tim Collins, Mary Jane Maples, and Andrew Boon

Publisher: Andrew Robinson

Managing Editor: Derek Mackrell

Additional Editorial Support: Jacqueline Eu

Director of Global Marketing: Ian Martin

Senior Product Marketing Manager: Anders Bylund

Heads of Regional Marketing:
Charlotte Ellis (Europe, Middle East and Africa)
Kiel Hamm (Asia)
Irina Pereyra (Latin America)

Senior Production Controller: Tan Jin Hock

Associate Media Researcher: Jeffrey Millies

Senior Designer: Lisa Trager

Operations Support: Rebecca G. Barbush,
Hayley Chwazik-Gee

Manufacturing Planner: Mary Beth Hennebury

Composition: Symmetry Creative Productions, Inc.

ISBN-13: 978-0-357-42644-9

National Geographic Learning
200 Pier 4 Boulevard
Boston, MA 02210
USA

Locate your local office at **international.cengage.com/region**

Visit National Geographic Learning online at **ELTNGL.com**
Visit our corporate website at **www.cengage.com**

Printed in China
Print Number: 04 Print Year: 2023

CONTENTS

SCOPE AND **SEQUENCE**

UNIT	FUNCTIONS	GRAMMAR	VOCABULARY	PRONUNCIATION	READ, WRITE, & WATCH
1 WHAT'S YOUR FAVORITE VIDEO GAME?					PAGE 6
	Talking about popular movies, singers, video games, etc. **Real English:** *Really?*	***Wh-* questions:** *what* and *who* *What's his favorite movie?* *Who's her favorite singer?* *What's your favorite video game?*	People Sports Games Parts of speech: nouns, verbs, adjectives	Contractions: *What's/Who's*	**Reading:** My Favorite Things **Writing:** Self-introduction **Video:** What's Your Favorite?
2 THIS PLACE IS AMAZING!					PAGE 18
	Describing places **Real English:** *Wow!*	**Using *be* and adjectives:** *The buildings are amazing.* *They're very new.* *Is the street long?*	Places Adjectives Conjunctions: *and, but*	Long and short *i* sounds	**Reading:** Amazing Places **Writing:** Poster **Video:** Ha Long Bay
3 WHERE'S THE LION?					PAGE 30
	Talking about location of things Describing animals on land and in the water **Real English:** *Look!*	**Asking for quantity and location:** *The bears are near the tree.* *How many animals are there?* *Where are the monkeys?* **Prepositions:** *in, on, under, in front of, behind, next to*	Animals Adjectives Prepositional phrases: *on the right, on the left, in the middle*	*There are* and *They're*	**Reading:** Strange Animals **Writing:** Photo description **Video:** Ocean Oddities
4 THIS IS MY FAMILY					PAGE 42
	Describing family members Talking about family activities **Real English:** *Yeah!*	**Using *have*:** *She has a brother.* *I have two sisters.* *They don't have any brothers.* *Do they have any cousins?*	Family members and relationships Prefix: *great-*	Reduction: *do* and *does*	**Reading:** From Japan to Hawaii **Writing:** Email **Video:** The Bhatti Family
5 I LIKE FRUIT!					PAGE 54
	Expressing likes and dislikes Talking about one's favorite food **Real English:** *Me, too.*	**Using *like*:** *I like fruit.* *I don't like vegetables.* *She doesn't like milk.* *Do you like juice?*	Food and drinks Collocations with *food*	Final *s* sounds	**Reading:** Foodscapes **Writing:** Descriptive paragraph **Video:** Our Favorite Food
6 WHAT TIME DOES CLASS START?					PAGE 66
	Talking about routines and school subjects **Real English:** *Oh, no!*	**Simple present:** *I always get up at 7 o'clock.* *He does homework in the afternoon.* *What time do you get up?* **Adverbs of frequency:** *always, usually, often, sometimes, never*	Phrasal verbs School subjects Collocations with *school*	Long and short *u* sounds	**Reading:** Kakenya's Dream **Writing:** Email **Video:** Kakenya's School

Welcome to the updated and expanded edition of *Time Zones*.

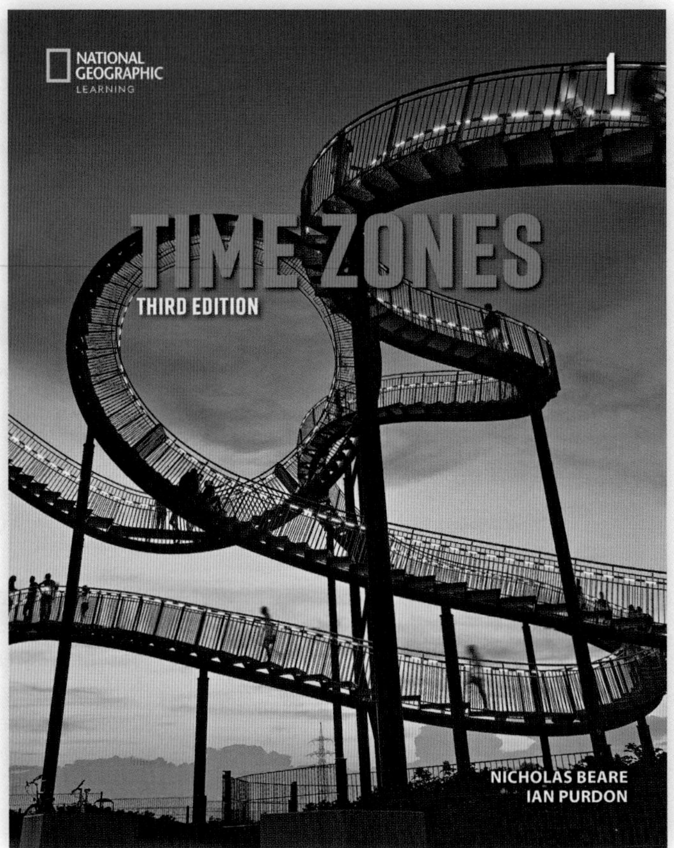

WHAT IS *TIME ZONES*?

Time Zones is a five-level, four-skills series that combines a communicative approach to learning English with up-to-date National Geographic content. It is designed to be engaging for all young students, from pre-teens to young adults.

HOW IS THE BOOK ORGANIZED?

Time Zones follows a familiar grammatical syllabus, with simple structures introduced in the lower levels, followed by increasingly complex structures in later levels. However, *Time Zones* also follows a rich, thematic content syllabus. Real-world content is used as a springboard for introducing the language that students need to become effective communicators in English.

As with the grammatical syllabus, *Time Zones* teaches the highest-frequency vocabulary in the earlier stages of the course, with relatively lower-frequency vocabulary appearing only in the higher levels of the series. Along the way, more specialized vocabulary is occasionally introduced so that students can develop a meaningful understanding of it, as well as be able to talk about the real world topics and issues introduced in *Time Zones*. Key vocabulary is recycled systematically throughout the series.

The vocabulary and grammar is well integrated throughout the series. For example, students might learn the grammatical structure *can* to talk about abilities in a unit on animals—learning to talk about what animals can and can't do—before going on to personalize the language and talk about themselves and their own abilities.

Ideally, the units of *Time Zones* will be taught in order and no units will be skipped. However, if your students have some background in English, you may wish to skip the **Starter Level**, which consolidates some of the core English that young students might have already encountered if they have been exposed to English learning before.

WHAT ARE THE PRINCIPLES BEHIND THE SERIES?

1. ENGLISH FOR INTERNATIONAL COMMUNICATION

Students today are living in an increasingly globalized world, with English continuing to become an important lingua franca. The distinction between "native" and "non-native" speakers of English is becoming even less distinct than in the past. In fact, the majority of communication in English is between two so-called "non-native" English speakers. While *Time Zones* uses standard American English as its basis—in terms of lexis and grammar—it also acknowledges, and embraces, the fact that English is a global language.

Time Zones positions students to be effective communicators in English in a world where English is a common means of international communication. Because of this, the *Time Zones* audio program includes speakers from other countries with a range of real-world accents. This allows students to become comfortable listening to speakers from around the world and encourages them to speak themselves. Additionally, this emphasis on global accents better prepares students for common international exams, which increasingly focus on various international English accents.

2. AUTHENTIC, REAL-WORLD CONTENT

Time Zones is built on the belief that authentic, real-world content is more motivating and more relevant to students than content that is contrived or artificial. Stories, photographs, and video from National Geographic and other real sources tap into student curiosity, motivate them to learn about the world, and get students talking in English as early in their studies as possible.

At the same time, this focus on authenticity provides students with many opportunities for personalization. Throughout the program, students apply the language they learn as they develop the ability to talk about the world, as well as about themselves and their own lives. For example, students may learn about extreme weather conditions—the coldest place on Earth—but will also be able to use this language to talk about themselves and their own everyday experiences.

3. GLOBAL CITIZENSHIP AND VALUES

Time Zones encourages students to think deeply about the values that all global citizens share. Throughout reading, listening, and video lessons, students of *Time Zones* learn about the world around them and its many varied cultures, as well as about global issues and events affecting everyone—including historical discoveries, scientific developments, and the health of the environment and the planet's inhabitants. Real stories about National Geographic Explorers and real-life global citizens prompt students to consider the effects of their own thoughts, beliefs, and actions on the whole world, and act as a springboard for short projects that go beyond the textbook.

4. ESSENTIAL SKILLS FOR SUCCESS

Students need more than strong communication skills to be successful. *Time Zones* recognizes that students need to be able to understand information presented in different ways—text, audio, video, charts, maps, and graphs—and be able to communicate about them in different settings and contexts. They also need to be able to work collaboratively in pairs and in group settings. Explicit and frequent practice in higher-order thinking skills are critical to future success in the classroom. Students using *Time Zones* will be exposed to all of these skills weaved into each unit of the program.

Time Zones also acknowledges that many students today are balancing long-term communication goals with the immediate need for exam preparation. Throughout the program, students are exposed to task types commonly found on international exams. This helps students practice test-taking strategies and builds their confidence before taking these high-stakes exams.

WHAT'S NEW IN *TIME ZONES*, THIRD EDITION?

- Two videos in every unit help students see more of the world and make personal connections with the unit theme.
- More grammar and vocabulary activities in each unit deliver more guided language practice for in-class use.
- Clear unit goals and review activities encourage learner independence and self-assessment.
- Audio recordings with a range of international accents expose learners to natural English.
- Updated technology resources make *Time Zones* easy to use in and out of the classroom.
- Different activities in the Workbook and Online Practice offer more practice opportunities out of the classroom.
- An expanded Starter Combo level with six complete units is ideal for short courses for true beginners.

TAKE A TOUR OF *TIME ZONES* TEACHER'S BOOK

The Teacher's Book of *Time Zones* is full of suggestions on how to get the most out of your class time. The following pages will help you understand the vast resources at your disposal. (Don't forget to read about the other components on page xix.)

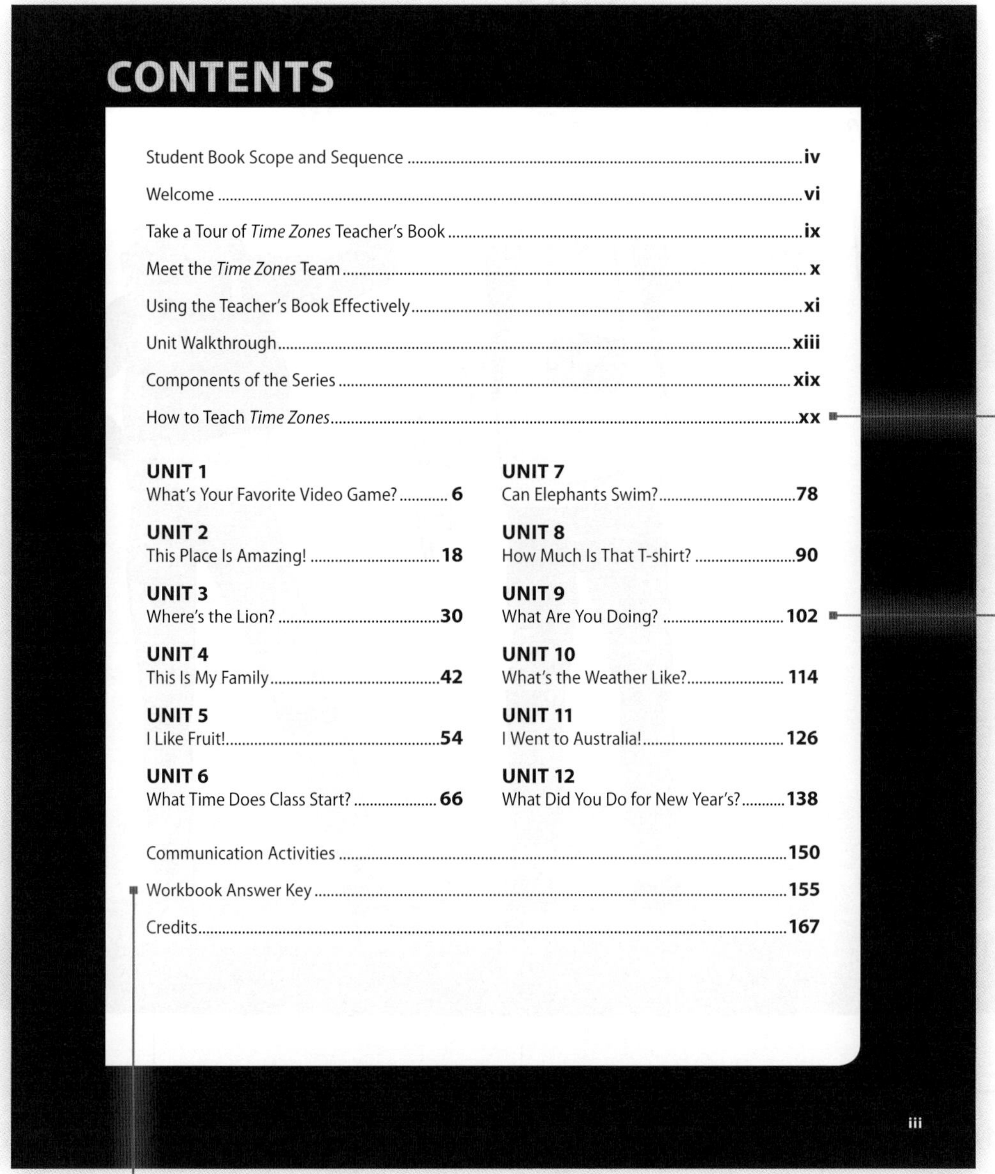

CONTENTS

iii

The **How to Teach Time Zones** section introduces techniques and tips to help you teach *Time Zones* more effectively.

Every level of *Time Zones* is divided into **12 units**. Each twelve-page unit is based on a particular theme, allowing students to learn about the world around them as they develop language skills.

The **Workbook** is an effective way for students to practice the language learned in *Time Zones*. Page xix gives more information about the Workbook. Answer keys for all of the Workbook activities are on pages 155–166.

MEET THE *TIME ZONES* TEAM

This is **Maya Santos** from Rio de Janeiro, in Brazil. She's into music, singing, and shopping.

This is **Ming Chen** from Shanghai, in China. He likes sports and animals.

This is **Stig Andersson** from Stockholm, in Sweden. He loves food, photography, and sports.

This is **Nadine Barnard** from Cape Town, in South Africa. She loves nature, movies, and music.

USING THE TEACHER'S BOOK EFFECTIVELY

The **reduced Student's Book pages** show answers for each activity. "Answers will vary." is used when there is no single correct answer for a particular question or activity.

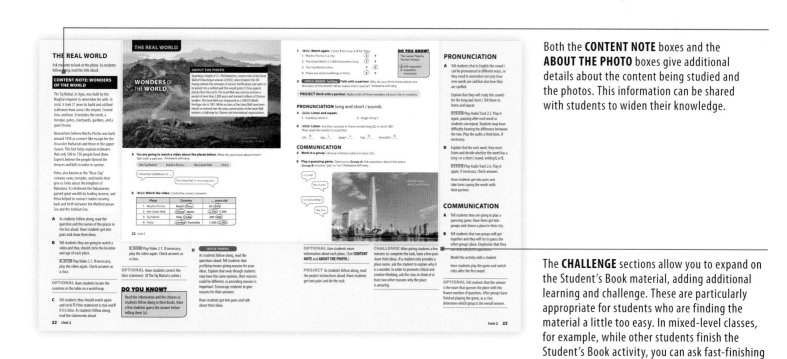

The **CONTENT AREA** box summarizes key vocabulary and the grammar point in the unit. It also gives optional suggestions for things you may want to prepare before class. **Other useful vocabulary** is related to the topic of the unit and is particularly helpful for students who are slightly more advanced and need a further challenge.

The **End of Unit Project** section provides a suggestion for a bigger project that students can do either inside or outside of class. The project extends and personalizes both the content and the language from the unit.

The **TEACHING NOTE** boxes contain tips for teachers, additional activity explanations, and explanations of language acquisition concepts. These notes are in easy-to-understand language so that they can be used to explain the concepts to students.

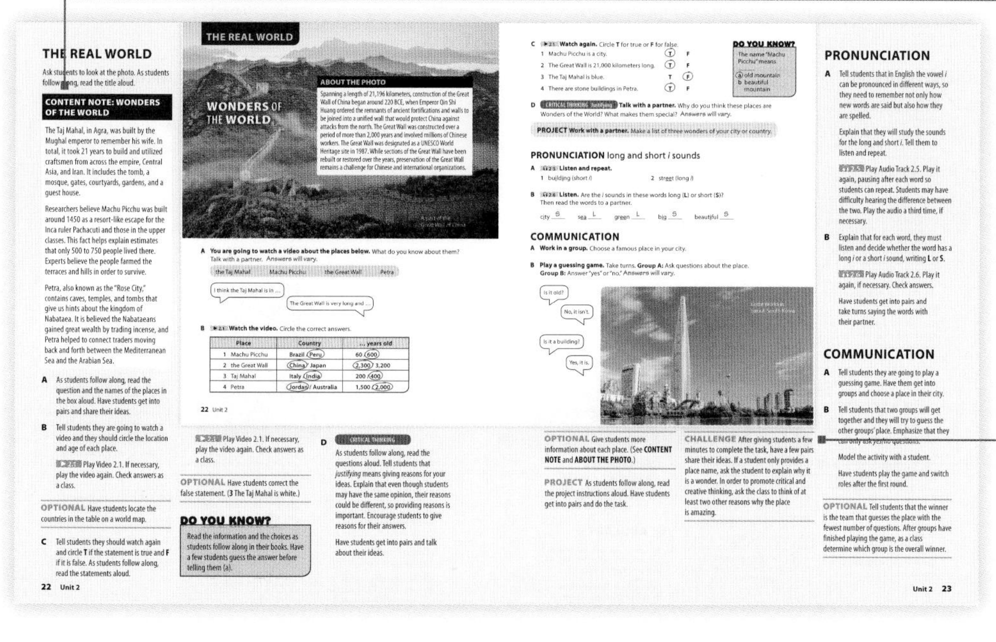

Both the **CONTENT NOTE** boxes and the **ABOUT THE PHOTO** boxes give additional details about the content being studied and the photos. This information can be shared with students to widen their knowledge.

The **CHALLENGE** sections allow you to expand on the Student's Book material, adding additional learning and challenge. These are particularly appropriate for students who are finding the material a little too easy. In mixed-level classes, for example, while other students finish the Student's Book activity, you can ask fast-finishing pairs and groups to work on these activities.

Three sections give suggestions for differentiated instruction. **SUPPORT** sections provide ideas to make the activities more accessible for lower-level students. **CHALLENGE** sections include ways to expand the learning or make them more difficult (for stronger students), and **OPTIONAL** sections expand the activities, providing more practice.

The **OPTIONAL** sections suggest additional activities to practice the Student's Book material. You can use these to provide your students with additional practice before moving on to new material or as review as you progress through the unit.

Additional Activities to Use with the Reading suggest various activities to expand the content, including reinforcing vocabulary, increasing students' awareness of the way vocabulary is used, expanding on the grammar used in the reading, personalizing the material, and practicing the unit's pronunciation point. You can select the activities that best meet your students' needs and your time constraints.

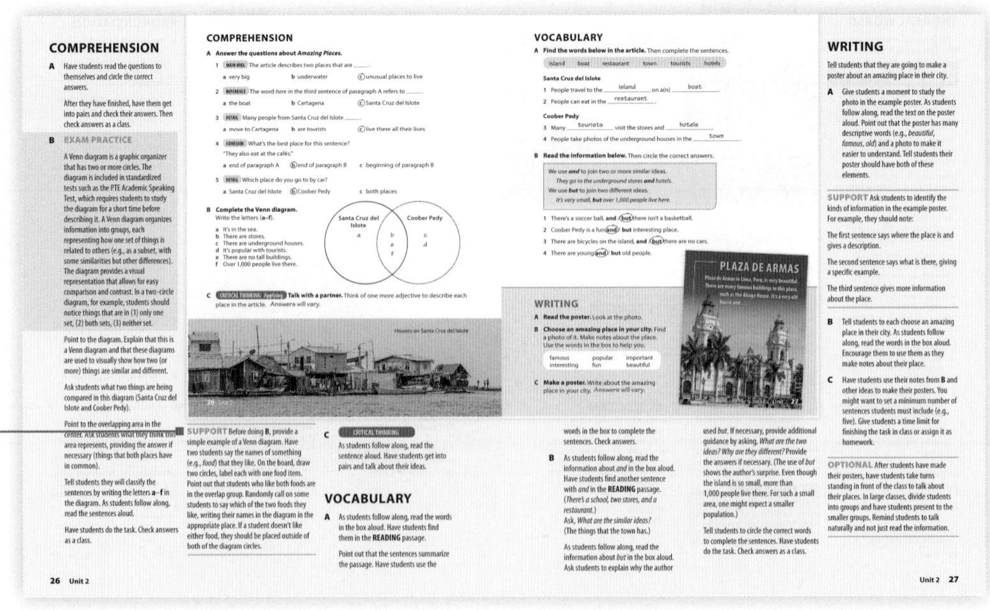

The **SUPPORT** sections provide suggestions for further explanation for students who are finding the Student's Book material a little challenging. These additional procedures help students review previously studied material and explore Student's Book material in more detail. These sections also provide additional practice of the language.

UNIT WALKTHROUGH

Time Zones, Third Edition uses amazing photography, updated videos, and inspiring stories of global citizens to encourage teenage learners to explore the world in English.

Through teacher-tested language lessons, carefully scaffolded practice activities, and teaching resources that keep classrooms engaged, *Time Zones*, Third Edition delivers the skills and language that learners need for wherever they're going next.

High-interest photography introduces the unit topic and target vocabulary, stimulates students' interest, and sparks classroom discussion.

Time Zones features real-world information from **four content areas**: People and Places, History and Culture, the Natural World, and Science and Technology.

2
THIS PLACE IS
AMAZING!
Copacabana Beach is a popular place in Rio de Janeiro, Brazil.
PREVIEW
A 2.1 Match the places with the pictures. Then listen and check your answers.
sea beach building store city street
OPEN
1 2 3 4 5 6
18
B Talk with a partner. Look at the photo. Which places from A do you see?
C Talk with a partner. Ask about their favorite places.
PEOPLE AND PLACES
UNIT GOALS
• talk about places in your city
• use language for describing places
• learn about amazing places around the world
19

Each **Preview** section includes a listening activity that provides authentic speaking models so students can improve their pronunciation and general communication skills.

The **Unit Goals** box tells students what they are going to learn in the unit. This can be particularly helpful for students who might otherwise focus on the details without seeing how they are related to one another.

The unit's target language is introduced through an entertaining conversation featuring the *Time Zones* team. Students can repeat the conversation, varying vocabulary and the speaker parts, to build fluency and confidence.

The **Real English** box highlights a functional phrase or discourse marker from the dialog that is commonly spoken by fluent speakers of English.

The **Language Focus** activities practice and reinforce the unit's grammar and language, moving from controlled and contextualized practice to freer practice.

Most **Language Focus** sections have a listening component, allowing students to become more comfortable with the language before producing it.

LANGUAGE FOCUS

A 2.2 **Listen and read.** Do Stig and Nadine like Amsterdam? Then repeat the conversation and replace the words in **bold**.

REAL ENGLISH Wow!

Stig: It's my first time in Amsterdam. What a **big** city! (**beautiful** / **clean**)

Nadine: It's my first time here, too. Look at those buildings, Stig!

Stig: They're houses. They're **amazing**. (**famous** / **beautiful**)

Nadine: Yes, they are. And they're **colorful**. (**old** / **small**)

Stig: There's another famous place in Amsterdam—the NEMO Science Museum.

Nadine: Wow! The design of the building is **interesting**. (**beautiful** / **great**)

Stig: The place is very popular with tourists.

Nadine: We're tourists, too! Let's go there. I want to take photos.

B 2.3 **Look at the chart.** Then circle the correct answers below.

DESCRIBING PLACES (USING *BE* AND ADJECTIVES)		
This place **is famous**. / The buildings **are amazing**. They**'re** very **new**. They**'re not old**. / They **aren't old**.		They're = They are They're not = They are not aren't = are not isn't = is not
Is the street **long**?	**Yes**, it **is**. **No**, it **isn't** / it**'s not**.	
Are the houses **big**?	**Yes**, they **are**. **No**, they **aren't** / they**'re not**.	

1 We use *are* with **one thing** / **more than one thing**.

2 We add *not* to make a **question** / **negative sentence**.

3 We use *Is*/*Are* at the beginning of a **question** / **sentence**.

20 Unit 2

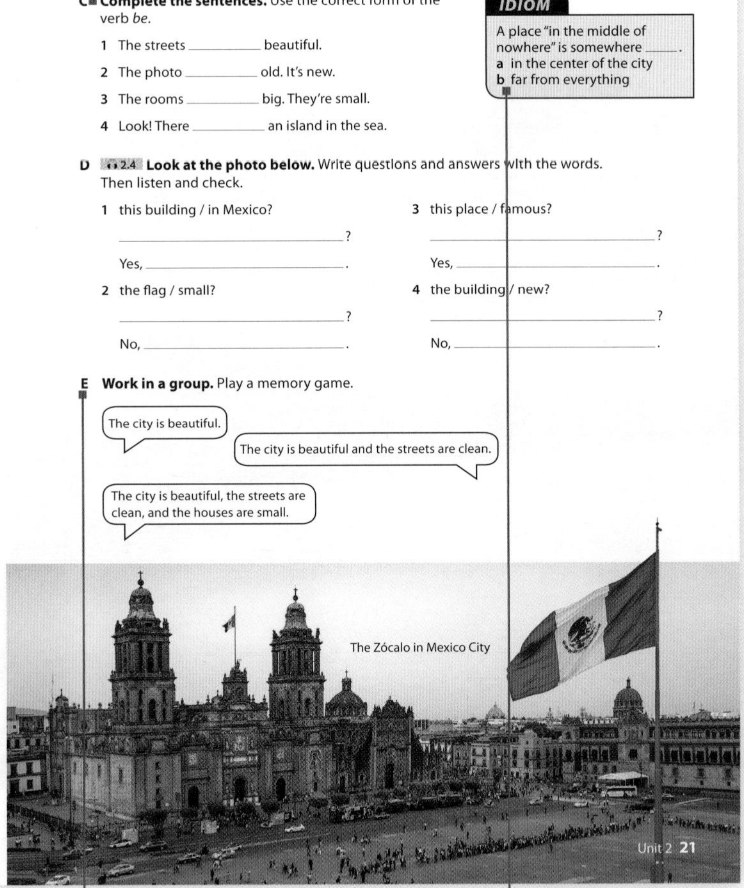

C **Complete the sentences.** Use the correct form of the verb *be*.

1 The streets ________ beautiful.

2 The photo ________ old. It's new.

3 The rooms ________ big. They're small.

4 Look! There ________ an island in the sea.

IDIOM

A place "in the middle of nowhere" is somewhere ________.
a in the center of the city
b far from everything

D 2.4 **Look at the photo below.** Write questions and answers with the words. Then listen and check.

1 this building / in Mexico?
________?
Yes, ________.

2 the flag / small?
________?
No, ________.

3 this place / famous?
________?
Yes, ________.

4 the building / new?
________?
No, ________.

E **Work in a group.** Play a memory game.

The city is beautiful.

The city is beautiful and the streets are clean.

The city is beautiful, the streets are clean, and the houses are small.

The Zócalo in Mexico City

Unit 2 21

The final activity in each Language Focus is an open-ended communicative activity, such as a game, role-play, or survey.

The **Idiom** box presents an idiom related to the unit topic. The idioms are all commonly used expressions and understanding them will increase students' communicative ability.

The Real World uses a short video to introduce students to more general knowledge about the world through personal stories and experiences of National Geographic Explorers, recent discoveries and research, scientific experiments, and more.

The **Pronunciation** section helps to build student confidence, using a listen-notice-repeat sequence. This section introduces and practices features of spoken English that are appropriate to students at each level. The pronunciation syllabus is topic-related and focuses on the unit's target language.

Project suggestions encourage students to personalize what they've learned in the lesson and go beyond the book to do research online, in their neighborhood, or in the classroom.

Do You Know? quizzes provide students with fun, real-world facts related to the content.

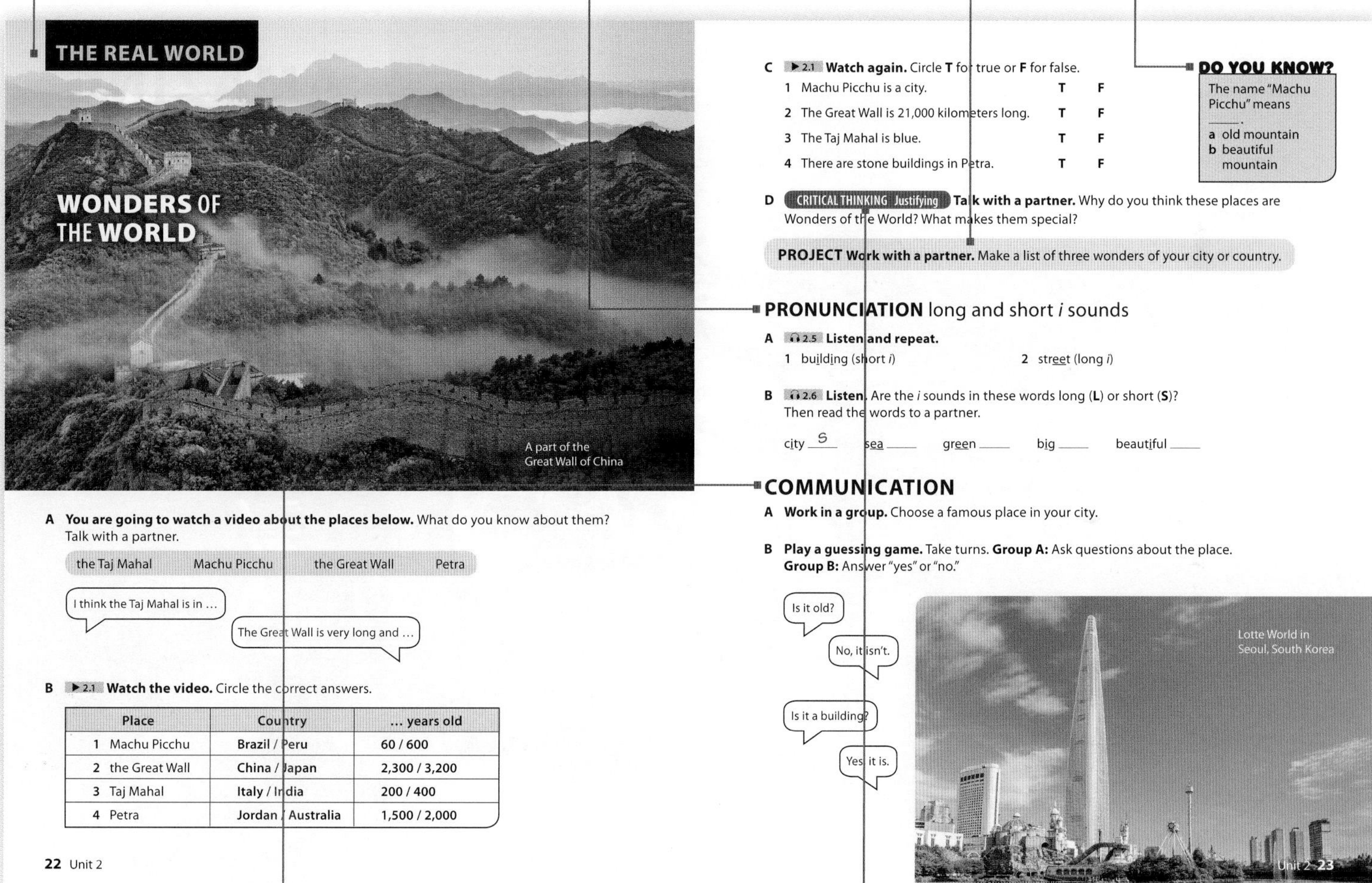

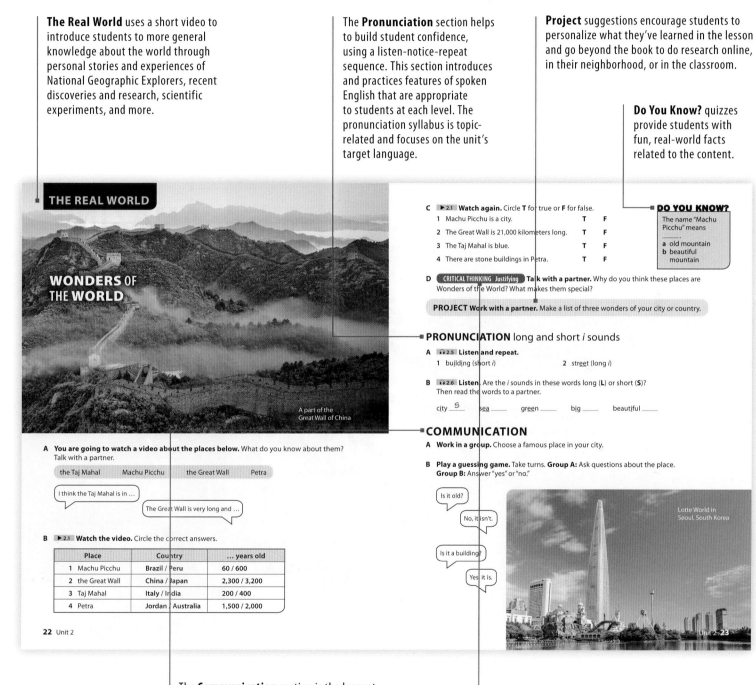

THE REAL WORLD

WONDERS OF THE WORLD

A part of the Great Wall of China

A **You are going to watch a video about the places below.** What do you know about them? Talk with a partner.

the Taj Mahal | Machu Picchu | the Great Wall | Petra

I think the Taj Mahal is in …

The Great Wall is very long and …

B ▶ 2.1 **Watch the video.** Circle the correct answers.

Place	Country	… years old
1 Machu Picchu	Brazil / Peru	60 / 600
2 the Great Wall	China / Japan	2,300 / 3,200
3 Taj Mahal	Italy / India	200 / 400
4 Petra	Jordan / Australia	1,500 / 2,000

22 Unit 2

C ▶ 2.1 **Watch again.** Circle **T** for true or **F** for false.

1 Machu Picchu is a city. **T** **F**
2 The Great Wall is 21,000 kilometers long. **T** **F**
3 The Taj Mahal is blue. **T** **F**
4 There are stone buildings in Petra. **T** **F**

DO YOU KNOW?
The name "Machu Picchu" means ______.
a old mountain
b beautiful mountain

D CRITICAL THINKING Justifying **Talk with a partner.** Why do you think these places are Wonders of the World? What makes them special?

PROJECT **Work with a partner.** Make a list of three wonders of your city or country.

PRONUNCIATION long and short *i* sounds

A 2.5 **Listen and repeat.**
1 building (short *i*) 2 street (long *i*)

B 2.6 **Listen.** Are the *i* sounds in these words long (**L**) or short (**S**)? Then read the words to a partner.

city S sea ____ green ____ big ____ beautiful ____

COMMUNICATION

A **Work in a group.** Choose a famous place in your city.

B **Play a guessing game.** Take turns. **Group A:** Ask questions about the place. **Group B:** Answer "yes" or "no."

Is it old?
No, it isn't.
Is it a building?
Yes, it is.

Lotte World in Seoul, South Korea

Unit 2 23

The **Communication** section is the longest communicative task of the unit. These pair or group activities allow students to use the language they have learned in a less structured speaking activity. These sections include activities such as games, surveys, information gap activities, and questionnaires.

Critical Thinking questions provide an opportunity for students to engage critically with the article by asking and answering questions related to the content.

The **Reading** section starts with a photograph and a pre-reading activity to engage students, introduce the topic, and activate prior knowledge and language. Students also practice skimming, scanning, prediction, and other skills that are essential for effective reading.

Audio recordings of each passage help students practice their listening, understand the pronunciation of new words, and study natural rhythm and intonation.

High-interest readings feature real-world information that has been adapted from National Geographic or other reliable sources. The reading passage introduces new vocabulary; however, the length and language level of each passage is carefully graded and controlled to ensure student understanding with little or no teacher support.

Activity A of the Comprehension section features multiple-choice questions to check students' basic comprehension. The multiple-choice questions follow the same format as many common international exams. Question types include main idea, purpose, detail, inference, cohesion, vocabulary, and understanding reference words.

Activity A of the Vocabulary section gives students more practice with target lexicon from the Reading passage.

Activity B explains and practices real-world, commonly used expressions such as phrasal verbs, collocations, and synonyms.

COMPREHENSION

A Answer the questions about *Amazing Places.*

1 MAIN IDEA The article describes two places that are ___.
a very big b underwater c unusual places to live

2 REFERENCE The word *here* in the third sentence of paragraph A refers to ___.
a the boat b Cartagena c Santa Cruz del Islote

3 DETAIL Many people from Santa Cruz del Islote ___.
a move to Cartagena b are tourists c live there all their lives

4 COHESION What's the best place for this sentence?
"They also eat at the cafés."
a end of paragraph A b end of paragraph B c beginning of paragraph B

5 DETAIL Which place do you go to by car?
a Santa Cruz del Islote b Coober Pedy c both places

B Complete the Venn diagram. Write the letters (**a–f**).

a It's in the sea.
b There are stores.
c There are underground houses.
d It's popular with tourists.
e There are no tall buildings.
f Over 1,000 people live there.

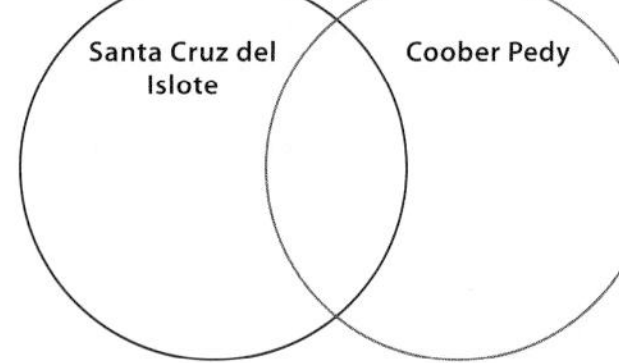

C CRITICAL THINKING Applying **Talk with a partner.** Think of one more adjective to describe each place in the article.

Houses on Santa Cruz del Islote

VOCABULARY

A Find the words below in the article. Then complete the sentences.

island boat restaurant town tourists hotels

Santa Cruz del Islote
1 People travel to the ___ on a(n) ___.
2 People can eat in the ___.

Coober Pedy
3 Many ___ visit the stores and ___.
4 People take photos of the underground houses in the ___.

B Read the information below. Then circle the correct answers.

> We use ***and*** to join two or more similar ideas.
> *They go to the underground stores **and** hotels.*
> We use ***but*** to join two different ideas.
> *It's very small, **but** over 1,000 people live here.*

1 There's a soccer ball, **and** / **but** there isn't a basketball.
2 Coober Pedy is a fun **and** / **but** interesting place.
3 There are bicycles on the island, **and** / **but** there are no cars.
4 There are young **and** / **but** old people.

WRITING

A Read the poster. Look at the photo.

B Choose an amazing place in your city. Find a photo of it. Make notes about the place. Use the words in the box to help you.

famous popular important interesting fun beautiful

C Make a poster. Write about the amazing place in your city.

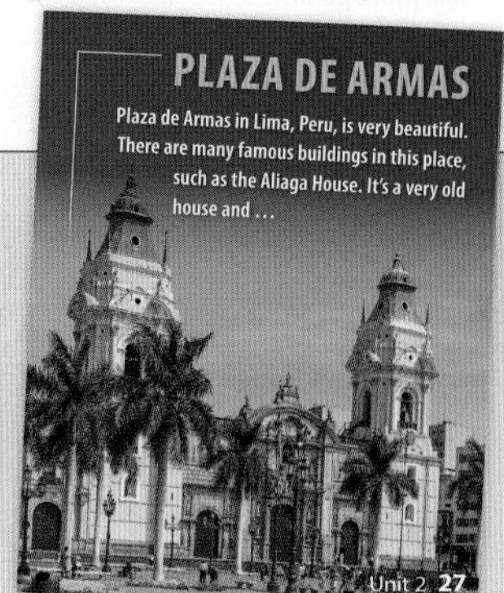

PLAZA DE ARMAS
Plaza de Armas in Lima, Peru, is very beautiful. There are many famous buildings in this place, such as the Aliaga House. It's a very old house and ...

Activity B contains graphic organizers, such as charts, word webs, and diagrams. These help students develop their critical thinking skills and help students gain a deeper understanding of the reading passage.

In the **Writing** section, students demonstrate their newly gained language skills through a variety of writing tasks, including writing emails, blog posts, and reports. A clear model is provided for each writing activity to support students as they create their own piece of personalized writing.

Each unit includes a short **Video** related to the unit theme. The video is scripted to be level appropriate and recycle the unit's target language.

The **Before You Watch** section is a pre-watching task that introduces the topic, engages students, and activate prior knowledge.

The **While You Watch** section helps students understand the video. These activities can be used to assess students' understanding and determine how many times to show the video.

The **Review** page allows students to show that they understand the grammar and main vocabulary that was introduced in the unit.

VIDEO

ABOUT THE VIDEO Ha Long Bay is a famous place in Vietnam.

HA LONG BAY

Before You Watch

Look at the photo. What do you think you can see at Ha Long Bay?

☐ tourists ☐ beaches ☐ boats ☐ tall buildings ☐ rocks

While You Watch

A ▶ 2.2 **Watch the video.** Check (✓) the information you hear.

☐ the number of islands
☐ island names
☐ famous food
☐ things to do on the islands
☐ where the hotels are

B ▶ 2.2 **Watch again.** Circle the correct answers.

1 There are **1,600** / **16,000** islands in Ha Long Bay.
2 Tourists stay on the **small** / **big** islands.
3 The shapes of the **rocks** / **buildings** in Ha Long Bay are interesting.
4 Tourists go to the islands by **car** / **boat**.

After You Watch

Talk with a partner. Do you know any other amazing places like Ha Long Bay? What are they like?

The islands in Ha Long Bay

28 Unit 2

REVIEW

A Complete the words for places.

1 s e __
2 b u __ __ __ __ __ g
3 s t __ __ e
4 c __ __ y
5 b __ a __ __
6 s t __ __ __ __ t

B Write sentences and questions with *is* or *are*. Use the words below.

1 the sea / blue — The sea is blue.
2 the boats / not small ______
3 the cities / big? ______
4 the island / beautiful? ______
5 the restaurants / popular ______
6 the beach / not clean ______

C Complete the sentences. Use *and* or *but*.

1 This is a clean ______ beautiful city.
2 There's a school in my town, ______ there isn't a park.
3 Ha Long Bay is a beautiful ______ amazing place.
4 There are many islands, ______ no one lives on them.
5 There are houses, stores, ______ restaurants on this street.

SELF CHECK Now I can ...

☐ talk about places in my city
☐ use language for describing places
☐ talk about amazing places around the world

Unit 2 29

The **After You Watch** activities allow students to respond to the video by analyzing and personalizing what they've learned.

Self Check *I can* statements allow students to assess their own learning and helps teachers evaluate learner confidence.

WORKBOOK

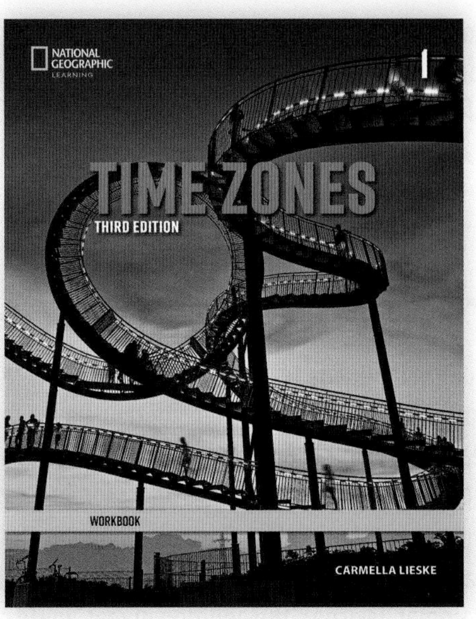

Reinforce Student's Book lessons with additional practice in the print Workbook. You may use the Workbook as additional class practice or set it as homework.

ONLINE PRACTICE ON THE SPARK PLATFORM

Keep students engaged with mobile-responsive Online Practice, including audio, video, and practice activities. Manage your classroom and track students' Online Practice progress in the Course Gradebook.

STUDENT'S EBOOK

Access the Student's eBook on the Spark platform, with embedded audio and video.

CLASSROOM PRESENTATION TOOL

Enrich your classroom lessons with interactive Student's Book and Workbook pages with embedded audio, video, and interactive activities on the Classroom Presentation Tool, available on the Spark platform.

EXAMVIEW® ASSESSMENT SUITE

Track learner progress with exam questions for every unit, plus mid-year and end-of-year tests.

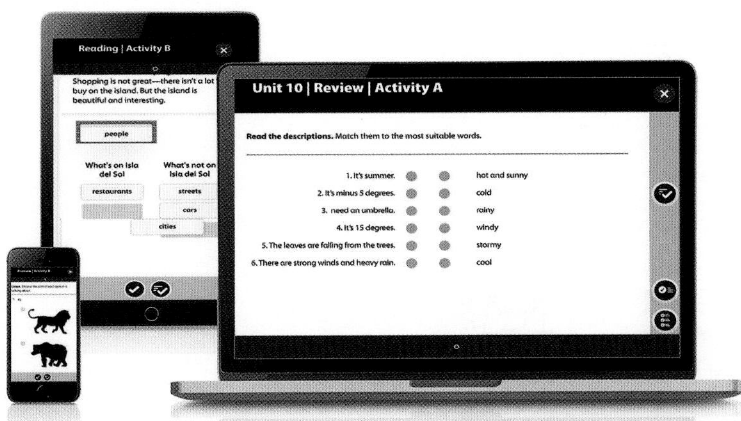

HOW TO TEACH *TIME ZONES*

More than ever before, students need to develop **C**ritical thinking, **C**reative thinking, the ability to **C**ommunicate with speakers from around the world, and the ability to work **C**ollaboratively. Often referred to as the **Four Cs**, these 21st Century Skills are essential for all students, and because of its real-world content, *Time Zones* provides you with amazing opportunities to help your students develop these skills.

TEACHING THROUGH CONTENT

Modern language teaching has moved away from discreet, non-contextual drills to context-based learning, utilizing ideas from Content-based Instruction (CBI) and Content and Language Integrated Learning (CLIL). In addition, the flipped classroom and active learning emphasize the importance of the student in the language acquisition process.

One goal of the modern classroom remains the utilization of class time and the maximization of learning, but there is an increased awareness that rather than only focusing on the language (e.g., grammar, lexicon), the addition of real-world content and subject matter via a foreign language enhances learning.

Although the primary aim of *Time Zones* is to introduce the student to English, the language is always contextualized so that the student develops an appreciation and understanding of topics which are essential in the 21st Century, including world cultures, the environment, health, history, science, and sociology.

A few ideas for utilizing the content include:

- Make full use of the National Geographic images to help students understand more about their world. Have students describe what they see in the photographs. Encourage them to make connections between the photographs and the content of the unit.
- Have students look up country or city names on a map to help develop their geographical awareness.
- Have students find out more about the content you are teaching them. This could be given as homework (e.g., find out one fact about a polar bear and share with the class the next week).

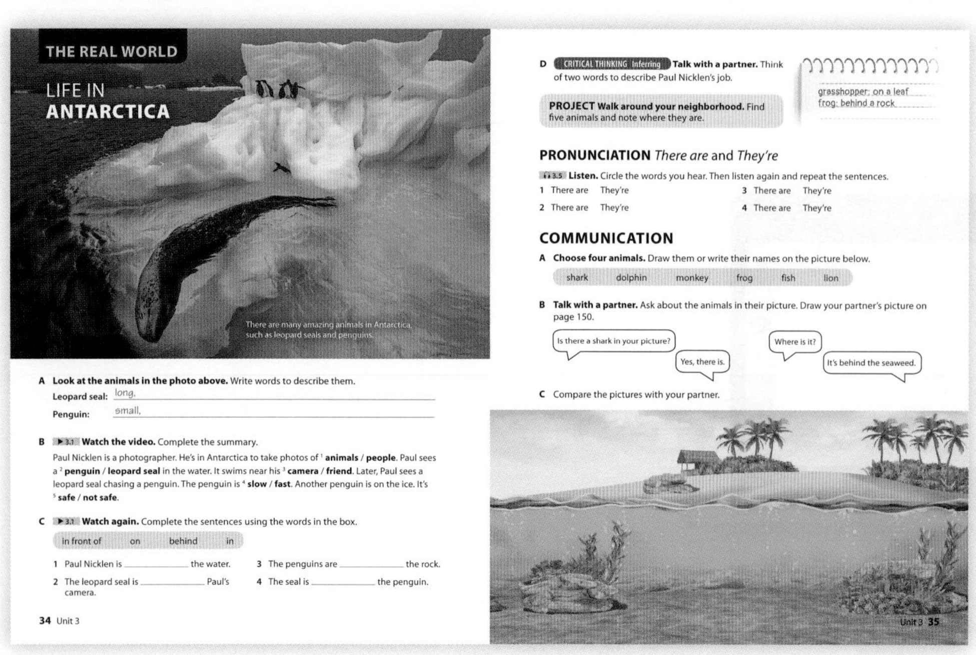

THE REAL WORLD

LIFE IN ANTARCTICA

There are many amazing animals in Antarctica, such as leopard seals and penguins.

A Look at the animals in the photo above. Write words to describe them.

Leopard seal: long,

Penguin: small,

B ▶ 3.1 **Watch the video.** Complete the summary.

Paul Nicklen is a photographer. He's in Antarctica to take photos of [1] **animals / people**. Paul sees a [2] **penguin / leopard seal** in the water. It swims near his [3] **camera / friend**. Later, Paul sees a leopard seal chasing a penguin. The penguin is [4] **slow / fast**. Another penguin is on the ice. It's [5] **safe / not safe**.

C ▶ 3.1 **Watch again.** Complete the sentences using the words in the box.

in front of | on | behind | in

1 Paul Nicklen is ______ the water.
2 The leopard seal is ______ Paul's camera.
3 The penguins are ______ the rock.
4 The seal is ______ the penguin.

34 Unit 3

D CRITICAL THINKING Inferring **Talk with a partner.** Think of two words to describe Paul Nicklen's job.

PROJECT Walk around your neighborhood. Find five animals and note where they are.

grasshopper: on a leaf
frog: behind a rock

PRONUNCIATION *There are* and *They're*

3.5 **Listen.** Circle the words you hear. Then listen again and repeat the sentences.

1 There are They're
2 There are They're
3 There are They're
4 There are They're

COMMUNICATION

A Choose four animals. Draw them or write their names on the picture below.

shark | dolphin | monkey | frog | fish | lion

B Talk with a partner. Ask about the animals in their picture. Draw your partner's picture on page 150.

Is there a shark in your picture?
Yes, there is.
Where is it?
It's behind the seaweed.

C Compare the pictures with your partner.

Unit 3 35

CONTENT TO DEVELOP GLOBAL CITIZENS

> **TIP**
>
> Encourage learners to think critically by comparing and contrasting content with their own cultures.

Teaching through content helps students see a real need or purpose for using the language. Furthermore, using topics or content that can stimulate the interest of the students can make learning the language a much more enjoyable experience. For example, imagine you prepare a lesson about "School." Your students can learn:

- About education around the world.
- Country names (e.g., Indonesia, China, Colombia).
- About schools and children around the world.
- Questions (e.g., *Where do you live? How do you travel to school?*).
- To share information about their own culture (e.g., *The school year starts in April.*).
- To talk about their own life (e.g., *I travel to school by bus.*).

By becoming global students, your students will understand more about the world they inhabit. Global students will:

- Develop a deeper understanding of the world as a whole.
- Develop a deeper understanding, tolerance, and respect for other cultures.
- Develop a deeper understanding and appreciation of their own culture within the context of a more global perspective.
- Develop a greater understanding of the issues the world faces.
- Think creatively about responding to global issues.
- Develop the skills needed to function in an ever-increasing global society.
- Realize a need for bilingualism or multilingualism and increase their motivation to study the target language.

TEACHING VOCABULARY

Successfully knowing a word requires a student to understand its meaning, its form, and its usage. In this respect, *Time Zones* provides students with the opportunity to encounter new words through incidental learning, repeated exposure to key vocabulary in different contexts, and by encouraging students to produce the vocabulary in communication activities.

Vocabulary is first introduced in the Preview tasks. It is expanded in the **Language Focus** and reinforced in the listening, **Reading**, **Vocabulary**, and **Video** activities.

Throughout each unit, students are given opportunities to practice using the words for themselves via both spoken and written activities. Some tips for vocabulary learning include:

- Have students keep a vocabulary notebook. Students write the word, the part of speech, a definition in English, and an example sentence using the word (e.g., I like to play tennis.).
- Review the vocabulary at the end of the unit. Give teams blank pieces of paper. Have them write words from the unit on each piece of paper. Put the pieces in a pile and shuffle. One student takes the first word, puts the paper on his or her forehead so the other group members can see the word but the student with the paper cannot. Group members try and get the student to say the word by giving hints in English (e.g., hobby—"*My ____ is music. I like to play the guitar.*" "*Is the word* hobby?" "*Yes, that's correct.*"). Repeat with the next student until all the words have been guessed.

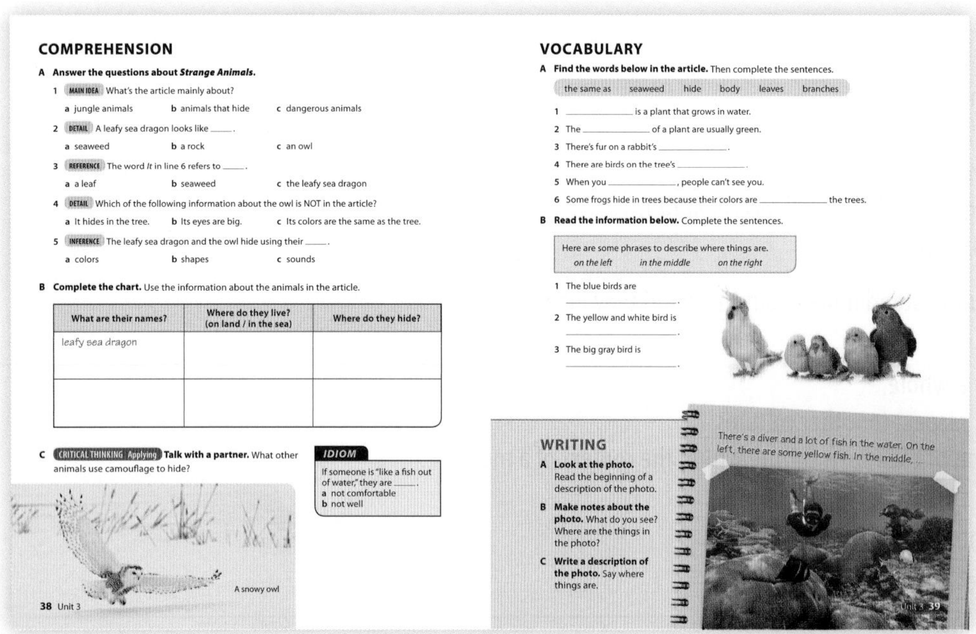

COMPREHENSION

A Answer the questions about *Strange Animals*.

1 MAIN IDEA What's the article mainly about?
a jungle animals b animals that hide c dangerous animals

2 DETAIL A leafy sea dragon looks like ____.
a seaweed b a rock c an owl

3 REFERENCE The word *It* in line 6 refers to ____.
a a leaf b seaweed c the leafy sea dragon

4 DETAIL Which of the following information about the owl is NOT in the article?
a It hides in the tree. b Its eyes are big. c Its colors are the same as the tree.

5 INFERENCE The leafy sea dragon and the owl hide using their ____.
a colors b shapes c sounds

B Complete the chart. Use the information about the animals in the article.

What are their names?	Where do they live? (on land / in the sea)	Where do they hide?
leafy sea dragon		

C CRITICAL THINKING Applying **Talk with a partner.** What other animals use camouflage to hide?

IDIOM
If someone is "like a fish out of water," they are ____.
a not comfortable
b not well

A snowy owl

38 Unit 3

VOCABULARY

A Find the words below in the article. Then complete the sentences.

the same as | seaweed | hide | body | leaves | branches

1 ____ is a plant that grows in water.
2 The ____ of a plant are usually green.
3 There's fur on a rabbit's ____.
4 There are birds on the tree's ____.
5 When you ____, people can't see you.
6 Some frogs hide in trees because their colors are ____ the trees.

B Read the information below. Complete the sentences.

Here are some phrases to describe where things are.
on the left *in the middle* *on the right*

1 The blue birds are ____.
2 The yellow and white bird is ____.
3 The big gray bird is ____.

WRITING

A Look at the photo. Read the beginning of a description of the photo.

B Make notes about the photo. What do you see? Where are the things in the photo?

C Write a description of the photo. Say where things are.

There's a diver and a lot of fish in the water. On the left, there are some yellow fish. In the middle, ...

Unit 3 39

TEACHING GRAMMAR COMMUNICATIVELY

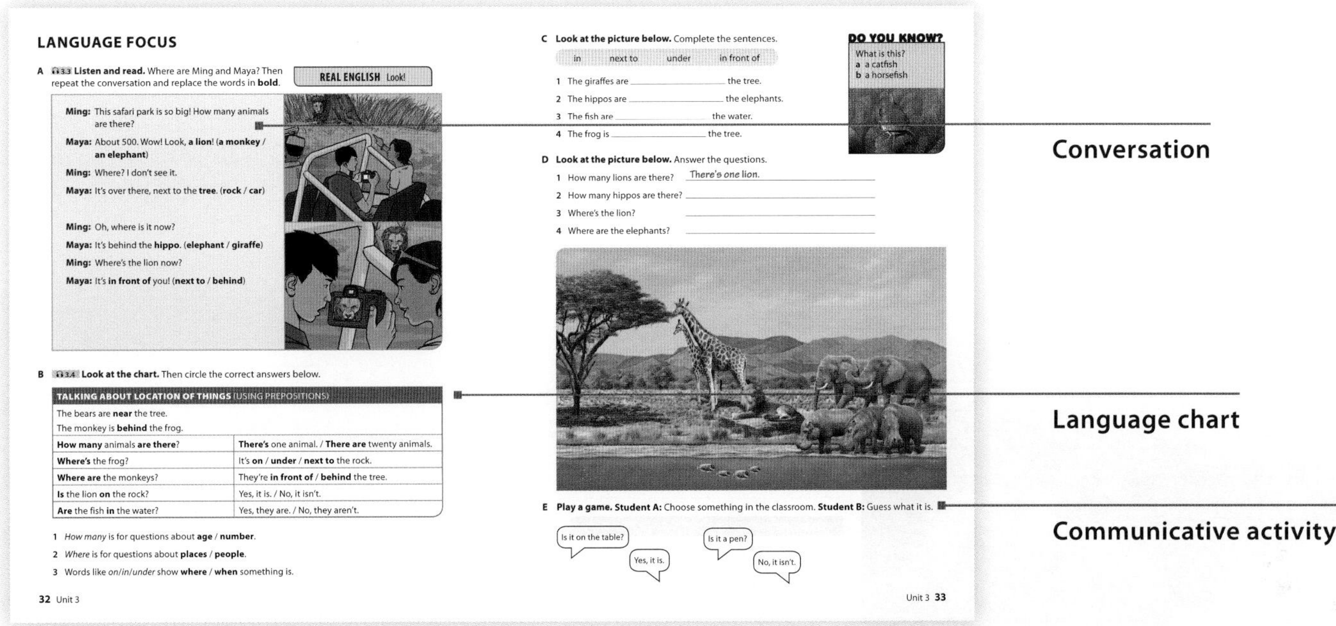
LANGUAGE FOCUS

A 1.3 Listen and read. Where are Ming and Maya? Then repeat the conversation and replace the words in bold.

REAL ENGLISH Look!

Ming: This safari park is so big! How many animals are there?
Maya: About 500. Wow! Look, a lion! (a monkey / an elephant)
Ming: Where? I don't see it.
Maya: It's over there, next to the tree. (rock / car)
Ming: Oh, where is it now?
Maya: It's behind the hippo. (elephant / giraffe)
Ming: Where's the lion now?
Maya: It's in front of you! (next to / behind)

B 1.3.4 Look at the chart. Then circle the correct answers below.

TALKING ABOUT LOCATION OF THINGS (USING PREPOSITIONS)	
The bears are near the tree. The monkey is behind the frog.	
How many animals are there?	There's one animal. / There are twenty animals.
Where's the frog?	It's on / under / next to the rock.
Where are the monkeys?	They're in front of / behind the tree.
Is the lion on the rock?	Yes, it is. / No, it isn't.
Are the fish in the water?	Yes, they are. / No, they aren't.

1 *How many* is for questions about age / number.
2 *Where* is for questions about places / people.
3 Words like *on/in/under* show where / when something is.

32 Unit 3

C Look at the picture below. Complete the sentences.

in | next to | under | in front of

1 The giraffes are ______ the tree.
2 The hippos are ______ the elephants.
3 The fish are ______ the water.
4 The frog is ______ the tree.

DO YOU KNOW?
What is this?
a a catfish
b a horsefish

D Look at the picture below. Answer the questions.

1 How many lions are there? *There's one lion.*
2 How many hippos are there? ______
3 Where's the lion? ______
4 Where are the elephants? ______

E Play a game. Student A: Choose something in the classroom. Student B: Guess what it is.

Is it on the table?
Yes, it is.
Is it a pen?
No, it isn't.

Unit 3 33

One of the important goals of the 21st Century English language classroom is to develop each student's communicative competence. This can be facilitated by:

- Getting students to communicate with one another in the target language.
- Providing active, meaningful tasks—tasks in which students need to use the target language.
- **Using content and language that is important and meaningful to the students.**
- Allowing students to make errors, particularly when working on activities to increase fluid speaking.

The aim of teaching grammar is therefore to equip students with the skills to communicate with the target language in a meaningful way.

In *Time Zones*, grammar is introduced in the **Language Focus** sections of each unit. First, the grammar is contextualized within a **conversation**, making it meaningful for students. Next, they focus on form. Students are then guided through the structures in several controlled activities until they communicate with one another in a final free **communicative activity**.

Tips for increasing communicative grammar teaching include:

- Have students personalize the language to make it more meaningful.
- Have students think of other contexts in which they can use the language (e.g., *How often do you go to school? What do you do on weekends?*).
- Think of interesting ways to get students to use the language (e.g., talking about a friend's hobbies and interests; comparing their interests with a partner's).

TEACHING LISTENING AND READING COMMUNICATIVELY

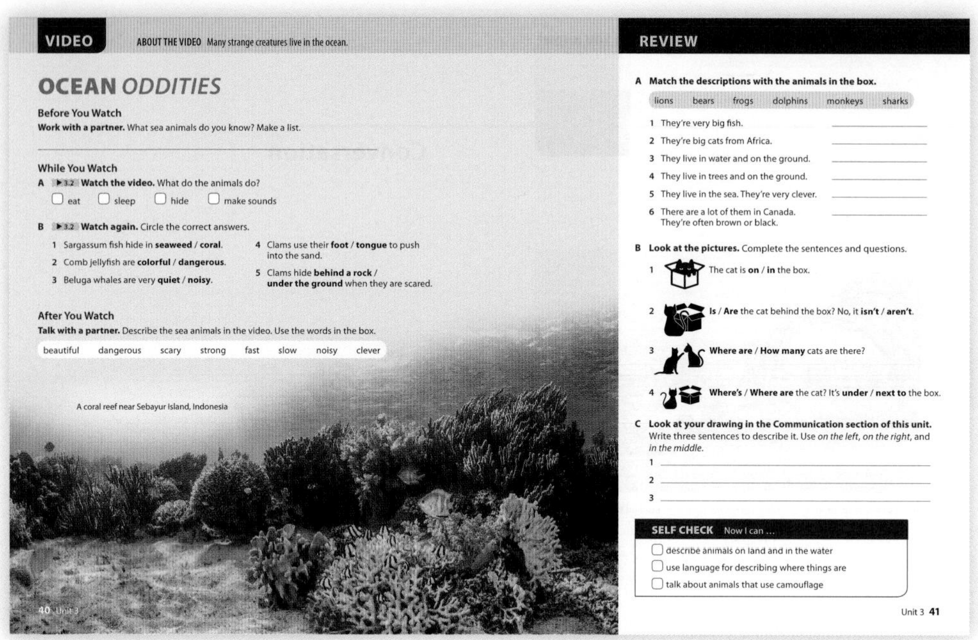
VIDEO ABOUT THE VIDEO Many strange creatures live in the ocean.

OCEAN *ODDITIES*

Before You Watch

Work with a partner. What sea animals do you know? Make a list.

While You Watch

A 3.2 **Watch the video.** What do the animals do?

☐ eat ☐ sleep ☐ hide ☐ make sounds

B 3.2 **Watch again.** Circle the correct answers.

1 Sargassum fish hide in **seaweed / coral**.
2 Comb jellyfish are **colorful / dangerous**.
3 Beluga whales are very **quiet / noisy**.
4 Clams use their **foot / tongue** to push into the sand.
5 Clams hide **behind a rock / under the ground** when they are scared.

After You Watch

Talk with a partner. Describe the sea animals in the video. Use the words in the box.

beautiful dangerous scary strong fast slow noisy clever

A coral reef near Sebayur Island, Indonesia

40 Unit 3

REVIEW

A **Match the descriptions with the animals in the box.**

lions bears frogs dolphins monkeys sharks

1 They're very big fish. ______
2 They're big cats from Africa. ______
3 They live in water and on the ground. ______
4 They live in trees and on the ground. ______
5 They live in the sea. They're very clever. ______
6 There are a lot of them in Canada. They're often brown or black. ______

B **Look at the pictures.** Complete the sentences and questions.

1 The cat is **on / in** the box.
2 **Is / Are** the cat behind the box? No, it **isn't / aren't**.
3 **Where are / How many** cats are there?
4 **Where's / Where are** the cat? It's **under / next to** the box.

C **Look at your drawing in the Communication section of this unit.** Write three sentences to describe it. Use *on the left, on the right,* and *in the middle.*

1 ______
2 ______
3 ______

SELF CHECK Now I can ...

☐ describe animals on land and in the water
☐ use language for describing where things are
☐ talk about animals that use camouflage

Unit 3 41

LISTENING AND VIDEO

Video can add a new and exciting dimension to classroom learning. There are many advantages to video. First, students can be exposed to a range of authentic content and encounter the target language in a natural context. Second, students are aided in their comprehension of the content with the use of visual cues as well as audio ones. In addition, video can accommodate students with different learning styles—both visual and auditory. Fourth, students' lives, including their free time, are filled with video. Video is part of their world, and it is a part of an authentic, motivating classroom. Finally, it is essential for 21st Century learners to understand and analyze various types of media, including video.

Both listening and watching are, by their nature, receptive skills, and many students benefit from a receptive period and working alone before being asked to communicate. Here are some ideas you can use to expand the video activities in *Time Zones* and make them more communicative:

- Have students look at the photo and predict what the video is about.
- Tell students to describe the photo in as much detail as possible.
- Ask students questions that activate their schemata so they think about the topic they will listen to.
- Have your students make and ask each other questions. You could provide a word list and have students make questions using specific words that will appear in the video (e.g., *fruits—What fruits do you like? What fruits don't you like?*).
- Encourage students to enjoy the video.
- The first time you play the video, allow students to watch it without doing a task. Have students watch and share what they saw with a partner.
- Have students check their answers with a partner after each task.
- Expand activities and games. For example, in Student's Book 1, Unit 4, students learn vocabulary for describing their extended family. Have students describe their own families to one another and have partners draw the other person's family tree.

USING VIDEO IN THE CLASSROOM

ADDITIONAL IDEAS FOR USING VIDEO IN THE CLASSROOM

BEFORE THE LESSON

Watch the video yourself. Make a note of language you feel may be difficult for your learners. Prepare activities to pre-teach the language.

BEFORE STUDENTS WATCH

Pre-teach any difficult language. For example, give students a handout where they match target words to definitions. Another idea is to make a list of questions that contain the target words for students to ask one another (e.g., *Have you ever been bird watching?*).

Have students predict the content of the video they are going to watch. For example, show students pictures that are related to the video and have students guess what the topic is.

Activate students' schemata and background knowledge of the topic of the video by discussing the photo and predicting the content (e.g., *I think the video is about people selling clothes.*).

WHILE STUDENTS WATCH

Preview the video without doing any Student's Book activities. Have students get into pairs. Play the video without sound. Have Student A watch the first half of the video while Student B turns his/her back. Student A should explain what he/she is seeing. Have students swap roles halfway through the video.

AFTER STUDENTS WATCH

Have students retell what they saw and heard in the video.

Have students make a dialog about the content.

TIP

Encourage learners to think critically by doing role-plays based on the video.

MAKING READING MORE COMMUNICATIVE

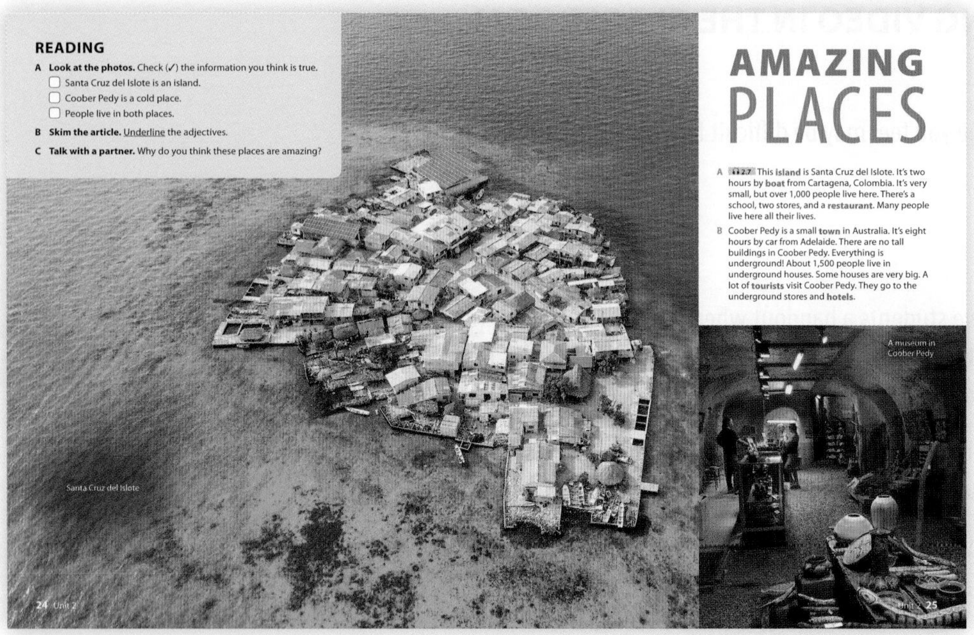

READING

A **Look at the photos.** Check (✓) the information you think is true.

- ☐ Santa Cruz del Islote is an island.
- ☐ Coober Pedy is a cold place.
- ☐ People live in both places.

B **Skim the article.** Underline the adjectives.

C **Talk with a partner.** Why do you think these places are amazing?

AMAZING PLACES

A 2.7 This **island** is Santa Cruz del Islote. It's two hours by **boat** from Cartagena, Colombia. It's very small, but over 1,000 people live here. There's a school, two stores, and a **restaurant**. Many people live here all their lives.

B Coober Pedy is a small **town** in Australia. It's eight hours by car from Adelaide. There are no tall buildings in Coober Pedy. Everything is underground! About 1,500 people live in underground houses. Some houses are very big. A lot of **tourists** visit Coober Pedy. They go to the underground stores and **hotels**.

Santa Cruz del Islote

A museum in Coober Pedy

24 Unit 2

Unit 2 25

Although reading is a receptive skill, it is very useful as a springboard to discussion in the communicative classroom. Here are some ideas you can use to get students communicating:

- Activate students' schemata by writing the title of the reading on the board. Have students predict what they will read about.
- Have students discuss what they see in the photograph (e.g., *A young child with a camera*).
- Photocopy the article and cut it into separate paragraphs. Before students study the passage, have students get into groups. Have each member read one of the paragraphs silently. Then have students explain the paragraph they have read to their group.
- Photocopy the article (or part of it) and cut it into separate sentences. After students have studied the passage, have students get into groups. Have each member take turns reading a sentence. Students then have to put the sentences in the correct order.
- Make the comprehension questions a race between groups. Elect one member of the group as the writer and give them a piece of chalk. Group members shout out the answers to their writer, who writes the answers on the board. The first team with all answers correct is the winner.
- The Critical Thinking task aims to get students talking about what they have read. Encourage students to give reasons for their answers.

GETTING STUDENTS TO COMMUNICATE

Students can be shy, reticent, afraid of making mistakes, fearful of appearing foolish in front of their classmates, and unwilling to take risks. As a result, students can be reluctant to produce the language and try to speak English in the classroom. The following are suggestions that may help you avoid too much teacher-talk and student silence.

- Create a classroom environment in which students feel safe and willing to take risks.
- Treat errors as a natural part of the learning process.
- Try to provide individual correction privately. In class, focus your discussion on mistakes that many students have been making, without singling out any students.
- When students are developing fluency, don't correct mistakes.
- Bring the students' own personal experiences into the tasks whenever possible.
- Incorporate movement into the classroom. Moving around can help students stay focused, engaged, and alert.
- Use the classroom space in innovative ways. Get your students to stand facing each other in a line. Have them do the speaking task and then physically move to the next person. Have them repeat the speaking task with a new partner (e.g., *What's your favorite hobby?*). Swap partners again and continue the activity.
- Regularly assign students different partners. This reduces complacency, increases social interaction, and develops flexibility to deal with various speakers.
- Encourage friendly competition among groups (e.g., *Which group can keep the conversation going the longest? Which group is the first to get survey answers from 10 different students?*).

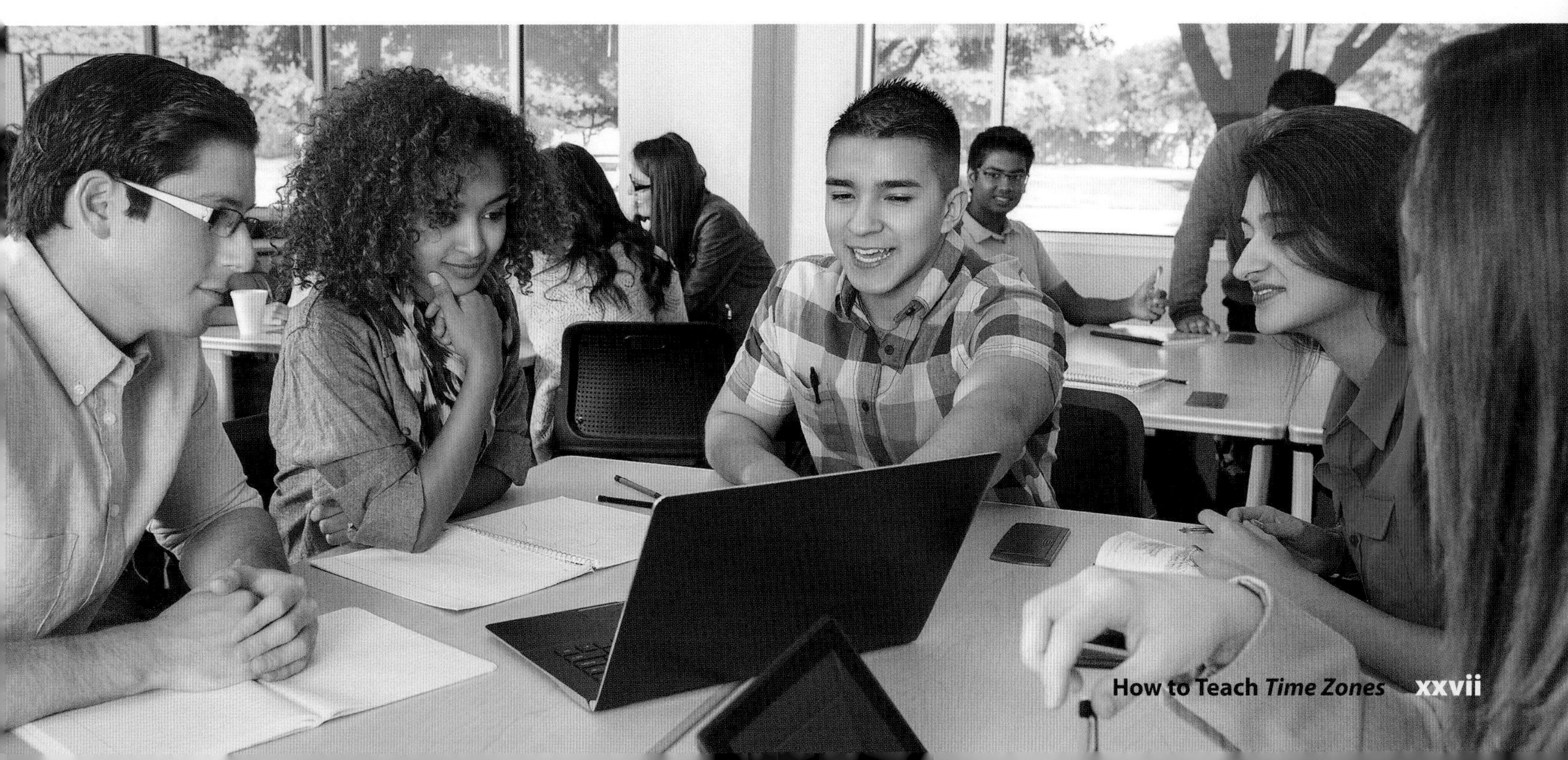

GETTING STUDENTS TO WRITE

Each unit of *Time Zones* has one short writing task that encourages students to reproduce the key language they have learned through a piece of writing. This helps develop students' communicative competence as they need to remember the vocabulary, spelling, and language structures while at the same time developing writing techniques such as cohesion, coherence, and paragraph structure. The writing task also gives students the opportunity to personalize the language, making it more meaningful to them. Some tips include:

- Develop students' critical thinking as they deduce the type of information needed. For example, if students must write a short email describing their hobbies, have students study the example and decide what kind of information should be included (e.g., greeting, their hobbies, a closing remark).
- Have students write a first draft with their textbooks closed. Then have students open their textbooks, look at the model writing as a guide, and write a second draft.
- Have students work with a partner, exchange first drafts, and read them. Have students write a comment under the partner's writing (e.g., *Wow! You play piano every morning. That's amazing!*).
- Have students read their first drafts to a partner or group of students. Encourage students to ask questions to clarify anything they did not understand. Have students write their second drafts while considering this feedback.
- Have students get into groups and share their writings. Then have a quiz about the group's writing (e.g., *What is Takashi's hobby? He likes to play the guitar.*).

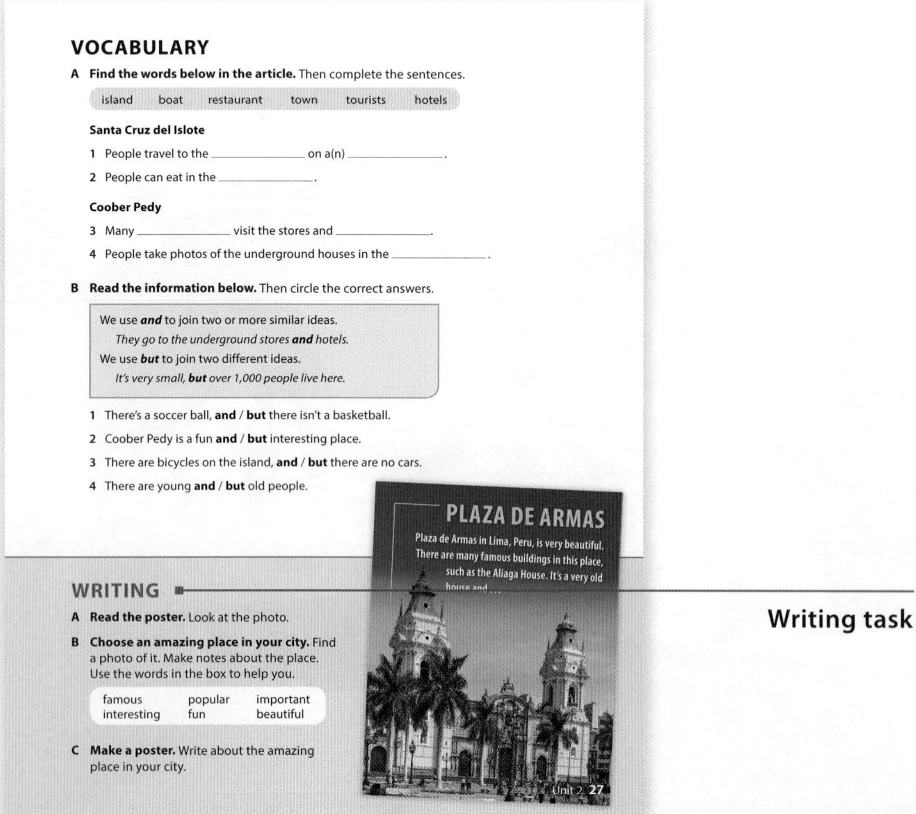

VOCABULARY

A Find the words below in the article. Then complete the sentences.

island boat restaurant town tourists hotels

Santa Cruz del Islote

1 People travel to the ____________ on a(n) ____________.

2 People can eat in the ____________.

Coober Pedy

3 Many ____________ visit the stores and ____________.

4 People take photos of the underground houses in the ____________.

B Read the information below. Then circle the correct answers.

We use ***and*** to join two or more similar ideas.
*They go to the underground stores **and** hotels.*
We use ***but*** to join two different ideas.
*It's very small, **but** over 1,000 people live here.*

1 There's a soccer ball, **and** / **but** there isn't a basketball.

2 Coober Pedy is a fun **and** / **but** interesting place.

3 There are bicycles on the island, **and** / **but** there are no cars.

4 There are young **and** / **but** old people.

WRITING

A Read the poster. Look at the photo.

B Choose an amazing place in your city. Find a photo of it. Make notes about the place. Use the words in the box to help you.

famous popular important interesting fun beautiful

C Make a poster. Write about the amazing place in your city.

PLAZA DE ARMAS
Plaza de Armas in Lima, Peru, is very beautiful. There are many famous buildings in this place, such as the Aliaga House. It's a very old house and . . .
Unit 2 27
Writing task

GOING BEYOND THE CLASSROOM

Homework is a great way to get students to think about what they have learned in class, to review lessons, and to practice the language outside of the classroom. This gives them more time for actually using the language.

As an example, let's take examples from Unit 1 in *Time Zones* Student's Book 1, What's Your Favorite Video Game?

- Students could write new words they have learned in the unit in their vocabulary notebook.
- Students could practice the Language Focus conversations at home, with friends, in front of a mirror, or in front of their pet dog!
- Students could do research about a sport that is popular in another country.
- Students could do a survey about favorite sports with friends from other classes.
- Students could write a short paragraph to describe a family member's or friend's favorites.
- Students could watch the unit video again, make some quiz questions, and test the class by asking them in the next lesson.
- Students can do activities from the Workbook.

TIP

Encourage students to think critically by offering them a choice of homework tasks (e.g., a piece of writing, internet research, or video task).

UNIT 1

WHAT'S YOUR FAVORITE VIDEO GAME?

CONTENT AREA: PEOPLE AND PLACES

Topic: favorites

Vocabulary: things: movie, app, video game, TV show; **people:** singer, writer, player, movie star; **sports:** soccer, baseball, basketball, table tennis; **adjectives:** cool, amazing, awesome, interesting, difficult, easy; **verbs:** travel, love, watch

Grammar: *Wh-* questions: *what*, *who*

Extra material: a world map

Other useful vocabulary: things: book, single, album, song; **people:** band, team; **sports:** rugby, cricket, tennis

END OF UNIT PROJECT Have students bring in pictures of their favorite books, movies, TV shows, singers, and bands.

Tell them the pictures should represent their favorites. Explain that for this project they do not need to do any writing.

In class, have students work in pairs and use their pictures to talk about themselves. Encourage students to ask questions about their partner's favorite things.

PREVIEW

Have students read the unit title to themselves as you read it aloud. Explain that in this unit they will learn to talk about things they like (their favorites). Point to the word *favorite* as you say this.

1

WHAT'S YOUR ***FAVORITE*** VIDEO GAME?

A Mexican gamer plays a game on the Oculus Quest VR headset.

6

A Tell students they are going to write the words that match the pictures. Point to the example as you explain *TV show*. If necessary, read the other words aloud and have students follow along in their books.

Have students write the words.

Explain that they will hear the five words or phrases and they should check their answers.

1.1 Play Audio Track 1.1. Play it again, if necessary. Check answers as a class.

B Explain that students will hear five words or phrases and they should circle the words they hear.

1.2 Play Audio Track 1.2. If necessary, tell students you will play the audio again and they should confirm their answers. Check answers as a class.

Direct students' attention to the write on lines. Ask them to write an example of each. Give students a few minutes to complete the task.

ABOUT THE PHOTO

This photo shows a female playing a video game on a virtual reality (VR) headset. Using a VR headset allows a player to be fully immersed in the game, moving around in the game's artificial world and interacting with virtual features or items. The Oculus Quest was launched on May 21, 2019. Created by Oculus VR, a division of Facebook Inc., the Quest is a standalone VR headset without wires or external sensors. It doesn't need to be plugged into a computer or console. The headset works in spaces big or small, and via the headset's unique tracking system, the Touch controllers realistically transport the player's hands and gestures into the game.

PREVIEW

A 1.1 **Match the words with the pictures.** Listen and check your answers.

movie singer app ~~TV show~~ video game

1 TV show 2 movie 3 video game

4 singer 5 app

B 1.2 **Listen and circle the words you hear.** Then write an example for each.

1 (a singer) / a movie star Answers will vary.
2 (a movie) / a video game
3 a TV show / (an app)
4 (a video game) / a movie
5 a movie / (a TV show)

C **Talk with a partner.** Take turns.
Student A: Say a word from **A**.
Student B: Say an example. Answers will vary.

PEOPLE AND PLACES

UNIT GOALS

- talk about your favorite things
- use language for talking about favorites
- learn about popular sports around the world

7

C Ask students to get into pairs. Explain that they should take turns saying a word from **A** and giving an example. Explain that they can use their ideas in **B** or other ideas.

Model the task with a student. Have students do the task.

CHALLENGE Ask the students to say some other words they associate with the vocabulary. (See **Other useful vocabulary**.)

UNIT GOALS

Direct students' attention to the **UNIT GOALS** box. Explain that these are some of the things students will learn in this unit. Point out that this unit is about people and places. As students follow along, read each of the unit goals to the class. Explain any words students do not know. Explain to students that at the end of the unit there is a self check. Tell the students this allows them to see if they have accomplished each goal.

OPTIONAL As part of the unit introduction, have students turn to page 17. Point out the **SELF CHECK** box. As students follow along, read the *I can* statements aloud. Give students a minute to compare these statements to the unit goals.

CONTENT NOTE: CULTURE

Aladdin is a musical. Both the live-action movie and the animated film are based on *The Thousand and One Nights*, a collection of stories from the Middle East and India. The exact authors are uncertain.

Minecraft, which is played by tens of millions of people, is a video game that allows players across devices to create a world. *Mario Kart*, a product of the *Super Mario* series, is a go-kart racing video game. *Overwatch* is a multiplayer, team-based, hero game.

Lady Gaga is a musician who has ventured into film. She has also created her own makeup line and become a multifaceted businessperson. She is best known for her vibrant clothes and provocative song lyrics.

Beyoncé is a singer-songwriter who has sold millions of albums and won various Grammy Awards.

The Grammy Award-winning singer-songwriter Ed Sheeran began writing music in his early teens.

Although the Avengers started as comic strip superheroes in the Marvel Comics' books, the characters are now often associated with the series of movies, starting with *The Avengers* in 2012, that have become box office successes.

Originally a Japanese horror movie from the 1950s, *Godzilla: King of the Monsters* was released in 2019 as part of the *Godzilla* and *Kong: Skull Island* series.

Ready Player One is a Steven Spielberg movie set in 2044. The story revolves around the race to find an Easter egg that will give the finder both control of a virtual reality called OASIS and OASIS's creator's fortune.

LANGUAGE FOCUS

A Tell students they will listen to a conversation with four short exchanges between Maya and Stig.

1.3 Play Audio Track 1.3 as students follow along in their books. If necessary, play the conversation again, pausing after each speaker so students can repeat.

As students follow along, read the question, *What's Maya's favorite movie?* Have students answer. You might want to ask the students why the exchange is funny. (Maya and Stig have all of the same favorites.)

SUPPORT Pointing to Maya's third utterance, ask students when they should use *she's* and when they should use *he's*. (They should use *she's* when talking about a female singer and *he's* when discussing a male one.)

Have students work in pairs and practice the conversation once. Point out the bold words and read them aloud as students follow along in their books. You might want to have students repeat the words after you say them. If necessary, explain the meaning of any words that students seem unfamiliar with.

Remind students that this is conversation practice, not reading practice. Ask students how Stig sounds as the conversation progresses (excited, surprised). Give students a funny example of reading out loud without showing any enthusiasm.

Tell students they will practice the conversation two more times, changing the bold words each time and swapping roles after the first time. Have them practice with both substitution choices.

LANGUAGE FOCUS

A 1.3 **Listen and read.** What's Maya's favorite movie? Then repeat the conversation and replace the words in **bold**. Her favorite movie is *The Avengers*.

REAL ENGLISH Really?

Maya: What's your favorite video game, Stig?

Stig: My favorite video game is ***Minecraft***. (***Mario Kart* / *Overwatch***)

Maya: That's my favorite video game, too! Who's your favorite singer?

Stig: My favorite singer is **Lady Gaga**. (**Beyoncé / Ed Sheeran**)

Maya: Really? **She's** my favorite singer, too! (**She's / He's**)

Stig: What's your favorite movie, Maya?

Maya: My favorite movie is ***The Avengers***. (***Godzilla* / *Ready Player One***)

Stig: That's **cool**! We like the same things! (**amazing / awesome**)

B 1.4 **Look at the chart.** Then circle the correct answers below.

TALKING ABOUT FAVORITES (USING *WHAT, WHO,* AND POSSESSIVE ADJECTIVES)		
What's your favorite movie?	**My** / **Our** favorite movie **is** *Spider-Man*.	What's = What is Who's = Who is
What's his favorite music app?	**His** favorite music app **is** Apple Music.	
What's their favorite color?	**Their** favorite color **is** orange.	
Who's her favorite singer?	**Her** favorite singer **is** Bruno Mars.	

1 *What* is for **things** / **people**.

2 *Who* is for **things** / **people**.

REAL ENGLISH

Direct students' attention to the expression in the **REAL ENGLISH** box. Explain that *Really?* is used in informal spoken English to show you are surprised by something. For example:

A: My favorite singer is Madonna.
B: Really? She's kind of old.

You may also want to explain that *Really?* can also be used when someone is impressed or happy. For example:

A: I got 99 percent on the test!
B: Really? Great job!

B Ask students to look at the chart.

1.4 Have students follow along as they listen to Audio Track 1.4.

Explain that we use *What's* when we are talking about a thing (*What's your favorite movie?*) and we use *Who's* when we are talking about a person (*Who's your favorite singer?*).

Ask students to look at the right side of the chart. Point out that the question words *What's* and *Who's* are contracted (or shortened) forms of *What is* and

C Complete the sentences. Circle the correct answers.

1 Hello, nice to meet you. **My** / **His** name is Jack.

2 What's **your** / **you** favorite color?

3 She's a singer. **Our** / **Her** name is Alexa.

4 Tom and Mina are writers. **They** / **Their** books are interesting.

5 This is Daniel. **Your** / **His** favorite country is Brazil.

D 1.5 **Complete the conversations.** Write the correct words. Then listen and check your answers.

1 **Nadine:** [1] What's Ana's favorite book?

Stig: [2] Her favorite book is *The Hunger Games*.

Nadine: [3] Who's her favorite writer?

Stig: Suzanne Collins.

2 **Ming:** [4] What's Carl's favorite video game?

Maya: [5] His favorite video game is *Fortnite*.

Ming: Hey! That's my favorite video game, too. [6] What's Carl's favorite movie?

Maya: *Guardians of the Galaxy*.

3 **Stig:** Ming, [7] What's your favorite season?

Ming: [8] My favorite season is spring.

Stig: What's [9] your favorite color?

Ming: Blue.

Stig: Really? Blue is [10] my favorite color, too.

E Work in pairs. Student A: Imagine you are a movie star or singer. **Student B:** Ask your partner about their favorite things. Answers will vary.

Hi, I'm Emma Watson.
Hi, Emma Watson. What's your favorite food?
My favorite food is salad.
What's your favorite movie?

Who is. Explain that both forms are correct, but when we speak we usually use the contracted form, which is more informal.

Ask students to look at the board.

Write *What's = What is*.

Then write *What is his favorite* ______ *?*

His favorite ______ *is X.*

Circle *is* in both the question and the answer. Point out that *is* is used no matter who the subject is (*my, their, her, his,* etc.).

Draw students' attention to the two statements under the chart. Explain that they summarize an important grammar point for this unit. Have students circle the correct answers. Check answers.

C As students follow along in their books, read the sentences aloud. Have students circle the correct answers. Check answers as a class.

D Ask students to read the conversations and write the correct words to complete them. Have students fill in the blanks. Tell students to listen to the conversations and check their answers.

1.5 Have students follow along as they listen to Audio Track 1.5. Play the audio. If necessary, play it again. Check answers as a class, writing them on the board as they are given.

SUPPORT Point to your book. Say *My book*. Point to a female student's book. Say *Her book*. Explain that when we use a person's name, we use an apostrophe *s* to show possession (e.g., *Ana's favorite book*). Give an example using a student's name: (*Student's name with apostrophe* s) *book*. Do the same with other female students.

Point to a male student's book. Say *His book* and (*Student's name with apostrophe* s) *book*. Repeat with other male students' names.

Ask a student about his or her favorite video game. Using that student's name, write *What's* ______ *'s favorite video game?* Call on another student to answer.

Continue with other objects as necessary.

E Tell students they are going to get into pairs and pretend to interview someone famous.

Model the conversation with a student. Point out that Student A is pretending to be a movie star or singer and Student B is the interviewer.

Have the students do the task. Then have them swap roles and do the task again.

THE REAL WORLD

As students follow along, read the title aloud. Then read the photo caption.

CONTENT NOTE: SOCCER AND SPORTS

Soccer, often called *football* outside of the United States, has the most spectators of any sport in the world. An estimated four billion people consider themselves to be soccer fans. Two teams of 11 players try to get the ball into the other team's goal. Only the goalkeeper (who stands in front of the goal) can touch the ball with his or her hands.

Popular sports around the world include basketball, baseball, soccer, tennis, table tennis, golf, and gymnastics. It's good to remember that students may be familiar with other sports that are well known and popular in their cultures even if they are not as popular in other regions of the world.

A Read the names of the sports aloud as students follow along in their books. Tell students they should match the pictures to the sports. Have students do the task. Check answers as a class.

OPTIONAL Ask students to look at the photo and say what sport the girls are playing (soccer).

DO YOU KNOW?

Read the question aloud, as students follow along in their books. Have them guess the answer before providing it (a).

CONTENT NOTE: CRICKET

Cricket, England's national summer sport, is played all around the world, but it is particularly popular in countries with historical ties to England. Two teams of 11 players play on an oval field. Teams take turns batting and pitching (called *bowling* in cricket). Some aspects of the game are similar to baseball. The team with the most runs at the end is the winner.

Girls from France and Germany play a friendly game.

ABOUT THE PHOTO

This photo shows a U16 (under 16) friendly match between France and Germany. Football, or soccer (as the game is called in some parts of the world), has a long history going as far back as 2500 BCE, with the game called *cuju* in ancient China. However, the evolution of the sport as we know it today took place in Britain in the mid-nineteenth century. The first international soccer match was between Scotland and England in 1872. Today, the sport is so popular that the Fédération Internationale de Football Association (FIFA) estimates that more than 250 million players around the world are actively involved in the sport.

A Match the pictures with the sports.

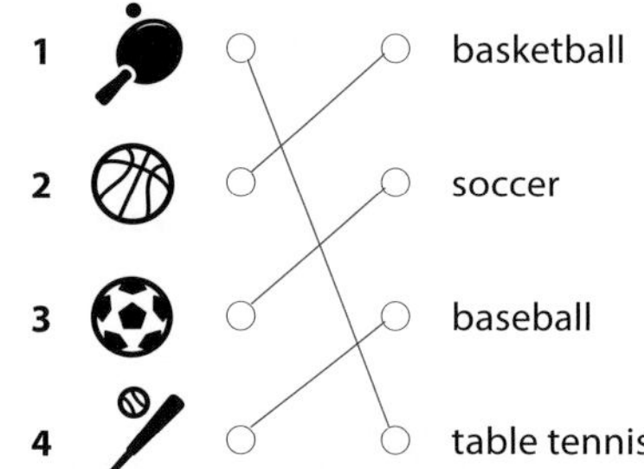

1 basketball
2 soccer
3 baseball
4 table tennis

DO YOU KNOW?

What sport is also the name of an insect?
(a) cricket
b soccer

B ▶ 1.1 **Watch the video.** Match the sports with the countries.

Brazil China the United States Japan

1 baseball Japan
2 table tennis China
3 basketball the United States
4 soccer Brazil

B As students follow along in their books, read the names of the countries aloud. Explain to students that they are going to watch a video talking about sports that are popular in these countries. Tell them that they should write the names of the countries.

▶ 1.1 Play Video 1.1. If necessary, play the video again.

Check answers as a class.

C Tell students they are going to watch the video again and they should complete the sentences with two words or a number.

▶ 1.1 Play Video 1.1. If necessary, play the video again.

Check answers as a class.

C ▶ 1.1 **Watch again.** Complete the sentences. Write two words or a number for each sentence.

1 Many Japanese students ___play baseball___ at school.

2 In China, both ___children___ and ___adults___ play table tennis.

3 Many basketball players are over ___2___ meters tall.

4 There are ___32___ national soccer teams in the World Cup Finals.

D CRITICAL THINKING Personalizing **Talk with a partner.** What's your country's favorite sport? Who are the famous players? Answers will vary.

PROJECT Talk to five friends or family members. Ask them about their favorite sport. Share your answers with a partner.

PRONUNCIATION contractions: *what's / who's*

A 1.6 **Listen and repeat.**

1 What is What's 2 Who is Who's

B 1.7 **Listen.** Circle the words you hear.

1 (What is) What's 3 What is (What's)

2 Who is (Who's) 4 (Who is) Who's

COMMUNICATION

A **Look at the chart.** Complete the questions with your ideas. Answers will vary.

Name	What's your favorite number?	What's your favorite color?	Who's your favorite ______?	What's your favorite ______?
Michiko	five	red		

B **Ask three classmates the questions in the chart.** Write their answers.

C **Work in a group.** Tell them the answers in your chart.

Michiko's favorite number is five. Her favorite color is red.

B Tell students they will listen to four questions. Explain that for each, they must decide whether the speaker uses two words or the contraction and circle the correct answer.

1.7 Play Audio Track 1.7. Play it again, if necessary. Check answers as a class by having four students write them on the board.

SUPPORT Give students more practice recognizing whether the speaker uses *is* or *'s*. Say *Who's* or *Who is*. Ask students who heard two words to raise their right hand and those who heard a contraction to raise their left hand. Continue to practice with increasingly longer phrases until you are using full questions (e.g., *Who's your favorite soccer player?*).

Then have students get into small groups and take turns asking questions, with the other students indicating which phrase was used.

D CRITICAL THINKING

As students follow along, read the questions aloud. Have students get into pairs and discuss the questions.

PROJECT As students follow along, read the project instructions aloud. Set a deadline by which students must talk with family and friends as homework. In the next class, have students get into pairs and compare answers.

PRONUNCIATION

A Tell students they will practice their pronunciation by repeating the words they hear.

1.6 Play Audio Track 1.6. Play it again, pausing after each word. Have the students repeat. Students may have difficulties hearing the difference between the words with and without the contractions. Play the audio again, if necessary.

COMMUNICATION

Tell students they are going to do a survey. Explain that they will go around the class and ask and answer questions with three students.

A As students follow along, read the first two questions and example answers aloud. If necessary, review when to use *Who's* and *What's*.

Tell students to complete the last two questions.

B Model the task with a student. Have students get up and interview three classmates.

C When students have finished, have them get into groups and tell each other their answers.

CHALLENGE Have students think of other questions to ask and answer during the class survey. For example: *What's your favorite subject in school? Who's your favorite teacher?*

READING

Ask one student to read the title aloud.

As students follow along in their books, read Susan Seubert's introduction.

Ask, *Who is this about? (Who is "my"?)* Have one student answer (*Susan Seubert*).

A Explain skimming. (See **TEACHING NOTE.**) As students follow along, read the statement and four main ideas aloud. Ask students to skim the article to find the main idea(s). Explain that this is a good way to understand a passage before reading it more closely.

Emphasize that they do not have to read every word because at this point they are just looking for the main ideas.

Have students do the task and check answers.

OPTIONAL The text can also be used as a listening activity. Once you have completed **A**, have students close their books. Tell students they will listen to a short passage about Susan Seubert's favorite things. Explain that they should remember the main ideas (i.e., favorites) that she talks about.

1.8 Play Audio Track 1.8. Ask students what some of her favorites are.

Have students open their books and continue with **B**.

B Explain scanning. (See **TEACHING NOTE.**) Tell students that they will scan the text and they should underline Susan's favorite things.

Have students do the task. When all the students have finished, check answers.

Have students read the interview more carefully so they can answer the **COMPREHENSION** questions.

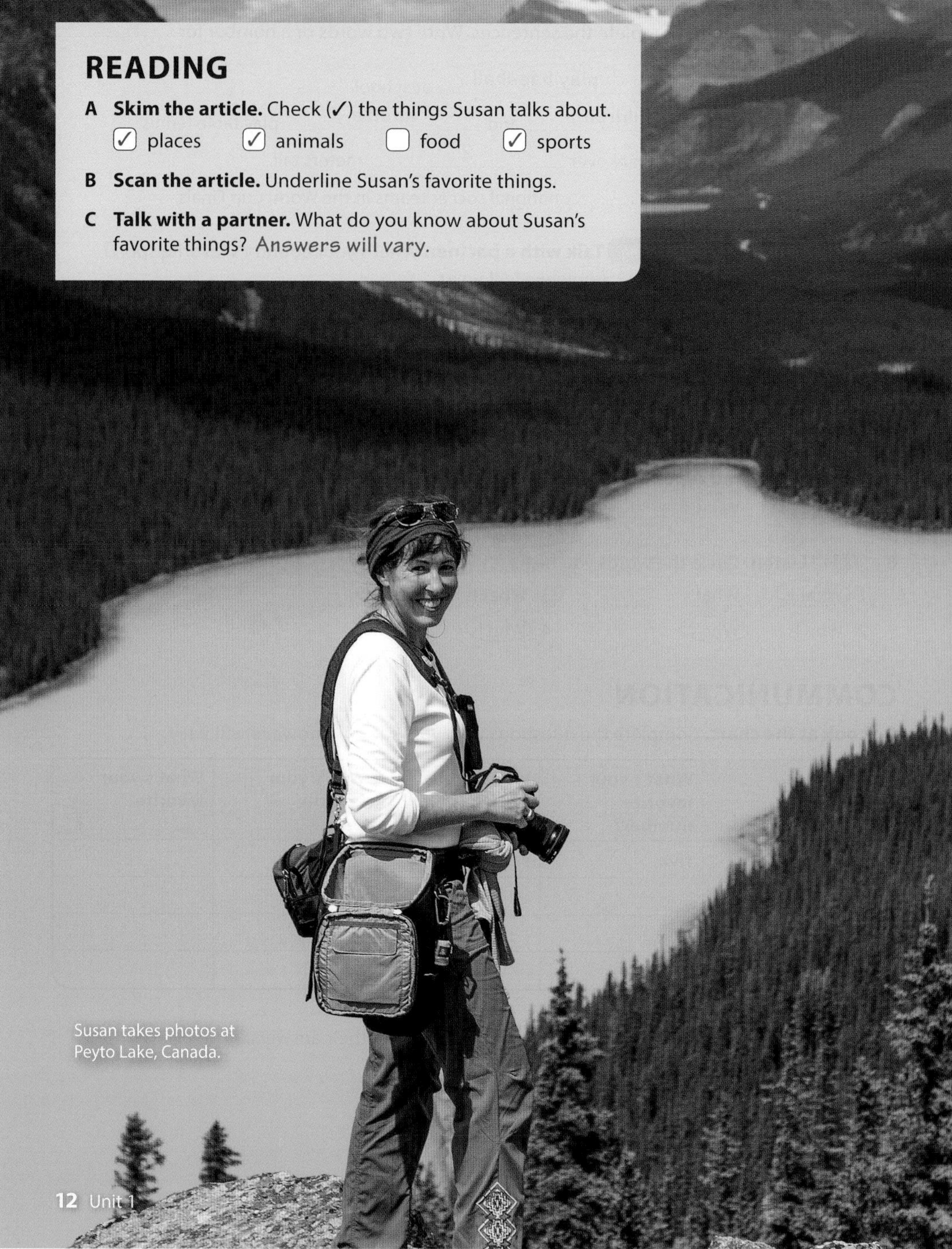

READING
A Skim the article. Check (✓) the things Susan talks about.
☑ places ☑ animals ☐ food ☑ sports
B Scan the article. Underline Susan's favorite things.
C Talk with a partner. What do you know about Susan's favorite things? Answers will vary.
12 Unit 1

Susan takes photos at Peyto Lake, Canada.

SUPPORT Help students understand new words without having to look them up in the dictionary. For example, explain that *travel* means *go to (a place)*. Use gestures to reinforce the new words.

C As students follow along, read the question aloud. Have students get into pairs and talk about their ideas.

TEACHING NOTE: SKIMMING AND SCANNING

Skimming is a reading technique. It is not the same as reading because you do not read every word. You look for key words to get the main idea(s) in the text. You can also use skimming to decide if you want to read the text more closely. Skimming is not searching for specific information.

ABOUT THE PHOTO

The main photo shows Peyto Lake, located in the Banff National Park in Alberta, Canada. It is a glacier-fed lake that is a popular sightseeing spot for tourists. During the summer, glacier rock flour from a nearby glacier flows into the lake, giving the lake its bright blue color.

The other photo shows South Georgia Island, located in the southern Atlantic Ocean. One of the most remote places on Earth, the island is around 160 kilometers long and 32 kilometers wide. Grytviken is the island's main settlement. A small number of scientists and support staff live on the island. The island is home to a few species of penguins and seals.

MY FAVORITE THINGS

1.8 Susan Seubert is a photographer for National Geographic. She takes photos of people and places.

Q: Susan, you **travel** to a lot of countries. What's your favorite place?

A: My favorite place is South Georgia Island in the Atlantic Ocean. It's amazing. There are many **interesting** animals there.

Q: What's your favorite animal?

A: I **love** giraffes. But I like to take photos of penguins. They're fun to **watch**.

Q: What's your favorite photo?

A: That's **difficult**! I think my favorite photo is Ansel Adams's "Moonrise, Hernandez." It's beautiful.

Q: Do you do sports? What's your favorite sport?

A: My favorite sport is ice skating. It looks **easy**, but it's actually very difficult.

Q: Final question—who's your favorite sportsperson?

A: Right now, it's Megan Rapinoe. She's an amazing soccer player!

Susan's photo of King penguins at Gold Harbor, South Georgia Island

Hints for skimming:

1 Read the title.

2 Look at the pictures.

3 Read the headings and notice how the text is arranged.

4 In longer texts, read the first and last sentences of each paragraph.

5 Try to notice key words.

Scanning is a reading technique to look for specific information or to find information in a list (e.g., *a phone number, the time a TV show starts, the page of an item in a catalog*).

Hints for scanning:

1 Don't read every word. It's not important to understand everything.

2 Think about the order of the information. Is it by date (chronological)? Is it alphabetical? Is it by time (like a bus schedule)?

3 When possible, use titles and headings to help you find the information quickly. With longer texts, also use header words at the top of sections, pages, and columns.

4 When searching for names or places, scan for capital letters.

5 When searching for a statistic or other numerical facts, look for numbers in the text.

Additional Activities to Use with the Reading

Vocabulary Building

Readings sometimes have words that will be new for the students. You can use these words in many ways. For example, have students write the words in a vocabulary notebook. The notebook can be ordered by unit or alphabetically. If you choose the latter, students should leave several blank pages between each letter.

Have students write easy explanations in English or draw pictures to help them remember the meanings of new words.

Encourage students to only use English in their notebooks.

Regularly collect the notebooks to provide feedback and/or correction as appropriate.

To reinforce the vocabulary, you can also:

1 Provide opportunities for students to regularly review their notebooks and use the words they have learned in previous lessons.

2 At the beginning of the next lesson, do warm-up activities using this vocabulary.

3 Include these new words on the students' spelling list.

4 Include these words on regular quizzes to test spelling, meaning, usage, and/or parts of speech.

COMPREHENSION

A EXAM PRACTICE

Multiple-choice questions are used on standardized tests around the world. Hints for students:

- Students should not spend too much time on one question, particularly when all questions are equally weighted. They can return to a question at the end if they have extra time.
- The students' understanding of meaning is tested. Repetition of words can be deceiving, so they should not choose an answer simply because it has some of the same words as the passage.
- When students are uncertain of the answer, they should eliminate wrong answers to increase the probability of correctly answering the item.

Have students read the questions to themselves and circle the correct answers.

After they have finished, check the answers as a class.

OPTIONAL Ask students additional true/false comprehension questions.

1. *That's difficult in line 13 means That's a difficult photo*. (False. It means *That's a difficult question*. Explain that it's difficult because she has many favorite photos.)
2. *Susan thinks ice skating is easy.* (False. She thinks it is difficult.)
3. *Megan Rapinoe is a soccer player.* (True.)
4. *Susan's picture of King penguins is from South Georgia Island.* (True. Students must look at the photo caption to answer this question.)

COMPREHENSION

A Answer the questions about *My Favorite Things*.

1 MAIN IDEA What's another title for the article?

a Susan's Photos   b Susan's Travels   ⓒ About Susan

2 DETAIL Susan likes the ____ on South Georgia Island.

ⓐ animals   b plants   c people

3 REFERENCE The word *They* in line 11 refers to ____.

a giraffes   ⓑ penguins   c Susan's photos

4 PURPOSE Susan talks about Ansel Adams when giving an example of ____.

ⓐ her favorite photo   b her favorite photographer   c a person she works with

5 DETAIL Which of the following is true about Susan?

a She works at home.   b She's a teacher.   ⓒ She likes sports.

B Complete the chart. Write Susan's favorite things and yours.

Susan's Favorite Things	My Favorite Things
South Georgia Island, giraffes, Ansel Adams's "Moonrise, Hernandez", ice skating, Megan Rapinoe	Answers will vary.

C CRITICAL THINKING Comparing **Talk with a partner.** How are you and Susan the same? How are you different? Answers will vary.

Susan's favorite animal is …
That's my favorite animal, too.

IDIOM

"I'm really into …" means ____.

a I think …

ⓑ I really like …

B Tell students that we sometimes use a chart to help us compare two things more easily. Explain that when we compare things, we look at how they are similar and how they are different.

Point to the headings in the chart, and read them aloud, as students follow along in their books.

Explain to the students that they should use the text on page 13 to complete the left side of the chart. Tell them to write their own answers on the right side of the chart.

Have students do the task. Check the answers for "Susan's Favorite Things."

C CRITICAL THINKING

As students follow along, read the questions aloud. Tell students they will use their charts in **B** to talk about these questions.

Model the conversation with a student. Have students get into pairs and discuss the questions.

VOCABULARY

A Complete the sentences. Use the words in the box.

travel interesting love watch difficult easy

1 My favorite food is pizza. I love it!
2 I'm not good at skiing. It's difficult for me.
3 The title of the book is interesting. I want to read it.
4 I want to travel around Southeast Asia.
5 Baseball is my favorite sport. I watch the games on TV.
6 This is my favorite photo app. It's easy to use.

B Read the information below. Look for these words in the article. Write them in the chart.

Nouns are names of people, things, and places.
Verbs are actions.
Adjectives describe things.

travel favorite sports animal fun do love interesting photographer

Nouns	Verbs	Adjectives
sports, animal, photographer	travel, do, love	favorite, fun, interesting

WRITING

A Read the sentences.

B Make notes about each space. What kind of information goes there (e.g., a name, a noun, or a number)?

C Write about yourself and a friend. Complete the sentences. Answers will vary.

My name is ______. I am from ______. My favorite ______ is ______ and my favorite ______ is ______. I am ___ years old and my best friend is ___ years old. ______ name is ______. His/Her favorite ______ is ______.

Unit 1 15

IDIOM

As students follow along in their books, read the statement aloud. Have them guess the answer before explaining that *be into* means to be very interested in something. For example:

He's really into Taylor Swift. He listens to her music all the time.

She's into tennis. She plays it every day.

CHALLENGE Have students get into pairs and make sentences using the idiom. After a few minutes, have pairs share their sentences with the class, and provide guidance on usage problems.

VOCABULARY

A As students follow along, read the words in the box aloud. Have students find them in the **READING** passage.

Have students use the words in the box to complete the sentences. Check answers as a class.

B As students follow along, read the information in the box aloud. Explain that verbs are things we do.

Have students find the words in the article and write them in the chart.

Check answers as a class.

SUPPORT Before students do the task, say some words (e.g., *book*, *good*) and do some gestures (e.g., *running*) and have students classify the words as nouns, verbs, and adjectives.

WRITING

Tell students that they are going to write a short paragraph.

A As students follow along, read the example paragraph aloud.

B As a class, have students discuss what information they need for each blank (e.g., age, favorite thing). Have students make notes with ideas for their paragraph.

C Have students use their notes from **B** and complete the sentences about themselves and a friend. Give them a time limit for finishing the task or assign it as homework.

OPTIONAL After students finish, have them get into groups, randomly exchange papers, and take turns reading each other's paragraphs so they can guess who wrote them. Emphasize that they must omit the first sentence with the student's name. Have group members guess who the person is.

VIDEO **ABOUT THE VIDEO** Learn about everyone's favorite things.

WHAT'S *YOUR* FAVORITE?

Before You Watch

Talk with a partner. Say three of your favorite things. *Answers will vary.*

While You Watch

A ▶ 1.2 **Watch the video.** Check (✓) the things the speaker talks about.

- [x] colors
- [x] food
- [x] sports
- [x] people
- [ ] singers
- [x] movies
- [x] countries
- [ ] apps

B ▶ 1.2 **Watch again.** Circle **T** for true or **F** for false.

1	Andre's favorite color is red.	T	Ⓕ
2	Jenny's favorite food is pizza.	Ⓣ	F
3	Gordon and Alyssa's favorite sport is soccer.	Ⓣ	F
4	Matthew's favorite movie is the same as Jasmine's.	Ⓣ	F
5	Sarah's favorite country is the Netherlands.	T	Ⓕ

C ▶ 1.2 **Watch again.** Circle the correct answers.

1 Samira's favorite color is (**yellow**) / **white**.

2 David's favorite food is **the same as** / (**different from**) Jenny's.

3 Nichola is **Kalam's** / (**Alexandra's**) best friend.

4 Danielle is from **China** / (**Canada**).

After You Watch

Talk with a partner. What are their favorite things? Are they the same as or different from the people in the video? *Answers will vary.*

ABOUT THE PHOTO

This picture shows Doi Inthanon, the highest peak in Thailand at a height of 2,565 meters above sea level. Surrounding the mountain is a national park covering 482 square kilometers. Doi Inthanon was named after Inthawichayanon, one of the last kings of Chiang Mai, who was concerned about the forests in northern Thailand and wanted to preserve them. The summit of Doi Inthanon offers visitors amazing views in the early morning. Other attractions include several waterfalls and the two chedis that were built to honor the 60th birthday anniversaries of King Bhumibol Adulyadej and Queen Sirikit.

VIDEO

Tell students they are going to watch a video. As students follow along, read the title and the sentence about the video aloud.

OPTIONAL Tell students that thinking about a video before watching it will make it easier to understand.

Before watching the video, ask students to predict things they might see. For example: favorite sports.

After watching the video, ask students how many of their predictions were correct.

BEFORE YOU WATCH

As students follow along in their books, read the statement aloud. Have students get into pairs and think of three of their favorite things.

OPTIONAL Have students find Thailand on a world map.

WHILE YOU WATCH

A Tell students they will watch the video and they should check the things that the speaker talks about. As students follow along, read the items aloud.

▶ 1.2 Play Video 1.2. Encourage students who are uncertain to listen for the answers as they watch the video again in **B**.

B Explain to students that they will watch the video again, and they should circle **T** if the statement is true and **F** if the statement is false. As students follow along, read the statements aloud.

▶ 1.2 Play Video 1.2.

Check answers as a class. Then check answers in **A**.

SUPPORT Before reading the statements to the students, explain true and false by pointing to something that is not blue. Say *blue* and use gestures to indicate to students that this is not true. Tell them this is *false*. Repeat with several more objects, asking students to determine if each is true or false.

C Explain to students that they will watch the video again, and they should circle the correct answers to complete the sentences. As students follow along, read the statements aloud.

▶ 1.2 Play Video 1.2.

Check answers as a class.

OPTIONAL Download the video scripts from the *Time Zones* website. After students have watched the video, have students read along as you play the video. Play it again, pausing as necessary so students can repeat.

AFTER YOU WATCH

Tell students they will get into pairs and talk about the video.

As students follow along in their books, read the questions aloud.

Have them get into pairs and do the task.

REVIEW

A Complete the sentences. Use the words in the box.

movie video games singer app TV show

1 That song is great. Who's the singer?
2 My favorite TV show is on every Monday at 8 o'clock.
3 Instagram is my favorite app for photos.
4 My favorite movie is *Guardians of the Galaxy*.
5 I play video games on my computer.

B Complete the questions and answers.

1 **A:** What's your favorite color?
B: It's blue.
2 **A:** What's John's favorite movie?
B: His favorite movie is *X-Men*.
3 **A:** Who's Sofia's favorite writer?
B: Her favorite writer is J. R. R. Tolkien.
4 **A:** Carla's favorite TV show is *Sherlock*.
B: What's her favorite video game?

C Look at the word groups. Cross out the odd one in each group.

1 do watch ~~favorite~~
2 do ~~animal~~ love
3 sports animal ~~difficult~~
4 ~~go~~ photo soccer
5 amazing ~~country~~ interesting

SELF CHECK Now I can ...

- [ ] talk about my favorite things
- [ ] use language for talking about favorites
- [ ] talk about popular sports around the world

The top of Doi Inthanon in Thailand

REVIEW

Explain to students that they are going to review the material from the unit and this will help them remember what they have studied.

A Explain that activity **A** reviews vocabulary from the unit. Have students use the words in the box to complete the sentences. Check answers as a class.

CHALLENGE As students recall other vocabulary that was important in the unit, write it on the board (e.g., *difficult*, *travel*, *interesting*, *love*, *watch*, *easy*). Have students get into pairs and take turns making sentences using the words. After students have finished, randomly call on pairs to share one of their sentences. As you repeat back the sentences, make corrections to grammar and vocabulary usage.

B Explain that activity **B** reviews the grammar from the unit. Have students write the correct words to complete the questions and answers. Have students get into pairs and check answers, before you randomly call on students to give the answers.

OPTIONAL Have students get into pairs and practice the conversations. When they have finished, have students personalize the answers.

C Point out that activity **C** reviews words from **VOCABULARY** activities **A** and **B**.

Explain that there are three words, but one is different than the other two. As students follow along in their books, read the three words in **1** aloud. Ask students why *favorite* is not the same. (It is an adjective, whereas the other two are verbs.)

Have students cross out the odd word in each group. Check answers.

SELF CHECK

These *I can* statements provide vital feedback on students' perceived ability to use the language from the unit. If you find students are reluctant to check that they can do the skills, consider asking them to rate themselves from 1 (not very confident) to 3 (very confident).

OPTIONAL Have students complete the **SELF CHECK** before doing the **REVIEW** activities. After reviewing the unit, have students once again check their confidence for each statement.

UNIT 2

THIS PLACE IS AMAZING!

CONTENT AREA: PEOPLE AND PLACES

Topic: places

Vocabulary: places: sea, beach, building, store, city, street, hotel, island, town, restaurant; **adjectives:** big, beautiful, clean, famous, old, small, great; **things:** boat, tourists

Grammar: the verb *be* and adjectives

Extra material: a world map

Other useful vocabulary: places: palace, museum, monument, stadium, temple, shrine, church, mosque, mountain, wall, rock, cave; **other words:** underground, house

END OF UNIT PROJECT Have students do some research about a famous place in their country that is not their own city. Explain that when they meet people from other countries, they sometimes explain famous places. Remind them that they made a list of three wonders of their country on page 23. Tell them they can use one of these places if they want.

Ask them to do research and use it to write several sentences. Explain that they should imagine they are talking to someone who knows nothing about their country. Tell them they can bring in a map. Alternatively, provide maps (paper or digital).

To provide structure, ask students to answer the following questions: Say,

What is the name of the place?

Where is it? (Tell them to bring a map to show the other students.)

What is it like? (e.g., *This place is beautiful.*)

What are the (beaches) like? (*The beaches are very nice.*)

In class, tell students to play a guessing game. Have them get into small groups and take turns reading their reports without saying the name of the place. Other group members should listen and guess the place. After students have discovered what the place is, tell group members to ask questions about their partners' place.

2

THIS PLACE IS AMAZING!

Copacabana Beach is a popular place in Rio de Janeiro, Brazil.

PREVIEW

A 2.1 **Match the places with the pictures.** Then listen and check your answers.

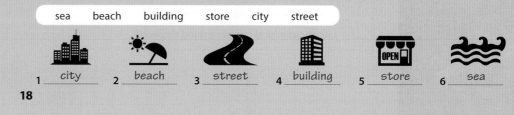

sea beach building store city street

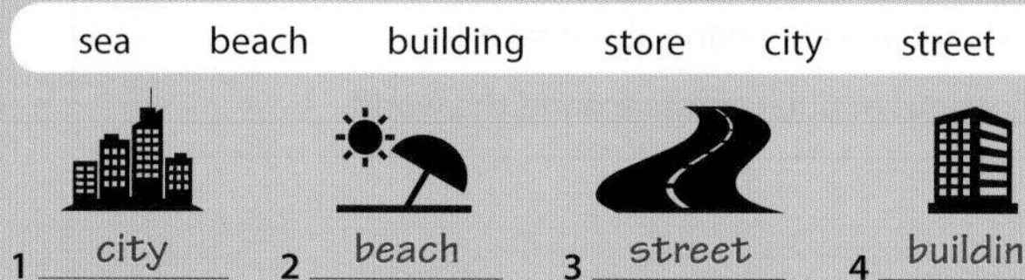

1 city 2 beach 3 street 4 building 5 store 6 sea

18

TEACHING NOTE: EXPECTATIONS IN CLASS

During the first few weeks of class, tell your students about your expectations for the class. For example:

Ask students to take notes and be active learners.

Encourage them to speak in English.

Remind students to not text during class.

ABOUT THE PHOTO

This photo shows Copacabana Beach, one of the most famous beaches in the world. It is four kilometers long and is a popular place with tourists and local people. Many sports facilities are located along the beach, such as volleyball nets and soccer courts, where people can enjoy a game of beach volleyball or beach soccer. Kiosks offering local food and drinks, and beach vendors hawking their wares add to the air of activity on the beach. Copacabana Beach is host to one of the largest outdoor parties in the world—more than two million people gather there for the annual New Year's Eve celebrations.

PEOPLE AND PLACES

B **Talk with a partner.** Look at the photo. Which places from **A** do you see? *city, beach, streets, buildings, sea*

C **Talk with a partner.** Ask about their favorite places. *Answers will vary.*

UNIT GOALS

- talk about places in your city
- use language for describing places
- learn about amazing places around the world

19

If you do not allow students to use their phones in class (e.g., to search for words and information), tell them to put their cell phones and other technology away so it doesn't distract them.

PREVIEW

Have students read the unit title to themselves as you read it aloud. Explain that in this unit they will learn to talk about and describe amazing places.

A Explain to students that they should match the places with the pictures. As students follow along, read the words in the box aloud. Have students do the task.

Tell students they should listen and check their answers.

2.1 Play Audio Track 2.1. Play it again, if necessary. Check answers as a class.

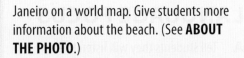

OPTIONAL Have students read the photo caption. Then have them find Brazil and Rio de Janeiro on a world map. Give students more information about the beach. (See **ABOUT THE PHOTO**.)

B Read the question aloud, as students follow along in their books. Have students get into pairs and talk about their ideas.

SUPPORT Using the photo, ask students additional questions until they become comfortable with the vocabulary. For example: point to the beach. Ask, *What color is the beach?*

C Tell students to get into pairs and take turns asking and answering questions about their favorite places. If necessary, before students start, ask them to brainstorm questions they can ask, such as *What's your favorite store?*

CHALLENGE Ask students to name some other places. (See **Other useful vocabulary**.) Have students work with a partner again and talk about their favorites among these places.

UNIT GOALS

Direct students' attention to the **UNIT GOALS** box. Explain that these are some of the things students will learn in this unit. Point out that this unit is about people and places. As students follow along, read each of the unit goals to the class. Explain any words students do not know. Remind students that at the end of the unit there is a self check that allows them to see if they have accomplished each goal.

TEACHING NOTE: UNIT GOALS

Discussing the unit goals is an important part of introducing the unit. It gives students a framework to better understand what they are going to learn. It also allows them to activate prior knowledge and experiences about the topic and vocabulary, so they can organize the content to understand and learn it more efficiently.

LANGUAGE FOCUS

A Tell students they will listen to a conversation with four short exchanges between Stig and Nadine.

2.2 Play Audio Track 2.2 as students listen and follow along in their books. If necessary, play the conversation again, pausing after each speaker so students can repeat.

As students follow along, read the question, *Do Stig and Nadine like Amsterdam?* Have students answer.

Have students work in pairs and practice the conversation once. Point out the bold words and read them aloud as students follow along in their books. You might want to have students repeat the words after you say them. If necessary, explain the meaning of any words that students seem unfamiliar with.

Tell students they will practice the conversation two more times, changing the bold words each time and swapping roles after the first time.

OPTIONAL Have students practice the conversation again, substituting words to personalize it. Ask pairs to volunteer to present their own conversations in the front of the class.

REAL ENGLISH

Direct students' attention to the expression in the **REAL ENGLISH** box. Explain that the expression *Wow!* is used in informal spoken English to show you are surprised.
For example:

A: There's a man with a monkey!
B: Wow!

Tell students that *Wow!* can also be used when the speaker is impressed. For example:

A: My dog won first prize in the pet show!
B: Wow! That's great.

LANGUAGE FOCUS

A 2.2 **Listen and read.** Do Stig and Nadine like Amsterdam? Then repeat the conversation and replace the words in **bold**. Yes, they do.

REAL ENGLISH Wow!

Stig: It's my first time in Amsterdam. What a **big** city! (**beautiful** / **clean**)
Nadine: It's my first time here, too. Look at those buildings, Stig!
Stig: They're houses. They're **amazing**. (**famous** / **beautiful**)
Nadine: Yes, they are. And they're **colorful**. (**old** / **small**)

Stig: There's another famous place in Amsterdam—the NEMO Science Museum.
Nadine: Wow! The design of the building is **interesting**. (**beautiful** / **great**)
Stig: The place is very popular with tourists.
Nadine: We're tourists, too! Let's go there. I want to take photos.

B 2.3 **Look at the chart.** Then circle the correct answers below.

DESCRIBING PLACES (USING *BE* AND ADJECTIVES)		
This place **is famous**. / The buildings **are amazing**. They**'re** very **new**. They**'re not old**. / They **aren't old**.		They're = They are They're not = They are not aren't = are not isn't = is not
Is the street **long**?	**Yes**, it **is**. **No**, it **isn't** / it**'s not**.	
Are the houses **big**?	**Yes**, they **are**. **No**, they **aren't** / they**'re not**.	

1 We use *are* with **one thing** / **more than one thing**.
2 We add *not* to make a **question** / **negative sentence**.
3 We use *Is/Are* at the beginning of a **question** / **sentence**.

20 Unit 2

B Ask students to look at the chart.

2.3 Have students follow along as they listen to Audio Track 2.3.

Read the first three lines from the left side of the chart aloud as students follow along in their books. Explain that the subject of the first sentence (*this place*) doesn't have an *s* (is singular) so *is* is used. Draw students' attention to the next subject (*buildings*). Explain that it is plural (*buildings*), so the verb is *are*.

On the board, write *My school* ______ *amazing*. Underneath, write *The stores* ______ *amazing*. Ask students to provide the missing verbs (*is*, *are*). Continue with other examples, as necessary.

Draw students' attention to the contractions on the right side of the chart. Point out that *they're* is the contraction (shortened form) of *they are*. Explain the other contractions.

C Complete the sentences. Use the correct form of the verb *be*.

1 The streets are beautiful.
2 The photo isn't old. It's new.
3 The rooms aren't big. They're small.
4 Look! There is an island in the sea.

IDIOM

A place "in the middle of nowhere" is somewhere ____.
a in the center of the city
(b) far from everything

D 2.4 **Look at the photo below.** Write questions and answers with the words. Then listen and check.

1 this building / in Mexico?
Is this building in Mexico?
Yes, it is.

2 the flag / small?
Is the flag small?
No, it isn't.

3 this place / famous?
Is this place famous?
Yes, it is.

4 the building / new?
Is the building new?
No, it isn't.

E Work in a group. Play a memory game. Answers will vary.

The city is beautiful.

The city is beautiful and the streets are clean.

The city is beautiful, the streets are clean, and the houses are small.

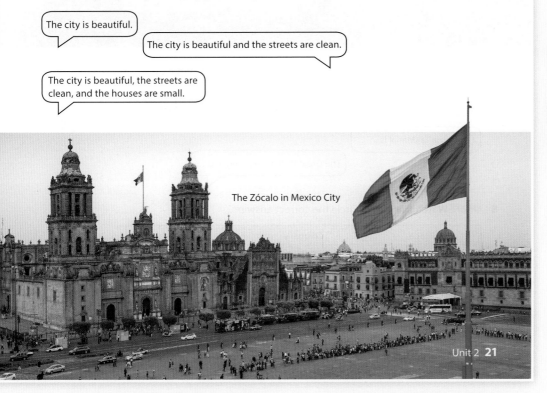

The Zócalo in Mexico City

Unit 2 21

Read the first question in the chart aloud. Draw circles around the verb (*is*) in the question and answer to emphasize that it is repeated in both. Explain that the subject (*the street*) is referred to by *it* in the answer.

Read the second question in the chart aloud and ask students why *are* rather than *is* is used, providing the answer if necessary (the question asks about *houses* not *a house*). Point out that *are* is repeated in the answers.

Emphasize that questions starting with *Is* and *Are* are *yes/no* questions.

Draw students' attention to the three statements under the chart. Have students do the task. Check answers.

C Tell students that *is* and *are* are forms of the verb *be*. Tell students that they should complete the sentences using the correct form of the verb *be*. Have students do the task. Check answers.

IDIOM

Read the statement aloud, as students follow along in their books. Have students guess the answer before providing it (b). Tell students that *in the middle of nowhere* is used to emphasize how remote something is.

D Ask students to look at the photo and make questions and answers with the words provided. Have students do the task.

Explain to students that they will listen and check their answers.

2.4 Play Audio Track 2.4. Check answers as a class.

OPTIONAL Have students get into pairs and take turns asking and answering the questions.

E Tell students they are going to play a memory game in a group.

Explain that they will take turns adding new information to a sentence, but they must also remember the previous information.

Model the game with two students. Point out that the third student repeated the first and second students' information before adding his or her own (about the houses).

Check understanding of how the game works.

Have the students play the game.

SUPPORT Making new sentences and remembering what was previously said can be quite difficult for students. To help them, before playing the game, give them time to write out several sentences that they can use for the game.

THE REAL WORLD

Ask students to look at the photo. As students follow along, read the title aloud.

CONTENT NOTE: WONDERS OF THE WORLD

The Taj Mahal, in Agra, was built by the Mughal emperor to remember his wife. In total, it took 21 years to build and utilized craftsmen from across the empire, Central Asia, and Iran. It includes the tomb, a mosque, gates, courtyards, gardens, and a guest house.

Researchers believe Machu Picchu was built around 1450 as a resort-like escape for the Inca ruler Pachacuti and those in the upper classes. This fact helps explain estimates that only 500 to 750 people lived there. Experts believe the people farmed the terraces and hills in order to survive.

Petra, also known as the "Rose City," contains caves, temples, and tombs that give us hints about the kingdom of Nabataea. It is believed the Nabataeans gained great wealth by trading incense, and Petra helped to connect traders moving back and forth between the Mediterranean Sea and the Arabian Sea.

A As students follow along, read the question and the names of the places in the box aloud. Have students get into pairs and share their ideas.

B Tell students they are going to watch a video and they should circle the location and age of each place.

▶ 2.1 Play Video 2.1. If necessary, play the video again. Check answers as a class.

OPTIONAL Have students locate the countries in the table on a world map.

C Tell students they should watch again and circle **T** if the statement is true and **F** if it is false. As students follow along, read the statements aloud.

THE REAL WORLD

ABOUT THE PHOTO

Spanning a length of 21,196 kilometers, construction of the Great Wall of China began around 220 BCE, when Emperor Qin Shi Huang ordered the remnants of ancient fortifications and walls to be joined into a unified wall that would protect China against attacks from the north. The Great Wall was constructed over a period of more than 2,000 years and involved millions of Chinese workers. The Great Wall was designated as a UNESCO World Heritage site in 1987. While sections of the Great Wall have been rebuilt or restored over the years, preservation of the Great Wall remains a challenge for Chinese and international organizations.

A part of the Great Wall of China

A **You are going to watch a video about the places below.** What do you know about them? Talk with a partner. *Answers will vary.*

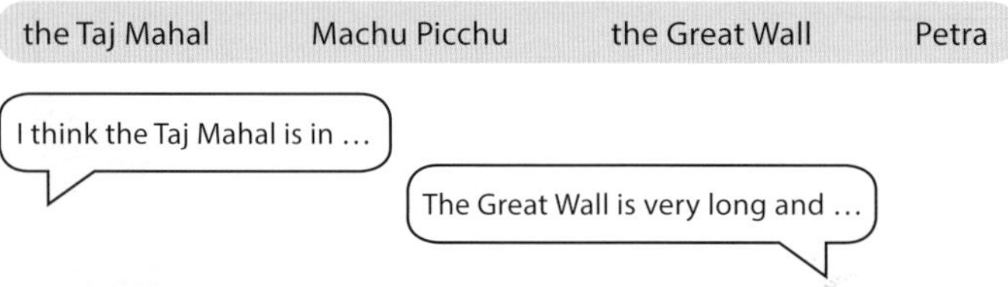

the Taj Mahal
Machu Picchu
the Great Wall
Petra
I think the Taj Mahal is in …
The Great Wall is very long and …

B ▶ 2.1 **Watch the video.** Circle the correct answers.

Place	Country	... years old
1 Machu Picchu	Brazil / (Peru)	60 / (600)
2 the Great Wall	(China) / Japan	(2,300) / 3,200
3 Taj Mahal	Italy / (India)	200 / (400)
4 Petra	(Jordan) / Australia	1,500 / (2,000)

22 Unit 2

▶ 2.1 Play Video 2.1. If necessary, play the video again. Check answers as a class.

OPTIONAL Have students correct the false statement. (**3** The Taj Mahal is white.)

DO YOU KNOW?

Read the information and the choices as students follow along in their books. Have a few students guess the answer before telling them (a).

D CRITICAL THINKING

As students follow along, read the questions aloud. Tell students that *justifying* means giving reasons for your ideas. Explain that even though students may have the same opinion, their reasons could be different, so providing reasons is important. Encourage students to give reasons for their answers.

Have students get into pairs and talk about their ideas.

C ▶ 2.1 **Watch again.** Circle **T** for true or **F** for false.

1 Machu Picchu is a city. (T) F

2 The Great Wall is 21,000 kilometers long. (T) F

3 The Taj Mahal is blue. T (F)

4 There are stone buildings in Petra. (T) F

DO YOU KNOW?

The name "Machu Picchu" means ____.

(a) old mountain
b beautiful mountain

D CRITICAL THINKING Justifying **Talk with a partner.** Why do you think these places are Wonders of the World? What makes them special? *Answers will vary.*

PROJECT Work with a partner. Make a list of three wonders of your city or country.

PRONUNCIATION long and short *i* sounds

A 2.5 **Listen and repeat.**

1 building (short *i*) 2 street (long *i*)

B 2.6 **Listen.** Are the *i* sounds in these words long (**L**) or short (**S**)? Then read the words to a partner.

city S sea L green L big S beautiful S

COMMUNICATION

A Work in a group. Choose a famous place in your city.

B Play a guessing game. Take turns. **Group A:** Ask questions about the place. **Group B:** Answer "yes" or "no." *Answers will vary.*

Is it old?
No, it isn't.
Is it a building?
Yes, it is.

Lotte World in Seoul, South Korea

Unit 2 23

OPTIONAL Give students more information about each place. (See **CONTENT NOTE** and **ABOUT THE PHOTO**.)

PROJECT As students follow along, read the project instructions aloud. Have students get into pairs and do the task.

CHALLENGE After giving students a few minutes to complete the task, have a few pairs share their ideas. If a student only provides a place name, ask the student to explain why it is a wonder. In order to promote critical and creative thinking, ask the class to think of at least two other reasons why the place is amazing.

PRONUNCIATION

A Tell students that in English the vowel *i* can be pronounced in different ways, so they need to remember not only how new words are said but also how they are spelled.

Explain that they will study the sounds for the long and short *i*. Tell them to listen and repeat.

2.5 Play Audio Track 2.5. Play it again, pausing after each word so students can repeat. Students may have difficulty hearing the difference between the two. Play the audio a third time, if necessary.

B Explain that for each word, they must listen and decide whether the word has a long *i* or a short *i* sound, writing **L** or **S**.

2.6 Play Audio Track 2.6. Play it again, if necessary. Check answers.

Have students get into pairs and take turns saying the words with their partner.

COMMUNICATION

A Tell students they are going to play a guessing game. Have them get into groups and choose a place in their city.

B Tell students that two groups will get together and they will try to guess the other groups' place. Emphasize that they can only ask *yes/no* questions.

Model the activity with a student.

Have students play the game and switch roles after the first round.

OPTIONAL Tell students that the winner is the team that guesses the place with the fewest number of questions. After groups have finished playing the game, as a class determine which group is the overall winner.

READING

Have one student read the title aloud.

A Ask students to look at the photos. Read the captions aloud as students follow along.

As students follow along, read the three statements in **A** aloud. Have students check the ones they think are true.

Ask a few students which statements they checked. Discuss as a class.

B Tell students to skim the text and underline the adjectives. If necessary, remind students that an adjective is a word that describes something (i.e., a noun or pronoun). Have students do the task.

When all the students have finished, check answers as a class.

Give students time to read the text in more detail before moving on to **C**.

Ask students to once again look at the statements in **A** and decide which are true.

OPTIONAL The text can also be used as a listening activity. Have students close their books. Tell students they will listen to the passage.

2.7 Play Audio Track 2.7. Ask students to get into pairs and discuss what information they heard. Then have them read the article more carefully.

C As students follow along in their books, read the question aloud. Point out that the question asks for their opinion so there is no correct answer.

Have students get into pairs and do the task.

OPTIONAL Have students find Colombia and Adelaide, Australia, on a world map. Then tell students more about Santa Cruz del Islote and Coober Pedy. (See **CONTENT NOTE** and **ABOUT THE PHOTO**.)

READING
A Look at the photos. Check (✓) the information you think is true.
✓ Santa Cruz del Islote is an island.
☐ Coober Pedy is a cold place.
✓ People live in both places.
B Skim the article. Underline the adjectives.
C Talk with a partner. Why do you think these places are amazing?
Answers will vary.
Santa Cruz del Islote
24 Unit 2

ABOUT THE PHOTO

The main photo shows an aerial view of Santa Cruz del Islote, an island described as being the size of two football fields. While tourists can visit the island, there's nowhere for them to spend the night on the island. The nearest hotel is on Múcura Island, a short distance away by boat.

The other photo shows an underground museum in Coober Pedy, a small town located in northern South Australia. It is estimated that the town has a population of 2,500. (See **CONTENT NOTE** for more information.)

CONTENT NOTE: SANTA CRUZ DEL ISLOTE AND COOBER PEDY

Santa Cruz del Islote, one of 10 islands in the San Bernardo Archipelago, is one of the most densely populated places in the world. Unique in many ways, the islanders contend that there is no crime on the island. As a result, there are no police officers. There are also no mosquitos, which the locals believe is the result of a lack of beaches and mangrove trees. There is limited access to water and electricity on the island, and while seafood is easily available to the residents, all other food and household goods have to be brought in by boat.

Coober Pedy is famous as a mining town. Approximately 70 percent of the world's opals come from the town, but the city is not for the faint of heart. It can get hot, particularly in January when temperatures regularly reach 42°C during the day. This heat is part of the reason people started living underground. In 1985, the town was the backdrop for the movie *Mad Max Beyond Thunderdome*.

AMAZING PLACES

A 2.7 This **island** is Santa Cruz del Islote. It's two hours by **boat** from Cartagena, Colombia. It's very small, but over 1,000 people live here. There's a school, two stores, and a **restaurant**. Many people live here all their lives.

B Coober Pedy is a small **town** in Australia. It's eight hours by car from Adelaide. There are no tall buildings in Coober Pedy. Everything is underground! About 1,500 people live in underground houses. Some houses are very big. A lot of **tourists** visit Coober Pedy. They go to the underground stores and **hotels**.

A museum in Coober Pedy

Unit 2 25

Additional Activities to Use with the Reading

Additional Comprehension Questions

1 *How many restaurants are on Santa Cruz del Islote?* (one)

2 *How far is Coober Pedy from Adelaide?* (eight hours)

3 *Are all of the buildings in Coober Pedy one or two stories tall?* (yes)

4 *Which place has more people?* (Coober Pedy)

Vocabulary Extension

Draw students' attention to the words in orange. Help students understand and remember the words.

Have students name some towns near them.

Using gestures if necessary, ask students to raise their hands if they have used a boat. Also ask questions. For example:

Hawaii has many islands. Is it famous in (your country)?

What's your favorite restaurant?

Do a lot of tourists visit (your area)?

What's a famous hotel in (your area)?

Question Construction

Have students get into pairs. Ask,

Is Santa Cruz del Islote a store? (No, it isn't.)

Is Coober Pedy an island? (No, it isn't.)

Are the hotels in Coober Pedy underground? (Yes, they are.)

Point out that there are many factual questions they can ask about the reading. Tell students to take turns asking and answering other factual questions about the reading passage.

Grammar (Focused)

Explain that *is*/*are very* (adjective) is the same as *is*/*are* (adjective) but adding *very* makes the adjective stronger. Have students underline all the instances of *is very* + (adjective) and *are very* + (adjective) in the article (*it's very small*, *are very big*).

Personalization and Presentation

Have students do research about another small island. Ask them to bring in pictures of the island and prepare some basic information to present to the class. For example:

- location (e.g., distance from a city)
- number of people
- things on the island

In class, have students get into small groups and take turns talking about their islands.

COMPREHENSION

A Have students read the questions to themselves and circle the correct answers.

After they have finished, have them get into pairs and check their answers. Then check answers as a class.

B EXAM PRACTICE

A Venn diagram is a graphic organizer that has two or more circles. The diagram is included in standardized tests such as the PTE Academic Speaking Test, which requires students to study the diagram for a short time before describing it. A Venn diagram organizes information into groups, each representing how one set of things is related to others (e.g., as a subset, with some similarities but other differences). The diagram provides a visual representation that allows for easy comparison and contrast. In a two-circle diagram, for example, students should notice things that are in (1) only one set, (2) both sets, (3) neither set.

Point to the diagram. Explain that this is a Venn diagram and that these diagrams are used to visually show how two (or more) things are similar and different.

Ask students what two things are being compared in this diagram (Santa Cruz del Islote and Coober Pedy).

Point to the overlapping area in the center. Ask students what they think this area represents, providing the answer if necessary (things that both places have in common).

Tell students they will classify the sentences by writing the letters **a**–**f** in the diagram. As students follow along, read the sentences aloud.

Have students do the task. Check answers as a class.

COMPREHENSION

A Answer the questions about *Amazing Places.*

1 MAIN IDEA The article describes two places that are ____.

a very big b underwater (c) unusual places to live

2 REFERENCE The word *here* in the third sentence of paragraph A refers to ____.

a the boat b Cartagena (c) Santa Cruz del Islote

3 DETAIL Many people from Santa Cruz del Islote ____.

a move to Cartagena b are tourists (c) live there all their lives

4 COHESION What's the best place for this sentence?

"They also eat at the cafés."

a end of paragraph A (b) end of paragraph B c beginning of paragraph B

5 DETAIL Which place do you go to by car?

a Santa Cruz del Islote (b) Coober Pedy c both places

B Complete the Venn diagram. Write the letters (**a–f**).

a It's in the sea.
b There are stores.
c There are underground houses.
d It's popular with tourists.
e There are no tall buildings.
f Over 1,000 people live there.

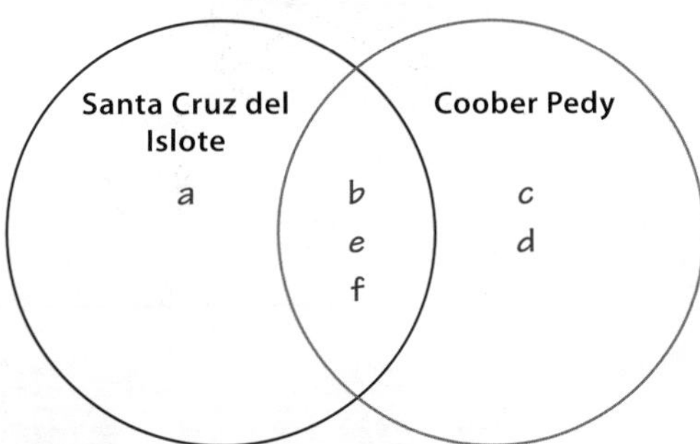

C CRITICAL THINKING Applying **Talk with a partner.** Think of one more adjective to describe each place in the article. Answers will vary.

Houses on Santa Cruz del Islote

26 Unit 2

SUPPORT Before doing **B**, provide a simple example of a Venn diagram. Have two students say the names of something (e.g., *food*) that they like. On the board, draw two circles, label each with one food item. Point out that students who like both foods are in the overlap group. Randomly call on some students to say which of the two foods they like, writing their names in the diagram in the appropriate place. If a student doesn't like either food, they should be placed outside of both of the diagram circles.

C CRITICAL THINKING

As students follow along, read the sentence aloud. Have students get into pairs and talk about their ideas.

VOCABULARY

A As students follow along, read the words in the box aloud. Have students find them in the **READING** passage.

Point out that the sentences summarize the passage. Have students use the

VOCABULARY

A Find the words below in the article. Then complete the sentences.

island boat restaurant town tourists hotels

Santa Cruz del Islote

1 People travel to the island on a(n) boat.

2 People can eat in the restaurant.

Coober Pedy

3 Many tourists visit the stores and hotels.

4 People take photos of the underground houses in the town.

B Read the information below. Then circle the correct answers.

> We use ***and*** to join two or more similar ideas.
>
> *They go to the underground stores **and** hotels.*
>
> We use ***but*** to join two different ideas.
>
> *It's very small, **but** over 1,000 people live here.*

1 There's a soccer ball, **and** / (**but**) there isn't a basketball.

2 Coober Pedy is a fun (**and**) / **but** interesting place.

3 There are bicycles on the island, **and** / (**but**) there are no cars.

4 There are young (**and**) / **but** old people.

WRITING

A Read the poster. Look at the photo.

B Choose an amazing place in your city. Find a photo of it. Make notes about the place. Use the words in the box to help you.

famous	popular	important
interesting	fun	beautiful

C Make a poster. Write about the amazing place in your city. Answers will vary.

PLAZA DE ARMAS

Plaza de Armas in Lima, Peru, is very beautiful. There are many famous buildings in this place, such as the Aliaga House. It's a very old house and . . .

Unit 2 27

words in the box to complete the sentences. Check answers.

B As students follow along, read the information about *and* in the box aloud. Have students find another sentence with *and* in the **READING** passage. (*There's a school, two stores, and a restaurant.*)
Ask, *What are the similar ideas?* (The things that the town has.)

As students follow along, read the information about *but* in the box aloud. Ask students to explain why the author used *but*. If necessary, provide additional guidance by asking, *What are the two ideas? Why are they different?* Provide the answers if necessary. (The use of *but* shows the author's surprise. Even though the island is so small, more than 1,000 people live there. For such a small area, one might expect a smaller population.)

Tell students to circle the correct words to complete the sentences. Have students do the task. Check answers as a class.

WRITING

Tell students that they are going to make a poster about an amazing place in their city.

A Give students a moment to study the photo in the example poster. As students follow along, read the text on the poster aloud. Point out that the poster has many descriptive words (e.g., *beautiful*, *famous*, *old*) and a photo to make it easier to understand. Tell students their poster should have both of these elements.

SUPPORT Ask students to identify the kinds of information in the example poster. For example, they should note:

The first sentence says where the place is and gives a description.

The second sentence says what is there, giving a specific example.

The third sentence gives more information about the place.

B Tell students to each choose an amazing place in their city. As students follow along, read the words in the box aloud. Encourage them to use them as they make notes about their place.

C Have students use their notes from **B** and other ideas to make their posters. You might want to set a minimum number of sentences students must include (e.g., five). Give students a time limit for finishing the task in class or assign it as homework.

OPTIONAL After students have made their posters, have students take turns standing in front of the class to talk about their places. In large classes, divide students into groups and have students present to the smaller groups. Remind students to talk naturally and not just read the information.

VIDEO

Tell students they are going to watch a video about a famous place in Vietnam.

As students follow along, read the title and the sentence about the video aloud.

You might want to have students find Vietnam and then Ha Long Bay on a world map.

CHALLENGE Before watching the video, ask students what they know about Vietnam. Have them name places, food, and any other things they are familiar with.

CONTENT NOTE: HA LONG BAY

About 165 kilometers from Hanoi (the capital of Vietnam), the Ha Long Bay area is a UNESCO World Heritage site. *Ha Long* means "descending dragon" in Vietnamese, and a Vietnamese legend says a dragon sprayed jewels across the area to protect the people. According to the legend, over time these jewels became the limestone formations that are now famous around the world.

Ha Long Bay is also scientifically important because in other parts of the world, formations like these are not in the water. In addition, many of the islands have been undisturbed by humans, partially because people do not live on them.

VIDEO **ABOUT THE VIDEO** Ha Long Bay is a famous place in Vietnam.

HA LONG BAY

Before You Watch

Look at the photo. What do you think you can see at Ha Long Bay?

☑ tourists ☑ beaches ☑ boats ☐ tall buildings ☑ rocks

While You Watch

A ▶ 2.2 **Watch the video.** Check (✓) the information you hear.

☑ the number of islands
☐ famous food
☑ where the hotels are
☐ island names
☑ things to do on the islands

B ▶ 2.2 **Watch again.** Circle the correct answers.

1 There are 1,600 / **16,000** islands in Ha Long Bay.
2 Tourists stay on the **small** / big islands.
3 The shapes of the rocks / **buildings** in Ha Long Bay are interesting.
4 Tourists go to the islands by **car** / boat.

After You Watch

Talk with a partner. Do you know any other amazing places like Ha Long Bay? What are they like?
Answers will vary.

The islands in Ha Long Bay

28 Unit 2

BEFORE YOU WATCH

Have students look at the photo. Then, as students follow along in their books, read the question aloud. Have students check their guesses.

WHILE YOU WATCH

A Tell students they will watch the video and they should check the information they hear. As students follow along, read the information aloud.

▶ 2.2 Play Video 2.2. Check answers as a class.

B Explain to students that they will watch the video again, and they should circle the correct answers to complete the sentences. If necessary, read the sentences aloud as students follow along in their books.

▶ 2.2 Play Video 2.2. Play the video again, if necessary. Check answers as a class.

Have students look at their predictions in **BEFORE YOU WATCH**. Discuss why each option was correct or incorrect.

You might want to tell students more about Ha Long Bay. (See **CONTENT NOTE**.)

CHALLENGE Have students discuss which fact surprised them the most, giving reasons for their answers.

AFTER YOU WATCH

Tell students they are going to get into pairs and talk about the video.

As students follow along in their books, read the questions aloud.

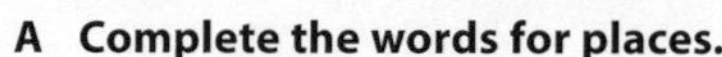

REVIEW

ABOUT THE PHOTO

This photo shows an aerial view of Ha Long Bay, located in Quảng Ninh Province, Vietnam. Containing an estimated 1,600 islands and islets, many featuring spectacular limestone karst landforms, Ha Long Bay has an area of around 1,500 square kilometers. (See **CONTENT NOTE** for more information.)

A Complete the words for places.

1 s e a
2 b u i l d i n g
3 s t o r e
4 c i t y
5 b e a c h
6 s t r e e t

B Write sentences and questions with *is* or *are*. Use the words below.

1 the sea / blue — The sea is blue.
2 the boats / not small — The boats aren't small.
3 the cities / big? — Are the cities big?
4 the island / beautiful? — Is the island beautiful?
5 the restaurants / popular — The restaurants are popular.
6 the beach / not clean — The beach isn't clean.

C Complete the sentences. Use *and* or *but*.

1 This is a clean ___and___ beautiful city.
2 There's a school in my town, ___but___ there isn't a park.
3 Ha Long Bay is a beautiful ___and___ amazing place.
4 There are many islands, ___but___ no one lives on them.
5 There are houses, stores, ___and___ restaurants on this street.

SELF CHECK Now I can ...

- ☐ talk about places in my city
- ☐ use language for describing places
- ☐ talk about amazing places around the world

Have them get into pairs and do the task.

CHALLENGE Ask, *Do you want to go to Vietnam? Do you want to see the caves? Do you want to climb the rocks?* Have students discuss their answers in pairs, small groups, or as a class, giving reasons for their answers.

REVIEW

Explain that students are going to review the material from the unit and this will help them remember what they have studied.

A Explain that activity **A** reviews vocabulary from the unit. Explain that they should write letters to complete the words.

Have students do the task. Check answers as a class.

CHALLENGE As students recall other vocabulary that was important in the unit, write it on the board (e.g., *museum*, *underground*). Have students get into pairs and take turns making sentences using the words. After students have finished, randomly call on pairs to share one of their sentences. As you repeat back the sentences, make corrections to grammar and vocabulary usage.

B Explain that activity **B** reviews the grammar from the unit. Have students use *is* or *are* and the words to make sentences and questions.

Have students do the task and then check answers as a class.

C Point out that activity **C** reviews words from **VOCABULARY** activity **B**.

Have students write the correct words to complete the sentences. Check answers.

SUPPORT Write sentence 1 on the board. Cover up *and beautiful*. Read the sentence aloud. Cover up *clean and*. Read the sentence aloud. Explain that even though part of the information is removed, the sentence remains. Emphasize that *and* gives us more information. Repeat with sentences 3 and 5.

Discuss why the two ideas in 2 and 4 are different, providing explanations if necessary. (Number 2 contrasts what exists—a school—and what does not exist—a park. Number 4 contrasts the abundance of islands with the lack of people.)

SELF CHECK

These *I can* statements provide vital feedback on students' perceived ability to use the language from the unit. If you find students are reluctant to check that they can do the skills, consider asking them to rate themselves from 1 (not very confident) to 3 (very confident).

OPTIONAL Have students complete the **SELF CHECK** before doing the **REVIEW** activities. After reviewing the unit, have students once again check their confidence for each statement.

UNIT 3

WHERE'S THE LION?

CONTENT AREA: THE NATURAL WORLD

Topic: animals

Vocabulary: animals: dolphin, bear, frog, lion, monkey, shark, elephant, hippo, giraffe; **adjectives:** fast, noisy, clever, scary, dangerous, slow, quiet, strong; **things:** tree, rock, car, seaweed, coral, body, leaves, branches; **other words:** hide, the same as

Grammar: asking for quantity and location; prepositions of place

Extra material: a world map

Other useful vocabulary: animals: zebra, cheetah, leopard, rhinoceros (rhino), crocodile; **sea animals:** tuna, clownfish, puffer fish, conch, crab, crown-of-thorns starfish, shrimp, lobster, seahorse, sea urchin, sponge, squid

END OF UNIT PROJECT Have students do a research project about their favorite animal. Ask them to use their research to write a short report.

To provide structure, suggest some questions for students to answer. Ask,

What animal is it?

Where does it live?

What is it like? (Is it shy? Is it big?)

How long does it live?

Does it use camouflage?

In class, have students work in pairs and take turns reading their reports. Have students ask questions about their partner's animal.

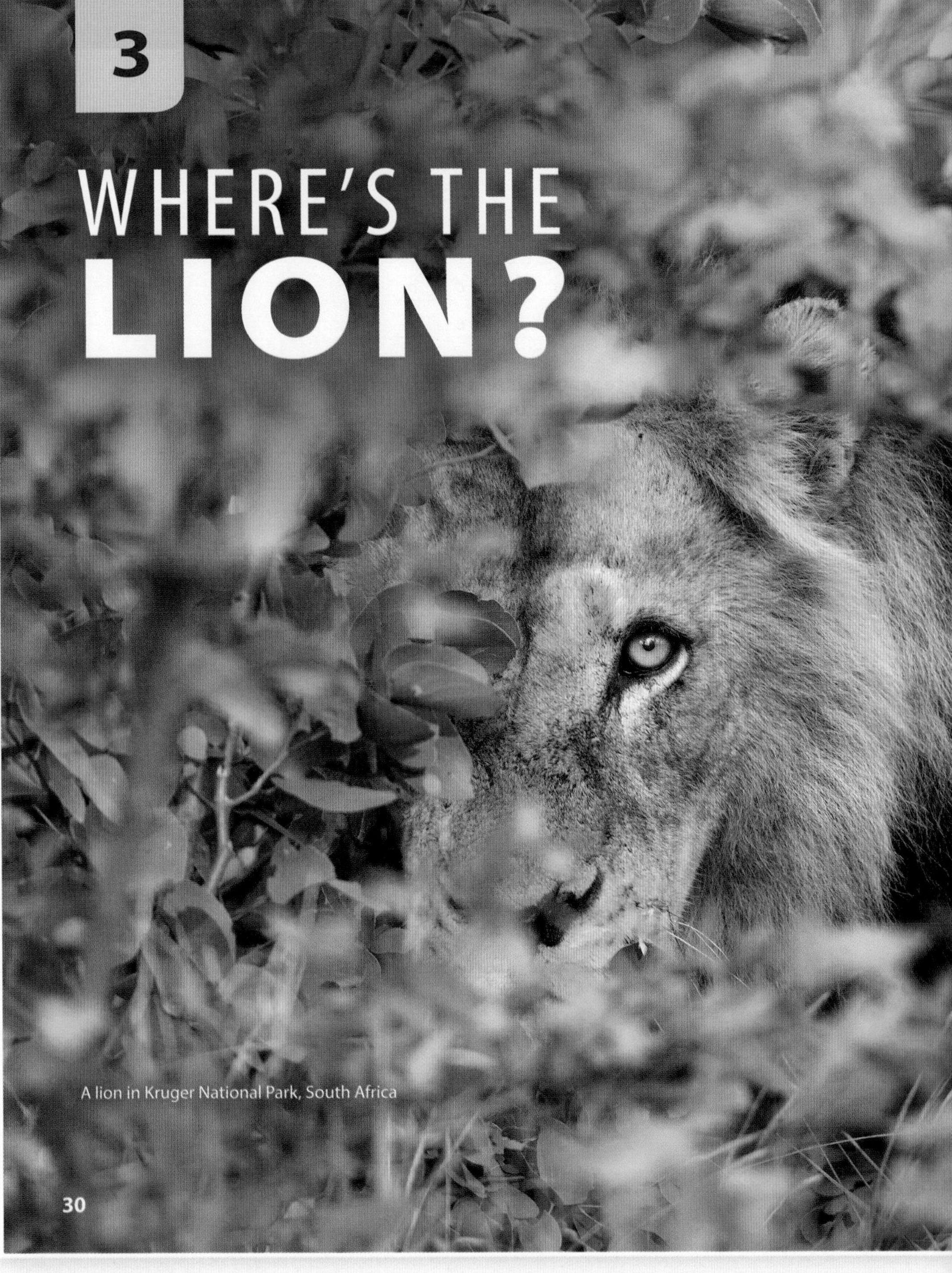

A lion in Kruger National Park, South Africa

PREVIEW

Have students read the unit title to themselves as you read it aloud. Explain that in this unit they will learn to talk about animals.

SUPPORT Review the adjectives in Unit 2. Say an adjective and have students name or point to something. For example: if you say *big*, students might say *the school*. Continue with other adjectives.

A Explain to students that they should write the names of the animals under the pictures. If necessary, before playing the audio track, read the animals' names aloud and have students follow along in their books. Have students do the task. Tell students they should listen and check their answers.

3.1 Play Audio Track 3.1. Play again, if necessary. Check answers.

ABOUT THE PHOTO

This photo shows a male African lion in South Africa's Kruger National Park. African lions can grow to a body length of between 1.4 to 2 meters and weigh between 120 to 190 kilograms. Lions live in groups, called prides. A pride is a family unit usually made up of related females and their cubs, and may include up to three male lions. The males' role is to defend the pride's territory, whereas the females are the pride's primary hunters. With African lion numbers declining due to factors such as habitat loss, the illegal wildlife trade, and human-wildlife conflict, it is estimated that there are only around 20,000 African lions left in the wild.

PREVIEW

A 3.1 **Match the animals with the pictures.** Listen and check your answers.

monkey lion shark frog dolphin bear

1 lion 2 bear 3 frog

4 dolphin 5 monkey 6 shark

B 3.2 **Listen.** What does each person say about the animals below? Complete the sentences. Two words are extra.

fast clever dangerous quiet
noisy scary slow strong

1 Dolphins are clever.
2 Monkeys are fast.
3 Frogs are noisy, and sharks are scary.
4 Lions are quiet, and bears are strong.

C **Talk with a partner.** Describe the animals in **A**. Use words from **B**. *Answers will vary.*

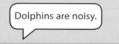

Dolphins are noisy.

THE NATURAL WORLD

UNIT GOALS

- describe animals on land and in the water
- use language for describing where things are
- learn about animals that use camouflage

31

SUPPORT Draw a Venn diagram with two circles, labeling one *land* and the other *water*. Have students classify the animals according to where they live (**land:** lion, bear, monkey; **water:** dolphin, shark; **both:** frog). You may want to explain that frogs are amphibians, so they live both in the water and on land.

B Ask students to follow along as you read the words in the box aloud. Tell them they will hear people talk about the animals in **A**, and they should complete the sentences using the words in the box. Point out that they will not need two of the words.

3.2 Play Audio Track 3.2. Play again, if necessary. Check answers.

SUPPORT Ask the students additional questions until they become comfortable with the vocabulary. For example, point to the picture of the shark. Ask, *What color is a shark? Is a shark dangerous?*

Ask other questions about the animals. For example: *Is a bear big? Are bears colorful?*

Explain that some questions require an opinion and there is no wrong/right answer. Ask, *Is a monkey interesting? Do you think a dolphin is amazing? Are frogs popular?*

CHALLENGE Randomly call on a few students and ask them if they agree with the statements in **B**. For example: *Do you think dolphins are clever?* Encourage them to give reasons for their answers.

C Tell students they will take turns saying sentences about the animals in **A** using the words in **B**. As students follow along in their books, model the example.

Have students get into pairs. Remind them that there may be more than one possible sentence. Have students do the task.

TEACHING NOTE: MAKING PAIRS

Allowing students to make their own pairs lets them work with a partner they feel comfortable with. On other occasions, it may be better for you to choose partners.

You may want to choose partners in different ways so students have the opportunity to meet more classmates and work with a variety of students. One way to control the assigning of partners is to divide the class in half, group A and group B, and allow students to find their own partner from the opposite group.

UNIT GOALS

Direct students' attention to the **UNIT GOALS** box. Explain that these are some of the things students will learn in this unit. Point out that this unit is about the natural world. As students follow along, read each of the unit goals to the class. Explain any words students do not know. Remind students that at the end of the unit there is a self check that allows them to see if they have accomplished each goal.

LANGUAGE FOCUS

A Tell students they will listen to a conversation with four short exchanges between Ming and Maya.

3.3 Play Audio Track 3.3 as students listen and follow along in their books. If necessary, play the conversation again, pausing after each speaker so students can repeat.

As students follow along, read the question, *Where are Ming and Maya?* Have students answer.

Have students work in pairs and practice the conversation once. Point out the bold words and read them aloud as students follow along in their books. You might want to have students repeat the words after you say them. If necessary, explain the meaning of any words that students seem unfamiliar with.

Tell students they will practice the conversation two more times, changing the bold words each time.

Ask students to swap roles after they have practiced the conversation once. Have them practice with both substitution choices.

OPTIONAL Have students practice the conversation again, substituting words to personalize it.

LANGUAGE FOCUS

They're at a safari park.

A 3.3 **Listen and read.** Where are Ming and Maya? Then repeat the conversation and replace the words in **bold**.

REAL ENGLISH Look!

Ming: This safari park is so big! How many animals are there?

Maya: About 500. Wow! Look, **a lion**! (**a monkey** / **an elephant**)

Ming: Where? I don't see it.

Maya: It's over there, next to the **tree**. (**rock** / **car**)

Ming: Oh, where is it now?

Maya: It's behind the **hippo**. (**elephant** / **giraffe**)

Ming: Where's the lion now?

Maya: It's **in front of** you! (**next to** / **behind**)

B 3.4 **Look at the chart.** Then circle the correct answers below.

TALKING ABOUT LOCATION OF THINGS (USING PREPOSITIONS)	
The bears are **near** the tree. The monkey is **behind** the frog.	
How many animals **are there**?	**There's** one animal. / **There are** twenty animals.
Where's the frog?	It's **on** / **under** / **next to** the rock.
Where are the monkeys?	They're **in front of** / **behind** the tree.
Is the lion **on** the rock?	Yes, it is. / No, it isn't.
Are the fish **in** the water?	Yes, they are. / No, they aren't.

1 *How many* is for questions about **age** / **number** (circled: number).
2 *Where* is for questions about **places** / **people**. (circled: places)
3 Words like *on/in/under* show **where** / **when** something is. (circled: where)

32 Unit 3

REAL ENGLISH

Direct students' attention to the word in the **REAL ENGLISH** box. Explain that *Look!* is used in spoken English to get someone's attention. For example:

(A and B are walking down the beach and looking at the ocean.)

A: Look! It's a shark!
B: It's really big!

CHALLENGE Explain to students that *Look!* and *Look out!* are quite different. *Look out!* is used to warn someone of impending danger. For example:

A: Look out! There's a car coming!

B Ask students to look at the chart.

3.4 Have students follow along as they listen to Audio Track 3.4.

As students follow along, read the first question in the chart aloud. Explain that it asks about quantity. Point to an object in the classroom. Say, *There is (a book)./ There are (two pencils).* Explain that these sentences tell us quantity (the number of things). Write the sentences on the board. Point out that when there is one thing, we use *is*, but when there are two or more things, we use *are*.

SUPPORT Have students get into pairs and practice asking and answering questions about things on their desks or in their schoolbags.

C Look at the picture below. Complete the sentences.

in | next to | under | in front of

1 The giraffes are *next to* the tree.

2 The hippos are *in front of* the elephants.

3 The fish are *in* the water.

4 The frog is *under* the tree.

DO YOU KNOW?

What is this?

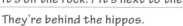

(a) a catfish

b a horsefish

D Look at the picture below. Answer the questions.

1 How many lions are there? *There's one lion.*

2 How many hippos are there? *There are three hippos.*

3 Where's the lion? *It's on the rock. / It's next to the elephants.*

4 Where are the elephants? *They're behind the hippos.*

E Play a game. Student A: Choose something in the classroom. **Student B:** Guess what it is.

Answers will vary.

Is it on the table?
Yes, it is.
Is it a pen?
No, it isn't.

C Tell students they should look at the picture below and complete the sentences. After giving them a minute to complete the task, check answers as a class.

OPTIONAL Have students make the questions that these sentences would answer, writing them on the board if necessary. Then have students get into pairs and take turns asking and answering the questions.

DO YOU KNOW?

Read the question as students follow along in their books. After students answer, tell them the catfish gets its name because of the catlike whiskers on its face.

D Ask students to look at the picture again and answer the questions. After students write the sentences, check answers.

E Tell students they are going to play a guessing game with a partner.

Explain that they must each choose one thing in the classroom for the other student to guess. Tell them that they will take turns asking and answering questions to find out what the object is.

Model the conversation with a student.

Have the students do the task.

TEACHING NOTE: MAKING ACTIVITIES INTO GAMES

To make the activity more like a game, tell the class that the student who guesses correctly using the fewest questions is the winner.

Using a classroom object, demonstrate *near*, *in*, *behind*, *on*, *under*, *next to*, *in front of*. For example: *The book is on the desk.* Emphasize that we use these words to tell others where something is.

Direct students' attention to the chart. Read the second and third questions and answers aloud. Explain that *where* is used to ask the location of something. Using classroom objects, ask students questions. For example: *Where's the pencil?* Randomly ask different students to answer.

Direct students' attention to the chart again. Read the last two questions and answers aloud. Point out that the questions ask about location and require a *yes/no* answer. Using classroom objects, ask students questions. For example: *Is the pencil under the desk?* Randomly ask different students to answer.

Draw students' attention to the three statements under the chart. Give students a moment to circle the correct answers. Check answers.

THE REAL WORLD

Ask students to look at the photo. As students follow along in their books, read the title and the photo caption aloud. Point to each animal to explain *penguin* and *leopard seal.*

OPTIONAL Have students find Antarctica on a world map.

CONTENT NOTE: PAUL NICKLEN

Paul Nicklen was born and lives in Canada. Although he was a biologist, he now specializes in photographing polar areas. He has won many prestigious awards, including the BBC Wildlife Photographer of the Year and the World Press Photo prize for photojournalism.

A Tell students to write adjectives to describe the animals. Have them do the task and then share their ideas with a partner or the class.

B Tell students they are going to watch a video and they should circle the correct words to complete the summary. As students follow along in their books, read the summary and answer choices aloud.

▶ 3.1 Play Video 3.1. If necessary, play the video again. Check answers as a class.

OPTIONAL Tell students more about Paul Nicklen. (See **CONTENT NOTE.**)

C Tell students they should watch again and complete the sentences using the words in the box. As students follow along in their books, read the words aloud.

▶ 3.1 Play Video 3.1. If necessary, play the video again. Check answers as a class.

THE REAL WORLD

LIFE IN ANTARCTICA

There are many amazing animals in Antarctica, such as leopard seals and penguins.

ABOUT THE PHOTO

This photo shows a leopard seal hunting a penguin. The leopard seal, sometimes called the sea leopard, is the second largest species of seal in the Antarctic. It is named for its black-spotted coat which has a pattern similar to that of the big cat. Leopard seals are fierce predators and they are the only species of seals to feed on warm-blooded prey. Leopard seals are solitary animals and generally hunt alone. When hunting penguins, the leopard seals often wait underwater at the edge of the ice and then catch the penguins just as they enter the water after jumping off the ice.

A **Look at the animals in the photo above.** Write words to describe them. Answers will vary.

Leopard seal: long,

Penguin: small,

B ▶ 3.1 **Watch the video.** Complete the summary.

Paul Nicklen is a photographer. He's in Antarctica to take photos of [1] **animals** / **people**. Paul sees a [2] **penguin** / **leopard seal** in the water. It swims near his [3] **camera** / **friend**. Later, Paul sees a leopard seal chasing a penguin. The penguin is [4] **slow** / **fast**. Another penguin is on the ice. It's [5] **safe** / **not safe**.

C ▶ 3.1 **Watch again.** Complete the sentences using the words in the box.

in front of | on | behind | in

1 Paul Nicklen is in the water.
2 The leopard seal is in front of Paul's camera.
3 The penguins are on the rock.
4 The seal is behind the penguin.

CHALLENGE Before playing the video again, give students additional questions.

1 *How many types of animals are in the water?* (There are two.)
2 *How big are leopard seals?* (They are four meters long.)
3 *Where do the penguins live?* (They live in Antarctica.)
4 *Which animal is dangerous?* (The leopard seal is dangerous.)

Have them watch the video to find the answers. Check answers as a class.

D CRITICAL THINKING

As students follow along, read the statement aloud. Have students get into pairs and talk about their ideas.

CHALLENGE After the class has talked about their ideas, encourage students to brainstorm three more adjectives that describe his job. This encourages them to analyze the content more, thereby promoting more critical thinking.

D CRITICAL THINKING Inferring **Talk with a partner.** Think of two words to describe Paul Nicklen's job. Answers will vary.

PROJECT Walk around your neighborhood. Find five animals and note where they are.

grasshopper: on a leaf
frog: behind a rock

PRONUNCIATION *There are* and *They're*

3.5 **Listen.** Circle the words you hear. Then listen again and repeat the sentences.

1 (There are) They're
2 There are (They're)
3 There are (They're)
4 (There are) They're

COMMUNICATION

A **Choose four animals.** Draw them or write their names on the picture below. Answers will vary.

shark dolphin monkey frog fish lion

B **Talk with a partner.** Ask about the animals in their picture. Draw your partner's picture on page 150.

Is there a shark in your picture?
Yes, there is.

Where is it?

It's behind the seaweed.

C Compare the pictures with your partner.

PROJECT As students follow along, read the project instructions aloud. Set a deadline by which students must finish their observations. In the next class, have students get into pairs and discuss what they saw.

PRONUNCIATION

Tell students they will listen to the pronunciation of *There are* and *They're*. Remind them that *They're* is the contraction of *They are*. Explain that they should circle the words they hear.

3.5 Play Audio Track 3.5. Play it again, if necessary. Check answers.

Tell students you will play the audio again, pausing after each sentence, and they should repeat. Do the task.

Students may have difficulty hearing the difference between the words. Play the audio again, if necessary.

SUPPORT Point to *There are* and *They're*. Explain that it is important to learn to hear the difference, but that when they are listening they should also use context to deduce what they hear. Ask students when *There are* and *They're* are used, providing examples if necessary. (*There are six sharks. They're [They are] blue*.) Have students get into pairs and practice the pronunciation as they make other sentences. For example: *There are lots of trees. There are three fish in the water. They're orange and white*. While students practice, walk around the room and provide assistance.

COMMUNICATION

A Tell students they are going to play a drawing game with a partner. As students follow along, read the names of the animals in the box aloud. Tell students they will choose four animals and draw them in the picture below. Explain that they can write the animals' names if they prefer. Allow time for students to draw their animals.

B When students have finished, tell them they will get into pairs and ask and answer questions to find out about their partner's picture. Model the conversation with a student.

Tell students they will listen to their partner's explanation and draw their partner's picture on page 150. Emphasize that they should not show their picture to their partner until they have finished. Give them time to do the task.

C When students have finished, have them compare their drawings on pages 35 and 150.

SUPPORT Before students start the activity, have them think about different questions and vocabulary they might use. Write the ideas on the board as they are given. For example: *How many sharks are there? There's one. Where is the shark? It's in the water near the dolphin.*

READING

A Ask students to look at the photos. As students follow along, read the sentences and answer choices aloud, and have students check the things they see in the photos. Then check their answers.

CONTENT NOTE: LEAFY SEA DRAGON

Leafy sea dragons are native to Australia. They are a kind of fish that is closely related to seahorses. They feed on plankton, crustaceans, and sea lice. They can grow to up to 30 centimeters in length and are usually green to yellow in color. Leafy sea dragons are frequently taken by divers who want them as pets. They also suffer from issues associated with pollution and loss of habitat. The species is now quite threatened.

B As students follow along in their books, read the title and the question aloud. Have students provide their ideas.

C Remind students that since they are skimming the passage, they should not read every word. Emphasize that skimming is an important skill that allows us to find specific information quickly. Tell students that they don't have to understand everything when they read a text quickly.

Have them skim the text and underline the places where animals hide.

When all the students have finished, check answers as a class.

Have students read the article in more detail so they can answer the **COMPREHENSION** questions.

OPTIONAL The text can also be used as a listening activity. Have students close their books. Tell students they will listen to the passage.

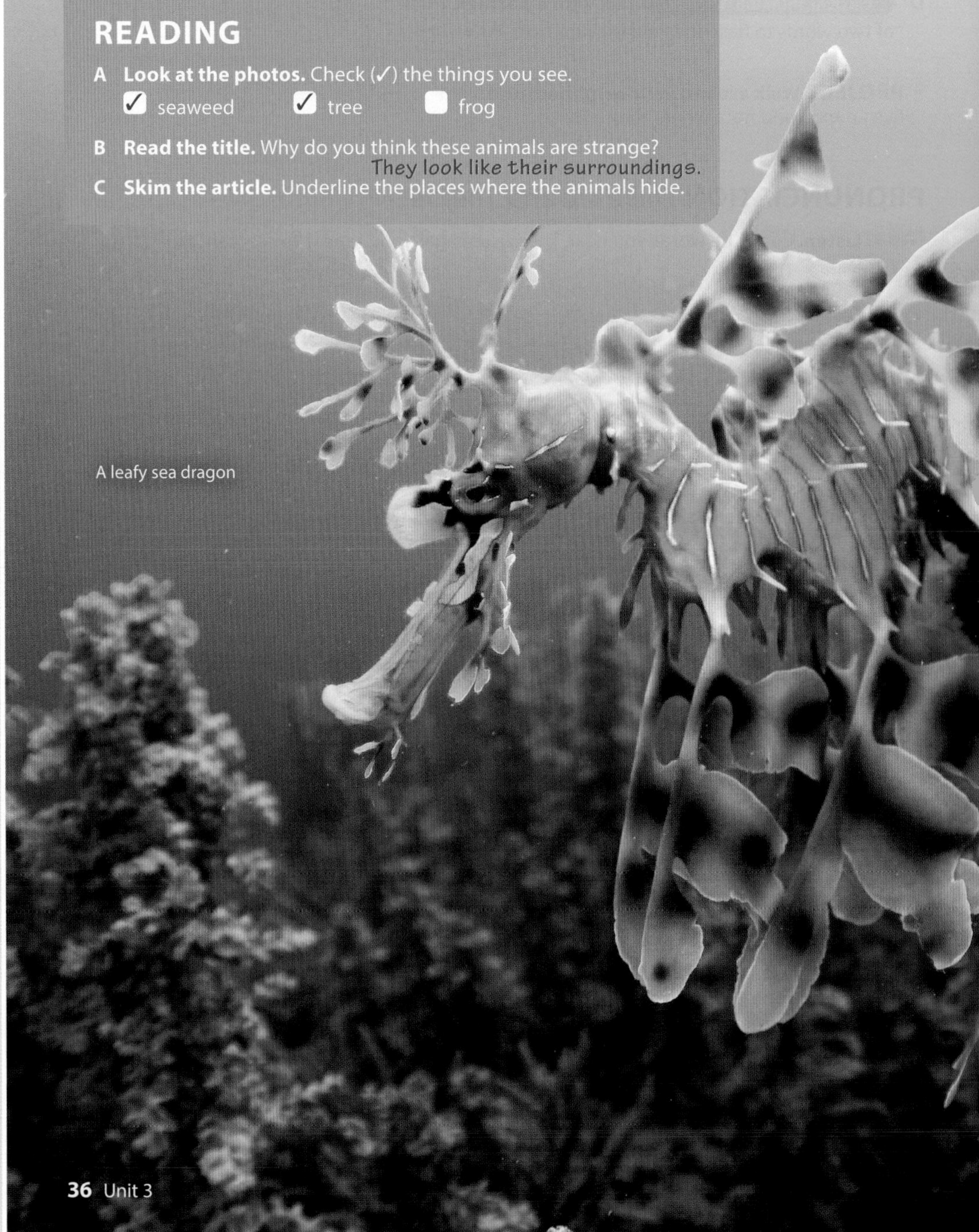

READING
A Look at the photos. Check (✓) the things you see.
✓ seaweed ✓ tree frog
B Read the title. Why do you think these animals are strange?
They look like their surroundings.
C Skim the article. Underline the places where the animals hide.
36 Unit 3

A leafy sea dragon

3.6 Play Audio Track 3.6. Ask students to get into pairs and discuss what information they heard. Then have them read the article more carefully.

Additional Activities to Use with the Reading

Sentence Construction

Remind students that in Unit 2 they studied when to use *and* (to join similar ideas) and *but* (to join different ideas), and review their usage if necessary.

Direct students' attention to the last sentence of the first paragraph. Have them form two sentences so they do not use *and*. (*Some animals in the sea are camouflaged. Some animals on land are camouflaged.*) Point out that by using *and* there is less repetition.

Have students find *but* in the second paragraph. Have them explain why it is used, providing assistance as necessary. (Two ideas are being contrasted—how the animal looks and what it really is.)

ABOUT THE PHOTO

The main photo shows a leafy sea dragon in the waters near Edithburg, South Australia. Named for their plantlike appearance that enables them to blend in with the seagrass and kelp formations in the reefs they live in, leafy sea dragons are so well camouflaged that neither prey nor predators recognize them. (See **CONTENT NOTE** for more information.)

The other photo shows an eastern screech owl, a small owl with a length of around 21.5 centimeters and a wingspan of around 53 centimeters. Eastern screech owls vary in color from gray to reddish-brown. They have a complex pattern of bands and spots that provides them with excellent camouflage against tree bark.

STRANGE ANIMALS

3.6 Do you know that some animals are camouflaged? This means their colors are **the same as** the colors around them. Some animals in the sea and on land are camouflaged.

Look at the photo on the left. This looks like **seaweed**, but it's not! It's a leafy sea dragon. It **hides** in the seaweed. It's the same color as the seaweed. Its **body** is also in the shape of **leaves**.

Look at the photo below. Do you see the owl in the tree? It's the same colors as the **branches** of the tree. Where are its eyes and its head?

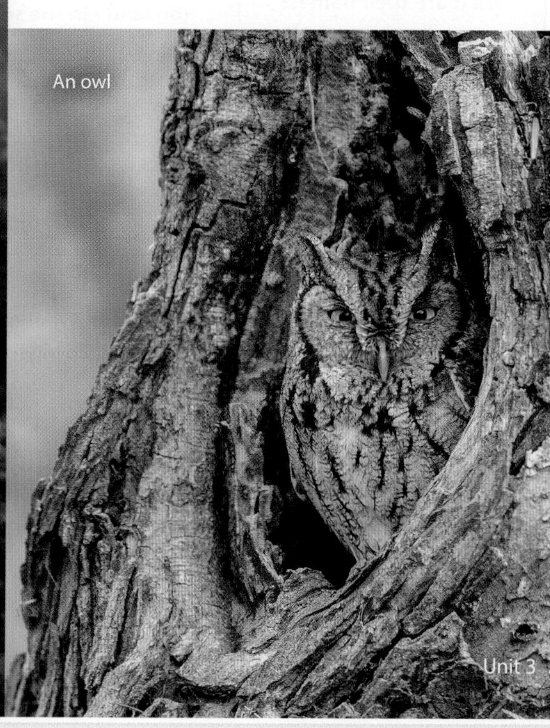
An owl

Unit 3 37

Using Pronouns

Have students look at the first paragraph. Ask them to identify the word the writer uses rather than repeating the words *the animals'* (*their*).

Ask students to look at the second paragraph. Ask them to find the word the writer uses to talk about *the leafy sea dragon* (*it* in *It hides in . . .* and *It's the same color . . .*).

Do the same with the third paragraph. (*The owl* is replaced by *it* in *It's the same . . .* and *the owl's* is replaced by *its*.)

Ask students why the writer uses *it* and *they* rather than repeating the words *animals, leafy sea dragon*, and *owl*.

After they have finished guessing, read through the second paragraph without using the pronouns. Ask students which version they prefer, and encourage them to provide reasons for their answers. (The version without pronouns is boring. It takes longer. It can actually make it more difficult to understand the meaning. Saying *the leafy sea dragon's* is difficult.)

Have students get into pairs and make simple sentences using pronouns. Then ask some students to write them on the board. Correct the sentences and discuss each one.

Vocabulary Extension

Have students find *the same as* in the first paragraph. Explain that we use this when two things are equivalent (not different).

Have students find *the same color as* in the second paragraph. Explain that although this is a different construction, the idea of being equivalent is similar.

On the board, write, *It's the same color as the seaweed.* Have students replace *it's* with *leafy sea dragon*. (*The leafy sea dragon is the same color as the seaweed.*)

Have students rewrite the sentence using *the same as*. (*The leafy sea dragon's color is the same as the color of the seaweed./The leafy sea dragon's color is the same as the seaweed's color.*)

Grammar (Focused)

If necessary, review the location words in the chart on page 32. Have students circle all of the location words (*in* and *on* in the first paragraph, *in* in the second and third paragraphs).

Ask students to identify the word that is most often used to give location (*in*). Randomly ask students to read the portion of each sentence with *in*. (*Some animals in the sea . . . It hides in the seaweed. Do you see the owl in the tree?*)

COMPREHENSION

A Have students read the questions to themselves and circle the correct answers.

After they have finished, you may want to ask them to get into pairs and check their answers. Then check answers as a class.

OPTIONAL Ask students additional true/false comprehension questions.

1 *Camouflaged animals hide in things that are the same color as them.* (True.)
2 *A leafy sea dragon is the same color as an owl.* (False. A leafy sea dragon is yellow and green, but an owl is mostly brown and black.)
3 *An owl has branches.* (False. It looks like a tree, but it does not have branches.)
4 *An owl doesn't have eyes.* (False. It has eyes. In the photo, they are yellow and black.)

B **EXAM PRACTICE**

Graphic organizers such as charts help students analyze information. While some charts allow students to compare and contrast two or more things, others allow students to summarize a passage by considering *who*, *what*, *when*, *where*, *why*, and *how*. Helping students become proficient with graphic organizers allows them to more easily classify information on standardized tests, even when the graphic organizers are not part of the test requirements. Charts also allow students to access both the logical part of the brain and the creative side. Scientists believe utilizing both sides enhances learning.

Have students follow along in their books as you read the questions in the chart aloud. Remind students to use information from the text on page 37 to complete the chart.

COMPREHENSION

A Answer the questions about *Strange Animals*.

1 MAIN IDEA What's the article mainly about?
a jungle animals (b) animals that hide c dangerous animals

2 DETAIL A leafy sea dragon looks like ____.
(a) seaweed b a rock c an owl

3 REFERENCE The word *It* in line 6 refers to ____.
a a leaf b seaweed (c) the leafy sea dragon

4 DETAIL Which of the following information about the owl is NOT in the article?
a It hides in the tree. (b) Its eyes are big. c Its colors are the same as the tree.

5 INFERENCE The leafy sea dragon and the owl hide using their ____.
(a) colors b shapes c sounds

B Complete the chart. Use the information about the animals in the article.

What are their names?	Where do they live? (on land / in the sea)	Where do they hide?
leafy sea dragon	in the sea	in the seaweed
owl	on land	in the tree

C CRITICAL THINKING Applying **Talk with a partner.** What other animals use camouflage to hide? Answers will vary.

IDIOM
If someone is "like a fish out of water," they are ____.
(a) not comfortable
b not well

A snowy owl

38 Unit 3

Have students do the task. Check answers as a class.

C CRITICAL THINKING

As students follow along, read the question aloud. Have students get into pairs and discuss the question. Encourage students to also talk about how they hide (e.g., what they hide in).

IDIOM

As students follow along in their books, read the statement and answer choices aloud. Have them guess the answer before providing it (a). Then explain that if someone is *like a fish out of water* it means they don't feel comfortable somewhere or in a certain situation.

VOCABULARY

A Find the words below in the article. Then complete the sentences.

the same as | seaweed | hide | body | leaves | branches

1 ___Seaweed___ is a plant that grows in water.

2 The ___leaves___ of a plant are usually green.

3 There's fur on a rabbit's ___body___.

4 There are birds on the tree's ___branches___.

5 When you ___hide___, people can't see you.

6 Some frogs hide in trees because their colors are ___the same as___ the trees.

B Read the information below. Complete the sentences.

Here are some phrases to describe where things are.
on the left *in the middle* *on the right*

1 The blue birds are ___in the middle___.

2 The yellow and white bird is ___on the left___.

3 The big gray bird is ___on the right___.

WRITING

A Look at the photo. Read the beginning of a description of the photo.

B Make notes about the photo. What do you see? Where are the things in the photo?

C Write a description of the photo. Say where things are.

Answers will vary.

There's a diver and a lot of fish in the water. On the left, there are some yellow fish. In the middle, ...

VOCABULARY

A As students follow along, read the words in the box aloud. Have students find them in the **READING** passage.

Have students use the words in the box to complete the sentences. Check answers.

SUPPORT Give students additional sentences and have them decide which word they should use to complete them. For example:

*Students don't have **bodies/branches**.*

Alternatively, use the word in a sentence and have students determine whether the sentence is true or false:

***Seaweed** is an animal.* (False. Seaweed is a plant.)

CHALLENGE On the board, write, *Their colors are the same as the colors around them.*

Have students replace *their* and *them*. (*The animals' colors are the same as the colors around the animals.*)

Have students rewrite the sentence using *the same color as*. (*The animals are the same colors as the things around them.*) Point out that they must add *things* to make the comparison.

B As students follow along, read the information in the box aloud. Put three things on the desk. Point to the one in the middle as you say *in the middle*. Do the same with *on the right* and *on the left*.

Have students complete the sentences. Check answers as a class.

WRITING

Tell students they are going to write a description of the photo.

A Have students study the photo. As students follow along, read the beginning of the example description aloud.

B Ask students the two questions. Have them make notes (e.g., words, locations) about things they see. If necessary, remind them that they can use the prepositions of location that they learned in **LANGUAGE FOCUS** activity **B** as well as the phrases they studied in **VOCABULARY** activity **B**.

C Have students use their notes from **B** and other ideas to write their descriptions. Give them a time limit for finishing the task or assign it as homework. You may want to set a minimum number of sentences they must write (e.g., five).

OPTIONAL Collect the descriptions and provide feedback on vocabulary and grammar usage.

VIDEO

Tell students that they are going to watch a video about ocean oddities.

Ask students to think about what *oddities* might mean, providing the answer if necessary (something or someone that is unusual or strange).

BEFORE YOU WATCH

As students follow along in their books, read the question aloud. Have students make a list of sea animals they know of. (See **Other useful vocabulary** for examples.)

OPTIONAL Read the photo caption aloud as students follow along. Have students find Indonesia on a world map.

WHILE YOU WATCH

A Tell students they will watch the video and they should check the things that the animals do.

▶ 3.2 Play Video 3.2. If necessary, play the video again. Check answers as a class.

B Explain to students that they will watch the video again and they should circle the correct words to complete the sentences. As students follow along in their books, read the sentences and the choices aloud.

▶ 3.2 Play the video. Play the video again, if necessary.

Check answers as a class.

SUPPORT On the board, write *The ocean is full of strange creatures.* Ask students to use the images they saw in the video and decide what *full of* means, providing the answer if necessary. (*Full of* is used to emphasize a large number of something, for example, creatures in the ocean. It means *there are a lot/it has many*.)

VIDEO **ABOUT THE VIDEO** Many strange creatures live in the ocean.

OCEAN *ODDITIES*

Before You Watch

Work with a partner. What sea animals do you know? Make a list.

Answers will vary.

While You Watch

A ▶ 3.2 **Watch the video.** What do the animals do?

☑ eat ☐ sleep ☑ hide ☑ make sounds

B ▶ 3.2 **Watch again.** Circle the correct answers.

1 Sargassum fish hide in (seaweed) / **coral**.
2 Comb jellyfish are (colorful) / **dangerous**.
3 Beluga whales are very **quiet** / (**noisy**).
4 Clams use their (**foot**) / **tongue** to push into the sand.
5 Clams hide **behind a rock** / (**under the ground**) when they are scared.

After You Watch

Talk with a partner. Describe the sea animals in the video. Use the words in the box.

beautiful	dangerous	scary	strong	fast	slow	noisy	clever

Answers will vary.

A coral reef near Sebayur Island, Indonesia

ABOUT THE PHOTO

This photo shows a coral reef in the Flores Sea in Indonesia. Coral reefs occupy less than one percent of the ocean floor but they support 25 percent of all marine creatures on this planet. Reefs are invaluable to Earth's biodiversity—their diversity is so rich that scientists don't have a definite count of all the species that live in the reefs, and they still discover new species every year. Many of the world's shallow water coral reefs have disappeared as a result of issues like climate change, overfishing, unsustainable coastal development, pollution, and destructive fishing practices, such as blast fishing and bottom trawling.

AFTER YOU WATCH

Tell students to get into pairs and describe the sea animals they saw in the video. Explain that they should use the words in the box. As students follow along in their books, read the words aloud. Have students get into pairs and do the task.

REVIEW

Explain that students are going to review the material from the unit and this will help them remember what they have studied.

A Explain that activity **A** reviews vocabulary from the unit. Point out that the names of some of the animals are in the box. Have students read the descriptions and write the names of the animals.

Check answers as a class.

CHALLENGE Tell students more about the animals. Alternatively, have students do research to learn more about the animals. (See **CONTENT NOTE**.)

REVIEW

A Match the descriptions with the animals in the box.

lions bears frogs dolphins monkeys sharks

1 They're very big fish. sharks

2 They're big cats from Africa. lions

3 They live in water and on the ground. frogs

4 They live in trees and on the ground. monkeys

5 They live in the sea. They're very clever. dolphins

6 There are a lot of them in Canada. They're often brown or black. bears

B Look at the pictures. Complete the sentences and questions.

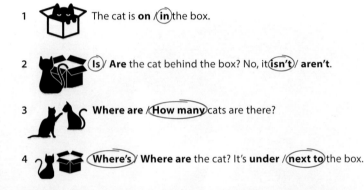

1  The cat is **on** / **in** the box.

2  **Is** / **Are** the cat behind the box? No, it **isn't** / **aren't**.

3  **Where are** / **How many** cats are there?

4 **Where's** / **Where are** the cat? It's **under** / **next to** the box.

C Look at your drawing in the Communication section of this unit. Write three sentences to describe it. Use *on the left*, *on the right*, and *in the middle*. Answers will vary.

1 ______

2 ______

3 ______

SELF CHECK Now I can ...

- ☐ describe animals on land and in the water
- ☐ use language for describing where things are
- ☐ talk about animals that use camouflage

Dolphins are actually a kind of whale. The largest dolphin, the orca, is often mistakenly referred to as a killer whale.

Monkeys live in groups called tribes, troops, or missions. There are 264 monkey species, which can be divided into two groups—those originally living in Asia and Africa and those from South America.

Based on fossil evidence, scientists believe sharks have been in the oceans for about 455 million years. Sharks do not, however, have bones.

B Explain that activity **B** reviews the grammar from the unit. Have students circle the correct words to complete the sentences and questions. Have students get into pairs and check answers, before you randomly call on students to give the answers.

C Point out that activity **C** reviews words from **VOCABULARY** activity **B**.

Tell students they should look at their **COMMUNICATION** section drawing and write three sentences. Point out that they should use *on the left*, *on the right*, and *in the middle*.

Have students write their sentences. Have several students write their sentences on the board. Correct them for grammar but also praise the students for some aspect of each sentence so they do not lose confidence.

CONTENT NOTE: ANIMAL FUN FACTS

African lions can weigh up to 190 kilograms. Lions are smaller than tigers. A lion's roar can be heard over eight kilometers away. Lions only catch about 30 percent of their prey. Lions eat about nine kilograms of meat a day.

There are eight different bear species around the world. Grizzly bears, native to North America, grow to be up to 2.5 meters long and can weigh as much as 450 kilograms.

Many male frogs have pockets on the sides of their mouth. The frogs can inflate them, making their croaks louder. The frogs use this to attract female frogs from farther away.

SELF CHECK

These *I can* statements provide vital feedback on students' perceived ability to use the language from the unit. If you find students are reluctant to check that they can do the skills, consider asking them to rate themselves from 1 (not very confident) to 3 (very confident).

UNIT 4

THIS IS MY FAMILY

CONTENT AREA: PEOPLE AND PLACES

Topic: families

Vocabulary: immediate family members: mother/mom, father/dad, brother, sister, baby sister, son, daughter, children, parents; **extended family members:** cousin, grandparents, grandfather, grandmother, great-grandfather, great-grandmother, nephew, niece, aunt, great-aunt, uncle, great-uncle; **other words:** tradition, especially, continue, add, local, enjoys

Grammar: verb *have*

Extra material: pictures of several coats of arms, photos of your immediate family, a map of the United States, a world map

Other useful vocabulary: family: husband, wife, baby brother; **extended family:** mother-in-law, father-in-law, brother-in-law, sister-in-law, half-brother/sister, stepbrother/sister, stepmother, stepfather, great-great-granddaughter, great-great-grandmother

END OF UNIT PROJECT Show pictures of coats of arms to the students. Then explain that a coat of arms usually has symbols or images of things that are important to a family or the family's history. Tell them these symbols can be anything, including animals, trees, rocks, and houses.

Draw a blank coat of arms on the board. Then ask students to draw the coat of arms onto a piece of paper.

Tell them to think of four symbols that represent their family and draw the symbols on their coat of arms.

When students have finished, have them work in pairs and take turns talking about their own coat of arms.

CONTENT NOTE: FAMILIES

The International Day of Families is on May 15. It was established by the United Nations to demonstrate the importance of families in communities around the world.

TEACHING NOTE: CULTURAL SENSITIVITY

Family situations vary in different societies, and what seems the norm in one place may not be relevant for students from a different country or background. Be aware of this in class.

There may be students with nontraditional family structures, and some may be self-conscious about this. Another potential

ABOUT THE PHOTO

This picture shows a family of four taking a photo along the Monteliusvägen in Stockholm, Sweden. The family is on vacation. Family travel is a good way for family members to bond, especially when longer working hours and other distractions prevent families from spending time with each other on a day-to-day basis. With cheaper airfares (a result of the competition between budget carriers and full-service carriers), air travel has become more affordable and many families take advantage of it to go on family vacations more than once a year.

PREVIEW

A Match the words with the people in the photo.

mother father brother sister

1 father
2 brother
3 mother
4 sister

B 4.1 **Listen.** Match the people to their descriptions.

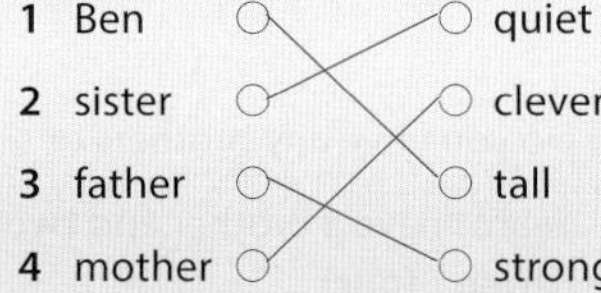

1 Ben — tall
2 sister — quiet
3 father — strong
4 mother — clever

C Talk with a partner. Ask and answer questions about your family.

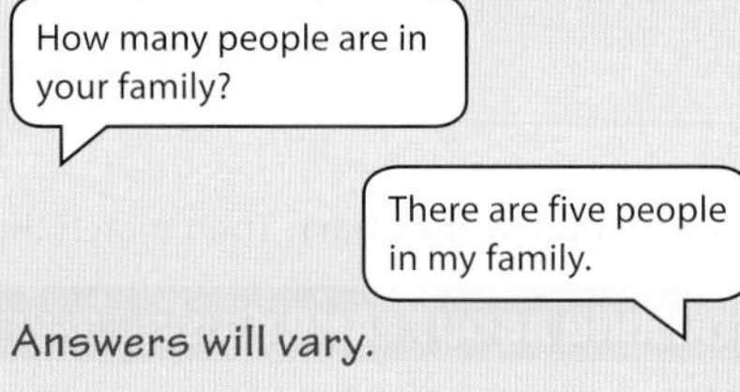

How many people are in your family?
There are five people in my family.

Answers will vary.

PEOPLE AND PLACES

UNIT GOALS

- describe people in your family
- use language for talking about family members
- read about family traditions

43

CHALLENGE Have students listen to the audio again and answer additional questions.

What is Ben's favorite sport? (soccer)

What is his sister good at? (singing)

What does his mother do? (teacher)

C Tell students they will take turns asking and answering questions about their family. Explain that they should use their own answers.

Model the conversation with a student. Tell students that when they count the number of people, they should include themselves, so a family with five members might have a mother, father, sister, brother, and the student.

Have students do the task. Check answers.

SUPPORT Before students begin, have them brainstorm other questions to ask about family members, writing them on the board as they are given. For example: *How many brothers do you have? How many sisters do you have?*

Tell students that when we count the number of brothers and sisters, we do not include ourselves. Give an example using the photo on the page or photos of your own family.

UNIT GOALS

Direct students' attention to the **UNIT GOALS** box. Explain that these are some of the things students will learn in this unit. Point out that this unit is about people and places. As students follow along, read each of the unit goals to the class. Explain any words students do not know. Remind students that at the end of the unit there is a self check that allows them to see if they have accomplished each goal.

issue is that their families, or some members of their family, may live far away, so the students feel homesick.

PREVIEW

Have students read the unit title to themselves as you read it aloud. Explain that in this unit they will learn to talk about the people in their family. Point to the word *family* as you say this.

A As students follow along, read the words in the box aloud. Ask students to look at the family in the photo and write the words on the correct line.

Give students a minute to complete the task. Check answers as a class.

B Explain that they will hear a short description of one family and they should match the people to their descriptions. As students follow along, read the descriptions aloud.

4.1 Play Audio Track 4.1. Play it again, if necessary. Check answers.

LANGUAGE FOCUS

A 4.2 **Listen and read.** What are Nadine and Maya looking at? Then repeat the conversation and replace the words in **bold**. They're looking at Maya's family photos.

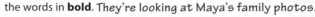

REAL ENGLISH Yeah!

Nadine: Hey, Maya, are those your family photos?

Maya: Yes, this is my family. That's my dad and that's my mom. They're in **Brazil** in this photo. (**Peru** / **Chile**)

Nadine: Are these your **sisters**? (**friends** / **brothers**)

Maya: No, they're my cousins.

Nadine: Do you have any brothers or sisters?

Maya: Yeah! I have a brother and **two** sisters. (**three** / **four**)

Nadine: Is that your **baby brother**? (**baby sister** / **baby cousin**)

Maya: No, that's me!

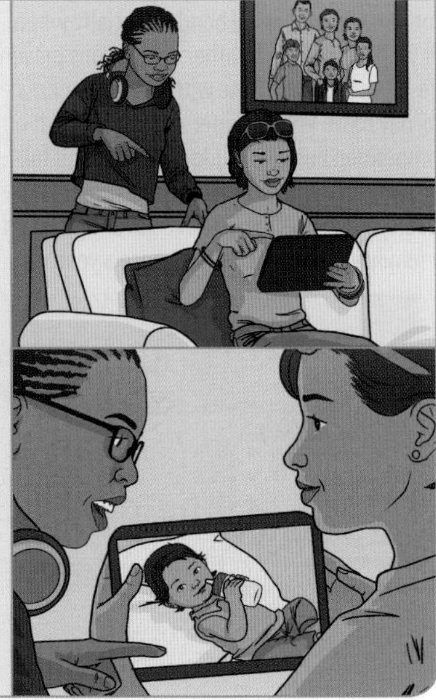

B 4.3 **Look at the chart.** Then match the parts of the sentences below.

TALKING ABOUT FAMILY (USING *HAVE*)		
I **have** two sisters. / I **don't have** any sisters. She **has** a brother. / She **doesn't have** any brothers. They **have** a brother. / They **don't have** any brothers.		don't = do not doesn't = does not
Do you **have** any brothers or sisters?	Yes, I **do**. / No, I **don't**.	
Does she **have** any brothers?	Yes, she **does**. / No, she **doesn't**.	
Do they **have** any cousins?	Yes, they **do**. / No, they **don't**.	

1 We use *have/has* — to make negative sentences.
2 We use *don't/doesn't* — to talk about people in our family.
3 We add *Do/Does* — at the beginning of questions with *have*.

LANGUAGE FOCUS

A Tell students they will listen to a conversation between Nadine and Maya.

4.2 Play Audio Track 4.2 as students listen and follow along in their books. As students follow along, read the question, *What are Nadine and Maya looking at?* Have students answer.

Tell students that family relationships are usually discussed in terms of the speaker or the subject of the sentence so we use expressions like *my grandmother, his brother,* and *your sister.*

Have students work in pairs and practice the conversation once. Point out the bold words and read them aloud as students follow along in their books.

Tell students they will practice the conversation two more times, changing the bold words each time and swapping roles after the first time.

REAL ENGLISH

Direct students' attention to the expression in the **REAL ENGLISH** box. Explain that *Yeah!* is used in informal spoken English to say *yes*. For example:

A: Do you like Taylor Swift?
B: Yeah! I think she's great.

B Ask students to look at the chart.

4.3 Have students follow along as they listen to Audio Track 4.3.

On the board, write *have* with *I* and *they* under it. Also write *has* with *she* under it. Say additional words and have students put them in the correct place in the chart (e.g., **have:** you, we, Bob and Connie; **has:** he, it, Bob).

Explain the contractions on the right side of the chart.

Explain to students that the three questions in the chart all start with *Do* or *Does* so students should answer with *Yes* or *No*. Point out that the first word of the second and third questions (*Does*, *Do*) and the subject (*she*, *they*) are repeated in the answer. Ask students why *you* in the first question is not repeated in the response, providing the answer if necessary. (Because if we answer *Yes, you do,* we are now talking about someone other than ourselves.)

Tell students to look for the word *any* in the questions. Explain that we use *any* in questions that ask about the existence of things. Point out that in these questions, we use the plural form (*brothers*, *sisters*, *cousins*).

SUPPORT Have the class make questions using *any* until they are comfortable with the new grammar. (e.g., *Do you have any books?*)

C 4.4 **Complete the sentences.** Write *has, have, doesn't have,* or *don't have*. Then listen and check your answers.

1 I ___have___ three sisters. (+)
2 He ___doesn't have___ any brothers. (–)
3 You ___don't have___ any cousins. (–)
4 She ___has___ a sister. (+)
5 They ___have___ two cousins. (+)
6 I ___don't have___ any brothers. (–)

IDIOM

"Like father, like son" means ___.
a everyone in a family is happy
(b) children are similar to their parents

D Complete the questions. Write *do, does,* or *have*. Then look at the photo below and answer the questions.

1 Do Carlos and Anita ___have___ children? Yes, they ___do.___
2 ___Does___ Samuel have three sisters? No, he doesn't.
3 Does Anita ___have___ a husband? Yes, she does.
4 ___Do___ Emma and Vera have a brother? Yes, they do.
5 ___Does___ Samuel have a brother? No, he doesn't.

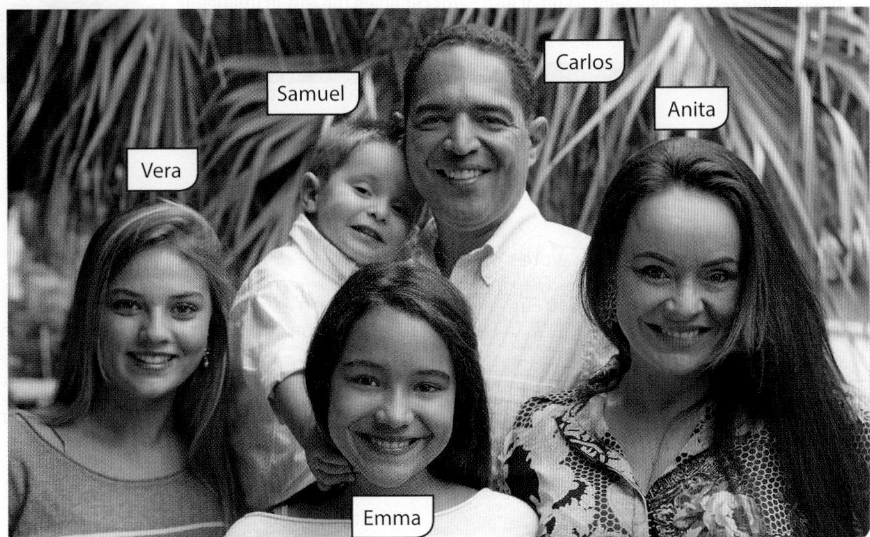

E Work with a partner. Ask and answer questions to make your partner's family tree. Look at Lisa's family tree on page 150 to help you. Answers will vary.

Draw students' attention to the three statements under the chart. Have students do the task. Check answers.

C Tell students that they should write *has, have, doesn't have*, or *don't have* to complete each statement. Explain the (+) and (–) signs, if necessary.

Have students do the task. Explain to students that they will listen and check their answers.

4.4 Play Audio Track 4.4. Check answers as a class.

IDIOM

"Like father, like son" is an idiom we use when a father and son share the same characteristic, trait, quality, or ability. For example: *I'm really good at sports. So is my dad. Like father, like son!*

D Ask students to write *do, does,* or *have* to complete each question. Point out the photo at the bottom of the page. Have students use the photo to answer the questions. Check answers as a class.

OPTIONAL Read the names aloud, having students repeat them. Then have students get into pairs and take turns asking and answering the questions.

E Explain what a family tree is. (See **CONTENT NOTE.**)

Have students look at Lisa's family tree on page 150. Point out how the relationships are provided.

Tell students they are going to ask and answer questions so they can draw their partner's family tree. Tell them to write the names of the people in their partner's family, and explain that the tree should demonstrate the relationships between the people.

Call on a few students to suggest questions they might use. (e.g., *What is your mother's name? Do you have any brothers and sisters?*)

Have them do the task. If some students finish more quickly, encourage them to add more generations to their family tree.

CONTENT NOTE: FAMILY TREE

A family tree is an easy way to show family relationships. It is called a tree because, like a tree, as it grows, it becomes larger and more extended. Each horizontal "branch" on the tree represents a generation. The youngest (current) generation is usually at the bottom and the older generations are at the top. Sometimes, a marriage is shown with an equals sign (=) or a line between two people, and children are shown by the lines coming down from this.

THE REAL WORLD

Ask students to look at the photo. Ask them who they think the people are.

CONTENT NOTE: FAMILIES

The immediate family can also be called the *nuclear family*. *Nuclear*, in *nuclear family*, comes from *nucleus*, denoting a central point. Traditionally, this core unit of mother, father, and children represents the idea of a husband and wife starting a new family of their own, and this is still somewhat common in Western thinking.

In the phrase *extended family*, *extended* relates to the idea of *expanding*, representing additional family members beyond the immediate ones, such as aunts, uncles, cousins, and grandparents.

A As students follow along, read the question aloud. Tell students they are going to watch a video and they should count how many people there are in Farah's immediate and extended family. Emphasize that they should not rely on the number of people in the photo.

▶ 4.1 Play Video 4.1. If necessary, play the video again. Check answers as a class.

B Tell students they will watch again and group the words in the box according to whether the person is a member of the immediate or extended family. As students follow along in their books, read the words aloud.

▶ 4.1 Play Video 4.1. If necessary, play the video again. Check answers as a class.

SUPPORT Have students group the words in **B** into three categories: *she* for words referring to females (*aunt*, *daughter*, *sister*, *grandmother*, *mom*, *niece*), *he* for words referring to males (*brother*, *grandfather*, *son*, *nephew*, *dad*), and *they* for words referring to people of both sexes (*parents*, *cousin*, *grandparents*).

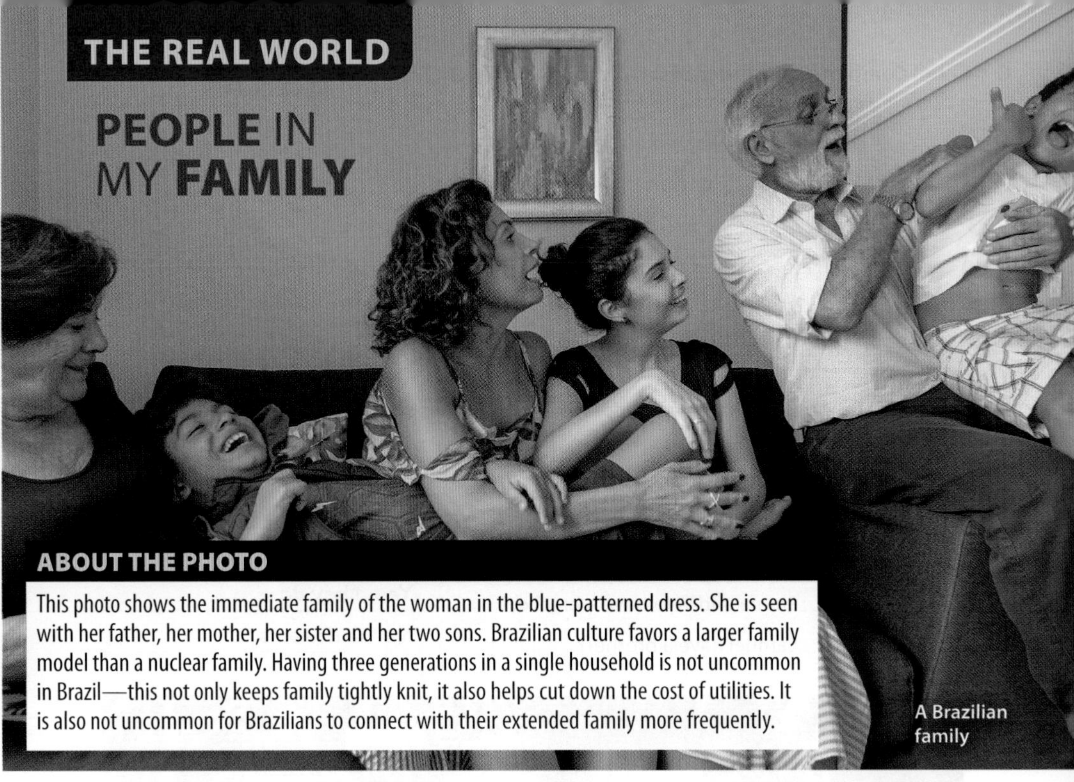

ABOUT THE PHOTO

This photo shows the immediate family of the woman in the blue-patterned dress. She is seen with her father, her mother, her sister and her two sons. Brazilian culture favors a larger family model than a nuclear family. Having three generations in a single household is not uncommon in Brazil—this not only keeps family tightly knit, it also helps cut down the cost of utilities. It is also not uncommon for Brazilians to connect with their extended family more frequently.

A Brazilian family

A ▶ 4.1 **Watch the video.** How many people are there in Farah's immediate and extended family?

a 5 b 8 (c) 14

B ▶ 4.1 **Watch again.** Write the words in the chart.

~~aunt~~ ~~brother~~ dad cousin son sister daughter nephew grandmother niece grandfather mom parents grandparents

IMMEDIATE FAMILY		EXTENDED FAMILY	
brother	sister	aunt	cousin
parents	son	grandmother	nephew
mom	daughter	grandfather	niece
dad		grandparents	

C Explain to students that they can use the words in **B** to help them answer the questions. Have them do the task and check answers as a class.

SUPPORT Have students get into pairs and take turns asking the questions. In order to help students remember the new vocabulary, tell students they shouldn't use their books when they answer. You may also want to have them practice again, using the names of their family members whenever possible.

D CRITICAL THINKING

As students follow along, read the statement and question aloud. Encourage students to give reasons for their answers. Have students get into pairs and talk about their ideas.

C Answer the questions.

1 Who's your uncle's daughter? She's my cousin.
2 Who's your dad's dad? He's my grandfather.
3 Who's your sister's daughter? She's my niece.
4 Who's your mom's brother? He's my uncle.
5 Who's your mom's sister? She's my aunt.

D CRITICAL THINKING Personalizing **Talk with a partner.** Tell them about the people in your extended family. Who are your favorite people? Answers will vary.

PROJECT Take or find photos of your immediate and extended family. Show them to your partner and name the people in the photos.

PRONUNCIATION reduction: *do* and *does*

4.5 **Listen.** Write the words you hear. Then read the questions to your partner.

1 Does she have a cousin?
2 Do they have an aunt?
3 Does he have a baby sister?
4 Do you have any aunts or uncles?

COMMUNICATION

Play a game. Ask the questions below. When someone answers "Yes," write their name in the box. The person who completes the greatest number of boxes is the winner. Answers will vary.

DO YOU HAVE ...		
a big family?	a pet fish?	a brother and sister?
two uncles?	four cousins?	two sisters?
three aunts?	a brother?	a dog or cat?

Do you have a big family?

No, I don't.

CHALLENGE Ask students to suggest some other family relations. (See **Other useful vocabulary**.) Explain that we only use *in-law* to refer to people in our immediate family (in other words, with *mother*, *father*, *sister*, and *brother*). If necessary, explain the difference between a stepbrother and half-brother. (A half-sibling shares a biological parent with you. A stepsibling joins your immediate family when one of your parents marries someone with children from a previous marriage.)

PROJECT As students follow along, read the project instructions aloud. Set a deadline by which students must bring their photos. In the lesson after the deadline, have students get into pairs and and talk with their partner about their photos.

CHALLENGE Have students talk about when their family gets together. (In the United States, families often get together for big holidays like Independence Day and Thanksgiving.) Ask students additional details. For example: *Who comes to the gathering? Where do you get together? What do you do?*

PRONUNCIATION

Tell students that when speaking naturally, *do* and *does* are often blended with the next word. Explain that this is called *reduction*. Tell them they are going to practice this. Explain that they will listen and should write the words they hear.

4.5 Play Audio Track 4.5. Play it again, if necessary. Check answers as a class.

Have students get into pairs and take turns reading the questions.

COMMUNICATION

Tell students they are going to play a game. Explain to students that they will stand up and move around the room, asking and answering questions with other students. Tell them that the winner is the person who has completed the most boxes when the game is over. Explain that they can only ask a classmate to write their name once, and then they should talk with a new person. Remind students to be truthful in their answers.

As students follow along in their books, model the game with a student.

Have students move around the room and play the game. After some students have finished, announce the end of the game and the winner(s).

READING

Have one student read the title aloud.

A Ask students to look at the photos. Read the question and the answer choices aloud as students follow along in their books.

Ask a few students to guess what the text is about. Have them give reasons for their answers (e.g., because the caption says *mochi*).

OPTIONAL Have students find Hawaii on a map of the United States and Japan on a world map.

CONTENT NOTE: MOCHI

Mochi is made of rice that has been steamed, pounded, and mashed before being formed into shapes. It is then baked, boiled, or steamed. Fillings such as red bean paste are usually put inside the pounded rice cakes. Although it is popular all year, mochi is also important during the New Year's holiday in Japan. It is considered to be good luck to eat it on New Year's Day. The sticky concoction can, however, be difficult to swallow, particularly for the elderly and young, and this can sometimes result in suffocation.

B Tell students that they will skim the text, and they should underline the words that represent family relationships.

Remind students that skimming is an important skill because it allows us to find specific information without spending a lot of time reading the text carefully.

Have students do the task.

When all the students have finished, check answers as a class.

Ask students if their predictions in **A** were correct, and check answers in **A**.

READING
A Look at the photos. What do you think the article is about? Check (✓).
✓ Japanese food ✓ a family store ☐ a vacation in Hawaii
B Skim the article. Underline the words that refer to family members.
C Scan the article. What is mochi? It's a traditional Japanese rice cake.
48 Unit 4

Mochi from Two Ladies Kitchen

SUPPORT If some students chose *a vacation in Hawaii* for **A**, explain that when we make predictions we sometimes make incorrect guesses and that is acceptable. If necessary, discuss why this option is incorrect. (Nora lives in Hawaii. There is no information about taking vacations in Hawaii.)

C As students follow along, read the question aloud. Randomly call on a student to answer.

Have students read the article in more detail so they can answer the **COMPREHENSION** questions.

ABOUT THE PHOTO

The main photo shows the colorful mochi made by Two Ladies Kitchen in Hilo, Hawaii. Although small, the store usually has a long line of customers. The most popular mochi in the store is the strawberry mochi, which features a large, whole, fresh strawberry wrapped inside the mochi with a bit of sweet red bean paste.

The other photo shows Nora Uchida, cofounder of Two Ladies Kitchen. Nora started Two Ladies Kitchen with her mother, Sachi Kishimoto, and her aunt, Tomi Tokeshi. Nora originally wanted to name the store Three Ladies Kitchen, but her mother said no because she didn't want the attention. (See **CONTENT NOTE** on page 49 for more information.)

FROM JAPAN *TO* HAWAII

A 4.6 Nora Uchida lives in Hawaii, but her grandparents are from Japan. Nora is Hawaiian. But she thinks her family's Japanese **traditions** are important.

B Nora remembers her grandmother's Japanese food—**especially** mochi. Mochi is a traditional Japanese rice cake. She **continues** her family's tradition, but in a Hawaiian way. She makes Japanese mochi, but **adds** fruit.

C Nora's store is called Two Ladies Kitchen. It is popular with tourists and the **local** people. Her parents often come to the store to help. Nora is happy to see people all over the world **enjoying** her mochi. "Mochi is love," she says.

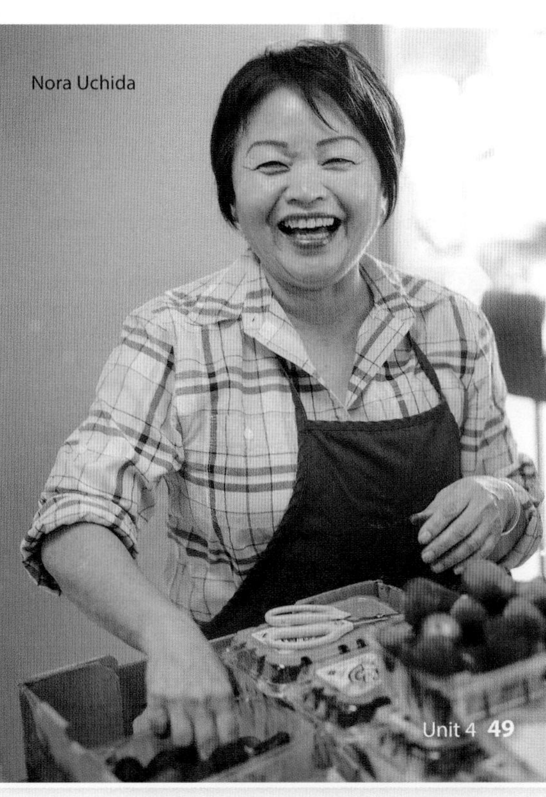

Nora Uchida

Unit 4 **49**

TEACHING NOTE: DICTIONARY SKILLS

It is very useful to teach students how to use an English dictionary. When teaching dictionary skills, explain that dictionaries include not only the meaning of the word but also the pronunciation, the part of speech, and sometimes example sentences.

Remind students that in a dictionary, words are organized alphabetically. So, when looking for the word *adds*, they must first find the *A* section, then look for words starting with *ad*, and then look for *add*. For longer words, they would continue in this manner until they have found the word. Also explain that dictionaries have the root of a word, so rather than finding *adds* in the dictionary they will find *add*.

Often, there is more than one definition for a word. Students should look beyond the first definition. They should find the most appropriate meaning for the context.

Although students should not rely too much on dictionaries, being able to use them effectively is an important skill.

OPTIONAL The text can also be used as a listening activity. Have students close their books. Tell students they will listen to the passage.

4.6 Play Audio Track 4.6. Ask students to get into pairs and discuss what information they heard. Then have them read the article more carefully.

CONTENT NOTE: TWO LADIES KITCHEN

Two Ladies Kitchen is in Hilo, which is on the Big Island of Hawaii. Started in the mid-1990s, the store sells more than 20 different flavors of mochi, ranging from mochi with traditional sweet red bean paste to unique mochi containing peanut butter, chocolate, or pieces of brownie. Unlike mochi in Japan, which tends to be round, the mochi is shaped to look like objects such as shells, fruit, flowers, and butterflies.

Additional Activities to Use with the Reading

Vocabulary Notebook

Remind students to write all the new words in a vocabulary notebook, including easy explanations for the words and example sentences.

Verbal Research Report

Have students use the internet to find out more about Nora Uchida. For example, ask them to find out who the other *lady* in *Two Ladies Kitchen* is. Also tell them to find out what inspired Nora Uchida to make unique mochi flavors. Encourage them to think of other questions and facts to research. In class, have students tell each other what they found out.

COMPREHENSION

A Have students read the questions to themselves and circle the correct answers.

After they have finished, have them get into pairs and check their answers. Then check answers as a class.

DO YOU KNOW?

Read the sentence aloud as students follow along in their books. Have them choose the correct answer (a). (See **CONTENT NOTE** on page 48.)

B EXAM PRACTICE

Students consider the organization of a passage when they match specific questions to the passage's paragraphs. This type of practice is beneficial for at least two reasons. First, it develops students' ability to quickly find specific information in a passage. After locating the paragraph that contains the information, they can then search for specific information. Second, this type of practice helps students prepare for exams such as the IELTS Reading Module, in which they must, among other things, complete summaries and answer questions. On the IELTS Exam, students must notice the maximum number of words from the passage (e.g., three) that can be used for each answer.

COMPREHENSION

A Answer the questions about *From Japan to Hawaii*.

1 MAIN IDEA What's another title for this article?

a Traditional Mochi (b) A Family Tradition c Hawaiian Food

2 DETAIL Nora likes her ____ mochi.

(a) grandmother's b mother's c aunt's

3 INFERENCE Nora's mochi is special because traditional Japanese mochi ____.

a isn't colorful b is small (c) doesn't usually have fruit

4 REFERENCE The word *It* in the second sentence of paragraph C refers to ____.

a Hawaii (b) Nora's store c fruit

5 DETAIL Why do Nora's parents come to the store?

(a) to help her b to buy mochi c to talk to her

B Read the article again. Which paragraph (**A–C**) has the answer to each question?

1 What is mochi? B

2 Where does Nora live? A

3 What's the name of Nora's store? C

4 What's in Nora's mochi? B

5 Who buys Nora's mochi? C

6 What country are Nora's grandparents from? A

C CRITICAL THINKING Applying **Talk with a partner.** Nora's mochi is both Japanese and Hawaiian. What are some other examples of food from two cultures? Answers will vary.

Food	Cultures

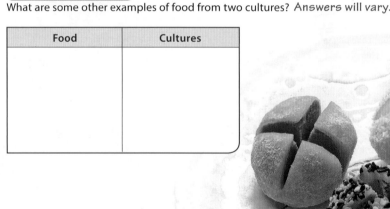

DO YOU KNOW?

Many Japanese eat mochi for ____.

(a) New Year

b Christmas

Explain the importance of understanding which paragraph contains the answer to a content question. (See **EXAM PRACTICE**.)

Have students follow along in their books as you read the questions aloud.

Have students do the task. Check answers as a class.

OPTIONAL Ask students additional comprehension questions.

1 *Nora lives in **Japan/the U.S.*** (the U.S.)

2 *Nora's grandparents are **American/Japanese***. (Japanese)

3 *Nora is probably often **in her store/at home***. (in her store)

4 ***Only tourists/Locals and tourists** buy Nora's mochi.* (Locals and tourists)

5 *Nora's store is called **Nora's Kitchen/Two Ladies Kitchen***. (Two Ladies Kitchen)

C CRITICAL THINKING

As students follow along in their books, read the statement and question aloud. Point out the chart that students should complete. Encourage students to give reasons why or provide evidence showing how the food represents two different cultures.

Have students get into pairs and do the task.

VOCABULARY

A As students follow along, read the words in the box aloud. Have students find them in the **READING** passage.

VOCABULARY

A Find the words below in the article. Then complete the sentences.

tradition | especially | continue | add | local | enjoys

1 I like everyone in my family, especially my grandmother.
2 We always have a party on my grandmother's birthday. It's a family tradition.
3 This restaurant is popular with local people because it has traditional food.
4 My dad doesn't add sugar to his coffee.
5 My family enjoys watching movies together.
6 It's important to continue family traditions.

B Read the information below. Then complete the family tree.

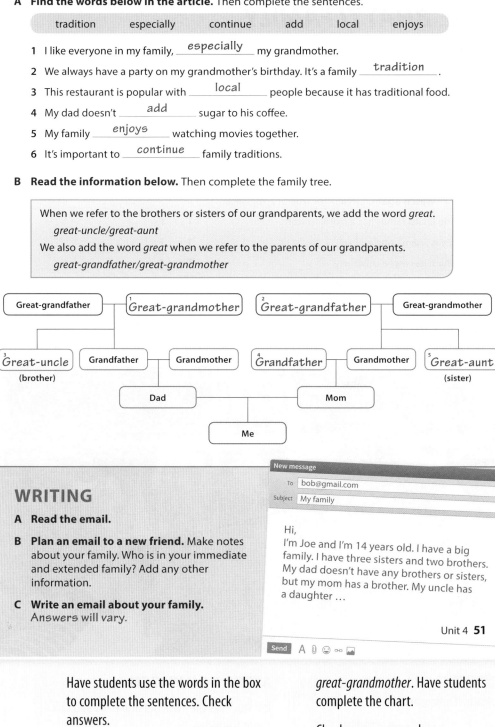

When we refer to the brothers or sisters of our grandparents, we add the word *great*.
great-uncle/great-aunt
We also add the word *great* when we refer to the parents of our grandparents.
great-grandfather/great-grandmother

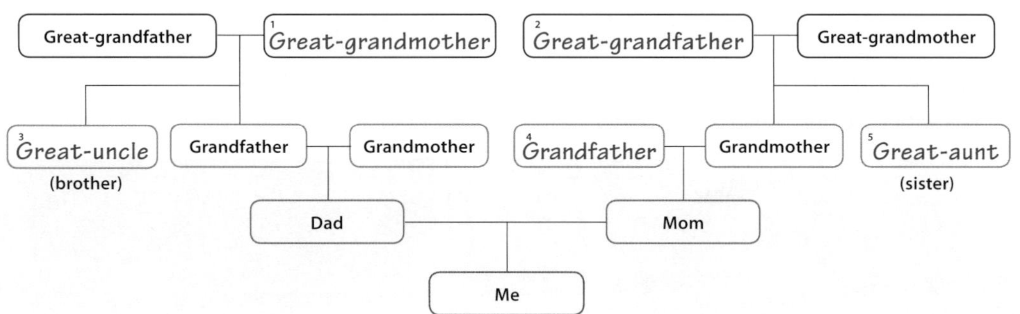

WRITING

A Read the email.

B Plan an email to a new friend. Make notes about your family. Who is in your immediate and extended family? Add any other information.

C Write an email about your family.
Answers will vary.

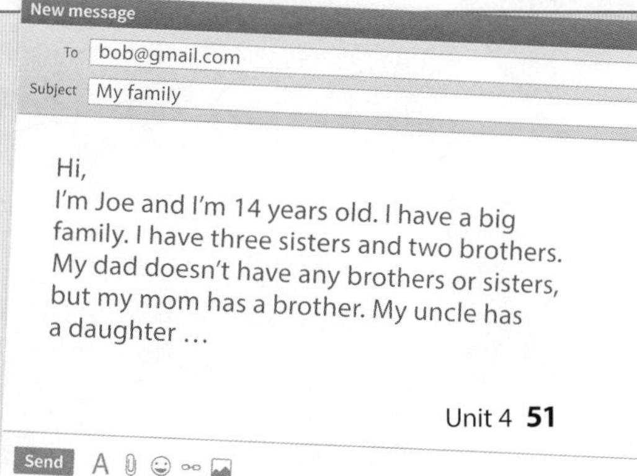

New message
To bob@gmail.com
Subject My family
Hi,
I'm Joe and I'm 14 years old. I have a big family. I have three sisters and two brothers. My dad doesn't have any brothers or sisters, but my mom has a brother. My uncle has a daughter …
Send

Have students use the words in the box to complete the sentences. Check answers.

B As students follow along, read the information in the box aloud. Explain that there is a pattern used to express family relationships outside the immediate family. Explain that *grand* + *parent* = *grandparent* (one generation removed from the immediate family). Tell students that for additional generations, we consecutively add *great*, so your grandmother's mother is *your great-grandmother*. Have students complete the chart.

Check answers as a class.

CHALLENGE Tell students that when speaking about younger generations, we say *daughter*, *granddaughter, great-granddaughter, great-great-granddaughter*, etc. Point to the *Great-grandfather* on the top left of the family tree. Have students describe his relationships to the *Grandfather* (son), *Dad* (grandson), and *Me* (great-grandson/great-granddaughter).

Tell students we continue adding *great* for each generation. Ask students to give the term for their grandmother's grandmother (*great-great-grandmother*). Have them get into pairs and take turns asking and answering questions about other relationships.

WRITING

Tell students they are going to write an email about their family. Ask students how often they send emails. Then ask them who they usually send emails to.

A As students follow along, read the email about Joe's family aloud. Ask who wrote it (Joe).

Point out to students how the email starts (*Hi*) and then explain that this kind of greeting is used with an informal email. Tell them that their email should include suitable greetings.

B Have students make notes about who the people are in their immediate and extended family. Then ask them to make notes with other information about their family members.

SUPPORT Ask students to identify the kind of information contained in the email (e.g., age of person writing the email, number of brothers and sisters, number of aunts and uncles).

C Have students use their notes from **B** to write their emails. You might want to give them a time limit for finishing the email, and set a minimum number of sentences they must write (e.g., five).

OPTIONAL After students have completed their emails, have them take turns reading them to a partner. Then have two pairs get together to form a group of four students. Have students take turns introducing their partner's family to the other pair.

VIDEO

Tell students they are going to watch a video about a family. Have students look at the photo and discuss how they think the people are related. Emphasize that they are brainstorming, which is a kind of creative thinking, and that there is no correct answer.

TEACHING NOTE: VIDEO AS HOMEWORK

You may want to assign the video page as homework. If your class has students of many different English abilities, this will allow the lower-level students to watch the video repeatedly and gain confidence in the content.

If you assign the video as homework, encourage the students to watch it several times.

During the following lesson, have a discussion about the video or give a short quiz. This will encourage students to do the homework.

BEFORE YOU WATCH

As students follow along in their books, read the sentence about the video aloud. Then read the questions. Have students get into pairs and talk about their ideas.

WHILE YOU WATCH

A Tell students they will watch the video and they should circle the correct answers to complete the sentences. As students follow along in their books, read the sentences aloud.

▶ 4.2 Play Video 4.2. Play the video again, if necessary.

Check answers as a class.

B Explain to students that they will watch the video again. Tell them that for each statement, they should circle **T** if they think it is true and **F** if they think it is false. As students follow along in their books, read the sentences aloud.

VIDEO ABOUT THE VIDEO The Bhattis have a family business.

THE *BHATTI FAMILY*

Before You Watch

Talk with a partner. Do you know any family businesses? What kind of business are they? *Answers will vary.*

While You Watch

A ▶ 4.2 **Watch the video.** Circle the correct answers.

1 The Bhatti family lives in **Canada** / **the United Kingdom**. (circled: the United Kingdom)

2 The Bhattis have a sale in their store every **year** / **six months**. (circled: year)

3 The Bhatti family is **small** / **big**. (circled: big)

B ▶ 4.2 **Watch again.** Circle **T** for True or **F** for False.

1	The Bhatti family has a clothing store.	(T)	F
2	Jay is Sham's uncle.	T	(F)
3	Sham has three children.	T	(F)
4	Mariam's grandfather works at the store.	(T)	F
5	After the sale, the Bhatti family has dinner together.	(T)	F

After You Watch

Talk with a partner. When do you see your extended family? What do you do? *Answers will vary.*

52 Unit 4

▶ 4.2 Play Video 4.2. Play the video again, if necessary.

Check answers as a class.

OPTIONAL Have students correct the false statements.

AFTER YOU WATCH

Tell students they will get into pairs and talk about the video.

As students follow along in their books, read the questions aloud.

Have them get into pairs and discuss their ideas.

REVIEW

ABOUT THE PHOTO

This photo shows siblings Jay and Sham who run the Bhatti family business. In a family business, two or more members of the family work for the business and the family controls a large amount of the business. Family businesses not only come in small sizes, they can also be large multinational companies. The biggest family company in the world is Walmart, owned by the Walton family.

A Complete the chart. Add the missing family words.

Male	Female
dad	mom
brother	sister
nephew	niece
uncle	aunt
grandfather	grandmother
son	daughter
p a r e n t s	
g r a n d p a r e n t s	
c o u s i n s	

B Complete the conversation. Use the correct form of *have* and *do*.

Tom: Sasha, do you [1] have any brothers and sisters?

Sasha: I have a brother, but I [2] don't have any sisters.

Tom: [3] Does your brother [4] have any children?

Sasha: Yes, he [5] does. He has a son, Jake.

Tom: Do you have any cousins?

Sasha: Yes, I [6] do. My aunt [7] has a daughter. She doesn't have any sons.

C Complete the sentences. Circle the correct answers.

1 Your dad's dad is your **grandfather** / **great-uncle**. (circled: grandfather)

2 Your grandfather's mom is your **grandmother** / **great-grandmother**. (circled: great-grandmother)

3 Your grandfather's brother is your **great-uncle** / **great-grandfather**. (circled: great-uncle)

Jay (left) and Sham (right) run the Bhatti family business.

SELF CHECK Now I can ...

- ☐ describe people in my family
- ☐ use language for talking about family members
- ☐ talk about family traditions

REVIEW

Explain to students that they are going to review the material from the unit and this will help them remember what they have studied.

A Explain that activity **A** reviews vocabulary from the unit. Point out that in the first part of the chart, they should write the male/female equivalent of the relationship already provided. Also explain that they should write letters to complete the three words at the bottom of the chart.

Have students do the task. Check answers as a class.

You may want to ask students why the bottom three words are not categorized as male/female. (The terms can be used for both men and women.)

CHALLENGE As students recall other vocabulary that was important in the unit, write it on the board (e.g., *tradition*, *especially*, *enjoy*). Have students get into pairs and take turns making sentences using the words. After students have finished, randomly call on pairs to share one of their sentences. As you repeat back the sentences, make corrections to grammar and vocabulary usage.

B Explain that activity **B** reviews the grammar from the unit. Have students write the correct words to complete the conversation. Have students get into pairs and check answers, before you randomly call on students to give the answers.

OPTIONAL Have students get into pairs and practice the conversation. When they have finished, have students personalize the conversation and practice again.

C Point out that activity **C** reviews words from **VOCABULARY** activity **B**.

Have students circle the correct words to complete the sentences. Check answers.

SELF CHECK

These *I can* statements provide vital feedback on students' perceived ability to use the language from the unit. If you find students are reluctant to check that they can do the skills, consider asking them to rate themselves from 1 (not very confident) to 3 (very confident).

SUPPORT For each skill, have students say sentences demonstrating their ability.

OPTIONAL Have students complete the **SELF CHECK** before doing the **REVIEW** activities. After reviewing the unit, have students once again check their confidence for each.

UNIT 5
I LIKE FRUIT!

CONTENT AREA: HISTORY AND CULTURE

Topic: food

Vocabulary: fruit: banana, apple, pineapple, cherry, watermelon, orange; **other food:** bread, chips, rice, soup, cookie, popcorn, burger, dessert, fries, sandwich; **drinks:** soda, milk, water, juice; **meat:** fish, chicken; **meals:** breakfast, lunch, dinner; **other words:** hungry, landscape, build, made of, real, fresh

Grammar: *like*; countable and uncountable nouns

Extra material: pictures of food you like and don't like, some menus, a bottle of water, a world map

Other useful vocabulary: fruit: grape, pear, peach, plum, grapefruit, lemon, lime, apricot, kiwi, mango, strawberry, nectarine, melon; **vegetables:** lettuce, spinach, cabbage, corn, pea, yam, broccoli, sweet potato; **other food:** hot dog, steak, pasta

ABOUT THE PHOTO

This photo shows a customer selecting fruit at a fruit stall in Borough Market. Established in the thirteenth century, Borough Market is the oldest market in London. Borough Market is a wholesale and retail market specializing in high-end fresh produce. The wide range of options for fresh produce draws locals and inspires new dish ideas, while the food stalls draw the tourists in for a quick bite or some dessert.

END OF UNIT PROJECT Have students write a short paragraph about a traditional food from their country. Encourage them to choose a food that they really like or that is very unusual.

Remind students that they studied some countries' popular dishes in the **VIDEO** section. Have students name traditional food that is popular among students. Then have them get into pairs, choose one food, and brainstorm the ingredients. Also have them brainstorm how to describe it.

Have students write their paragraphs individually.

Collect the students' papers. Shuffle them, pass them out, and have students take turns reading the descriptions of the food without naming it. Have the other students guess what food is being described.

CONTENT NOTE: WHAT YOU EAT

In this unit, students learn about what they eat. This is a good opportunity to tell them about their human footprint. When we eat an egg, we're not just eating an egg. We also have to consider the gasoline the truck used to deliver the egg to the store, the fuel used to make the energy to power the refrigerator to keep it cool, and the resources needed to cook it, not to mention all of the resources to produce it before it left the farm. All of these things together make up our human footprint—the impact we have on the planet and its resources.

A fruit stall at Borough Market in London

PREVIEW

A 5.1 **Listen.** What kinds of fruit do the speakers like? Complete the ***Like*** column.

bananas

apples

cherries

pineapples

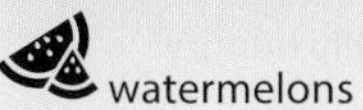
watermelons

oranges

Name	Like ☺	Don't Like ☹
Dino	bananas	pineapples
Sophie	watermelons	cherries
Miguel	apples	oranges

B 5.2 **Listen.** What kinds of fruit don't the speakers like? Complete the ***Don't Like*** column.

C **Talk with a partner.** What kinds of fruit do you like? What kinds of fruit don't you like?

Answers will vary.

I like apples and bananas.

I like watermelons, but I don't like oranges.

HISTORY AND CULTURE

UNIT GOALS

- talk about the food you like and don't like
- use language for describing likes and dislikes
- learn about food in different countries

55

PREVIEW

Have students read the unit title to themselves as you read it aloud. Explain that in this unit they will learn to talk about different foods, including *fruit*. Point to the word *fruit* and some of the fruit in the photo as you say it.

OPTIONAL Ask students to follow along in their books as you say the names of some of the foods in the picture aloud.

A Explain to students that they will hear a short conversation with three people talking about the fruit they like. Tell them to write the name of the fruit each person likes in the chart. As they follow along, read the names of the fruit and people aloud.

5.1 Play Audio Track 5.1. Play it again, if necessary.

Have students check answers with a partner and then elicit answers from the class.

SUPPORT Before playing the audio, explain *like* and *don't like*. Use the pictures you brought in. Hold up a picture. Make a happy face as you say *I like X*. Hold up another picture. Make an unhappy face as you say *I don't like X*.

B Explain to students that the conversation will continue with the three speakers talking about the fruit they don't like. Tell them to write the fruit the speakers don't like in the chart.

5.2 Play Audio Track 5.2. Play it again, if necessary.

Check answers as a class.

C Tell students they will take turns asking and answering the questions in **C**. Explain that they should use their own answers.

Model the conversation with a student. Then have students do the task.

CHALLENGE Before students start **C**, have them brainstorm other kinds of fruit. (See **Other useful vocabulary**.)

UNIT GOALS

Direct students' attention to the **UNIT GOALS** box. Explain that these are some of the things students will learn in this unit. Point out that this unit is about history and culture. As students follow along, read each of the unit goals to the class. Explain any words students do not know. Explain to students that at the end of the unit there is a self check that allows them to see if they have accomplished each goal.

LANGUAGE FOCUS

A 5.3 **Listen and read.** Does Nadine like Stig's food? Then repeat the conversation and replace the words in **bold**. *Yes, she does.*

REAL ENGLISH Me, too.

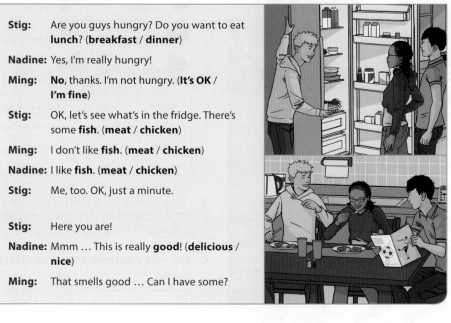

Stig: Are you guys hungry? Do you want to eat **lunch**? (**breakfast** / **dinner**)

Nadine: Yes, I'm really hungry!

Ming: **No**, thanks. I'm not hungry. (**It's OK** / **I'm fine**)

Stig: OK, let's see what's in the fridge. There's some **fish**. (**meat** / **chicken**)

Ming: I don't like **fish**. (**meat** / **chicken**)

Nadine: I like **fish**. (**meat** / **chicken**)

Stig: Me, too. OK, just a minute.

Stig: Here you are!

Nadine: Mmm ... This is really **good**! (**delicious** / **nice**)

Ming: That smells good ... Can I have some?

B 5.4 **Look at the chart.** Then circle the correct answers below.

TALKING ABOUT LIKES AND DISLIKES (USING *LIKE*)

		Countable	Uncountable
I **like** fruit. I **don't like** vegetables. He **likes** popcorn. She **doesn't like** milk. They **like** rice, but they **don't like** sandwiches.		sandwich(**es**) dessert(**s**) vegetable(**s**)	milk water bread
Do you **like** juice?	Yes, I **do**. No, I **don't**.		
Does he **like** oranges?	Yes, he **does**. No, he **doesn't**.		

1 We use *like* **before** / **after** a noun.

2 We use **have** / **do** to ask questions with *like*.

3 We add *-s* or *-es* to **countable** / **uncountable** nouns.

56 Unit 5

LANGUAGE FOCUS

A Tell students they will listen to a conversation between Nadine, Ming, and Stig.

5.3 Play Audio Track 5.3 as students listen and follow along in their books. If necessary, play the conversation again, pausing after each speaker so students can repeat.

As students follow along, read the question, *Does Nadine like Stig's food?* Have students answer.

Have students work in pairs and practice the conversation once. Point out the bold words and read them aloud as students follow along in their books.

Have students practice the conversation two more times, changing the bold words each time and swapping roles after the first time.

REAL ENGLISH

Explain that *Me, too* is used to show that we have something in common with other people or that we agree with a statement. For example:

A: I like fruit a lot.
B: Me, too!

B Ask students to look at the chart.

5.4 Have students follow along as they listen to Audio Track 5.4.

Explain that these are statements about likes and dislikes. Write *like/likes* and *don't like/doesn't like* on the board. Point out that they must be careful because the verb changes, depending on the subject of the sentence (*I like/She likes* ...). Say sentence subjects (e.g., *they, Sam, Matt and I*) and have students decide which verb should be used.

Read the questions and answers at the bottom of the chart aloud as students follow along in their books.

Ask students to look at the questions and find *like* in each one. Point out that the verb does not change even though the subject does. Emphasize they must use *like* in all questions (and should not use *likes*).

On the board, write, *Does he like oranges? Yes, he does.* Circle *does* in both, pointing out that it is repeated in both the question and the answer.

Explain to students that in English we refer to the person we are talking to by using *you/your* when asking questions. Expand on this by explaining that we would not ask Bob, *Does Bob like oranges?* Instead, we would ask him *Do you like oranges?*

Draw students' attention to the right side of the chart. Tell students that countable nouns are individual objects, people, or places that can be counted. Hold up a pen saying, *one pen*. Hold up two pens, saying, *one, two; two pens.*

C **Look at the photos below.** Are the foods countable or uncountable? Write **C** for countable and **U** for uncountable.

popcorn U   burger C   sandwich C   soda U

bread U   chips C   rice U   soup U

cookie C   vegetables C   milk U   juice U

D 5.5 **Complete the conversation.** Write *like*, *likes*, *don't like*, or *doesn't like*. Then listen and check your answers.

Mia: I'm hungry. Let's have lunch.

Raul: OK. Do you [1] like rice and beans?

Mia: Well, I like rice, but I [2] don't like beans.

Raul: How about Sarah? Does Sarah [3] like rice?

Mia: Yes, she does. She [4] likes beans, too.

Raul: How about Tim?

Mia: He [5] likes beans, but he [6] doesn't like rice.

Raul: Hmmm … Let's eat burgers. We all [7] like burgers!

E **Play tic-tac-toe.** Turn to page 151 and follow the instructions.

DO YOU KNOW?

What's this fruit called?

(a) snake fruit

b dragon fruit

Explain that uncountable nouns are things that are not individual objects and cannot be counted. If you brought in a bottle of water, ask, *How can we count water?* Tell them we need another word: *a bottle of water*. Tell them uncountable nouns need other words to be counted. Explain that uncountable nouns are always expressed as singular (with no plural *s*).

Draw students' attention to the three statements under the chart. Have students do the task. Check answers.

C Tell students to look at the pictures and decide if the food is countable or uncountable and write **C** or **U**.

Check answers as a class.

D Ask students to write *like*, *likes*, *don't like*, or *doesn't like* in each blank to complete the conversation.

Tell students they will listen to the conversation so they can check their answers.

5.5 Play Audio Track 5.5. Check answers as a class.

E Tell students they are going to play a game of tic-tac-toe in pairs. Have students turn to page 151.

A Have students get into pairs and take turns asking what food they like and don't like. Emphasize that they should remember their partner's answers.

B Explain that one student will be X and the other will be O and the goal is to get three letters in a row vertically, horizontally, or diagonally.

Tell them they will take turns making sentences about what their partner likes/doesn't like. If their sentence is correct, they get to write their letter (X or O) in one square in the chart.

Model the conversation with a student.

Have students play the game.

DO YOU KNOW?

Read the question and answer choices aloud, as students follow along in their books. Ask students to guess the answer before providing it (a).

CONTENT NOTE: AN UNUSUAL FRUIT

Salak, also known as snake fruit, is a kind of palm tree fruit that is originally from Indonesia. The fruit, about the size of a strawberry and shaped like a fig, got its name from the red-brown scaly skin on the outside, which reminds some people of the scales of snakes like the cobra and python.

THE REAL WORLD

Ask students to look at the photo. As students follow along in their books, read the title and the photo caption aloud.

CONTENT NOTE: SCHOOL LUNCHES

School lunches vary greatly around the world, but there is a trend toward healthier meals. In France, for example, lunch is considered the main meal of the day, so French schools serve four courses. The first is a salad or vegetable. Vegetables are also included with the main dish. Cheese, the third course, is followed by fruit four times a week and dessert once a week. There are many guidelines to control the nutritional content and decrease the amount of fat.

Similarly, Singapore has instituted guidelines to reduce fat, sugar, and salt while increasing whole grains, fruit, and vegetables.

A As students follow along in their books, read the questions aloud. Have students get into pairs and discuss the questions.

B Explain to students that they will watch a video about school lunches in four countries and they should match the lunches with the countries. As students follow along, read the countries' names aloud.

▶ 5.1 Play Video 5.1. If necessary, play the video again.

Check answers as a class.

OPTIONAL Have students find Germany, Russia, Brazil, Japan, and the United States on a world map.

C Tell students they are going to watch the video again and they should check the food that is in each country's school lunch.

THE REAL WORLD

SCHOOL MEALS

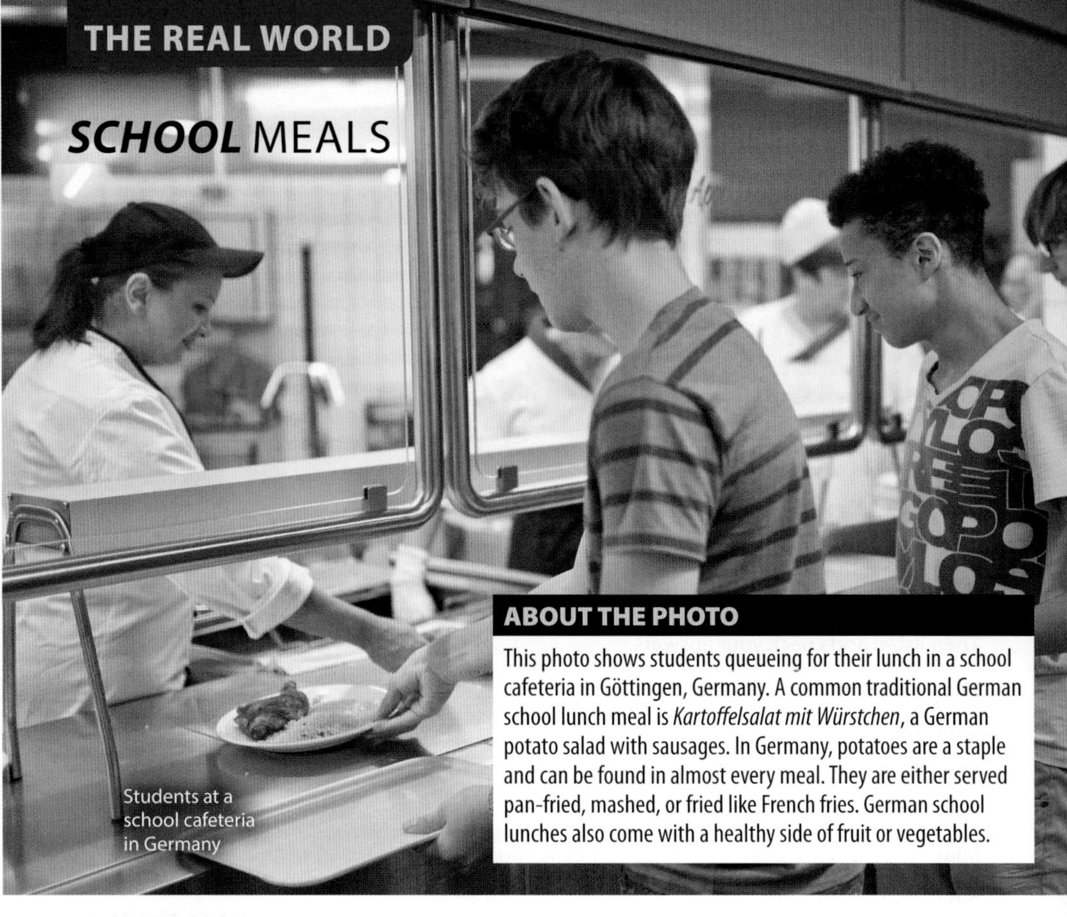

Students at a school cafeteria in Germany

ABOUT THE PHOTO

This photo shows students queueing for their lunch in a school cafeteria in Göttingen, Germany. A common traditional German school lunch meal is *Kartoffelsalat mit Würstchen*, a German potato salad with sausages. In Germany, potatoes are a staple and can be found in almost every meal. They are either served pan-fried, mashed, or fried like French fries. German school lunches also come with a healthy side of fruit or vegetables.

A Talk with a partner. Do you have lunch at school? What do you eat? *Answers will vary.*

B ▶ 5.1 **Watch the video.** Match the lunches with the countries.

Russia   Brazil   Japan   the United States

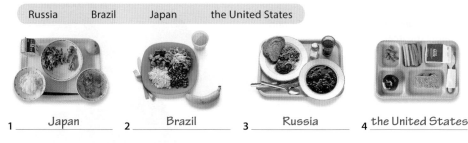

1 *Japan* 2 *Brazil* 3 *Russia* 4 *the United States*

58 Unit 5

▶ 5.1 Play Video 5.1. If necessary, play the video again.

Check answers as a class.

CHALLENGE Ask students to compare their school lunch with the lunches in **B**. Encourage them to compare the amount of meat, the number of fruit and vegetables, and the variety of colors. Also ask them to talk about whether they think the people in each country eat a bigger, smaller, or similarly sized lunch as them.

D CRITICAL THINKING

As students follow along, read the questions aloud. Have students get into pairs and discuss their answers.

PROJECT As students follow along, read the project instructions aloud. Set a deadline by which students must make their poster. In the next lesson, have students get into pairs and discuss their posters.

C ▶ 5.1 **Watch again.** Check (✓) the food items from each country.

	Japan	Brazil	Russia	USA
rice	✓	✓		
bread			✓	✓
soup	✓		✓	
meat	✓	✓	✓	
vegetables	✓	✓		✓
fruit/dessert	✓	✓		✓
drink (juice/milk)	✓	✓	✓	✓

D CRITICAL THINKING Personalizing **Talk with a partner.** Which of the school lunches do you like? Why? *Answers will vary.*

PROJECT Make a poster. What kind of lunch would you like in your school? Find photos of different food and drinks. Share your ideas with a partner.

PRONUNCIATION final *s* sounds

A 5.6 **Listen and repeat.**

1 *s*, drinks 2 *z*, bananas 3 *iz*, glasses

B 5.7 **Listen.** Write the sounds (*s*, *z*, *iz*) of the words. Then read the words to a partner.

1 chips s 2 oranges iz 3 desserts s

4 apples z 5 watermelons z 6 sandwiches iz

COMMUNICATION

Complete the chart below. Then turn to page 151 and follow the instructions. *Answers will vary.*

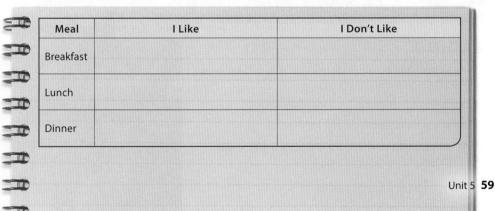

Meal	I Like	I Don't Like
Breakfast		
Lunch		
Dinner		

COMMUNICATION

Tell students they are going to make a meal plan with their favorite foods.

If you brought in some menus, show them to the students and explain that a menu lists the food you can buy at a restaurant. Tell them that their meal plan is like a menu because they will make a list of foods for three meals.

Point to the chart. Have students make lists of the foods they like and don't like to eat for specific meals.

Have students turn to page 151.

Explain to students that they should get into groups and talk about the foods they've written in their charts.

Tell students they must decide which foods to have for each meal, and everyone in the group should like all of the foods.

Have students do the task. When students have finished, ask a few groups to share their meal plans.

SUPPORT If students are having problems using *like* and *likes* when discussing their charts, ask them to form their own grammar rule. This is a good critical thinking skill.

like	I				
likes					

PRONUNCIATION

Tell students they will practice their pronunciation of final *s* sounds (e.g., *drinks, bananas, glasses*).

A Have students look at the words. Tell them that even though all of the words end in *s*, the pronunciation of the *s* sound is not the same. Explain that there are three different pronunciations for the final *s* sound, and they will practice all three of them.

5.6 Play Audio Track 5.6. Play it again, pausing after each word so students can repeat. Play the audio a third time, if necessary.

B Tell students they will listen to the words and write down which of the final *s* sounds the words have.

5.7 Play Audio Track 5.7. Play it again, if necessary. Check answers. Have students get into pairs and take turns reading the words. Remind them to be careful about using the correct *s* pronunciation.

READING

Have one student read the title aloud.

A Ask students to look at the photos. As students follow along, read the captions and then the question and the answer choices aloud. Have students circle their answer.

OPTIONAL Have students get into pairs and talk about the things they can see in the photos (fish, an island with pineapples, etc.).

B Tell students that they will skim the text and that they should underline the food words. Emphasize that they should not underline the word *food*.

Have students do the task.

When all the students have finished, ask students how many words they underlined (six). If several students missed some words, give them some more time to find the remaining food words.

Check answers as a class.

Ask them if their answer for **A** was correct.

SUPPORT Ask students additional questions to help them understand the text.

1. *What are the fish made from?* (fruit)
2. *What are the trees made from?* (pineapples)

C Tell students to get into pairs and think of a title for the photo with Carl. You might want to tell students that titles can be a statement or a question. You may also want to teach more about elements of a good title (See **TEACHING NOTE**).

Encourage students to have fun and be creative.

A coral seascape

READING

A **Look at the photos.** What are the things in these photos made of? Choose the correct answer.

a animals   **(b)** food   **c** paper

B **Skim the article.** Underline the food words.

C **Talk with a partner.** Think of a title for the photo with Carl Warner. Answers will vary.

60 Unit 5

OPTIONAL Have some pairs tell the class their title. If some titles are very long or vague, have the class work together to discuss how the titles can be improved.

After completing the task, give students the opportunity to read the article in more detail so they can fully comprehend it.

OPTIONAL The text can also be used as a listening activity. Have students close their books. Tell students they will listen to the passage.

5.8 Play Audio Track 5.8. Ask students to get into pairs and discuss what information they heard. Then have them read the article more carefully.

FOOD SCAPES

5.8 Carl Warner takes photos of interesting things. He also makes beautiful **landscapes** using food. These are called "foodscapes." It takes Carl four or five days to **build** each foodscape.

Look carefully at the photo with sea animals. What do you see? There's an ocean with a lot of fish and rocks. There's also sand. But are the fish **real**? The fish are **made of** fruit! There's an island and some trees. The trees are made of pineapples. In fact, it's all made of food—**fresh** fruit and vegetables!

What other foods do you see in the photo? Do you see melons and oranges? Now look at the photo below. What foods do you see in this photo?

ABOUT THE PHOTO

The main photo shows Carl Warner's foodscape of a coral seascape. Foodscapes are images of landscapes that are made with food. Warner gets his inspiration from walking through farmer markets in London, finding interestingly shaped vegetables and fruit. The creation of a foodscape can be a long process, taking from a week up to months to plan before building starts for the foodscape. Using traditional photography techniques of layout and composition, Warner makes the scene look very real. Many food items are used in the foodscapes, but there is no need to worry about food wastage—most of the food is consumed by Warner's team or donated to charity.

The other photo shows Carl Warner posing with another foodscape he created.

Carl Warner with his foodscape

Unit 5 61

TEACHING NOTE: A GOOD TITLE SHOULD …

- give a hint about the content.
- not be too long.
- be meaningful and related to the content.
- be interesting and make readers want to know more.
- be decided after the essay or paper has been written, not before.

Additional Activities to Use with the Reading

Paragraph Construction

Ask students to identify the number of paragraphs in the article (three).

Explain to students that a paragraph is a group of sentences about the same topic. Point out that each sentence does not start on a new line but instead follows the previous sentence.

Tell students that a paragraph has three parts: the beginning, the middle, and the end. Explain each part.

Tell students that the beginning of the paragraph introduces the idea. In the first paragraph, the introduction tells us *who* (Carl Warner) and *what* (Warner takes photos).

The middle of the paragraph explains the idea. In the first paragraph of *Foodscapes*, the middle of the paragraph tells us *how* Warner makes foodscapes (with food).

The end of the paragraph ties up the paragraph. In the first paragraph, we find out *how long* it takes to make a foodscape.

Have students work in pairs and analyze the beginning, middle, and end of the second paragraph. Then discuss answers as a class. (The beginning of the second paragraph describes the sea photo. The middle of the paragraph tells us about some of the things we can see in the foodscape. The end of the paragraph tells us about some of the food Warner used.)

Tell students that the third paragraph wraps up the article. Point out that it challenges us to observe more in the photo and use the new knowledge we just read to analyze another photo of a foodscape (the photo with Carl Warner).

Vocabulary

Help students understand new words without having to look them up in the dictionary. For example, explain that *landscape* (line 2) means *a picture of how things look outside*. Ask students to think of other words that could replace *build* (e.g., *make*, *create*) on line 4.

COMPREHENSION

A Answer the questions about *Foodscapes*.

1 MAIN IDEA What's the article mainly about?

(a) photos of food b how to take photos c sea animals

2 INFERENCE What's Carl Warner's job?

a gardener (b) photographer c cook

3 DETAIL What are the trees made of?

(a) pineapples b apples c oranges

4 REFERENCE The word *it's* in line 9 refers to ____.

a the island b the trees (c) everything in the photo

5 DETAIL In the second photo, Carl uses ____ to show the sea.

a fruit (b) vegetables c sand

B Complete the word web. Use information from the article.

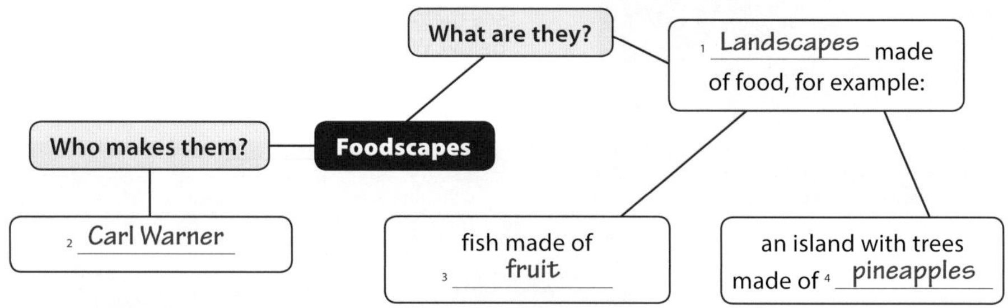

C CRITICAL THINKING Applying **Talk with a partner.** How can you make a similar picture? What kinds of fruit and vegetables do you need? Answers will vary.

COMPREHENSION

A Have students read the questions to themselves and circle the correct answers.

After they have finished, check answers as a class.

B **EXAM PRACTICE**

A word web, also known as a concept map or relationship chart, is another type of graphic organizer. Word webs can be used to classify and describe. They are also effective for demonstrating cause and effect.

In class, word webs can be used to brainstorm new ideas, but on tests students must be certain they do not include ideas that are not in the passage. Using a word web, students must reduce the reading passage into an easy-to-understand visual representation. To do this, students must determine which information is most important. As a result, students analyze information to establish relationships between ideas.

Point to the word web diagram. Have students follow along in their books as you read the words in the word web aloud.

Tell students that a word web can help us make connections between words and ideas. Explain that word webs can be used to help understand readings. Tell them that word webs can also be used to think of new ideas, and plan them out, before writing.

Explain to students that the main idea (the main topic) is in the center. Have students identify the color of the box (dark blue) and the main topic (*Foodscapes*).

Explain that the words that are directly related to the main topic are in the boxes directly connected to the main circle. Have them identify the color (gray shaded) and questions (*Who makes them? What are they?*).

Explain that the further the word is from the center (main topic), the more detail it usually gives.

Tell students that the remaining boxes contain more specific details and answer the questions that are in the gray-shaded boxes.

Have students use the text on page 61 to complete the diagram.

Check answers as a class.

CONTENT NOTE: CARL WARNER'S FOODSCAPES

Carl Warner makes many amazing foodscapes. If you look him up online, you can find photos of some of his work. His website also includes information about how and why he makes the foodscapes.

VOCABULARY

A **Find the words below in the article.** Then complete the sentences.

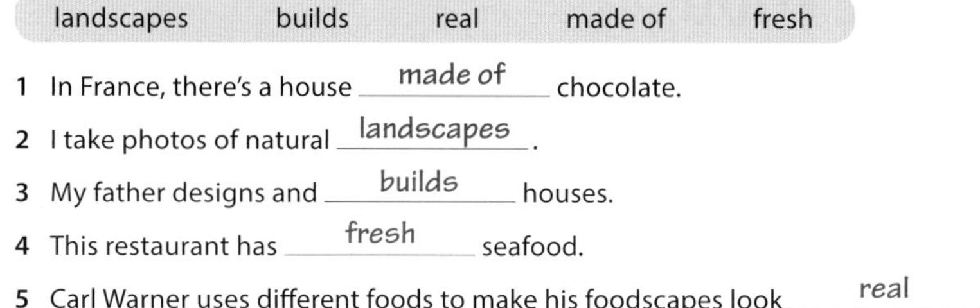

landscapes builds real made of fresh

1 In France, there's a house made of chocolate.
2 I take photos of natural landscapes.
3 My father designs and builds houses.
4 This restaurant has fresh seafood.
5 Carl Warner uses different foods to make his foodscapes look real.

B **Read the information below.** Then circle the correct answers.

We can make many phrases with the word *food*.
fresh food: food from markets
homemade food: food you cook at home
fast food: food you can make in a short time

1 This fruit salad is healthy because it's made of (**fresh**) / **fast** food.
2 I don't like food at restaurants. I like **fast** / (**homemade**) food.
3 Burgers and pizzas are examples of (**fast**) / **fresh** food.

IDIOM

Something that is "a piece of cake" is _____.
(a) easy to do
b difficult to do

WRITING

A **Look at the photo.** Read the beginning of a description about someone's favorite food.

B **Choose your favorite food.** Make notes about it. What is it? Why do you like it?

C **Write about your favorite food.** Answers will vary.

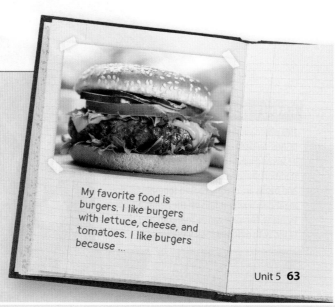

My favorite food is burgers. I like burgers with lettuce, cheese, and tomatoes. I like burgers because ...

Unit 5 **63**

C CRITICAL THINKING
Critical thinking includes the ability to reflect on and apply information. As students follow along, read the questions aloud. Have students get into pairs and discuss their ideas.

VOCABULARY

A As students follow along, read the words in the box aloud. Have students find them in the **READING** passage.

Have students use the words in the box to complete the sentences. Check answers as a class.

B As students follow along, read the information in the box aloud. Explain that a collocation is a set of two or more words that frequently appear together. Point out that these collocations deal with food.

Have students circle the correct answers to complete the sentences.

Check answers as a class.

WRITING

Tell students they are going to write about their favorite food.

A Ask student to look at the photo. Then, as students follow along, read the example description aloud. Point out that the author describes the burger and starts to give a reason why he likes burgers. Emphasize that they should include both of these points.

B Have students choose a favorite food and make notes about it. Remind students to write why they like it.

C Have students use their notes in **B** and other ideas to write their description. Give them a time limit for finishing the description and set a minimum number of sentences they should write (e.g., five).

CHALLENGE After students have completed their paragraphs, have them get into pairs and take turns reading them aloud to a partner. Have the partner ask them questions about the food. Encourage partners to also ask questions about things they do not understand.

Tell students that when we write we often revise our work by doing things such as correcting grammatical mistakes, adding information, editing unclear statements, and removing repetitive details. Explain that the second version of the work is called the second draft. Tell students that for some reports we might have three or more drafts.

Have students use their partner's questions to think about additional information they could include in their descriptions. Encourage them to include more details or examples and also make their descriptions clearer.

Have students write a second draft of their favorite food. Collect both drafts and provide feedback on their inclusion of more details.

VIDEO

Tell students they are going to watch a video about popular dishes in several countries.

As students follow along in their books, read the title and the sentence about the video aloud.

BEFORE YOU WATCH

Have students look at the photo. As students follow along, read the caption aloud. Ask, *Where is Brazil?* (South America.) This may help them brainstorm more information about feijoada.

As students follow along, read the two questions aloud. Have them get into pairs and discuss their ideas, and then call on several pairs to share their ideas.

CHALLENGE Ask students to get into pairs and describe how the food looks. Then ask them to discuss any similar food in their own country. Include questions such as: *What is the name of the dish? What is in it? When do you eat it? Do you usually eat it at home or in a restaurant?*

WHILE YOU WATCH

A Tell students they will watch the video and they should check the countries that the dishes in the video are from.

▶ 5.2 Play Video 5.2. Check answers.

OPTIONAL Have students find Brazil, Japan, and Italy on a world map.

B Explain to students that they will watch the video again. Tell them that for each statement they should circle the correct answer. As students follow along in their books, read the sentences aloud.

▶ 5.2 Play Video 5.2. Play the video again, if necessary.

Check answers as a class.

VIDEO **ABOUT THE VIDEO** Here are some popular dishes around the world.

OUR **FAVORITE FOOD**

Before You Watch

Look at the photo. What type of food is it? What do you think is in the dish? *Answers will vary.*

While You Watch

A ▶ 5.2 **Watch the video.** Check (✓) the countries the dishes are from.

☑ Japan	☐ the United States	☐ Australia
☑ Brazil	☐ China	☑ Italy

B ▶ 5.2 **Watch again.** Circle the correct answers.

1 Ramen is a type of **rice** / **(noodle)** dish.
2 There's **(seaweed)** / **salad** in some ramen.
3 Feijoada is a dish with black beans and **fruit** / **(meat)**.
4 People often eat feijoada with **(rice)** / **bread**.
5 Pizza marinara has only **cheese** / **(tomatoes)**.

After You Watch

Talk with a partner. Which dish in the video do you like? Why?
Answers will vary.

ABOUT THE PHOTO

This photo shows one of Brazil's most popular dishes, feijoada. This dish is a stew of black beans and meat (either pork or beef), and is traditionally served with a side of rice. The meat and beans are usually cooked together till the meat is so tender it falls off the bones. Enjoyed by many, this dish can be found all over the world with different local variations.

CONTENT NOTE: FEIJOADA AND RAMEN

Feijoada is considered the national dish of Brazil. It can be found in both casual diners and expensive restaurants. The name comes from the word *feijão*, which is Portuguese for "beans." In Brazil, Saturday is "the day of feijoada," demonstrating the dish's popularity. It is, however, more than a meal—it is considered to be an event that is shared with family and friends.

Although ramen may often be associated with Japan, it was originally made in China. The noodles are made of wheat, and in addition to seaweed, meat, and eggs, ramen may include chopped green onions, bean sprouts, slices of steamed fish cake, and/or corn.

AFTER YOU WATCH

Tell students they will get into pairs and talk about the video.

As students follow along in their books, read the questions aloud.

REVIEW

A Write the words in the chart.

watermelon	soda	water	milk	bread
banana	rice	pineapple	cookie	juice

Food	Drink
watermelon	soda
bread	water
banana	milk
rice	juice
pineapple	
cookie	

B Complete the sentences and questions. Use the correct form of *like*.

1 My sister ___likes___ (**like**) apples, but she ___doesn't like___ (**not like**) cherries.

2 I ___like___ (**like**) oranges, but I ___don't like___ (**not like**) apples.

3 **A:** ___Do___ you ___like___ (**like**) burgers?

B: Yes, I ___do___.

4 **A:** ___Does___ your sister ___like___ (**like**) soda?

B: No, she ___doesn't___.

C Circle the correct answers.

1 I make juice with **fresh** / **homemade** fruit.

2 My mother makes **fast** / **homemade** soup every Saturday.

3 McDonald's is an example of a **fast** / **homemade** food restaurant.

SELF CHECK Now I can …

- ☐ talk about the food I like and don't like
- ☐ use language for describing likes and dislikes
- ☐ talk about food in different countries

Feijoada is a popular dish in Brazil.

Unit 5 **65**

Have them get into pairs and do the task.

OPTIONAL Give students additional questions to discuss.

1 *Do you eat instant (cup) ramen? When? How often? Why? What is your favorite flavor?*

2 *Brazilians eat feijoada with rice. What food do you usually eat with rice?*

3 *How often do you eat pizza? What toppings do you usually have on your pizza? Do you like pizza that doesn't have cheese?*

REVIEW

Explain to students that they are going to review the material from the unit and this will help them remember what they have studied.

A Explain that activity **A** reviews vocabulary from the unit. Have students classify the words in the box as food or drink.

Check answers as a class.

CHALLENGE As students recall other vocabulary that was important in the unit, write it on the board (e.g., *build*, *fresh*, *real*). Have students get into pairs and take turns making sentences using the words. After students have finished, randomly call on pairs to share one of their sentences. As you repeat back the sentences, make corrections to grammar and vocabulary usage.

B Explain that activity **B** reviews the grammar from the unit. Have students write the correct words to complete the conversations. Have students get into pairs and check answers, before you randomly call on students to give the answers.

OPTIONAL Have students get into pairs and practice the conversations. When they have finished, have students personalize the answers and practice again.

C Point out that activity **C** reviews words from **VOCABULARY** activity **B**.

Have students circle the correct words.

Check answers.

SELF CHECK

These *I can* statements provide vital feedback on students' perceived ability to use the language from the unit. If you find students are reluctant to check that they can do the skills, consider asking them to rate themselves from 1 (not very confident) to 3 (very confident).

OPTIONAL Have students complete the **SELF CHECK** before doing the **REVIEW** activities. After reviewing the unit, have students once again check their confidence for each statement.

UNIT 6

WHAT TIME DOES CLASS START?

CONTENT AREA: PEOPLE AND PLACES

Topic: daily routines (schedules)

Vocabulary: about routines: get up, go to school, go home, do homework, have dinner, go to bed, soccer practice, wake up, have breakfast; **other words:** enough, finish, early, get married, dream, history

Grammar: *when* and *what time*; adverbs of frequency

Extra material: an analog clock, a world map, a book or article that has headings for the chapter/sections

Other useful vocabulary: get dressed, take a shower/bath, brush (my) teeth, wash (my) face, clean, exercise, make dinner, go for a walk, read; **additional adverbs of frequency:** occasionally, seldom, rarely, hardly ever

END OF UNIT PROJECT Have students make a clock showing their daily routine. Explain that they will draw a circle on a piece of paper and divide it into 24 evenly distributed spaces, one for each hour. Have students label some of the hours (e.g., 6:00, 12:00). Explain to students that they are going to keep track of how they spend an entire day. Tell them to use the wheel to record everything they do for the next 24 hours—from the time they get up, all the way to the time when they go to bed. Tell them they can color or otherwise mark actions that last many hours (e.g., the time when they are at school).

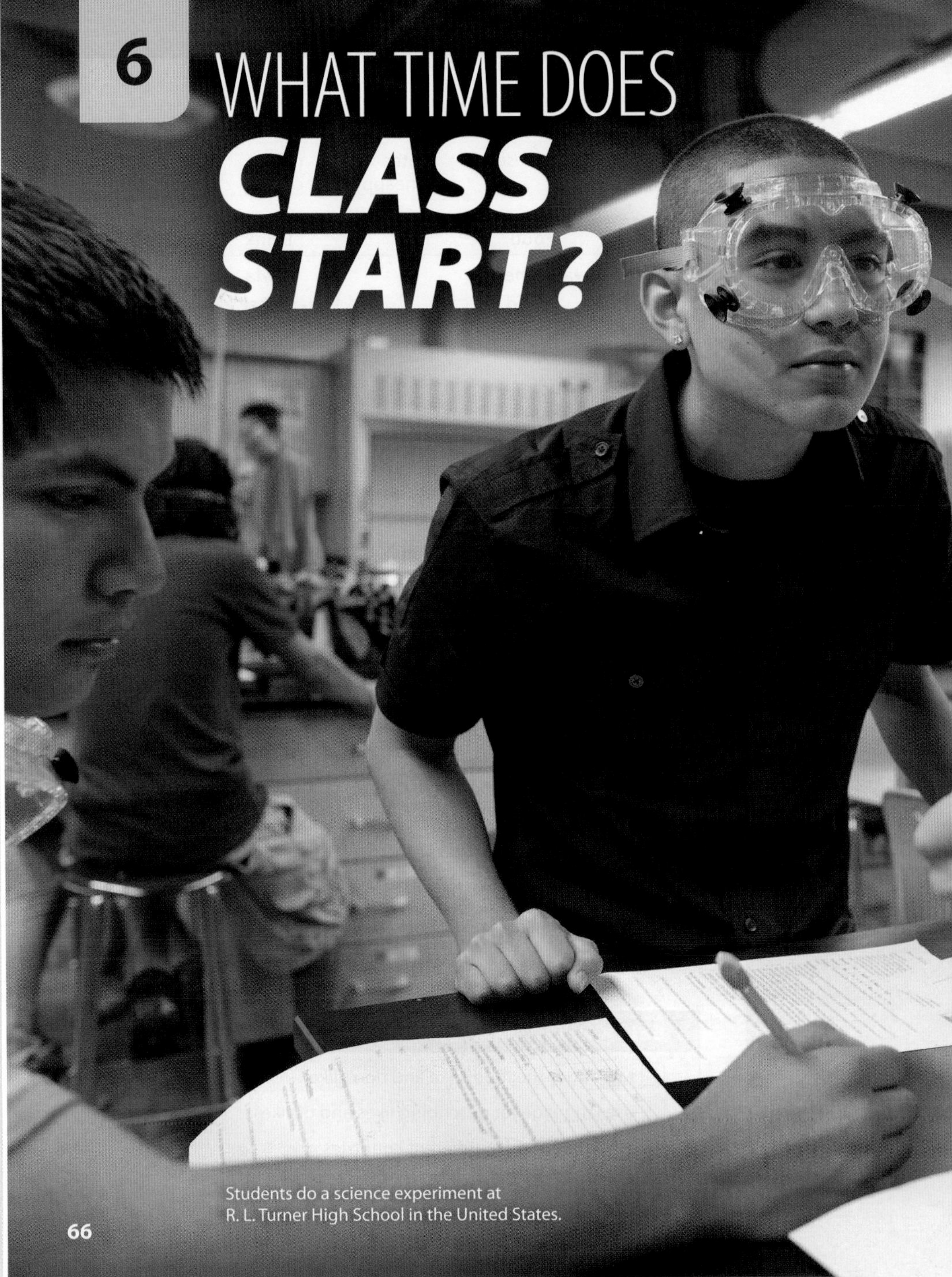
6
WHAT TIME DOES
CLASS
START?
66
Students do a science experiment at R. L. Turner High School in the United States.

In class, tell students to get into pairs and take turns talking about their day. Explain that they should complete a wheel with their friend's information.

Have students draw another blank wheel and do the task with their own information. When they have finished, have them compare how their days are similar and different.

CONTENT NOTE: TELLING THE TIME

Times that fall on the hour can be said in two ways. For example, for 8:00 we can say *eight o'clock*, but many speakers omit the *o'clock*, saying only *eight* (e.g., *It's eight*).

Twelve o'clock in the middle of the day is called *noon*, and 12 o'clock in the middle of the night is called *midnight*. *Midnight* does not refer to a broad range of time within the middle of the night.

ABOUT THE PHOTO

This photo shows high school students performing an experiment at R. L. Turner High School, in Texas, USA. Students at this school have a schedule with classes starting at 8:20 a.m. and school ending for the day at 3:35 p.m. Lunch break for students at this school is 25 minutes each day. On average, a school day in the USA lasts around 6.8 hours. Average school days in Asian countries like Singapore, Japan, and South Korea range from six to eight hours. Students in many Asian countries also attend private cram schools outside of regular school time, resulting in much longer school days for these students compared to students in western countries.

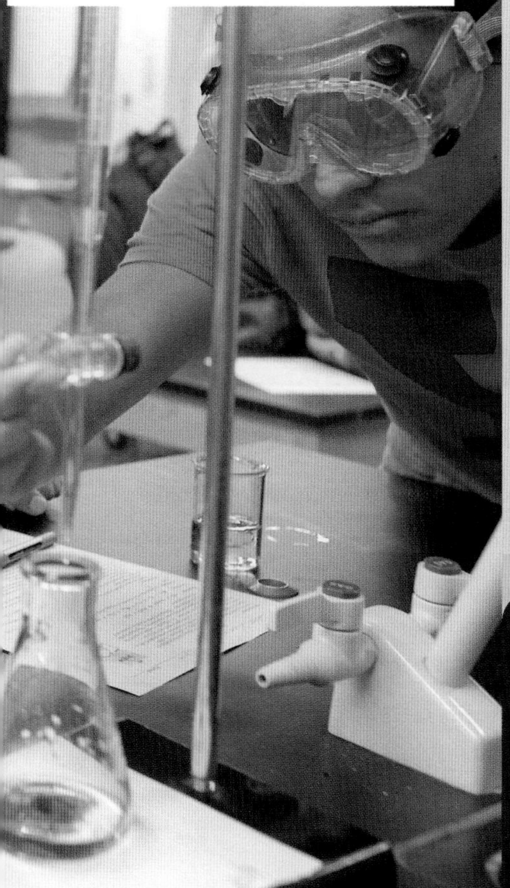

PREVIEW

A **Match.** Write the phrases under the pictures.

go to school | go to bed | go home
have dinner | get up | do homework

1 *get up* 2 *go to school*

3 *go home* 4 *do homework*

5 *have dinner* 6 *go to bed*

B 6.1 **Listen.** Write **S** (same) or **D** (different) for the time the speakers do each activity.

1 *S* 3 *D*
2 *D* 4 *S*

C **Talk with a partner.** Ask them when they do each activity in **A**. *Answers will vary.*

What time do you get up?

I get up at 6 o'clock.

PEOPLE AND PLACES

UNIT GOALS

- describe your daily routines
- use language for talking about how often you do things
- learn about schools around the world

67

PREVIEW

Have students read the unit title to themselves as you read it aloud. Explain that in this unit they will learn to talk about things they do every day.

A Explain to students that they should write the activities under the appropriate pictures. As they follow along, read the expressions in the box aloud.

Have students do the task. Check answers.

B Explain to students that they will listen to four short conversations about daily schedules, and they should write **S** if the speakers do the same activity at the same time and **D** if they do it at different times.

6.1 Play Audio Track 6.1. Play it again, if necessary.

Check answers.

C Explain to students that they will make pairs and take turns asking and answering questions about what time they do the activities in **A**.

Model the conversation with a student.

Have students do the task.

CHALLENGE If some students finish quickly, have them brainstorm other daily activities and ask and answer questions about them. (See **Other useful vocabulary**.)

Although schedules (such as plane and train timetables) use the 24-hour clock (e.g., *18:00* to refer to six o'clock in the evening), the 24-hour clock is not commonly used in conversation. A person looking at a train timetable would say *The train leaves at six o'clock tonight* (not *18 o'clock*).

Ante meridiem (a.m.) is also written as *am* (without the periods), *AM*, or *A.M.* In the United States, *a.m.* generally refers to the 12 hours between midnight and noon. Like *a.m.*, *post meridiem* (p.m.) is sometimes written as *pm* (without the periods), *PM*, or *P.M.* In the United States, *p.m.* generally refers to the 12 hours between noon and midnight.

The words *a.m.* and *p.m.* are more commonly used in written English than in spoken English. This is because, in speech, the context usually makes it clear whether a speaker means *a.m.* or *p.m.* When necessary, the speaker can use *in the morning* for *a.m.* and *in the afternoon/ evening* instead of *p.m.*

UNIT GOALS

Direct students' attention to the **UNIT GOALS** box. Explain that these are some of the things students will learn in this unit. Point out that this unit is about people and places. As students follow along, read each of the unit goals to the class. Explain any words students do not know. Remind students that at the end of the unit there is a self check that allows them to see if they have accomplished each goal.

LANGUAGE FOCUS

A 6.2 **Listen and read.** What time does Stig get up? Then repeat the conversation and replace the words in **bold**. *He gets up at 6:30.*

REAL ENGLISH Oh, no!

Stig: Hey, Ming. Are you at school?

Ming: Hi, Stig. Yeah, I usually have **soccer** practice at 6 o'clock before school. (**baseball** / **tennis**)

Stig: That's early! What time do you get up every day?

Ming: Well, I get up at **5:15** every day. What time do you get up, Stig? (**5 o'clock** / **5:30**)

Stig: I **get up** at 6:30. I go to school at 7:30. (**have breakfast** / **wake up**)

Ming: Stig … what time is it now?

Stig: Oh, no! It's 8 o'clock. I'm late!

Ming: **See you later**, Stig! (**Hurry up** / **Get moving**)

B 6.3 **Look at the chart.** Then circle the correct answers below.

TALKING ABOUT ROUTINES (USING ADVERBS OF FREQUENCY)		
What time do you **get up**? **When do** you **have breakfast**?	I **always get up** at 7 o'clock. I **usually have breakfast** at 7:30. I **often have breakfast** at 6:45.	100% always usually often
When does he **do homework**?	**Sometimes** he **does homework** in the afternoon, and **sometimes** he **does** it at night. He **never does** it in the morning.	sometimes
What time does school **start**?	It **starts** at 8 o'clock.	
When do they **go** to school?	They **go** to school at 7 o'clock.	0% never

1 The meaning of *when* and *what time* is **different** / **the same**.

2 We use a base verb with the words ***I*, *you*, *we*, and *they*** / ***he*, *she*, and *it*.**

3 We use *always*, *usually*, *sometimes*, *often*, and *never* **before** / **after** a verb.

LANGUAGE FOCUS

Tell students they will listen to a conversation between Ming and Stig about their daily schedules.

A 6.2 Play Audio Track 6.2 as students listen and follow along in their books.

Ask, *What time does Stig get up?* Have students answer.

Have students work in pairs and practice the conversation once. Point out the bold words and read them aloud as students follow along in their books.

Tell students they will practice the conversation two more times, changing the bold words each time and swapping roles after the first time. Have them practice with both substitution choices.

OPTIONAL Ask students how Ming and Stig are talking (via video chat). Have students discuss how often they use video chat, who they chat with, and why they like it. Encourage them to talk about any disadvantages of video chat.

REAL ENGLISH

Direct students' attention to the expression in the **REAL ENGLISH** box. Explain that we use *Oh, no!* in spoken English when we are negatively surprised or suddenly realize something that is not positive. For example:

A: Oh, no!
B: What's the matter?
A: I forgot my homework at home.

B Ask students to look at the chart.

6.3 Have students follow along in their books as they listen to Audio Track 6.3.

Read the questions in the chart aloud. Explain that questions with *What time* and *When* both ask about time. Point out that in the questions, the verb after the subject (*you*, *he*, *school*, *they*) never has an *s*.

Point out that in the questions, *do* and *does* follow the same pattern of use that they previously learned.

Draw students' attention to the right side of the chart with the graphic representation of the adverbs of frequency. Read the words aloud as students follow along in their books. Explain that these words describe how often someone does something. Point out that *always* means 100 percent of the time. To help students understand how to use the expressions, explain that *usually* is roughly 85 to 90 percent of the time; *often* is about 65 to 70 percent of the time; *sometimes* is about 50 percent of the time; and *never* means 0 percent. Explain that these percentages are just general guidelines.

Have students look at the answers to the questions (middle of the chart). Read the sentences aloud as students follow along in their books.

C 6.4 **Write sentences and questions.** Use the words given. Then listen and check your answers.

1 Liam / do homework / 8 o'clock
Liam does homework at 8 o'clock.

2 Hyun and Min / have breakfast / 9:30
Hyun and Min have breakfast at 9:30.

3 when / Eva / get up?
When does Eva get up?

4 what time / the students / go home?
What time do the students go home?

IDIOM

If you work "around the clock," you ____.
a work late at night
(b) work long hours

D Read the descriptions. Then circle the correct answers.

1 I get up at 6 o'clock every day. → I **(always)** / **never** get up at 6 o'clock.
2 I have breakfast at home three times a week. → I **usually** / **(sometimes)** have breakfast at home.
3 I always do my homework at home. → I **(never)** / **often** do my homework at school.
4 I go to bed at 9 o'clock on weekdays. I go to bed at 10 o'clock on weekends. → I **always** / **(usually)** go to bed at 9 o'clock.
5 I have dinner with my family Wednesdays to Sundays. → I **(often)** / **sometimes** have dinner with my family.

E Work with a partner. Choose one activity and one time and make a sentence. Say how often you do the activity. Take turns. Answers will vary.

Activity	Adverb	Time
get up	never	1:30
have breakfast	sometimes	3:00
go to school	often	6:00
go home	usually	7:30
do homework	always	8:00
go to bed		9:00

I usually get up at 6 o'clock.

A student in Beijing eats his breakfast before school.

CHALLENGE Explain that the adverbs of frequency come after *be* verbs. On the board, write *I am late*. Have students make three sentences (e.g., *I am always/usually/never late*).

You might want to also have students give more adverbs of frequency. (See **Other useful vocabulary**.) Have them use these adverbs in sentences about routines.

C Tell students to use the words to make sentences and questions.

Explain to students that they will listen to the sentences and should check their answers.

6.4 Play Audio Track 6.4. Check answers as a class.

IDIOM

Read the statement and answer choices aloud, as students follow along in their books. Have students guess the answer before providing it (b).

If you brought in an analog clock, use it to indicate hour after hour passing. Explain that *around the clock* is used to emphasize how many hours are being worked. (The literal meaning is 24 hours a day.)

D Explain to students that they will read the first sentence and then circle the word in the second sentence so that both sentences have the same meaning.

Have students do the task. Check answers.

E Tell students they are going to get into pairs and make sentences using the words in the chart.

Explain that each student should choose an activity, an adverb, and a time, and they should use these words to make a sentence.

Model the example with a student.

Have students take turns saying their sentences.

On the board, write, *I get up at 6:45*.

Explain that most of the adverbs of frequency (*always*, *usually*, *often*, *never*) come before verbs. Have students make three sentences with the adverbs and the sentence on the board (*I always/usually/never get up at 6:45*).

Help students to make a rule for *sometimes*. (It can be used at the beginning of the sentence for all verbs.) Using the sentence that is still on the board, have students make two sentences with *sometimes* (e.g., *Sometimes I get up at 6:45; Sometimes I am late*).

Draw students' attention to the three statements under the chart. Have students do the task. Check answers.

THE REAL WORLD

A Ask students to look at the photo. As they follow along, read the title and photo caption aloud. Then read the question and answer choices aloud and have students circle their answers.

CONTENT NOTE: BARRINGTON IRVING

Barrington Irving was the youngest person to fly around the world without anyone else in the airplane. It took him 97 days, during which he went through thunderstorms, monsoons, snowstorms, and sandstorms.

Irving wants to tell young people that determination, hard work, and passion are the crucial elements for success. His nonprofit organization's goal is to help more young people become interested in careers in the aviation, science, and math fields.

B Explain to students that they will watch a video and they should circle **T** if the statement is true and **F** if it is false. If necessary, read the statements aloud as students follow along in their books.

▶ 6.1 Play Video 6.1. If necessary, encourage students to listen for the answers as they watch the video again in **C**.

C Tell students they are going to watch the video again and they should check the things the students in the video do.

▶ 6.1 Play Video 6.1. If necessary, play the video again.

Check answers as a class. Also check answers in **B** and then **A**.

D CRITICAL THINKING

As students follow along, read the questions aloud. Have students get into pairs and discuss them.

THE REAL WORLD

THE FLYING CLASSROOM

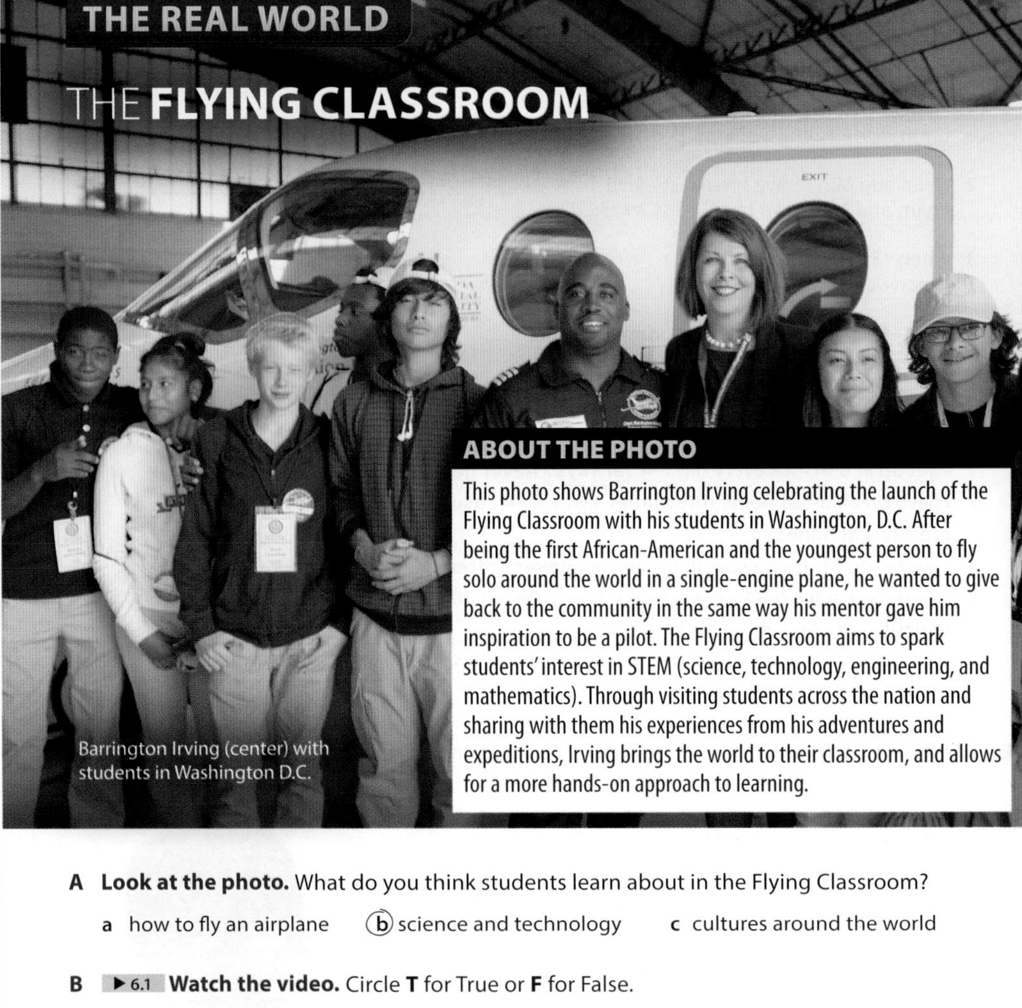

Barrington Irving (center) with students in Washington D.C.

ABOUT THE PHOTO

This photo shows Barrington Irving celebrating the launch of the Flying Classroom with his students in Washington, D.C. After being the first African-American and the youngest person to fly solo around the world in a single-engine plane, he wanted to give back to the community in the same way his mentor gave him inspiration to be a pilot. The Flying Classroom aims to spark students' interest in STEM (science, technology, engineering, and mathematics). Through visiting students across the nation and sharing with them his experiences from his adventures and expeditions, Irving brings the world to their classroom, and allows for a more hands-on approach to learning.

A **Look at the photo.** What do you think students learn about in the Flying Classroom?

a how to fly an airplane (b) science and technology c cultures around the world

B ▶ 6.1 **Watch the video.** Circle **T** for True or **F** for False.

1	Barrington Irving is a photographer.	T	(F)
2	The Flying Classroom has students from around the world.	(T)	F
3	Barrington wants students to be interested in science.	(T)	F
4	The students like the Flying Classroom.	(T)	F

C ▶ 6.1 **Watch again.** Check (✓) the things the students do in the video.

- [✓] use computers
- [✓] make robots
- [✓] do experiments
- [ ] visit an airport
- [✓] use VR glasses
- [ ] give a presentation

70 Unit 6

PROJECT As students follow along, read the project instructions aloud. Have students get into pairs and talk about their ideas. Encourage students to think of at least five things they want to do in the class.

CHALLENGE Tell students that the act of evaluating includes many different types of critical thinking, and they will practice four of them in this activity. First, they will get into pairs and then they will *decide* which things they want to do in the Flying Classroom.

Second, explain to students that two pairs will get together and they will *compare* their ideas. Have students do the task.

Third, tell students their groups of four will *assess* all of the ideas to decide which ones are the best, and then, using these ideas, they will create a new plan. Give students time to do the task.

Fourth, explain that the group (originally two pairs) will get together with another group and they must share their plans before trying to *convince* the other group that their plan is

D CRITICAL THINKING Evaluating **Talk with a partner.** Is the Flying Classroom a good way to learn? What do you like about it? *Answers will vary.*

PROJECT Work with a partner. Imagine the Flying Classroom is coming to your school. Write a list of things you want to do in the class.

PRONUNCIATION long and short *u* sounds

A 6.5 **Listen and repeat.**

1 lunch (short *u*) 2 usually (long *u*)

B 6.6 **Listen.** Are the *u* sounds in these words long (**L**) or short (**S**)? Then read the words to a partner.

1 hungry S 2 computer L 3 understand S 4 up S

5 subject S 6 student L 7 music L

COMMUNICATION

Do a survey. Write the times you do these activities. Then find two other students who do the activities at the same time as you. *Answers will vary.*

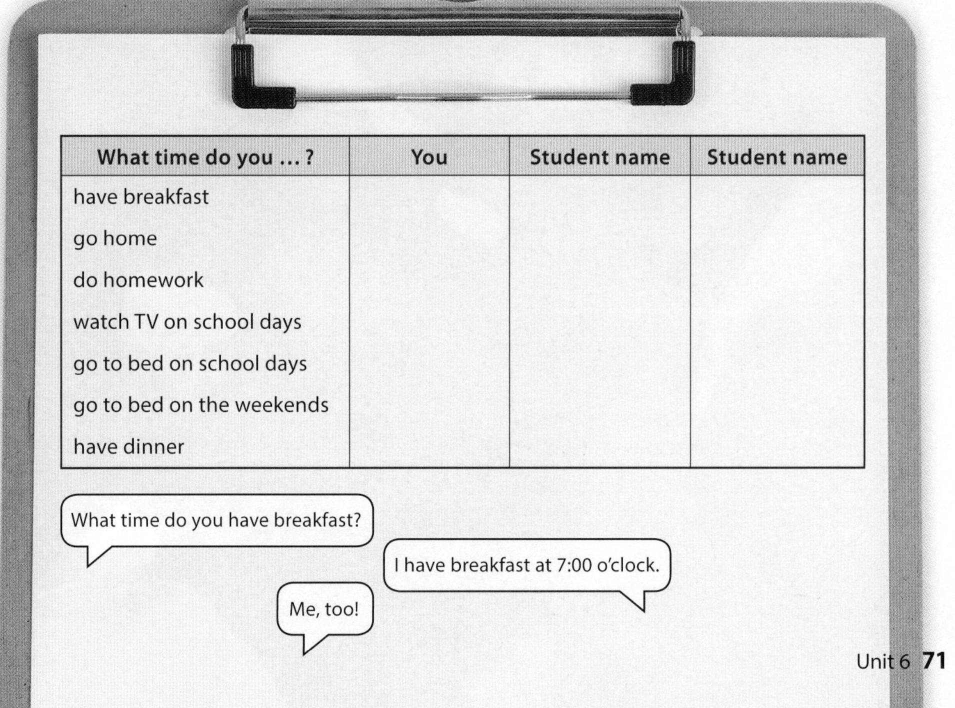

What time do you ... ?	You	Student name	Student name
have breakfast			
go home			
do homework			
watch TV on school days			
go to bed on school days			
go to bed on the weekends			
have dinner			

What time do you have breakfast?
I have breakfast at 7:00 o'clock.
Me, too!

better. Encourage students to discuss reasons for their opinions. Have students share their ideas in groups and then decide which of the two plans is better.

Have one or two groups share their ideas with the class.

PRONUNCIATION

Tell students they will practice saying long and short *u* sounds.

A Explain to students that in English the vowel *u* has many different pronunciations, so they need to remember the pronunciation of new words based on how the word is said rather than just the spelling.

Tell students that the long *u* sound is said *u* (like the name of the letter), while the short *u* sound is different (like the *u* in *cup*).

6.5 Play Audio Track 6.5. Play it again, pausing after each word so students can repeat.

B Explain that students must decide whether the pronunciation of each word has a long *u* or a short *u*, and write **L** or **S**, respectively.

6.6 Play Audio Track 6.6. Play it again, if necessary. Check answers.

Have students get into pairs and take turns saying the words with their partner.

OPTIONAL After students have practiced, have students use the words in sentences so they can practice saying the words in context.

COMMUNICATION

Tell students they are going to do a survey.

Ask students to follow along as you read the questions in the chart aloud.

Tell students to write their answers in the *You* column.

Explain that they will interview other students and should try to find two students who do each of the activities at the same time as them.

Point to the headings, *Student name*. Tell them they should write the students' names in these columns. Emphasize that each column should have different names, and each line may have different names.

Model the conversation with a student.

Have students stand up, move around the room, and interview each other.

READING

As students follow along in their books, read the title aloud. Explain that *Kakenya* is the name of a woman.

A Ask students to look at the photo and think about what the article is about. As they follow along, read the answer choices aloud. Have students circle their answer.

B Tell students they will skim the text and find out what Kakenya's dream is. As students follow along, read the answer choices aloud. Have students do the task.

Check answers. Ask students if their answer in **A** was correct.

After completing the task, give students the opportunity to read the article in more detail so they can comprehend it more fully.

OPTIONAL The text can also be used as a listening activity. After finishing **B**, have students close their books. Tell students they will listen to the passage.

6.7 Play Audio Track 6.7. Ask students to get into pairs and discuss what information they heard. Then have them read the article more carefully.

C Have students look at the symbols for each school subject. Read each subject name aloud as students follow along in their books. Tell students to scan the article and circle the subjects that Kakenya's students study.

Check answers as a class.

SUPPORT For each symbol, ask students if they study that subject. Use simple questions to reinforce the school subjects. For example: *Do you like math? Who is your history teacher?*

READING

A **Look at the photo.** What do you think the article is about?
a city life **b** a big family (**c**) a school in Africa

B **Skim the article.** What is Kakenya's dream?
a to write books
(**b**) to help educate Maasai girls
c to help girls get married

C **Scan the article.** Circle the subjects Kakenya's students study.

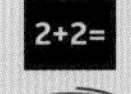

(math)

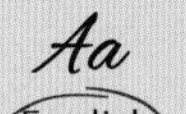

(English)

(science)

(PE)

(art)

music

(geography)

TEACHING NOTE: SCANNING

To provide additional practice with scanning, explain it in more detail by using the following steps to help students understand it.

1 Take out a dictionary. Tell students you want to find a word. (You could choose a word from the reading.)

2 Open to page 1 and, with great exaggeration, begin reading each word aloud. Explain to students what a waste of time this is.

3 Ask students how you can find the word more quickly. (Look at the headwords. Find the correct two pages. Then use alphabetical order to find the correct section. Finally, find the exact word.)

4 Explain that this is scanning and they already know how to scan and regularly use it.

5 Have students use scanning to find words in their dictionaries.

KAKENYA'S DREAM

A 6.7 School life is not easy for some Maasai people in Kenya. In some schools, there are 70 students in one classroom. Schools don't always have books. Sometimes there aren't **enough** teachers, or there isn't enough money.

B This is especially true for Maasai girls. Not many Maasai girls in Kenya **finish** elementary school. Many Maasai girls have to leave school **early** to **get married**. Kakenya Ntaiya has a **dream**. She has a school for girls because she wants to help Maasai schoolgirls in her village.

C Today, 200 girls go to Kakenya's school, and they love it. They study English and Swahili (an African language). They also study math, science, geography, **history**, art, and PE. Kakenya wants her students to have better lives.

Kakenya and her students

ABOUT THE PHOTO

This photo shows Kakenya and her students celebrating together at Kakenya's school. In Kenya, only 48 percent of Maasai girls are enrolled in primary school despite government efforts to make primary school education free. Maasai girls are usually kept busy at home with chores, or are married off at a young age in exchange for a dowry. It is not uncommon in Maasai culture to measure a girl's worth using a herd of goats or cattle. This often leads to parents finding the dowry more important than education.

Unit 6 73

Additional Activities to Use with the Reading

Increasing Cultural Awareness

Have students say what continent Kenya is on (Africa) and then find the country on a world map. Ask students to use the map or their digital devices to identify Kenya's capital (Nairobi).

Pronunciation Practice

6.7 Have students read along as you play Audio Track 6.7.

Play it again, pausing as necessary, so students can repeat. Have them practice reading the article several times.

Play the audio a final time, and have students read along aloud as they listen.

Critical Thinking

Have students compare their educational environment with the one discussed in the article. Have students compare:

- the number of students in the school and in one classroom.
- the availability of textbooks.
- the possible shortage of teachers.
- the reasons for going to school.
- the proportion of female students who don't finish elementary school.

Linguistic Awareness

Tell students that a *lingua franca* is a language that people with different first languages (mother tongues) use to communicate with each other. Ask students what their first language is. Then ask them what languages they use as lingua francas (e.g., English).

Tell students about Swahili. (See **CONTENT NOTE.**) Ask students to get into pairs and discuss why the area might need a lingua franca. (There are many tribes, each with its own dialect or language. Swahili helps people communicate.)

CONTENT NOTE: SWAHILI

Arabic has greatly influenced the Swahili language. Swahili has 15 main dialects. Swahili is used by people living on the east coast of Africa, from Kenya in the north to the southern border of Tanzania. Swahili is often used as the lingua franca in Tanzania, Kenya, Congo, and Uganda.

It is estimated that between 5 and 15 million people speak Swahili as their first language. When people who use Swahili as a second or other language are included, however, the number of people who speak Swahili swells to 60 to 150 million people.

COMPREHENSION

A Have students read the questions to themselves and circle the correct answers.

After they have finished, check answers as a class.

B EXAM PRACTICE

The task of matching a paragraph to an appropriate heading is used in standardized tests such as the reading section of the IELTS exam. This item tests students' ability to comprehend the main idea of each paragraph. To do this, students must not only read the first and last sentences of each paragraph but also scan the body of each paragraph to understand enough details that they don't choose one of the distractors.

On the IELTS exam, there are more headings than paragraphs so that students cannot use the process of elimination to find an answer. Before reading the passage, students should quickly read the headings.

If you brought in a book or article that has headings, show it to the students, explaining that headings are short titles that help the reader understand and preview the main idea of a page or section of a longer passage.

Explain to students that they should match the paragraph with the correct heading.

Have them do the task. Check answers as a class.

C CRITICAL THINKING

As students follow along, read the first question aloud. Have them get into pairs and answer it. Encourage them to give reasons for their answers.

Point to the diagram. Explain to students that this type of diagram allows us to look at how two things are similar and different. Ask students what two things are being compared (how the student's school and Kakenya's school are similar and different).

Read the second question aloud, as students follow along in their books. Have students work in pairs and complete the chart.

Discuss ideas as a class.

COMPREHENSION

A Answer the questions about *Kakenya's Dream*.

1. MAIN IDEA What's another title for this article?
   a Life after School b Living in Kenya (c) A School for Girls
2. DETAIL How many students are there in some village school classrooms?
   (a) 70 b 90 c 100
3. VOCABULARY "Especially true" in the first sentence of paragraph B means ____.
   a not true b only true (c) even more true
4. DETAIL Why do some Maasai girls not finish school?
   a They leave Kenya. (b) They get married. c They move to another house.
5. INFERENCE Which of the following about Kakenya can you infer from the article?
   (a) She's from Kenya. b Her school is free for girls. c Her students have good grades.

B Match. Choose the correct heading for each paragraph in the article.

1 Paragraph A — Student life at Kakenya's school
2 Paragraph B — Going to school in Kenya
3 Paragraph C — Kakenya's dream

(Headings as printed: Kakenya's dream / Student life at Kakenya's school / Going to school in Kenya)

C CRITICAL THINKING Comparing **Talk with a partner.** What do you think of Kakenya's school? Is your school similar to or different from Kakenya's? Answers will vary.

Similarities	Differences

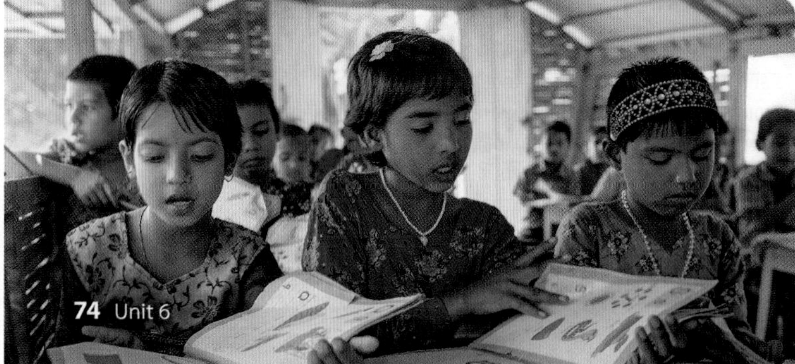

74 Unit 6

DO YOU KNOW?

This classroom in Bangladesh is ____.

a on a bus
(b) on a boat

CONTENT NOTE: KAKENYA'S SCHOOL

Kakenya Ntaiya grew up in a rural part of Kenya where, even now, only 17 percent of the female students study beyond elementary school. Her organization, Kakenya's Dream, has an all-girls school that opened in 2009 and continued to expand through 2017. In addition to dormitories where the students live, the school campus has facilities such as a library and art and science facilities.

VOCABULARY

A Find the words below in the article. Then complete the sentences.

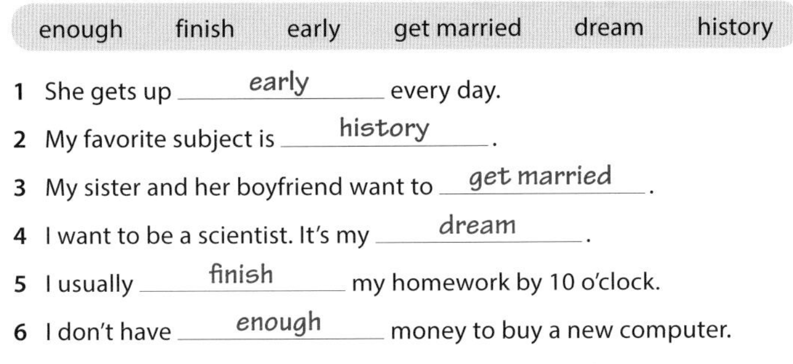

enough | finish | early | get married | dream | history

1 She gets up ___early___ every day.
2 My favorite subject is ___history___.
3 My sister and her boyfriend want to ___get married___.
4 I want to be a scientist. It's my ___dream___.
5 I usually ___finish___ my homework by 10 o'clock.
6 I don't have ___enough___ money to buy a new computer.

B Read the information below. Complete the timeline using the words in the box.

There are different types of schools for students of different ages. Here are some examples: *high school, elementary school, college, kindergarten, middle school.*

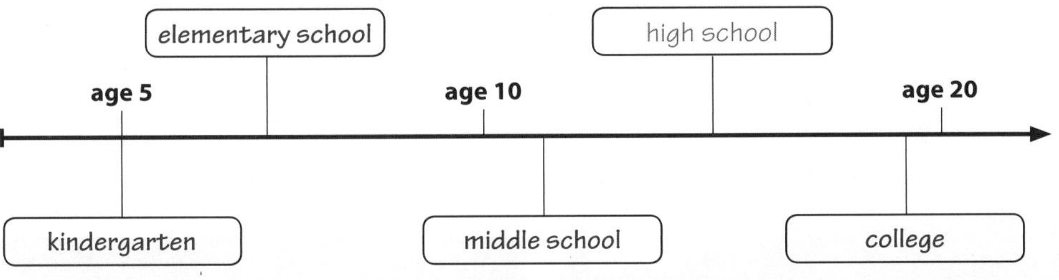

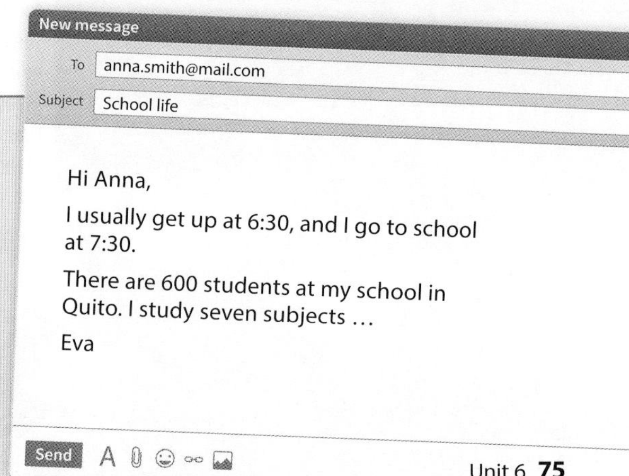

New message
To anna.smith@mail.com
Subject School life
Hi Anna,
I usually get up at 6:30, and I go to school at 7:30.
There are 600 students at my school in Quito. I study seven subjects …
Eva
Send
Unit 6 75

WRITING

A Read the email.

B Plan your reply. Make notes about your school life. What time do you go to school? What do you study at school?

C Write a short email. Describe your school. Start with "Hi Eva, …".
Answers will vary.

After students graduate, the girls continue to receive assistance in the form of mentoring, tutoring, career advice, and help so that they can apply to and attend universities around the world.

DO YOU KNOW?

Read the statement and answer choices aloud, as students follow along in their books. Have them guess the answer before providing it (b).

VOCABULARY

A As students follow along, read the words in the box aloud. Have students find them in the **READING** passage.

Have students use the words in the box to complete the sentences. Check answers as a class.

TEACHING NOTE: VOCABULARY

Learners have different ways of effectively remembering new lexicon. In class, teachers should consider combining direct teaching of vocabulary with strategies students can learn to memorize words. Students can also learn vocabulary indirectly through the teacher's use, thus emphasizing the importance of using English in the classroom whenever pragmatic.

B As students follow along, read the information in the box aloud.

Have students write the school types in the timeline.

Check answers as a class.

WRITING

Tell students they are going to write an email about their school.

A As students follow along in their books, read the example email aloud.

B Tell students they should imagine they are going to reply to Eva. As they follow along, read the questions aloud. Have them make notes about their school life, including answers to the questions.

C Have students write a short email describing their school. Point out that they should start with *Hi Eva*.

Give students a time limit for finishing the email and set a minimum number of sentences they must write (e.g., five).

SUPPORT Teach students some of the important elements in an email (e.g., the greeting, paragraphs starting on new lines, closings, ending with the author's name).

VIDEO

Tell students they are going to watch a video about Kakenya's school. Remind students that they have already learned some things about the school in the **READING**.

CHALLENGE Tell students that a uniform is clothing that all of the people in one group, such as at a school, wear. Have students look at the photo. Ask, *Do students at Kakenya's school wear uniforms?* Ask them if students at their school wear uniforms.

Have students get into small groups to brainstorm some of the positive reasons for schools requiring uniforms (e.g., social status and economic disparity become less obvious).

Have groups share their ideas with the class.

BEFORE YOU WATCH

As students follow along in their books, read the title, the sentence about the video, and the question aloud.

Have students circle their answers to complete the statements.

WHILE YOU WATCH

A Tell students they will watch the video and they should check the topics that are in the video. As students follow along in their books, read the topics aloud.

▶ 6.2 Play Video 6.2. Encourage students to confirm their answers as they watch again in **B**.

OPTIONAL Help students understand the power of images by playing the video once without any sound. Have them get into pairs and discuss what they saw and deduce what topics were included in the video. Play the video a second time with sound so students can check their ideas.

VIDEO **ABOUT THE VIDEO** Kakenya Ntaiya helps girls get an education.

KAKENYA'S SCHOOL

Before You Watch

Circle the correct answers. What do you remember about Kakenya's school?

1 This school is in **Kenya** / **Uganda**. (circled: Kenya)

2 The school is for girls living in **cities** / **villages**. (circled: villages)

While You Watch

A ▶ 6.2 **Watch the video.** Check (✓) the topics the video talks about.

- [x] the history of Kakenya's school
- [ ] Kakenya's family
- [x] life at Kakenya's school
- [x] Kakenya's future plans
- [ ] students' after school activities

B ▶ 6.2 **Watch again.** Circle **T** for true or **F** for false.

1	Kakenya's school starts at first grade.	T	(F)
2	The students walk to school every day.	T	(F)
3	There are meals for students at the school.	(T)	F
4	The teachers live at Kakenya's school.	(T)	F
5	Kakenya wants to have more students in her school.	(T)	F

After You Watch

Talk with a partner. Kakenya says, "Help a girl, help a family." What do you think this means?
Answers will vary.

ABOUT THE PHOTO

This photo shows students at Kakenya's school playing together outdoors. This is a rare and precious moment for these girls. Maasai girls typically don't continue their education past primary school. Their main role in the Maasai culture is to be a caretaker of the home. This means that education for girls is often seen as unnecessary by the Maasai elders. Kakenya hopes to empower these girls by providing them with equal opportunity for an education.

76 Unit 6

B Explain to students that they will watch the video again. Tell them that for each statement, they should circle **T** if the statement is true and **F** if it is false. As students follow along in their books, read the statements aloud.

▶ 6.2 Play Video 6.2. Play it again, if necessary.

Check answers as a class. Also check answers in **A** and **BEFORE YOU WATCH**.

SUPPORT On the board, write, *It is a boarding school. All girls live there. They eat meals at the school.* Explain that we can often use the words around an unfamiliar word to understand it. Tell them this is called *using context*. Ask, *What is a boarding school?* Have students use context to explain what a boarding school is (a school where the students eat and live instead of going home each night).

A Complete the daily routine phrases.

1 I get ___up___ at 6 o'clock every day.

2 I always ___have/eat___ breakfast at 6:15.

3 I usually ___go to___ school at 7 o'clock.

4 I go ___home___ at 4 o'clock every day.

5 I do my ___homework___ after school.

6 I go to ___bed___ at 10:30.

B Complete the questions. Circle the correct answers.

1 **A: Where / What time** do you get up?
B: At 7 o'clock.

2 **A: When / Why** do you go to school?
B: At 8:30.

3 I go to school early every day. I'm **never / always** on time.

4 **A: Who / When** do you go out with your friends?
B: On Saturday.

5 The library is a good place to study. I **usually / never** do my homework there.

C Complete the sentences. Circle the correct answers.

1 Students go to **college / middle school** before high school.

2 Students usually study one main subject at **college / high school**.

3 Students 3 to 6 years old usually go to **kindergarten / elementary school**.

Students at Kakenya's school

SELF CHECK Now I can ...

- [ ] describe my daily routines
- [ ] use language for talking about how often I do things
- [ ] talk about schools around the world

CONTENT NOTE: KAKENYA CENTER FOR EXCELLENCE

In addition to having high academic standards at the school, Kakenya's Dream provides after-school health and leadership training that is open to both boys and girls. Students learn about leadership, gender equality, self-defense, and other life skills.

REVIEW

Explain to students that they are going to review the material from the unit and this will help them remember what they have studied.

A Explain that activity **A** reviews vocabulary from the unit. Have students write the correct words and phrases to complete the sentences. Check answers as a class.

B Explain that activity **B** reviews the grammar from the unit. Have students circle the correct words to complete the sentences. Have students get into pairs and check answers, before you randomly call on students to give the answers.

OPTIONAL Have students get into pairs and practice the conversations. When they have finished, have students personalize the answers.

C Point out that activity **C** reviews words from **VOCABULARY** activity **B**.

Have students circle their answers. Check answers.

AFTER YOU WATCH

Tell students they are going to get into pairs and talk about the video.

As students follow along in their books, read the statement and question aloud.

Have them get into pairs and talk about their ideas.

Have students share their ideas with the class, providing one suggestion (e.g., by enabling a girl to have an education now, in the future her family will probably have a higher standard of living), if necessary.

CHALLENGE Remind students that Kakenya's dream is to change the world. Ask students to get into pairs and talk about what their dreams are. If they cannot think of any dreams, ask them to think about what they are passionate about. Encourage them to continue to find a long-term goal as they continue to study the book.

SELF CHECK

These *I can* statements provide vital feedback on students' perceived ability to use the language from the unit. If you find students are reluctant to check that they can do the skills, consider asking them to rate themselves from 1 (not very confident) to 3 (very confident).

UNIT 7

CAN ELEPHANTS SWIM?

CONTENT AREA: THE NATURAL WORLD

Topic: abilities

Vocabulary: animals: chimp, parrot, crow; **actions:** climb, fly, jump, dance, swim, use tools, do a handstand, skateboard, play the drums/piano/keyboard, drive; **other words:** smart, communicate, understand, point, hot, like

Grammar: talking about abilities using *can*

Extra material: English magazines (particularly sports, fashion, and entertainment magazines), pictures of famous athletes, a world map

Other useful vocabulary: sports: table tennis, volleyball; **instruments:** guitar, trombone, trumpet, violin; **actions:** draw, carve, sculpt, design

TEACHING NOTE: MODAL VERBS

Can and *can't* are modal verbs—verbs that work with other verbs to express ability, possibility, necessity, and permission. *Can* and *can't* do not change, no matter what the subject is (*I*, *you*, *he*, *she*, etc.).

Modal verbs are also called modals, modal auxiliary verbs, and modal auxiliaries. Modal verbs include *could*, *might*, *must*, and *should*.

END OF UNIT PROJECT Tell students they are going to make a class magazine. Give students a few minutes to look through some English magazines.

Explain that they will each write two paragraphs about someone they like who can do something amazing. If necessary, have students brainstorm the types of people they might include (e.g., athletes, musicians, artists).

As a class, talk about the kinds of information they might include in their stories: the person's name, the person's birthday, where the person lives, things the person likes to do, and some information about the person's special ability.

Ask students what they usually find in a magazine article (photos and the story). Emphasize that their magazine article should have one or more photos (cut out from other magazines, printed from the internet, sketched by the students) that make the reader more interested in the topic.

Point out that each article has a title, with the author's name usually next to or under the title. Ask students what else they notice about the title. (The title is usually in a larger font.) Tell them their magazine page should follow this pattern.

PREVIEW
A 7.1 Match the words with the pictures. Listen and check your answers.
climb fly jump dance swim use tools
1 swim 2 climb 3 jump
4 dance 5 use tools 6 fly
B 7.2 Listen. Write the things the animals can do. Use the words in A.
1 Birds can fly.
2 Chimps can use tools.
3 Parrots can dance.
4 Frogs can jump.
5 Elephants can swim.
6 Monkeys can climb.
C Talk with a partner. What can you do?
Answers will vary.
I can swim.
I can dance.
ABOUT THE PHOTO
This photo shows an elephant swimming off the coast of the Andaman Islands, located in the Bay of Bengal. Elephants are said to be expert swimmers by nature, just that their skill isn't demonstrated often because their natural habitats aren't usually near the ocean. It was originally thought that elephants arrived on the islands by swimming from India and Sri Lanka. The elephants were used to transport logs on the islands until logging was banned in 2002. Most of the elephants were sent back to the mainland, while some others, like the one in this photo, remained.
THE NATURAL WORLD
UNIT GOALS
• describe your abilities
• use language for talking about abilities
• learn about intelligent animals
79

An elephant in the Andaman Islands, India

Point out that in magazines the paragraphs aren't always right next to each other. Sometimes, for example, there is a photo between them. Tell them they should be creative and design the paragraphs and photos so it is like a magazine article.

In order to give the class magazine more variety, have students decide who they will write about and make sure students aren't writing about the same person.

Have students create their magazine pages.

After students have finished their pages, ask them what is on the cover of the magazines (photos and the magazine title). Have students work as a class and think of a title for their magazine.

After students write their magazine articles, grade them without making any marks on the actual magazine pages.

Before the next lesson, make a cover for the magazine, with the students' title and one or more appropriate photos. Also compile all of the students' pages to form the magazine.

In the next lesson, show the final result to the students and allow them to see each other's work.

PREVIEW

Have students read the unit title to themselves as you read it aloud. Explain that in this unit they will learn to talk about things they can do.

Read the photo caption aloud, as students follow along in their books.

A As students follow along, read the names of the activities in the box aloud. Tell students they should write the names of the activities under the pictures.

Explain to students that they will listen and they should check their answers.

7.1 Play Audio Track 7.1. Check answers.

B Explain to students that they will hear information about what various animals can do, and they should use the words in **A** to complete the sentences.

7.2 Play Audio Track 7.2. Check answers.

C Tell students they will get into pairs and take turns saying sentences about what they can do. Explain that they should use their own answers.

Model the conversation with a student.

Have students do the task.

UNIT GOALS

Direct students' attention to the **UNIT GOALS** box. Explain that these are some of the things students will learn in this unit. Point out that this unit is about the natural world. As students follow along, read each of the unit goals to the class. Explain any words students do not know. Remind students that at the end of the unit there is a self check that allows them to see if they have accomplished each goal.

LANGUAGE FOCUS

A 7.3 **Listen and read.** Is Nadine a good singer? Then repeat the conversation and replace the words in **bold**. Yes, she is.

REAL ENGLISH Don't be shy.

Ming:	The school concert is **next month**. What should we do? (**in two months** / **in three weeks**)
Stig:	Let's start a band! I can play the **drums**. (**piano** / **keyboard**)
Ming:	I can play the guitar, but I can't sing.
Stig:	Nadine, can you sing?
Nadine:	No, **I can't**. (**I'm bad at it** / **I'm a terrible singer**)
Ming:	Don't be shy. **I'm sure** you can sing. Look, here's a microphone. (**I know** / **I think**)
Nadine:	Um, OK …
Stig:	Wow! Nadine, you *can* sing. You're awesome!

B 7.4 **Look at the chart.** Then circle the correct answers below.

TALKING ABOUT ABILITIES (USING *CAN*)		
I **can** speak two languages. She **can** play the piano.		can't = cannot
Can you swim?	Yes, I **can**. / No, I **can't**.	
What **can** monkeys do?	They **can** climb trees, but they **can't** fly.	
Can he play baseball?	No, he **can't**, but he **can** play tennis.	

1 We use **can** / **can't** in negative sentences. (circled: **can't**)

2 We use a base verb **before** / **after** *can* and *can't*. (circled: **after**)

3 We make a *can* question using **Can you … ?** / **Do you … ?** (circled: **Can you … ?**)

LANGUAGE FOCUS

A Tell students they will listen to a conversation between Ming, Stig, and Nadine.

7.3 Play Audio Track 7.3 as students listen and follow along in their books. If necessary, play the conversation again, pausing after each speaker so students can repeat.

As students follow along in their books, read the question, *Is Nadine a good singer?* Have students answer.

Have students work in pairs and practice the conversation once. Point out the bold words and read them aloud as students follow along in their books. Have students practice the conversation two more times, changing the bold words each time and swapping roles after the first time.

OPTIONAL Have students practice the conversation again, substituting words to personalize it. Ask pairs to volunteer to present their own conversations in the front of the class.

REAL ENGLISH

Direct students' attention to the expression in the **REAL ENGLISH** box. Explain that *Don't be shy* is used in English to encourage someone to do something when they are hesitant or lack confidence.

B Ask students to look at the chart.

7.4 Have students follow along as they listen to Audio Track 7.4.

Tell students that we use *can* with another verb to show ability. Have students identify the verbs in the statements (*speak*, *play*), the questions (*swim*, *do*, *play*), and the responses (*climb*, *fly*, *play*).

Draw students' attention to the second question in the chart. Explain that *What can monkeys do?* is a broad question and, when answering, any ability is acceptable. Remind them that it is not a *yes/no* question.

Contrast this with the next question, *Can he play baseball?*, which is specific to one ability and requires a clear *yes* or *no* answer.

Ask a student, *What can you do?* Randomly call on individual students to answer using full sentences. Then ask, *Can you play tennis?* Continue asking and answering with other activities.

Have students look at the right side of the chart. Remind students about the contractions they encountered in previous units. On the board, write, *can't* = *cannot*. Point this out in the chart.

SUPPORT Direct students' attention to the second response. Ask students why *but* is used, providing the answer if necessary. (Two different ideas—can and cannot—are presented.)

Put pictures of famous athletes on the board. Point to one picture and say, *He can run, and he*

C Complete the sentences and questions. Circle the correct answers.

1 She can **play** / **plays** the piano and guitar. (play)
2 Can you draw well? No, I **don't** / **can't**. (can't)
3 **Have** / **Can** birds swim? Yes, some of them can swim. (Can)
4 Can he dance? Yes, he **can** / **can't**. (can)

D 7.5 **Complete the conversation.** Write *can* or *can't*. Listen and check your answers.

Yuko: Hey Taka, look at this! It's a painting by Phong the elephant. Phong is from Thailand.

Taka: Wow! 1 Can elephants paint?

Yuko: Not usually, but Phong 2 can. Phong 3 can play music, too.

Taka: Amazing! What other things 4 can Phong do? Can he dance?

Yuko: No, he 5 can't dance, and he 6 can't skateboard either. He's an elephant!

E Check (✓) the things you can do. Write one more in the chart. Then ask a partner.

Can you ... ?	You	Your partner
dance		
do a handstand		
skateboard		
play the drums		
drive		

Answers will vary.

Can you dance?

Yes, I can. What about you?

can swim. Point to another picture and say, *She can play tennis, but she can't play golf*. Have students make sentences with other pictures.

Draw students' attention to the three statements under the chart. Have students circle the correct words to complete the sentences. Check answers.

C Tell students they should circle the correct words to complete the sentences and questions. Have students do the task.

Check answers.

D Tell students they should write *can* or *can't* in each of the blanks to complete the conversation. Explain to them that they should use context to know which word to use.

Tell students they will listen to the conversation and should check their answers.

7.5 Play Audio Track 7.5. Check answers.

CONTENT NOTE: PHONG THE ELEPHANT

In addition to painting, Phong is a member of the Thai Elephant Orchestra, a group of musical elephants living in northern Thailand. The orchestra was created by elephant conservationist Richard Lair, who worked with the American musician Dave Soldier to make huge instruments for the elephants to play.

E As students follow along in their books, read the questions in the chart aloud. Have them add one more ability to the chart.

CHALLENGE Have students brainstorm other abilities. (See **Other useful vocabulary**.)

Tell students they should check the things they can do in the *You* column.

Tell students they will make pairs and take turns asking and answering the questions, checking the things their partner can do.

Model the conversation with a student.

Have students do the task.

SUPPORT Have students make sentences using *and* and *but* to talk about how they are similar to, and different from, their partner.

OPTIONAL Tell students they are going to use the information in the chart to play a true-lie game.

Explain that they should say three sentences about themselves and their partner, and that two of the sentences should be true but one should be a lie. Tell them that the class must decide which sentence isn't true.

Give students time to create their sentences.

Have students play the game.

THE REAL WORLD

Ask students to look at the photo. As students follow along in their books, read the title and the photo caption aloud. You might want to have students find France on a world map.

A Explain to students that *evidence* is information that proves (shows us) something is true. Tell students that there are many things we should not believe without evidence.

Tell students they are going to watch a video and they should check the evidence that crows are clever. As students follow along in their books, read the statements aloud. You might want to tell students that more than one statement could be evidence.

▶ 7.1 Play Video 7.1. If necessary, play the video again. Check answers as a class.

B Explain to students that they will watch the video again and should complete the flowchart. If necessary, explain that a flowchart is a kind of graphic organizer that provides a visual representation of a series of actions or events. Point out to students that flowcharts have arrows that indicate the direction of the steps.

▶ 7.1 Play Video 7.1. Play it again, if necessary.

Check answers as a class.

OPTIONAL Ask students other comprehension questions.

1. *At what type of place do the crows work?* (They work at a theme park.)
2. *How many crows work with Gaborit?* (Six.)
3. *Do people who don't work at the park like the crows?* (Yes. The visitors like to watch them, suggesting they think the crows are interesting.)

THE REAL WORLD

CLEVER CROWS

Christophe Gaborit at Puy de Fou theme park in France

ABOUT THE PHOTO

This photo shows Christophe Gaborit, a falconer at the Puy du Fou theme park in western France, with one of the crows trained by him to pick up trash such as small pieces of paper and cigarette butts around the park in exchange for food. These crows not only provide the park with a cheap and efficient way to keep litter at bay, they help in teaching people to pick up their own litter. Crows are considered to be very intelligent, and some people even keep them as pets due to their intelligence. They can be trained quickly to do simple tasks.

A ▶ 7.1 **Watch the video.** Check (✓) the evidence in the video that shows crows are clever.

- ☑ The birds know the kinds of things to find.
- ☑ The birds understand how to get a reward.
- ☐ The birds fly to Christophe when he calls their names.

B ▶ 7.1 **Watch again.** Complete the flowchart.

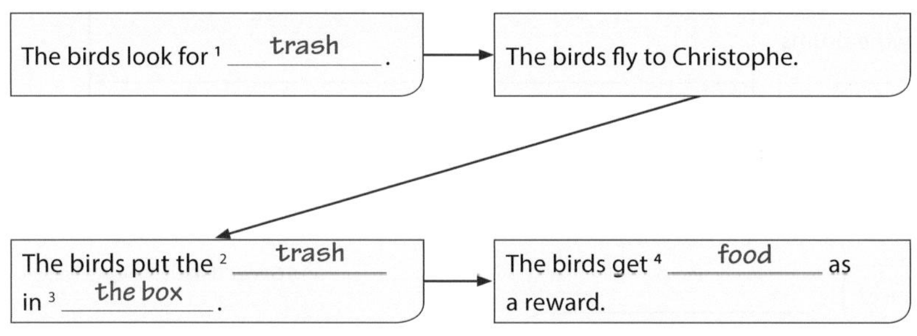

The birds look for [1] trash.
The birds fly to Christophe.
The birds put the [2] trash in [3] the box.
The birds get [4] food as a reward.

C Tell students they should use the words in the box to complete the paragraph. As students follow along in their books, read the words aloud. Have students do the task.

Check answers.

CHALLENGE Have students get into pairs and discuss which facts in **A**, **B**, and **C** are the most surprising, giving reasons for their answers.

D CRITICAL THINKING

As students follow along, read the questions aloud. Encourage students to give reasons for their answers.

Have students get into pairs and talk about their ideas.

PROJECT As students follow along, read the project instructions aloud. Give students time to do research or set a deadline to bring the research to class.

Have students share what they discovered.

C **Complete the paragraph.** Use the words in the box.

correct | remember | problems | teach | different

Crows are clever in many ways. For example, they can solve [1] problems. In one experiment, scientists [2] teach crows to use a tool to get food from a box. The scientists then take away the tool and box. One hour later, they show the crows [3] different tools. The birds usually choose the [4] correct tool. Many hours later, scientists give the box to the birds. About 90 percent of the crows [5] remember how to use the tool to get food!

D CRITICAL THINKING Applying **Talk with a partner.** What other animals can help us? How do these animals help us? Answers will vary.

PROJECT Go online. Find two more examples of things birds can do. Share your examples with the class.

PRONUNCIATION *can* and *can't*

A 7.6 **Listen and repeat.**

1 I can sing.

2 I can't play the piano.

B 7.7 **Listen.** Circle the words you hear. Then read the sentences to a partner.

1 I (**can**) / **can't** swim.

2 She **can** / (**can't**) speak French.

3 They (**can**) / **can't** dance.

4 We **can** / (**can't**) play tennis.

COMMUNICATION

Add two more abilities to the list. Then work in a group. Find out what each person can or can't do.

Can you sing a song in English?

Yes, I can.

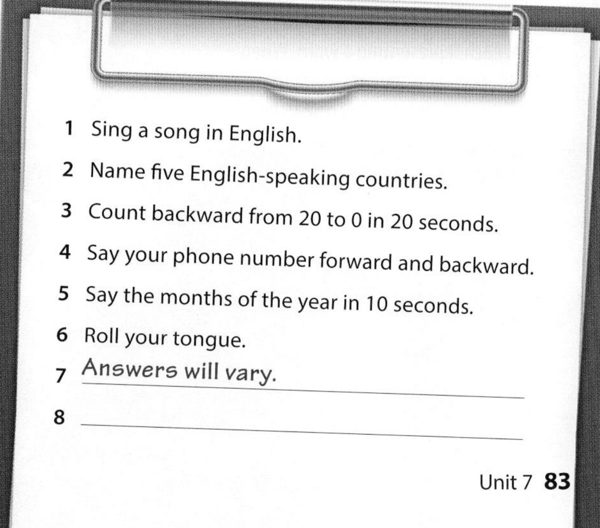

1 Sing a song in English.
2 Name five English-speaking countries.
3 Count backward from 20 to 0 in 20 seconds.
4 Say your phone number forward and backward.
5 Say the months of the year in 10 seconds.
6 Roll your tongue.
7 Answers will vary.
8

Unit 7 83

PRONUNCIATION

Tell students they will practice the pronunciation of *can* and *can't*.

Explain how important the pronunciation of these words is because the two are easily misunderstood if not pronounced clearly.

A 7.6 Play Audio Track 7.6. Play it again, pausing after each sentence so students can repeat.

B Tell students to listen to the four sentences and decide whether the speaker uses *can* or *can't* and circle the correct answer.

7.7 Play Audio Track 7.7. Play it again, if necessary. Students may have difficulties hearing the difference between *can* and *can't*, so you may need to play the audio a third time.

Randomly call on students to write their answers on the board. Check answers.

COMMUNICATION

Tell students they are going to do a survey. You might want to explain a survey in more detail. (See **TEACHING NOTE**.)

Explain that they will work in a group, asking and answering questions with other students. If necessary, read each of the items aloud as students follow along in their books.

Have students look at the last two lines. Tell students they should write their own ideas here.

Remind students that they must turn the statements into questions.

Model the conversation with a student.

Have students get into groups and do the task.

OPTIONAL When students have finished asking questions, have them tally their findings (e.g., four people can sing a song in English).

Ask groups to discuss which results are the most surprising and why.

Randomly call on some groups to share their insights with the class.

TEACHING NOTE: QUESTIONNAIRES AND SURVEYS

Questionnaires and surveys ask people about their opinions, abilities, and beliefs. For example, they are used to gather opinions on products, satisfaction with services, and attitudes toward politicians and celebrities. Surveys are common in the United States. Some market research companies administer these surveys (often by phone) and then consolidate and report the data.

READING

Ask students to look at the photos. Have a student read the title and photo captions aloud.

OPTIONAL Have students get into pairs and describe the photos in as much detail as possible. Ask them to keep track of how many sentences they make, and afterwards, determine which pair made the most sentences. Have that pair share their descriptions with the class.

CHALLENGE Tell students that *smarts* is an adaptation of the adjective *smart*. Explain that *smarts* is a slang term used mainly in the United States to mean *intelligence* or *expertise*.

CONTENT NOTE: BONOBOS

Bonobos are only found in one place, in the forests south of the Congo River in the Democratic Republic of Congo, Africa. Bonobos consume fruit, nuts, and vegetation, but they also eat small mammals, eggs, and soil. Bonobos are an endangered species because of poaching and habitat loss. Civil unrest near their homes has made it easier for poachers to kill the bonobos.

A As students follow along in their books, read the question and choices aloud.

Tell students to skim the article and pay attention to why Kanzi is special. Remind them that they shouldn't read every word. Tell them it is OK if they do not understand all of the text at this point.

Have students circle their answer.

B Remind students that *scanning* is a reading technique used to look for specific information. Remind students that when they scan, it is not important to understand or read every word.

Have students scan the article to find out where Kanzi lives.

Check answers as a class.

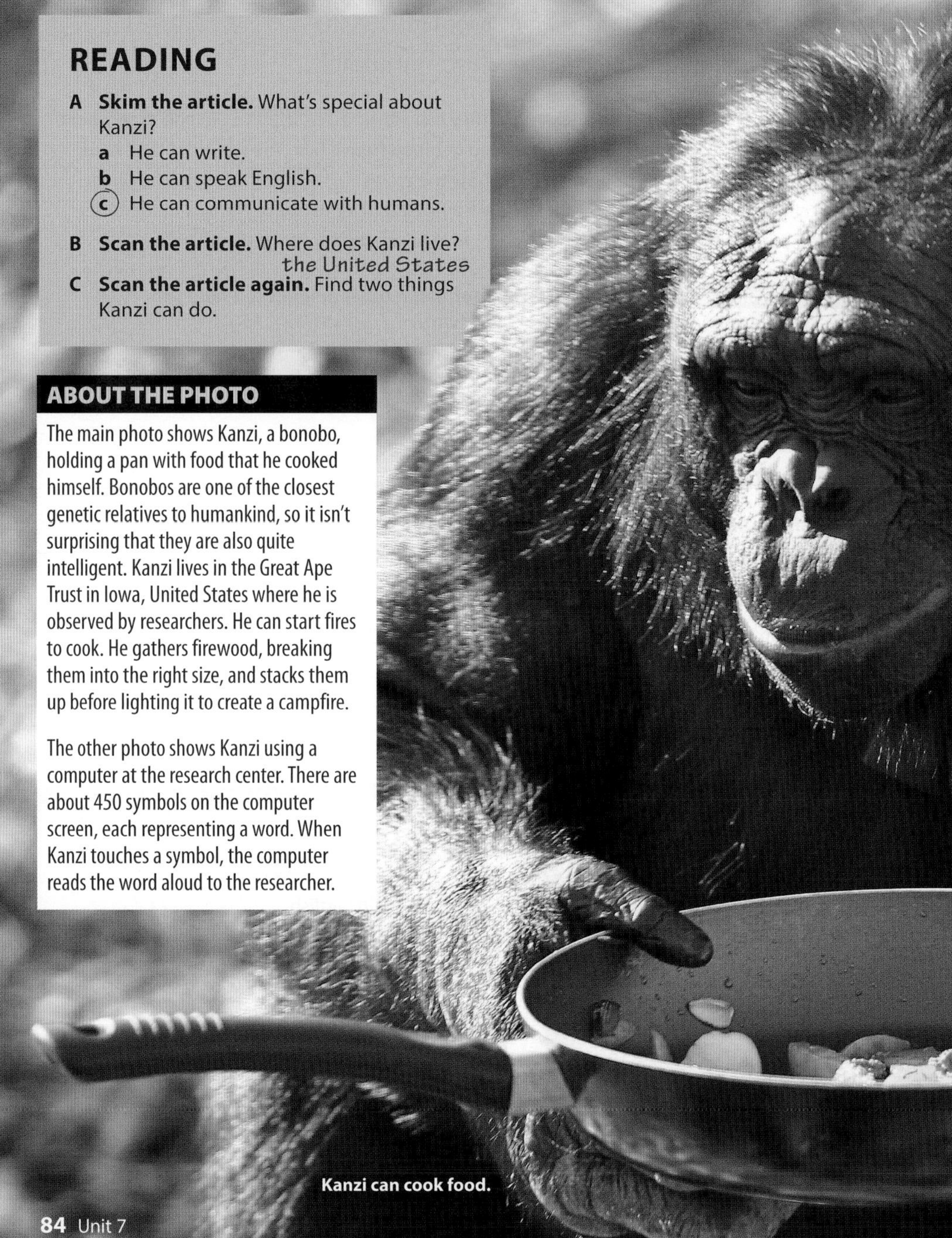

READING

A **Skim the article.** What's special about Kanzi?

- **a** He can write.
- **b** He can speak English.
- **(c)** He can communicate with humans.

B **Scan the article.** Where does Kanzi live? *the United States*

C **Scan the article again.** Find two things Kanzi can do.

Kanzi can cook food.

ABOUT THE PHOTO

The main photo shows Kanzi, a bonobo, holding a pan with food that he cooked himself. Bonobos are one of the closest genetic relatives to humankind, so it isn't surprising that they are also quite intelligent. Kanzi lives in the Great Ape Trust in Iowa, United States where he is observed by researchers. He can start fires to cook. He gathers firewood, breaking them into the right size, and stacks them up before lighting it to create a campfire.

The other photo shows Kanzi using a computer at the research center. There are about 450 symbols on the computer screen, each representing a word. When Kanzi touches a symbol, the computer reads the word aloud to the researcher.

C Ask students to scan the article again and find two things Kanzi can do, underlining his abilities.

Have students do the task. Check answers.

Ask students if their answer for **A** was correct.

Give students time to read the text in more detail before moving on to **COMPREHENSION**.

OPTIONAL The text can also be used as a listening activity. Have students close their books. Tell students they will listen to the passage.

7.8 Play Audio Track 7.8. Ask students to get into pairs and discuss what information they heard. Then have them read the article more carefully.

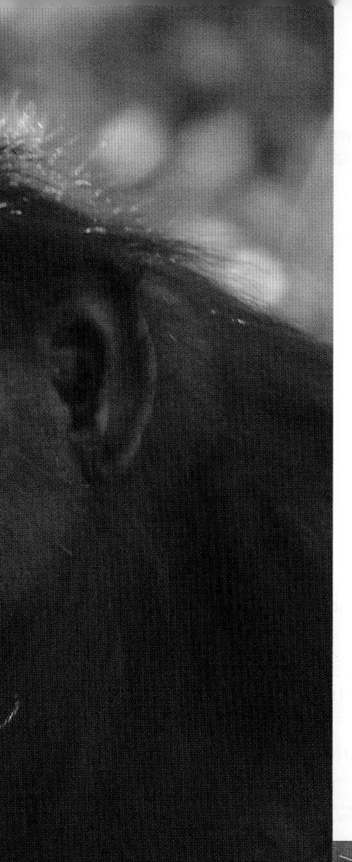

ANIMAL SMARTS

A 7.8 This is Kanzi, a bonobo. Bonobos are from Africa. There are only about 10,000 to 50,000 bonobos in the world today.

B Kanzi lives in a research center in the United States. He is very **smart**. He can **communicate** with humans.

C Kanzi can **understand** about 3,000 English words. He can't speak, but he can use a computer to say about 500 words. He **points** to pictures on the computer to say these words. He uses between 30 and 40 words every day.

D Kanzi can make a fire and cook marshmallows. He knows that fires are **hot**. Kanzi can't sing, but he can play the piano. Researchers teach Teco, a young bonobo at the center, to use a computer. Now Teco can use a computer, just **like** Kanzi.

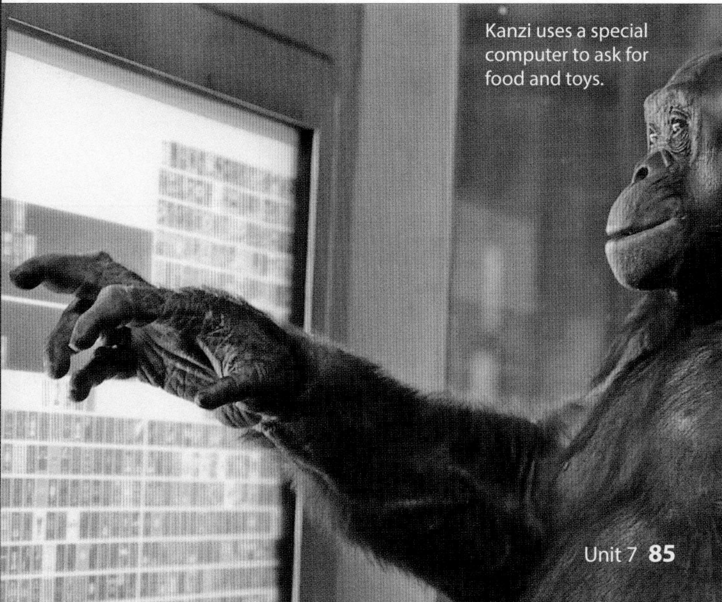

Kanzi uses a special computer to ask for food and toys.

Unit 7 85

Additional Activities to Use with the Reading

Additional Comprehension Questions

1 *Where are bonobos from?* (Africa.)

2 *Is Kanzi a male (i.e., boy) chimpanzee?* (Yes, he is. The text refers to Kanzi as *he*, indicating he is male.)

3 *Imagine Kanzi uses different words each day. How many days does it take him to use all of the words he knows?* (Since Kanzi says 30 to 40 words a day but can say 500 words, it would take between 12 and 16 days.)

Pronunciation Practice

Have students circle all of the instances of *can* (six) and *can't* (two) in the article on page 85.

Tell students that in statements *can* is often not as strongly stressed as *can't*. Explain that you will play the passage, and they should notice whether each is stressed or not.

7.8 Play Audio Track 7.8.

Play the audio again, pausing after each *can/can't* sentence so students can repeat.

Question Construction

Have students get into pairs and take turns asking and answering factual questions about the reading. For example: *Can Kanzi use a computer to say about 500 words?* (*Yes, he can.*)

Distinguishing Fact from Opinion

Ask students to decide whether each of the sentences from the article is a fact or opinion, giving reasons for their answers.

1 *Kanzi is very smart.* (Opinion. Although there is evidence that he is smart, not everyone may agree. Some people may think Kanzi is not extraordinary, whereas others may assert that Kanzi is *extremely intelligent*, which is even stronger than *very smart*. As a result, this is an opinion.)

2 *Kanzi uses 30 to 40 words every day.* (Fact. We could count the number each day to prove this is true.)

3 *Teco can use a computer.* (Fact. This can be demonstrated.)

Developing Creative Thinking

Ask students to brainstorm questions they would ask the researchers who work with Kanzi.

Developing Critical Thinking

Have students brainstorm other things Kanzi can (probably) do, writing them on the board as they are given. For example: *Kanzi can jump. Kanzi can run*. Have students give reasons for their ideas. For example: *Chimpanzees can usually jump and run, so Kanzi probably can, too.*

COMPREHENSION

A **EXAM PRACTICE**

On some standardized multiple-choice tests, for example, the MET Go! exam, students must choose the best response from three choices. On many other exams, including the Michigan Language Assessment (MET), TOEFL, TOEFL Jr., and IELTS, four choices are provided.

For all tests, students must determine how each option is different so they do not inadvertently mark the wrong answer. Many students find it helpful to quickly read the multiple-choice questions before reading the passage. This allows them to identify the key points to look for, but they should not spend too much time previewing the questions.

Have students read the questions to themselves and circle the correct answers.

After they have finished, check answers as a class.

B Point to the chart and explain that it helps us visualize the things that Kanzi can and can't do. Have students follow along in their books as you read the item already written in the chart aloud.

Have students do the task. Check answers as a class.

COMPREHENSION

A **Answer the questions about *Animal Smarts*.**

1 MAIN IDEA What's the article about?
 (a) a smart animal
 b bonobos in Africa
 c a zoo in the United States

2 DETAIL How does Kanzi communicate?
 a by making sounds b by writing words (c) by pointing to pictures

3 COHESION The best place for the sentence "These words include *bowl* and *yogurt*" is at the end of ______.
 a paragraph A (b) paragraph C c paragraph D

4 INFERENCE Which of these is NOT an example of Kanzi using tools?
 a making a fire (b) understanding words c playing the piano

5 DETAIL According to the article, Teco can ______.
 (a) use a computer b make a fire c play the piano

IDIOM

If you "can't make heads or tails of something," you ______.
a aren't good at something
(b) don't understand something

B **Complete the chart.** According to the article, what can Kanzi do?

Kanzi can ...	Kanzi can't ...
understand 3,000 English words communicate use a computer make a fire cook marshmallows play the piano	speak sing

C CRITICAL THINKING Analyzing **Match each ability with an example from the article.**

1 Kanzi understands a human language. — He knows 3,000 English words.
2 Kanzi can communicate his thoughts. — He points to pictures on a computer.
3 Kanzi knows how to use fire. — He cooks food.

86 Unit 7

OPTIONAL Tell students they will play a game. Explain that they will get into small groups. The first person must say a sentence about Kanzi. (*Kanzi can play the piano.*) The next person must say the first sentence and add another sentence without taking any notes. (*Kanzi can play the piano. Kanzi can't sing.*) The third student says the first two sentences and then adds another sentence. If a student can't remember, the group members can use gestures to give hints. The game continues until the group has said everything they can remember about Kanzi, or you call time.

C CRITICAL THINKING

Tell students about why we give examples. (See **TEACHING NOTE**.) Tell students they should match the ability with the example.

Check answers.

TEACHING NOTE: GIVING EXAMPLES

We give examples for several reasons. First, examples help clarify our ideas for the listener/reader. Second, examples extend and expand on our ideas. When our first statement is broad, an example provides a more specific context. Third, examples support and provide proof that helps substantiate our arguments.

VOCABULARY

A Find the words below in the article. Then complete the sentences.

smart communicate understand point hot like

1 My sister is good at everything. She's very smart.
2 Don't touch the bowl. It's hot.
3 The internet helps people communicate over long distances.
4 Bonobos can walk on two legs like humans.
5 In some cultures, it's not nice to point at people.
6 I can't speak Japanese, but I understand Spanish.

B Read the information below. Then circle the correct answers.

We can use the word *make* in many phrases.
make a fire: start a fire
make a call: call someone
make dinner: cook dinner
make plans: think of things to do

1 You need some wood to make **dinner** / **a fire**.
2 It's the weekend. Let's make **plans** / **a call** to go somewhere.
3 Are you hungry? Do you want me to make **dinner** / **a fire**?
4 Do you have a cellphone? I need to make **plans** / **a call**.

DO YOU KNOW?

Elephants ___ hear with their feet.
a can
b can't

WRITING

A Read the beginning of a report about someone's abilities.

B Choose a person or an animal you know. Make a list of things they can and can't do.

C Write a short report about the person or animal. Answers will vary.

My friend Lucy is friendly and very smart. She can't sing, but she can play the piano. She can surf but she can't do a handstand ...

Unit 7 **87**

VOCABULARY

A As students follow along, read the words in the box aloud. Have students find them in the **READING** passage.

Have students use the words in the box to complete the sentences. Check answers.

B As students follow along, read the information in the box aloud.

Tell students they should read the sentences below and circle the correct words to complete them. Have students do the task.

Check answers as a class.

DO YOU KNOW?

Read the sentence and answer choices aloud, as students follow along in their books. Ask a few students to give their answer before providing it (a).

WRITING

Tell students they are going to write a short report about things that a person or animal they know can and can't do.

A As students follow along, read the beginning of the example report aloud.

B Have students choose a person or animal and make a list of things they can and cannot do.

C Have students write a short report about the person or animal.

Give students a time limit for finishing the report, and set a minimum number of sentences they must write (e.g., five).

SUPPORT Have students find *and* in the example writing. Remind them that we use *and* to connect two ideas. Hold up a book and pencil. Say, *This is my book, and this is my pencil.* Point out that you repeated *this is my*. Then say, *This is my book and pencil.*

On the board, write, *My friend Lucy is friendly and very smart.* Ask students what information is not repeated (*My friend Lucy is*). Explain that by combining two sentences into one, the ideas are clearer and the writing sounds more developed.

Tell students that we can't use *and* when the ideas are very different. Say, *This is my book, and I can play the piano.* Point out that the two ideas have nothing to do with each other. Tell them that in this case, they shouldn't use *and* to connect the ideas.

Call on some students to make similar sentences.

OPTIONAL After students have completed their reports, have them take turns reading them with a partner. As students do this, walk around the class, noting grammatical mistakes. Discuss these mistakes when students have finished.

VIDEO

Tell students that they are going to watch a video about dolphins.

BEFORE YOU WATCH

As students follow along in their books, read the title and the sentence about the video aloud. Then, as students follow along, read the quiz question and statements aloud. Have them circle their answers.

Check answers.

OPTIONAL Before watching the video, ask students to predict some things they might see (e.g., a group of dolphins, dolphins sleeping). After watching the video, ask students how many of their predictions were correct.

CONTENT NOTE: DOLPHINS

Dolphins, which can live in both fresh and salt water, are fast swimmers (up to 30 kilometers per hour). One of the most widely recognized dolphins is the bottlenose dolphin, partially because it is able to adapt to living in aquariums and other places of confinement better than some other types of dolphins. The bottlenose dolphin has the longest social memory, sometimes remembering another dolphin's whistle 20 years after interacting with it.

VIDEO **ABOUT THE VIDEO** Dolphins are beautiful, friendly animals. They're also very intelligent.

Intelligent **Dolphins**

Before You Watch

Take a quiz. What do you know about dolphins?

1 Dolphins live **alone** / **in groups**.

2 Dolphins use **sound** / **smell** to find fish.

3 Dolphins sleep with **both eyes closed** / **one eye open**.

While You Watch

A ▶ 7.2 **Watch the video.** Choose the sentence that best describes the main idea.

a Scientists want to study how dolphins use tools to get food.

b Dolphins are smart because they can think of different ways to solve problems.

c Scientists know dolphins are smart, but they want to learn more about them.

B ▶ 7.2 **Watch again.** Circle **Yes**, **No**, or **Not Sure** for each sentence.

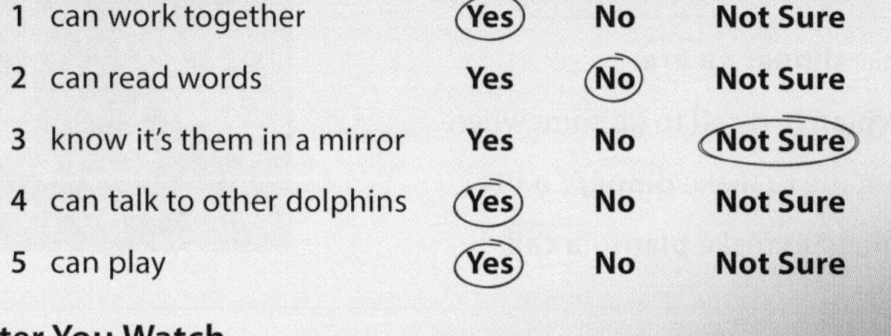

Dolphins ...

1	can work together	**Yes**	**No**	**Not Sure**
2	can read words	**Yes**	**No**	**Not Sure**
3	know it's them in a mirror	**Yes**	**No**	**Not Sure**
4	can talk to other dolphins	**Yes**	**No**	**Not Sure**
5	can play	**Yes**	**No**	**Not Sure**

After You Watch

Talk with a partner. What do you think is the most surprising thing dolphins can do? Why? Answers will vary.

ABOUT THE PHOTO

This photo shows bottlenose dolphins swimming at the Roatan Institute for Marine Sciences at Anthony's Key Resort in Roatan, Honduras. A bottlenose dolphin can grow up to 4.2 meters in length and weigh up to 500 kilograms. Dolphins produce sounds in different ways in air and underwater. They make sounds in air by releasing air through their blowholes. Underwater, the sounds are generated inside the dolphin's head, under the blowhole, but without air escaping from the blowhole. The sounds that dolphins make underwater help them to navigate, find food, gather information about their surroundings, as well as communicate with other dolphins.

88 Unit 7

WHILE YOU WATCH

A Tell students they will watch the video and they should choose the sentence that best describes the main idea. As students follow along in their books, read the sentences aloud.

▶ 7.2 Play Video 7.2. Tell students they can continue to think about the main idea as they watch the video again in **B**.

B Explain to students that they will watch the video again. Tell them that for each statement they should circle **Yes** if dolphins have the ability, **No** if dolphins cannot do the task, and **Not Sure** if they don't know. As students follow along in their books, read the sentences aloud.

▶ 7.2 Play Video 7.2. Play the video again, if necessary.

Check answers as a class.

Check answers in **A**. Discuss why the other two choices are incorrect (e.g., **a** is not mentioned in the video; **b** is incorrect because the video doesn't talk about problem solving).

CHALLENGE Have students discuss why the answer to 3 is *Not Sure* (e.g., we cannot know for sure what a dolphin is thinking).

AFTER YOU WATCH

Tell students they are going to get into pairs and talk about the video.

As students follow along in their books, read the questions aloud.

Have them get into pairs and do the task.

A Complete the sentences. Circle the correct answers.

1 I like to **climb** / **jump** mountains.
2 This music makes me want to **fly** / **dance**.
3 I don't like the water because I can't **climb** / **swim**.
4 Penguins are birds, but they can't **dance** / **fly**.
5 Chimps can **fly** / **use tools** to get food or water.
6 Animals like frogs and kangaroos can **jump** / **use tools** very well.

B Write sentences, questions, and answers using *can* or *can't*.

1 He / not / swim.
He can't swim.

2 frogs / use tools?
Can frogs use tools?
No, they can't.

3 chimps / climb?
Can chimps climb?
Yes, they can.

Bottlenose dolphins at the Roatan Institute for Marine Science in Honduras

C Complete the sentences. Use the words in the box.

a fire	a call	dinner	plans

1 Kanzi knows how to make a fire.
2 I usually make dinner for my family at 7 p.m.
3 Please give me the phone. I want to make a call.
4 We need to make plans for our vacation next month.

SELF CHECK Now I can ...

- ☐ describe my abilities
- ☐ use language for talking about abilities
- ☐ talk about intelligent animals

REVIEW

Explain to students that they are going to review the material from the unit and this will help them remember what they have studied.

A Explain that activity **A** reviews vocabulary from the unit. Explain that they should circle the correct words to complete the sentences.

Have students do the task. Check answers as a class.

B Explain that activity **B** reviews the grammar from the unit. Have students use *can* or *can't* and the words to make sentences and questions.

Have students do the task and then check answers as a class.

C Point out that activity **C** reviews words from **VOCABULARY** activity **B**.

Have students use the expressions in the box to complete the sentences. Check answers.

CHALLENGE Remind students that a collocation is a set of words that occur together more often than usual. Have students research or provide students with other collocations with *make* (e.g., *make a decision*, *make someone angry*, *make the bed*, *make a cake*, *make a mess*). Have them make sentences with each collocation.

TEACHING NOTE: PREPARATION TIME

Students often need time to prepare before discussing their opinions. To help them feel like they had a successful discussion, give students time to think about and take notes on both their ideas and the language they will use. If students are finding it difficult to think of ideas, as a class, have them brainstorm several ideas along with pertinent vocabulary.

After they have prepared, have them do the activity.

SELF CHECK

These *I can* statements provide vital feedback on students' perceived ability to use the language from the unit. If you find students are reluctant to check that they can do the skills, consider asking them to rate themselves from 1 (not very confident) to 3 (very confident).

UNIT 8

HOW MUCH IS THAT T-SHIRT?

CONTENT AREA: HISTORY AND CULTURE

Topic: shopping, clothes

Vocabulary: items: backpack, wallet, hat, cap, watch; **clothes:** T-shirt, shoes, shirt, sneakers, sweatshirt; **other words:** creative, customer, try, pay, instead, common

Grammar: expressions for buying and selling—*how much, I'd like, would you like*

Extra material: several TV commercials, a picture of a Pocky or Pepero snack, a world map

Other useful vocabulary: **clothes and shoes:** pants, jeans, shorts, sweater, dress, boots, slippers, skirt, socks; **accessories:** necklace, bracelet, ring, purse, scarf, belt

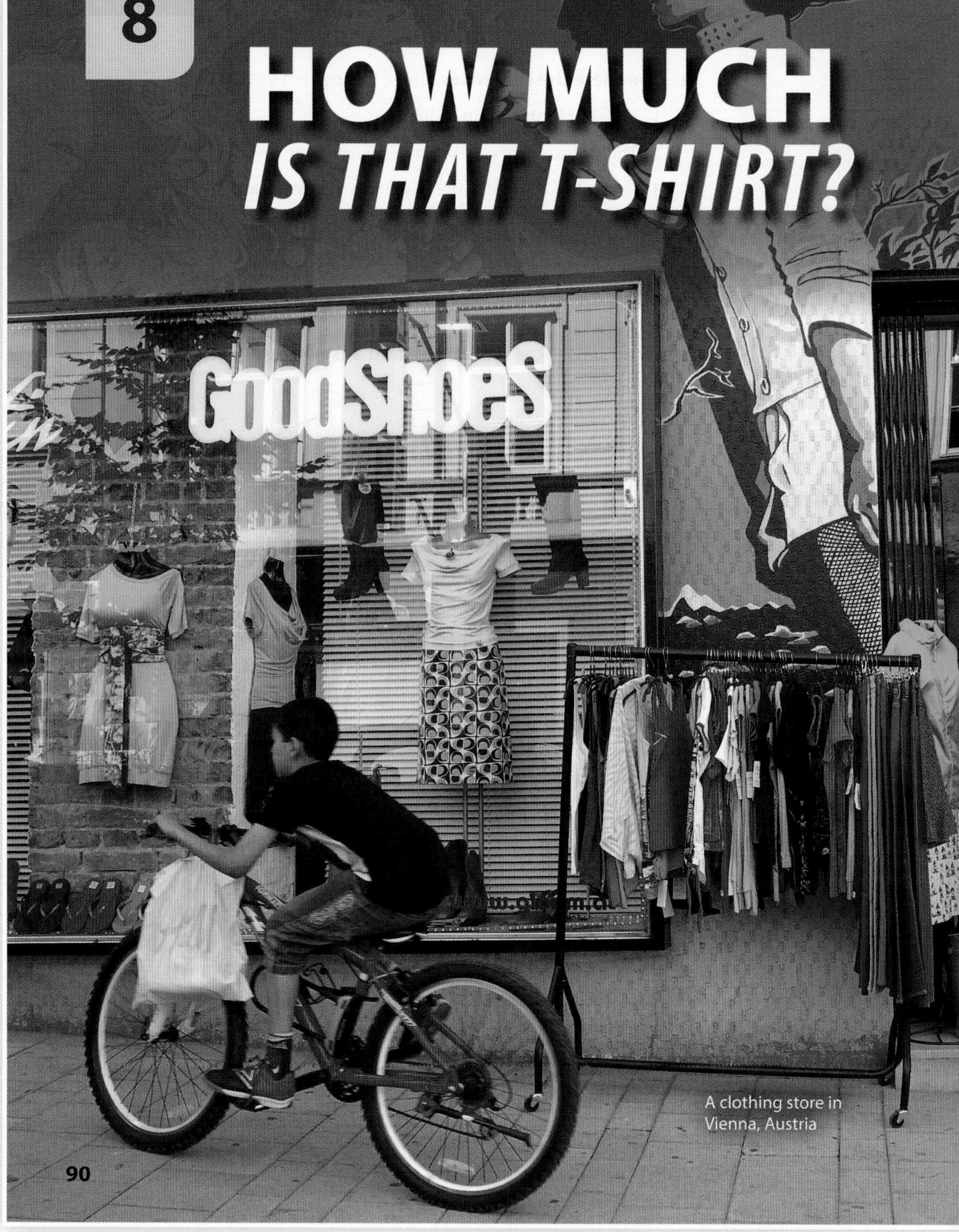

A clothing store in Vienna, Austria

END OF UNIT PROJECT Have students get into pairs and make their own commercial for their favorite store.

Ask students to name a few popular TV commercials. If you brought in a few commercials, show them to the students. Point out that most commercials are short—about 30 to 60 seconds.

Ask students what makes them interesting (humor, the excitement they create).

Ask students what commercials usually have (some talking and movement or pictures).

Have the class talk about the kinds of information they could put in their commercial. Say,

> *Where is the store?* (The store is in the mall.)
>
> *What can you buy at the store?* (There are clothes for everyone. You can get T-shirts, jeans, and baseball caps.)
>
> *How much do things at the store cost?* (The hats are only $10.)
>
> *Why is it a popular store?* (The clothes are cool!)

Have the students get into pairs and decide what their commercial will be about.

Have them write a short script for the commercial. Remind them that it shouldn't only have facts because otherwise it won't be very exciting.

If your students have smartphones, you can assign this project as homework. For example, they can use the clothes in their homes and make a commercial while using their scripts.

In class, have the students act out (or show) their commercials.

You might want to have students vote on the best commercial.

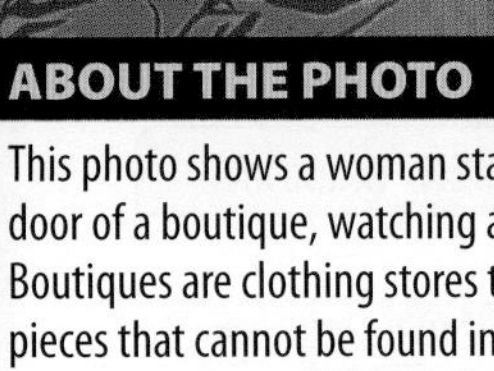

ABOUT THE PHOTO

This photo shows a woman standing at the front door of a boutique, watching as a boy cycles past. Boutiques are clothing stores that often sell unique pieces that cannot be found in chain stores. These boutiques are typically smaller than large clothing stores in malls, and usually specialize in specific brands, hence only providing a limited range of clothing.

PREVIEW

A 8.1 **Listen.** Number the items the people want to buy in the order you hear them (**1–5**).

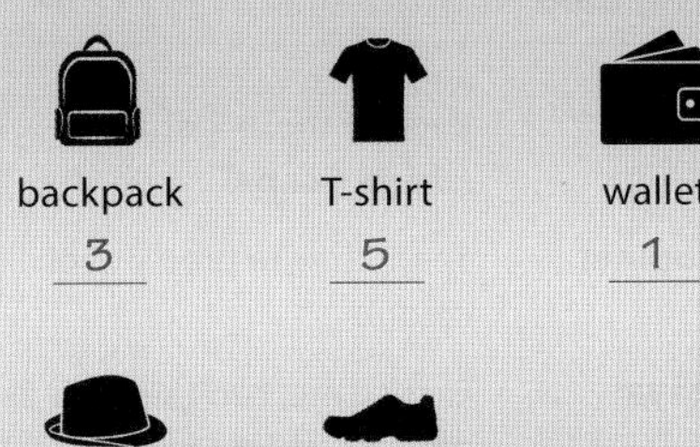

backpack 3 | T-shirt 5 | wallet 1 | hat 4 | shoes 2

B 8.2 **Listen.** Circle the correct answers.

1 The backpack is **black** / **large**.
2 The T-shirt is **white** / **small**.
3 The shoes are **cheap** / **expensive**.
4 The hat is **small** / **large**.
5 The wallet is **cheap** / **black**.

C **Talk with a partner.** Do you like to shop? Where do you usually go? Answers will vary.

Where do you like to shop?

I usually go to the mall near my house.

HISTORY AND CULTURE

UNIT GOALS

- describe your personal items
- use language for shopping
- learn about shopping trends

91

PREVIEW

Have students read the unit title to themselves as you read it aloud. Explain that in this unit they will learn to talk about shopping, clothes, and the prices of items.

A Explain to students that they will hear five short conversations between a person who works in a store and someone who wants to buy something in the store. As students follow along, read the names of the items aloud.

Tell students to number the items in the order they hear them, from one to five.

8.1 Play Audio Track 8.1. Play it again, if necessary. Check answers.

SUPPORT Using items in the photo, ask, *Do you like this T-shirt? What color are these shoes?* Repeat with other items.

B Tell students they will listen to five sentences, and they should circle the correct words to complete the sentences. If necessary, read the sentences aloud.

8.2 Play Audio Track 8.2. Play it again, if necessary. Check answers.

C As students follow along in their books, read the two questions aloud. Tell students they will get into pairs and take turns asking and answering the questions.

Model the conversation with a student. Have students do the task.

UNIT GOALS

Direct students' attention to the **UNIT GOALS** box. Explain that these are some of the things students will learn in this unit. Point out that this unit is about history and culture. As students follow along, read each of the unit goals to the class. Explain any words students do not know. Remind students that at the end of the unit there is a self check that allows them to see if they have accomplished each goal.

CONTENT NOTE: TALKING ABOUT PRICES

There are several rules for saying dollar prices in American English.

1 Use both words (*dollars* and *cents*). \$9.95 is said *nine dollars (and) ninety-five cents*.

2 Use no words (*dollars*, *cents*, or *and*). Instead, use only numbers. \$9.95 is said *nine ninety-five.*

3 Do not use just one word. \$9.95 cannot be said *nine and ninety-five cents. Nine dollars and ninety-five* is also incorrect.

4 There is an exception for one dollar. \$1.50 can be said *a dollar fifty* because we are using *a* rather than the number one.

In very informal conversation, and sometimes on television commercials, the slang word *buck(s)* is used rather than *dollar(s)*, particularly to emphasize that something is cheap. For example: *All this for only 95 bucks!*

LANGUAGE FOCUS

A 8.3 **Listen and read.** What's wrong with Maya's T-shirt? Then repeat the conversation and replace the words in **bold**. *It's too big.*

REAL ENGLISH Excuse me.

Maya:	Look at these **T-shirts**! (**shirts** / **caps**)
Nadine:	Yeah, they're pretty cool. I like the colors.
Maya:	Excuse me, can I see this **T-shirt**, please? (**shirt** / **cap**)
Salesperson:	Sure, here you go.
Maya:	How much is it?
Salesperson:	It's **$10**. Would you like to buy it? (**$15** / **$20**)
Maya:	Yes, please.
Maya:	Oh no—**it's too big**! (**it's too small** / **there's a hole in it**)

B 8.4 **Look at the chart.** Then circle the correct answers below.

TALKING ABOUT PRICES		
How much is this T-shirt? **How much are** those sneakers?	It's cheap. It's only $20. They're $50.	I'd = I would
I'd like that wallet, please.	Here you are. / Here you go.	
Would you like this hat?	Yes, please. No, thanks. **I'd like** that one.	
Would you like to see these backpacks?	No, thanks. **I'd like to see** those ones, please.	

1 We use *How much* to ask the **price** / **size** of something.
2 We use *I'd like* to **say what we want** / **ask more information about something**.
3 We use *Would you like* to **say** / **ask about** what someone wants.

LANGUAGE FOCUS

A Tell students they will listen to a conversation between a salesperson, Maya, and Nadine.

8.3 Play Audio Track 8.3 as students listen and follow along in their books.

As students follow along, read the question, *What's wrong with Maya's T-shirt?* Have students answer.

Have students work in pairs and practice the conversation once. Point out the bold words and read them aloud as students follow along in their books. Tell students they will practice the conversation two more times, changing the bold words each time and swapping roles after the first time.

SUPPORT Write $ on the board. Say, *This is a dollar sign.* Have students find the dollar signs on pages 92 and 93. Write *$10* on the board. Tell them we say *ten dollars*. Write additional prices on the board and have students practice saying them.

TEACHING NOTE: *PRETTY COOL*

Pretty cool is an informal way of admiring something. *Cool* is not related to temperature. *Pretty*, in this context, does not mean *beautiful*. It is an adverb, not as strong as *very*, which means *fairly* or *quite* (e.g., *I'm pretty hungry*; *That movie was pretty good*).

REAL ENGLISH

Direct students' attention to the expression in the **REAL ENGLISH** box. Explain that *Excuse me* is used in spoken English when you need to interrupt or bother someone. It's a polite way of getting someone's attention, usually to give him or her information or to ask a question. For example:

(in a library)
A: Excuse me, you dropped your notebook.
(in a restaurant, calling a waiter—getting someone's attention)
A: Excuse me, can we have the check, please?

B Ask students to look at the chart.

8.4 Have students follow along as they listen to Audio Track 8.4.

Write the first two questions and answers from the chart on the board.

Explain to students that these questions ask about the price of an item. Point out that *is* is used for just one item and *are* is used for more than one item.

Call on students to come to the board and underline *is* and *are* in the answers. (They need to spot them in the contractions *It's/They're*).

Draw students' attention to the right side of the chart. Tell students that *I'd* means *I would*.

C 8.5 **Complete the conversation.** Then listen and check your answers.

1 **A:** How much is this wallet?
B: It's $12.

2 **A:** How much are those watches?
B: They're $50.

3 **A:** How much is this hat?
B: It's cheap. It's $10.

4 **A:** How much are those books?
B: They're $15.

IDIOM

"It's a steal" means the price is ____.
(a) cheap
b expensive

D 8.6 **Complete the conversation.** Listen and check your answers. Then practice the conversation with a partner.

Buyer: Excuse me, can I see that sweatshirt, please?
Seller: [1] Would you like to see the blue one?
Buyer: No, I'd [2] like to see the red one, please.
Seller: [3] Here you go. It's $30.
Buyer: Hmm, it's too expensive. [4] How much is the blue one?
Seller: It's $25.
Buyer: OK, great. [5] I'd like the blue one, please.

E **Work with a partner.** You are at a store. **Student A:** You are a customer. **Student B:** You are a store assistant. Put some personal items on your desk and try to sell them. Answers will vary.

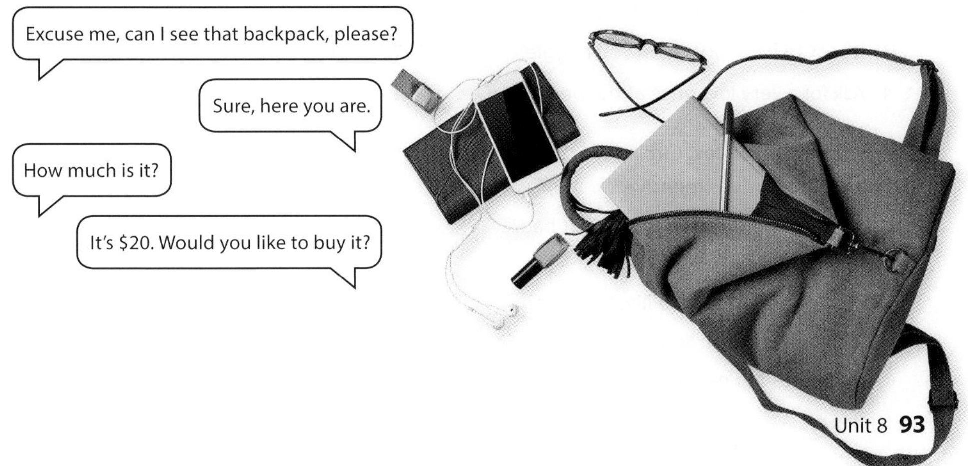

Excuse me, can I see that backpack, please?
Sure, here you are.
How much is it?
It's $20. Would you like to buy it?

Tell students they will listen to the conversations and they should check their answers.

8.5 Play Audio Track 8.5. Check answers as a class.

TEACHING NOTE: *CHEAP*

The word *cheap* can sometimes have a negative connotation. *Cheap* should be used with care, because it sometimes implies that the item is of poor quality.

IDIOM

As students follow along in their books, read the sentence and answer choices aloud. Have students guess the answer before providing it (a). Explain that we use the idiom when we can buy something at a very good price (compared to what we usually pay or expect to pay).

As students follow along in their books, read the two *Would you like . . .* questions and answers aloud. Explain that these questions and answers are about *wants*. Explain that *I'd like* is a more formal way of saying *I want*. Point out that the response is *Yes, please* or *No, thanks*.

Point out that when there is one item, the answer has *one*. Explain that *one* is a generic word that substitutes for the object (in this case, *hat*).

Point out that when there is more than one item, the answer uses *those* rather than *that*.

Draw students' attention to the three statements under the chart. Have students circle the correct answers. Check answers.

C Tell students they should refer back to the chart in **B** and write expressions to complete the conversations.

D Tell students they should write expressions to complete the conversation.

Tell students they will listen to the conversation and should check their answers.

8.6 Play Audio Track 8.6. Check answers as a class.

Have students get into pairs and practice the conversation twice, taking turns as the buyer and the seller.

E Tell students they are going to play a shopping game.

Tell students to get into pairs and put some things on their desks "to buy and sell."

Explain that Student A will be the customer and Student B will be the store assistant.

Model the conversation with a student, then have students do the task. Have students switch roles and go shopping again.

THE REAL WORLD

As students follow along in their books, read the title aloud. Ask students to look at the photo and follow along as you read the caption aloud. Tell students they are going to learn about haggling. Tell students that when we haggle, two people are usually involved: the buyer and the seller.

OPTIONAL Ask students if any of them have ever tried haggling before. If they have, ask them to briefly share their experiences.

CONTENT NOTE: HAGGLING (1)

Some people suggest the following ways are effective for getting better prices when haggling:

1 Don't wear expensive jewelry, carry designer bags, or otherwise look extremely affluent.

2 Go at the end of the day, rather than first thing in the morning. Sellers may be anxious to sell something rather than pack it up again that evening. In addition, if they didn't have good sales that day, they may settle for lower prices.

3 Hesitate, think, and always make a counteroffer.

A As students follow along, read the three items aloud. Tell them to watch the video and write the prices.

▶ 8.1 Play Video 8.1. If necessary, play the video again.

Check answers as a class.

B Explain to students that they will watch the video again and they should circle **T** if the sentence is true and **F** if it is false. As students follow along, read the sentences aloud.

▶ 8.1 Play Video 8.1. Play it again, if necessary. Check answers.

THE REAL WORLD

HAGGLING

A mirror seller at a market in Morocco

ABOUT THE PHOTO

This photo shows a man selling mirrors in Jemaa el-Fnaa, a market place in the medina quarter of Marrakesh, Morocco. This historic market square is filled with snake charmers, fortune tellers, and storytellers. It is a popular place to visit for both tourists and locals. In 2001, the market square inspired the creation of UNESCO's "Proclamation of Masterpieces of the Oral and Intangible Heritage of Humanity."

A ▶ 8.1 **Watch the video.** Write the prices.

Andrew's first price: £ 250 Dan's first price: £ 170 Final price: £ 200

B ▶ 8.1 **Watch again.** Circle **T** for true or **F** for false.

1	You can haggle at a pawnbroker's.	(T)	F
2	Say "no" if you don't like the price.	(T)	F
3	It's OK to be angry when you haggle.	T	(F)
4	Ask for a very low price at the beginning.	T	(F)

C **Read the sentences.** Circle **B** for Buyer or **S** for Seller. Then put the sentences in order (**1–6**).

5	"It's still very expensive."	(B)	S
1	"Excuse me, how much is that bag?"	(B)	S
6	"OK, you can have it for $35."	B	(S)
2	"It's $50. Would you like to buy it?"	B	(S)
4	"I can't do that. You can have it for $40."	B	(S)
3	"No, it's too expensive. How about $30?"	(B)	S

C Explain to students that they should read the sentences and decide who says each one. Have them circle **B** if the buyer would say it or **S** if the seller would say it.

When students have finished, ask them to put the conversation in the correct order, from one to six. Check answers.

OPTIONAL Have students get into pairs and practice the conversation twice, swapping roles after the first time.

D CRITICAL THINKING

As students follow along, read the questions aloud. Have students get into pairs and discuss them.

PROJECT As students follow along, read the project instructions aloud. Set a deadline by which students should talk to their friends and families.

Have students get into pairs and report their findings.

D CRITICAL THINKING Personalizing **Talk with a partner.** Do people haggle in your country? Do you like haggling? *Answers will vary.*

PROJECT Talk to your friends and family. Where can people haggle in your city?

PRONUNCIATION saying prices

8.7 **Listen.** Circle the prices you hear. Then read the prices to a partner.

1	($100)	$200	4	($207.90)	$27.90
2	($20.95)	$29.75	5	$56.50	($50.60)
3	$10.25	($10.35)	6	($6.10)	$64.10

COMMUNICATION

A **Work with a partner. Student A:** Look at the photo. Choose three things you want to buy. Ask Student B for their prices. Haggle to get cheap prices. Write the final price in the chart. **Student B:** You're a seller. Think of a price for each item.

B **Switch roles.** Choose different items and give different prices. *Answers will vary.*

Item	Student B's price	Final price
1		
2		
3		

How much are those earphones?
They're $40.
That's expensive.
How about $30?

COMMUNICATION

Tell students they are going to play a haggling game. Explain that they are going to pretend to buy three things.

Have students get into pairs and decide who is Student A and who is Student B.

A Explain that Student A should choose three items in the photo and haggle with Student B over the price of the items. Point out that they should write Student B's price and the final price in the chart.

Model the conversation with a student. Remind them that they have to practice haggling.

Have students do the task.

B Tell students they will switch roles and Student B should choose different items than Student A. Emphasize that they should also use different prices.

Have students do the task.

When students have finished, randomly call on some students and ask about their experiences.

CONTENT NOTE: HAGGLING (2)

Haggling, or bargaining, is more common in some countries than others, but even in countries where it is common, it may be unusual to try to bargain in shopping malls or other places where the prices are fixed. There are a few points that help you get a better price.

- The shopkeeper will always start with a very high price, so pay attention to what the locals paid. This will give you a better idea of how much you might be able to pay.
- Have fun. Getting angry won't help the situation, but it could make it much worse.

PRONUNCIATION

Tell students they will practice saying prices. Tell students that there are quite a few countries that use dollars as their currency. For example, Canada uses the Canadian dollar, and the United States uses the American dollar. Explain that in Canada and the United States there are 100 cents in one dollar.

OPTIONAL On the board write *95¢* and *$0.95*. Tell students that a price less than one dollar can be written in either way and is said *ninety-five cents.*

Tell students they will hear some prices and they should circle the correct price.

8.7 Play Audio Track 8.7. Play it again, if necessary. Check answers as a class.

Have students get into pairs and take turns reading the prices.

READING

CONTENT NOTE: POP-UP STORES

Until 2017, pop-up stores were limited to companies experimenting with new marketing campaigns, fashion-week stores, and internet companies testing the feasibility of building a physical store. Now, however, large companies, including Amazon, use pop-up stores because of their low-risk nature. Some use them as seasonal stores, selling holiday goods, whereas others find them beneficial for determining whether a location could support a permanent store. Large stores are even creating pop-ins (pop-up shops within another store), and these continually changing, exciting small stores encourage shoppers to regularly return to the larger stores.

Ask a student to read the title aloud. Then have students look at the photo.

OPTIONAL Have students look at the photo and describe what they see (e.g., *There is a woman; She is talking on her phone; She is wearing a coat*).

A As students follow along in their books, read the definition of *pop up* aloud. Then read the question. Have students get into pairs and discuss their ideas.

B Tell students that they are going to skim the article and they should check the questions that the article answers.

Have them do the task. Check answers.

Ask students if their ideas in **A** were correct.

OPTIONAL Ask students if they have ever seen a pop-up store. If they have, have them talk about where, when, and what was being sold.

READING

It's a store that is only open for a short time.

A **Read the definition of the phrase *pop up*.** What do you think a pop-up store is? Talk with a partner.

pop up *verb* to appear suddenly

B **Skim the article.** Check (✓) the questions it answers.

- [x] What are pop-up stores?
- [ ] When did the first pop-up store open?
- [x] Why are pop-up stores popular?

C **Scan the article.** Find an example of a pop-up store. *The Picture House/ In-N-Out Burger*

IT'S A POP-UP STORE!

8.8 On a quiet street in London, people stop to take photos of a store window. It's a restaurant—but it's only there for two days. The restaurant, called The Picture House, is a pop-up store.

Pop-up stores are only open for a short time—usually a few days or weeks. Sometimes, they're only open for a few hours, like In-N-Out Burger, a fast food restaurant that had a pop-up store in Singapore.

Pop-up stores are a fun and **creative** way for businesses to find new **customers**. They're cheap to open, so businesses can **try** new things. For example, customers at The Picture House don't **pay** for their meals. **Instead**, they take photos of their food and put them on social media.

Pop-up stores are **common** in many cities today. Look around—is there one near you?

ABOUT THE PHOTO

This photo shows a Kate Spade pop-up store. The store was open in December 2010, in Bryant Park, New York City. Pop-up stores allow retailers to take advantage of current trends and seasonal events such as Christmas. Combining the theme of Christmas with the winter season, the store was built to look like an igloo. Not only did cute penguin statues greet customers at the front of the store, but they were also given hot cocoa as a welcome gesture.

A pop-up store in Bryant Park, New York City

C Tell students that they will scan the article, and they should find an example of a pop-up store.

Have students do the task. Check answers.

Have students read the article in more detail so they can answer the **COMPREHENSION** questions.

OPTIONAL The text can also be used as a listening activity. Have students close their books. Tell students they will listen to the passage.

8.8 Play Audio Track 8.8. Ask students to get into pairs and discuss what information they heard. Then have them read the article more carefully.

Sentence Construction

Ask students to find the sentence on lines 4 and 5. Tell students that the phrase *called The Picture House* provides additional information about *The restaurant.* Point out that there are commas before and after the phrase. Explain that this phrase can be removed and the sentence will still be grammatically correct. Provide an example (e.g., *The restaurant is a pop-up store*).

Tell students that it is often possible to replace the noun that is being described with the phrase that gives more details. Have students find an example in the second paragraph and make the substitution. (*Sometimes, they're only open for a few hours, like a fast-food restaurant in Singapore.*)

Avoiding Repetition

Tell students that repeating the same word over and over in a short text can be boring. Ask students to find the words the author used instead of *pop-up stores* (they), *customers* (they), and *photos* (them).

Question Construction

Have students get into pairs and take turns asking and answering factual questions about the reading (e.g., *Where is the Kate Spade pop-up store?* [*It's in New York City*]).

Vocabulary Expansion

Have students brainstorm clothes and accessories that they might see in a pop-up store. (See **Other useful vocabulary**.)

Content Expansion

Have students research another pop-up store on the internet and tell the class about it. You might want to ask students to print pictures of the store, which may be helpful when explaining it to their classmates.

Additional Activities to Use with the Reading

Additional Comprehension Questions

1 *Are pop-up stores always restaurants?* (No. As the photo on pages 96 and 97 demonstrates, there are pop-up stores that carry clothes. There are also many other kinds of pop-up stores.)

2 *What two adjectives does the author use to describe pop-up stores?* (fun, creative)

3 *How do The Picture House customers pay for their food?* (They help other people learn about the restaurant by taking photos and putting them on social media.)

Idea Support

Draw students' attention to *For example* on line 14. Tell students we use this when we want to explain our ideas or give more specific information. Ask students what the author is giving an example of (trying a new method of paying/trying a new way of getting attention).

COMPREHENSION

A **EXAM PRACTICE**

Multiple-choice items can be either questions or statements with a blank. There are many kinds of items, including detail, purpose, main idea, inference, and reference. Multiple-choice questions usually follow the order of the reading (or listening) passage. Hints for mastering these test items include:

- Remember that even though some of the answer choices are true, they may not be the correct answer.
- Differentiation of fact, opinion, feeling, and argument may be necessary.
- Pay attention to *don't*, *always*, *never*, *sometimes*, and other words that may change the meaning of the question or answer.
- Make sure you are on the correct number. It is easy to fill in the circle for the wrong number, potentially affecting more than one answer.

Have students read the questions to themselves and circle the correct answers.

After they have finished, check answers as a class.

CHALLENGE Ask students to discuss whether social media reviews can always be trusted, giving reasons for their answers. Then ask, *Why is The Picture House unique?* (Rather than paying money, the customers give the restaurant social media coverage.)

Ask students if the customers should mention this when they post the photos. Also ask them if this is "fair" to those people seeing the photos, particularly if they don't realize the customers' incentive. Encourage students to provide reasons for their opinions.

COMPREHENSION

A **Answer the questions about *It's a pop-up store!***

1 PURPOSE The purpose of the article is to ____.

a describe interesting pop-up stores
ⓑ explain what pop-up stores are
c compare pop-up stores with regular stores

2 INFERENCE Which of the following is an example of a pop-up store?

ⓐ a store that's open for 10 days
b a store that has a three-hour sale
c a store that sells things at cheap prices

3 REFERENCE The word *they* in line 15 refers to ____.

a the meals　b pop-up stores　ⓒ restaurant customers

4 DETAIL The example of The Picture House shows how businesses use pop-up stores to ____.

a help the poor　ⓑ do something different　c get young customers

5 DETAIL Pop-up stores DON'T help businesses ____.

a save money　b find new customers　ⓒ make new items to sell

DO YOU KNOW?

At Magnum's pop-up store, people ____.

a get free ice cream
ⓑ design their own ice cream

B **Complete the chart.** Compare The Picture House and In-N-Out Burger.

Name	The Picture House	In-N-Out Burger
What type of store is it?	restaurant	fast food restaurant
Where is it?	London	Singapore
How long is it open?	two days	a few hours

C CRITICAL THINKING Evaluating **Talk with a partner.** Do you think pop-up stores are a good idea? Are there any disadvantages? Answers will vary.

DO YOU KNOW?

Read the question and answer choices aloud, as students follow along in their books. Ask a few students to give their answer before providing it (b).

CONTENT NOTE: MAGNUM POP-UP STORE

Every year, Magnum, the ice cream company, opens their Pleasure Store, a pop-up store, on London's Regent Street. The Magnum pop-up store has a dipping bar where the ice cream is enveloped in chocolate of colors ranging from gold to electric blue. In 2019, the pop-up had an experiential Play Room, where customers could visit masterclasses for up-and-coming artists in music, dance, fashion, and film. This activity demonstrates Magnum's principle: pleasure without fear.

B Tell students they should complete the chart to compare the two pop-up stores mentioned in the article. Have students do the task. Check answers as a class.

VOCABULARY

A Find the words below in the article. Then complete the sentences.

creative customers try pay instead common

1 This store is popular with many customers.
2 I think this T-shirt looks good. I want to try it on.
3 She always has interesting ideas. She's really creative.
4 In this store you can use your phone to pay for things.
5 Everyone uses this music app these days. It's very common.
6 We can't play soccer because it's raining. Let's play video games instead.

B Read the information below. Then complete the sentences with the phrasal verbs.

We can make phrasal verbs with *up*.
wake up: stop sleeping
give up: stop trying
look up: find information in a book or online

1 I wake up when I hear my alarm clock in the morning.
2 You can look up the meaning of words in a dictionary.
3 Learning a language is difficult, but don't give up.

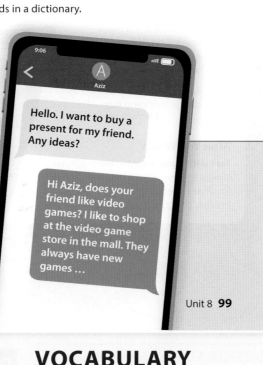

9:06

Hello. I want to buy a present for my friend. Any ideas?
Hi Aziz, does your friend like video games? I like to shop at the video game store in the mall. They always have new games ...

WRITING

A Read the text messages.

B Choose a store or place you like to shop at. Make notes about it. What are the prices of things? Why do you like the place?

C Write a text message reply to Aziz.
Answers will vary.

C CRITICAL THINKING

As students follow along, read the questions aloud. Have students get into pairs and discuss them.

TEACHING NOTE: PERSONALIZATION

Encourage students to personalize the content. This encourages them to apply the content to their own context. It also gives them the opportunity to use the language presented in the unit.

VOCABULARY

A As students follow along, read the words in the box aloud. Have students find them in the **READING** passage.

Have students use the words in the box to complete the sentences. Check answers.

B As students follow along, read the information in the box aloud.

Have students write the correct phrasal verbs to complete the sentences.

Check answers as a class.

CHALLENGE Have students research other phrasal verbs with *up* and share them with the class. Alternatively, provide students with more phrasal verbs (e.g., *take up*, *set up*, *make up*). Have students get into pairs and take turns making sentences with them.

WRITING

Tell students they are going to write a text message. Explain that because text messages are often between people who know each other well they tend to use informal English.

A As students follow along, read the text message from Aziz aloud. Point out that the message, like many text messages, is relatively short. Also point out that he doesn't use a final closing or include his name.

As students follow along in their books, read the example reply aloud.

B Tell students they will write a text reply to Aziz, and they should suggest a store or place that they like to shop at, giving reasons why they like the place. Point out that they should also discuss the prices.

Have students choose their place and make notes about the place, the prices, and why they like it.

C Have students use their notes in **B** and write their text message.

Give a time limit for finishing the text message, and set a minimum number of sentences they must write (e.g., six).

SUPPORT Ask questions to help students think of the information they can include. Ask, *Where do you like to shop? What is the place called? Where is it? What can you buy there?*

VIDEO

Tell students they are going to watch a video about Singles Day. As students follow along in their books, read the title, the sentence about the video, and the photo caption aloud. You might want to have students find China on a world map.

BEFORE YOU WATCH

As students follow along, read the question and answer choices aloud. Have students circle their answer.

CHALLENGE Before students look at their books, read the question aloud. Have students get into groups and brainstorm what the holiday is. Then have a few groups share their ideas with the class.

WHILE YOU WATCH

A Tell students they will watch the video and they should circle the correct answers to complete the sentences. As students follow along in their books, read the sentences aloud.

▶ 8.2 Play Video 8.2. Play it again, if necessary.

Check answers.

OPTIONAL Before watching the video, ask students to predict things they might see (e.g., people using their phones to shop). Then, after watching the video, ask students how many of their predictions were correct.

B Explain to students that they will watch the video again and they should complete the sentences with two words or a number. As students follow along, read the sentences aloud.

▶ 8.2 Play Video 8.2. Play it again, if necessary.

Check answers. Then check answers for **BEFORE YOU WATCH**.

VIDEO **ABOUT THE VIDEO** Singles Day is a big event in China.

SINGLES DAY

Before You Watch

Guess. What is Singles Day?

(a) It's a day when people shop online.

b It's a holiday for people to shop.

c It's a day when unmarried people can buy things at cheap prices.

While You Watch

A ▶ 8.2 **Watch the video.** Circle the correct answers.

1 Alibaba **makes a special app** / (**has a TV program**) for Singles Day.

2 Stores give **flowers** / (**discounts**) on Singles Day.

3 Singles Day is very popular (**in parts of Asia**) / **around the world**.

B ▶ 8.2 **Watch again.** Complete each sentence with two words or a number.

1 Another name for Singles Day is *11.11*.

2 Singles Day is popular in China because people usually buy things on *their phones*.

3 In 2018, Alibaba made one billion dollars in the first *90* seconds of its event.

4 Singles Day is the biggest online shopping day in *the world*.

After You Watch

Talk with a partner. Are there special shopping days in your country? Do you know any special shopping events in other countries? *Answers will vary.*

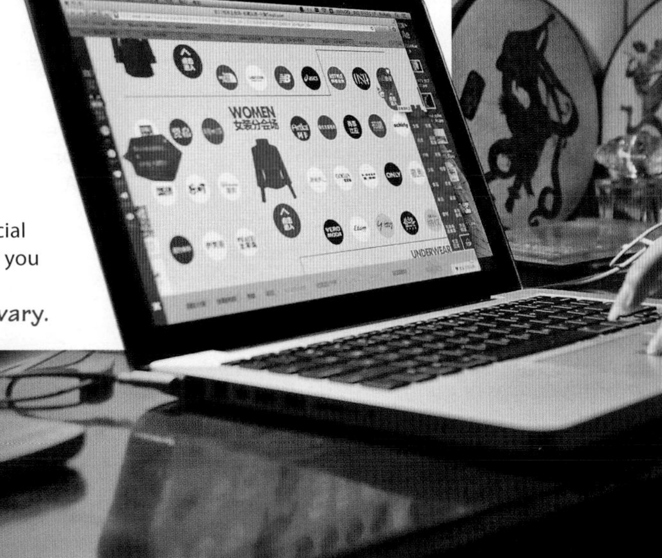

ABOUT THE PHOTO

This photo shows a student in China shopping online at midnight on November 11. Singles Day is a major online shopping day in China, and is popular around Asia. Said to be larger than U.S. equivalents Black Friday and Cyber Monday combined, it is the world's largest shopping event. Singles Day 2019 had 200,000 brands from 78 countries participating. In a lead-up to Singles Day 2019, e-commerce company, Alibaba, organized a countdown gala in Shanghai on November 10, featuring performances by popular stars such as Taylor Swift. It was reported that for Singles Day 2019, Alibaba achieved sales of over a billion dollars within the first minute.

OPTIONAL Ask students additional comprehension questions.

1 *What is Alibaba?* (A Chinese company.)

2 *According to the video, what kinds of things do people buy?* (Clothes, cameras, pet food, everything.)

3 *In what year did Alibaba have the first 11.11 event?* (2009.)

CONTENT NOTE: SINGLES DAY

In China, Singles Day is also called "bare sticks holiday" because of the aesthetic look of four ones in a row. Shoppers tend to buy presents for themselves, rather than for other people. Because of the huge volume of sales, companies across Southeast Asia are making bigger marketing campaigns to bring customers to their websites for the day. Not surprisingly, over 70 percent of the people use mobile devices to shop.

REVIEW

A student in China shops online at midnight on November 11.

A Complete the sentences. Use the words in the box.

backpack T-shirt shoes hat wallet

1 I usually change into a T-shirt at home.
2 I can't see his hair because he has a hat on.
3 I can't find my phone. It's not in my backpack.
4 I can't walk in these shoes. They're very uncomfortable.
5 Could you pay for me, please? I don't have my wallet with me now.

B Complete the conversation.

Customer: Excuse me. [1] I'd like to see that backpack, please.
Seller: [2] Would you like to see the large one?
Customer: No, the small one. [3] How much is it?
Seller: It's $29.90.
Customer: OK. I'd like to have it, please.
Seller: [4] Here you go.
Customer: Thank you.

C Complete the sentences. Circle the correct answers.

1 Try again! Don't **give up** / **look up** now.
2 I **give up** / **wake up** at 7 o'clock in the morning.
3 Please **look up** / **give up** the phone number of the restaurant online.

SELF CHECK Now I can ...

- describe my personal items
- use language for shopping
- talk about shopping trends

In contrast to the focus on buying for oneself, there is a tendency for shoppers on Black Friday and Cyber Monday (both in November in the United States) to shop for others in preparation for the December holiday season.

AFTER YOU WATCH

As students follow along in their books, read the questions aloud.

Have them get into pairs and do the task.

OPTIONAL Tell students that 11.11 is called Pocky Day in Japan, and in South Korea, it is called Pepero Day. If you brought a picture of a Pocky or Pepero snack, show it to students and explain that both snacks are similar and feature a cookie-like stick covered with chocolate or other flavors. Have them guess the reason why 11.11 is called Pocky Day or Pepero Day, providing it if necessary. (The snack stick looks like a 1.)

REVIEW

Explain to students that they are going to review the material from the unit and this will help them remember what they have studied.

A Explain that activity **A** reviews vocabulary from the unit. Explain that they should use the words in the box to complete the sentences.

Have students do the task. Check answers as a class.

CHALLENGE As students recall other vocabulary that was important in the unit, write it on the board (e.g., *buyers*, *customers*). Have students get into pairs and take turns making sentences using the words. After students have finished, randomly call on pairs to share one of their sentences. As you repeat back the sentences, make corrections to grammar and vocabulary usage.

B Explain that activity **B** reviews the grammar from the unit. Have students write words to complete the conversation.

Check answers as a class.

C Point out that activity **C** reviews words from **VOCABULARY** activity **B**.

Have students circle the correct words to complete the sentences. Check answers.

SELF CHECK

These *I can* statements provide vital feedback on students' perceived ability to use the language from the unit. If you find students are reluctant to check that they can do the skills, consider asking them to rate themselves from 1 (not very confident) to 3 (very confident).

OPTIONAL Have students complete the **SELF CHECK** before doing the **REVIEW** activities. After reviewing the unit, have students once again check their confidence for each statement.

UNIT 9

WHAT ARE YOU DOING?

CONTENT AREA: SCIENCE AND TECHNOLOGY

Topic: technology

Vocabulary: **actions:** take a photo, check email, call a friend, chat, play a game, text, write an email, use a computer; **technology:** robot, techie; **other words:** engineer, pyramid, repair, machine, instruction, material, program, plan

Grammar: present progressive

Extra material: a world map

Other useful vocabulary: **related to technology:** spam/spamming, phishing, junk mail, inbox, virus(es), security, firewall, hard drive; **actions:** download, upload, surf (the internet), browse (the internet)

END OF UNIT PROJECT Have students use their creative thinking and write a paragraph about a new technology they would like to create.

In this unit, students learn to talk about technology. Ask them to name some technology that we didn't have five years ago. Remind them that we are always making new and exciting technological breakthroughs.

Ask students what they would invent if they could make anything.

Tell students to write a short paragraph about the new technology they would make and give examples of how they would use it.

Read this example to students:

> *I love to eat, and I really like to smell the food. I want a computer that can share smells. With my computer, I can smell my friend's cake when I chat with her over the internet. I can do research and smell things at a festival in another country, too.*

9

WHAT ARE YOU DOING?

The Falls at Night

Visitors take selfies in front of Niagara Falls, Canada.

102

After students have written their paragraphs, have them get into small groups and take turns telling the rest of the group about their ideas. Encourage group members to ask questions if they don't understand anything about the new technology.

When all the students have finished, have each group decide which idea was best. Have those students share their ideas with the entire class.

TEACHING NOTE: SIMPLE PRESENT AND PRESENT PROGRESSIVE TENSES

The simple present tense is used for static situations (*I live in the United States*), universal truths (*Water boils at 100°C*), general actions and occupations (*I like coffee*; *I drive a taxi*), habitual actions (*I always go to school at 7:45*), and actions that are not specific to a point in time. The present progressive takes the *-ing* form and is used for actions that are occurring now (*I am playing tennis [right now]*).

ABOUT THE PHOTO

This photo shows visitors taking selfies of themselves while visiting Niagara Falls, Canada. The word *selfie* is slang for *self-portrait*. History indicates that the first self-portrait ever taken was in 1839 by Robert Cornelius. He used a daguerreotype camera and took the photo of himself by removing the lens cap of the camera, running into frame and sitting for a minute, then covering up the lens again. Taking a selfie is now easily accomplished as long as you have a digital camera or a smartphone. Many people around the world enjoy sharing their selfies on social media platforms like Facebook and Instagram.

PREVIEW

A 9.1 **Listen.** Number what each person is doing in the order you hear it (**1–6**).

4 taking a photo
1 texting
2 calling a friend
5 chatting
6 playing a game
3 checking email

B **How techie are you?** Complete the survey on page 152 and see your results.

C **Talk with a partner.** Compare your results.

I text a lot. I always chat with my friends through texts.

Me, too! But I don't play games on my phone.

Answers will vary.

SCIENCE AND TECHNOLOGY

UNIT GOALS

- describe your activities
- use language for talking about actions in progress
- learn about how technology helps improve lives

103

CHALLENGE Ask, *Are emailing and texting the same?* (No.) *How are they different?* (We send emails through an email account. Traditionally, we did this from a computer, but we now often send them through an app on our smartphones. We send texts with our phones, smartphones, and sometimes other devices.)

B Explain to students that they will complete a survey on page 152 to see how techie they are. If necessary, explain that *techie* means a person who is very good at, or who really likes, technology.

Have students do the task.

CHALLENGE Have students talk about when, where, and how often they use each kind of technology.

C Tell students they will get into pairs and take turns talking about the results of their surveys in **B**.

Model the conversation with a student.

Have students do the task.

CHALLENGE Have students brainstorm other things they might do when using technology. (See **Other useful vocabulary**.)

PREVIEW

Have students read the unit title and the photo caption to themselves as you read it aloud. Explain that in this unit they will learn to talk about technology and things they are doing right now.

OPTIONAL Have students name various kinds of technology they use regularly.

A Explain to students that they will hear six short conversations between two people talking about what they are doing. As students follow along, read the names of the activities aloud.

Tell students to number the items in the order they hear them, from one to six.

9.1 Play Audio Track 9.1. Play it again, if necessary. Check answers.

UNIT GOALS

Direct students' attention to the **UNIT GOALS** box. Explain that these are some of the things students will learn in this unit. Point out that this unit is about science and technology. As students follow along, read each of the unit goals to the class. Explain any words students do not know. Remind students that at the end of the unit there is a self check that allows them to see if they have accomplished each goal.

LANGUAGE FOCUS

Ming is in the same café as Maya.

A 9.2 **Listen and read.** Where is Ming? Then repeat the conversation and replace the words in **bold**.

REAL ENGLISH I'm just . . .

Ming: Hey, Maya. What are you doing?

Maya: Hi, Ming! I'm just **sitting** in a café. (**having lunch** / **writing an email**)

Ming: Do you want to go to **the movies**? (**Stig's house** / **the mall**)

Maya: OK. Where are you?

Ming: Well, I'm in a café, too …

Maya: **You are**? Which one? (**Really** / **Yeah**)

Ming: I'm standing **behind** you! (**in front of** / **next to**)

B 9.3 **Look at the chart.** Then circle the correct answers.

TALKING ABOUT WHAT SOMEONE IS DOING (USING PRESENT PROGRESSIVE)	
What **are** you **doing**? What**'s** he **doing**?	I**'m texting**. He**'s checking** his email.
Is she **listening** to music? **Are** they **using** the computer? Who **are** you **chatting** with?	**Yes**, she **is**. / **No**, she **isn't**. **Yes**, they **are**. / No, they **aren't**. **I'm chatting** with a friend.

1 We use the present progressive to talk about things we **usually do** / **are doing now**.

2 We usually form the present progressive by adding **-ing** / **-s** to the base verb.

3 At the beginning of a question, we use **a be** / **an -ing** verb or a *wh-* word.

LANGUAGE FOCUS

A Tell students they will listen to a conversation between Ming and Maya.

9.2 Play Audio Track 9.2 as students listen and follow along in their books. If necessary, play the conversation again, pausing after each speaker so students can repeat.

As students follow along, read the question, *Where is Ming?* Have students answer.

Have students work in pairs and practice the conversation once. Point out the bold words and read them aloud as students follow along in their books. You might want to have students repeat the words after you say them. If necessary, explain the meaning of any words that students seem unfamiliar with.

Tell students they will practice the conversation two more times, changing the bold words each time and swapping roles after the first time.

REAL ENGLISH

Direct students' attention to the expression in the **REAL ENGLISH** box. Explain that *I'm just ...* is used in English to soften statements or tell the other person that they don't mind being interrupted. For example:

A: What are you doing?
B: Oh, I'm just reading. (Here, *just* implies that *reading* is not an overly important action for the speaker.)

B Ask students to look at the chart. Tell them that the chart teaches the language needed to talk about actions that are currently taking place (present progressive tense).

9.3 Have students follow along as they listen to Audio Track 9.3.

Point out that when talking about what someone is currently doing, both the *be* verb (*am*, *is*, *are*) and the *-ing* form of the action verb are used.

As students follow along, read the first, second, and last questions aloud. Ask students to look at the questions and say how they end differently. (The *Who* question has *with* at the end.) Remind them that *with* shows there are other participants in the action—that it is not done alone.

Have students follow along as you read the answers to the first two questions. Point out that in both the questions and answers, the action verb always ends in *-ing*.

C **Complete the questions.** Then match the questions to the correct answers.

1 Is she texting Mira? (text) — Yes, they are.
2 Are you using this computer? (use) — No, she isn't.
3 Who 's Jean chatting with? (chat) — He's taking a photo.
4 Are they watching a movie? (watch) — She's talking to a friend.
5 What 's Hakim doing ? (do) — Yes, I am. I'm checking my email.

D 9.4 **Complete the conversation.** Use the correct form of the words in the box. Listen and check your answers.

chat do play eat study

Rita: Hey Bianca, what [1] are you doing ? [2] Are you studying for the test?

Bianca: No, I'm not. [3] I'm playing a game on my computer. What about you?

Rita: [4] I'm just chatting with friends and eating lunch.

Bianca: Oh, what [5] are you eating ?

Rita: Pasta. It's my favorite food!

E **Work with a partner.** Play tic-tac-toe. Take turns to choose a verb. Make a sentence using the *-ing* form of the verb. If your sentence is correct, write an **X** or **O** in the space.

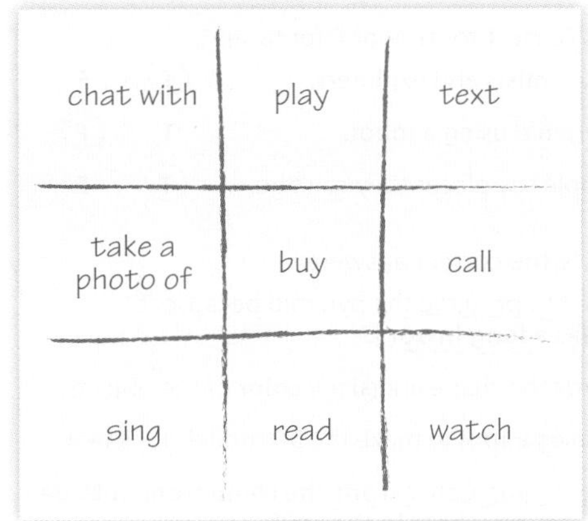

chat with
play
text
take a photo of
buy
call
sing
read
watch

My brother is chatting with his friends.

Answers will vary.

C Explain to students that in this activity, they must do two things. First, they must complete the questions using the correct form of the words in parentheses. Next, they should match the questions to the correct answers.

Have students fill in the blanks. Then tell students to read the answer options. Have them match each completed question to the correct answer.

Check answers as a class.

OPTIONAL Have students get into pairs and practice asking and answering the questions.

D Tell students they should use the correct form of the verbs in the box to complete the conversation. If necessary, read the words in the box aloud as students follow along. Have them do the task.

Tell students they will listen to the conversation and they should check their answers.

9.4 Play Audio Track 9.4. Check answers by calling on students and writing the answers on the board.

OPTIONAL Have students get into pairs and practice the conversation twice.

E Tell students they are going to get into pairs and play a game where they take turns choosing a verb and making a sentence with its *-ing* form. Tell students that if the sentence is correct, the speaker marks his or her symbol (i.e., either an **X** or an **O**).

Model the example.

Have students get into pairs and play the game.

SUPPORT Help students make three rules for formulating sentences using the present progressive tense. This is an important critical thinking skill. (1) The answers to the questions always have a *be* verb and the *-ing* form of the verb. (2) For all question subjects except *you*, the *be* verb is the same in both the question and the answer. (3) When the subject of the question is *you*, the *be* verb is changed for the answer. (The question has *are*, but the answer has *am*.)

Direct students' attention to the *Is* and *Are* questions. Explain that, like other questions with *Is* and *Are*, the answer is *yes* or *no*. If necessary, elicit examples of questions with other subjects to help students recall the use of *Is* and *Are*. For example: *Is he watching a DVD?*

Draw students' attention to the three statements under the chart.

Have students circle the correct answers. Check answers.

THE REAL WORLD

CONTENT NOTE: COREY JASKOLSKI

Corey Jaskolski wants people to see the world from different perspectives, so he helps archaeologists, filmmakers, biologists, and other scientists explore things with technology. He has degrees in physics, math, electrical engineering, and computer science.

Ask students to look at the photo. As students follow along in their books, read the title and the photo caption aloud.

A Tell students they are going to watch the video and they should circle **T** if the statement is true and **F** if it is false. As students follow along in their books, read the sentences aloud.

▶ 9.1 Play Video 9.1. Wait to check answers.

TEACHING NOTE: CHECKING ANSWERS

Because students will be watching the video again in **B**, after showing the video once, explain the **B** activity. Encourage students to double-check their **A** answers while they also do **B**. This will allow slower learners to complete **A** while working on **B**. After watching the video again in **B**, check answers for both **A** and **B**.

B Tell students they are going to watch the video again and they should circle the correct answers to complete the sentences.

▶ 9.1 Play Video 9.1. If necessary, play the video again. Check answers. Also check answers for **A**.

C As students follow along in their books, read the words in the box aloud. Tell students the paragraph gives more information about Corey and his work.

Have students use the words to complete the paragraph.

Check answers.

THE REAL WORLD

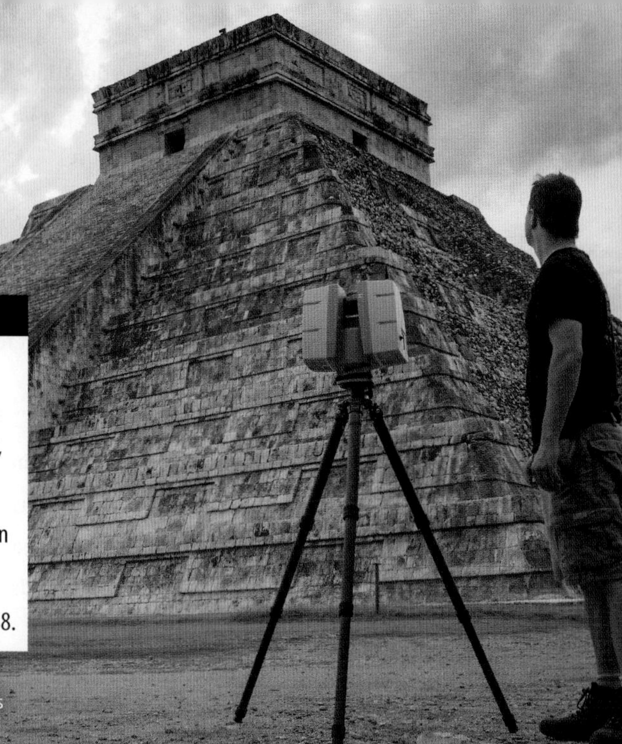

STUDYING THE PAST

ABOUT THE PHOTO

This photo shows Corey Jaskolski, a National Geographic Fellow and engineer, doing a 3D scan of one of the ancient pyramids in Mexico that the Maya people built. The digital preservation project, led by Jaskolski, aims to help researchers gain a better understanding of the cultural and climatic conditions that resulted in the formation of Chichén Itzá. Chichén Itzá is one of the most important archaeological sites in the Americas, and it was designated as a UNESCO World Heritage Site in 1988.

Corey Jaskolski is an engineer. He studies amazing places around the world.

A ▶ 9.1 **Watch the video.** Circle **T** for true or **F** for false.

1	Corey builds tools for scientists and explorers.	(T)	F
2	Corey is exploring a pyramid using a robot.	T	(F)
3	Corey's work helps people see places they can't go.	(T)	F

B ▶ 9.1 **Watch again.** Circle the correct answers.

1 Corey and his team want to preserve the pyramid because it **is in bad condition** / **has a long history**.

2 The laser scanner records the shape and **size** / **color** of the objects.

3 Corey **takes photos** / **uses a tool** to make the 3D models look real.

4 To take photos of secret rooms, Corey **scans the room from outside** / **puts a small camera through a hole in the wall**.

D CRITICAL THINKING

As students follow along, read the questions aloud. Tell students that they should get into pairs and talk about their ideas.

PROJECT As students follow along, read the project instructions aloud. Have students get into pairs and talk about their ideas. Encourage them to give reasons for their choices.

TEACHING NOTE: DIGITAL LITERACY

Digital literacy includes the ability to find, use, manipulate, and evaluate information, including images. With the advent of modern technology, it is increasingly important for students to think critically about media, including photos, because they can be digitally altered to appear real. Considering how to effectively and accurately use digital media (e.g., how Corey is using it) is another important aspect of digital literacy.

C Complete the paragraph. Use the words in the box.

learn	engineer	dark	technology	robot

Corey is a(n) [1] ___engineer___. He's very interested in science and [2] ___technology___. He has many inventions, such as an underwater [3] ___robot___. Underwater caves are difficult to study because they're [4] ___dark___ and deep. But Corey's robot can take very clear underwater photos. These help scientists [5] ___learn___ more about places people can't usually go.

D CRITICAL THINKING Evaluating **Talk with a partner.** Would you rather explore Chichen Itza with a 3D model or go there in person? Why? *Answers will vary.*

PROJECT Make a list. What places in your country do you think Corey should scan and record?

PRONUNCIATION intonation in questions

9.5 **Listen.** Is the intonation on the last word rising (↗) or falling (↘)? Listen again and repeat.

1 Are they watching a movie? 
3 Do you read blogs? 
2 What's she writing? 
4 What game are you playing?  

COMMUNICATION

Find the differences. Student A: Look at the picture below. **Student B:** Look at the picture on page 153. Ask and answer questions about the pictures. *Answers will vary.*

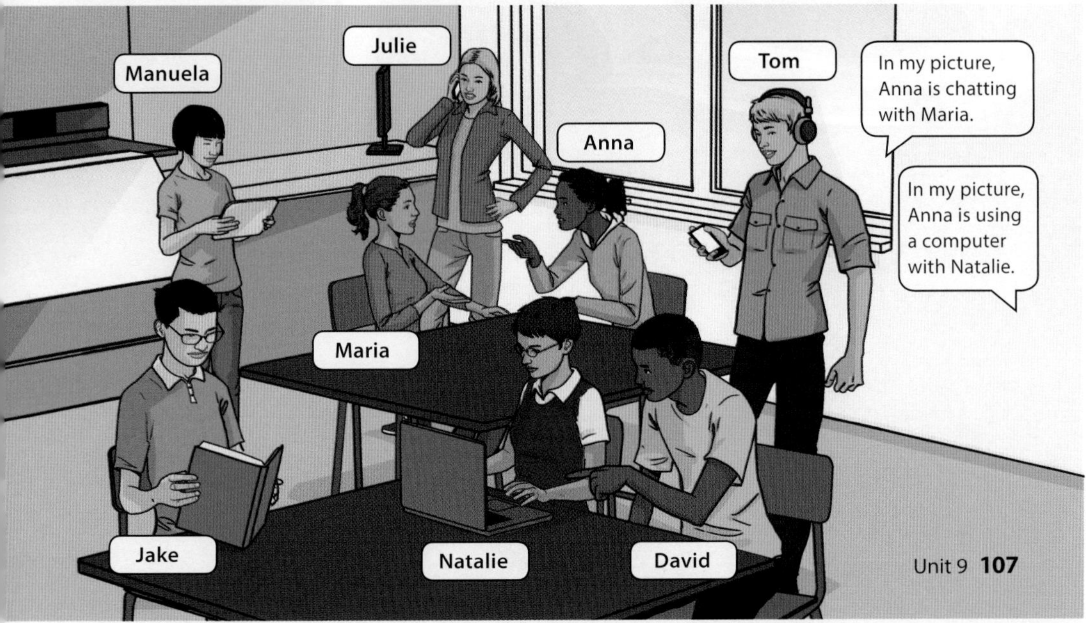
Manuela
Julie
Tom
In my picture, Anna is chatting with Maria.
Anna
In my picture, Anna is using a computer with Natalie.
Maria
Jake
Natalie
David

PRONUNCIATION

Tell students that they are going to learn about intonation in questions.

Explain to students that when we speak naturally, we do not use the same intonation for every word. Say, *Are you happy today?* in an even, monotone voice, with identical stress on all words. Then say, *Are you happy today?* with a rising intonation at the end of the question.

Ask students if they recognize the difference. Tell them they will now practice speaking with different intonations for *Wh-* and *yes/no* questions.

Ask students to read the questions to themselves. Explain that questions end with either a rising or falling intonation. Tell them to listen and circle the correct mark.

9.5 Play Audio Track 9.5. Play it again, if necessary. Check answers.

Tell students you will play the audio again and they should repeat each question.

9.5 Play Audio Track 9.5, pausing after each question so students can repeat.

SUPPORT Write the questions on the board. Include the arrows. Remind students that the *What* questions ask for specific information, whereas the *Are* and *Do* questions require *yes/no* answers.

Point out that our intonation falls (or decreases) when we ask a question requiring specific information, whereas our intonation rises (or increases) at the end of a question requiring a *yes/no* answer. Practice this again by reading each question aloud with the correct intonation. As you do this, point at the arrow, and then have students repeat.

COMMUNICATION

Tell students they are going to play a game. Explain that they will work in pairs to find the differences in two similar pictures. Tell them that to do this they will take turns asking and answering questions.

Emphasize that they should not look at their partner's picture.

Have students get into pairs. Tell Student Bs to look at the picture on page 153.

Model the conversation with a student.

Have them do the task.

When students have finished, check answers.

SUPPORT Tell students that after they find the differences they should write sentences in their notebooks about them.

READING

As students follow along in their books, read the title and the photo caption aloud.

OPTIONAL Ask, *Does our school have a 3D printer? Do you have one at home?* Have students who have access to a 3D printer share their experiences (e.g., when they got the printer, what they have printed, when and why they printed it).

CONTENT NOTE: 3D PRINTING

3D printing (three-dimensional printing) refers to making a three-dimensional object by laying hundreds or thousands of two-dimensional cross sections on top of each other. It has become a popular way to check the design of new things (prototypes) because it is relatively cheap and quick.

A As students follow along in their books, read the question and answer choices aloud. Have students scan the article to find the answer. Remind them that when they scan, they shouldn't read every word.

Check answers.

TEACHING NOTE: HELPING STUDENTS SCAN

Encourage students to scan quickly by saying the time that has elapsed every 10 or 15 seconds. If students are taking too long to find the answer, review how to quickly and efficiently scan a text.

B Have students skim the article and underline the things that 3D printers can make.

Check answers.

After completing **B**, give students the opportunity to read the article in more detail so they can more fully comprehend it and answer the **COMPREHENSION** questions.

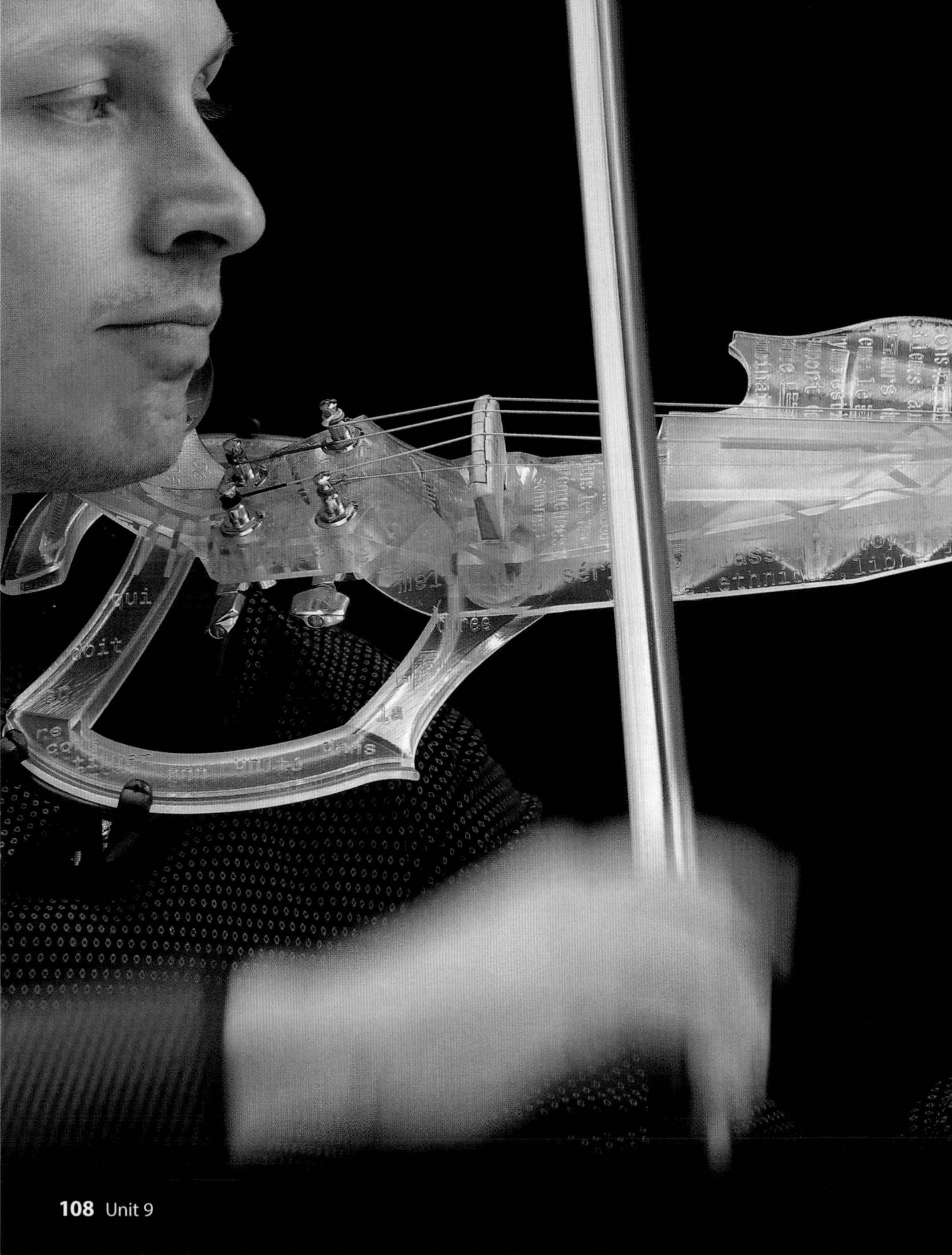

108 Unit 9

OPTIONAL The text can also be used as a listening activity. Have students close their books. Tell students they will listen to the passage.

9.6 Play Audio Track 9.6. Ask students to get into pairs and discuss what information they heard. Then have them read the article more carefully.

C As students follow along in their books, read the question aloud. Have students get into pairs and discuss their ideas.

Additional Activities to Use with the Reading

Personalizing

Ask students to talk about which facts surprised them the most and why.

Developing Creative Thinking

Tell students that word webs can be used to brainstorm new ideas. Emphasize that there are no wrong answers when brainstorming. Explain that the ideas may diverge greatly from the original idea, but that's OK.

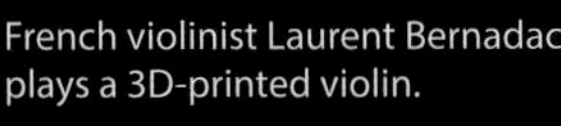

French violinist Laurent Bernadac plays a 3D-printed violin.

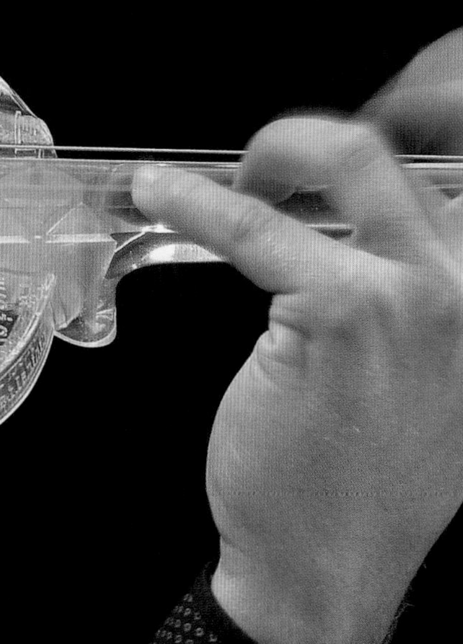

ABOUT THE PHOTO

This photo shows French engineer and famous violinist Laurent Bernadac playing a 3D-printed violin. 3D printing technology has advanced so far that we can now print simple human organs such as ears. This is done using an integrated tissue-organ printer, where the "ink" is made up of cells mixed with a gel. The cells are given the appropriate nutrients and grow around a base structure, and once complete, the new organ is ready. With advances continuing to be made for 3D organ printing, it is hoped that in the years to come, there will be similar successes in printing complex organs.

READING

A **Scan the article.** What large objects can 3D printers make? Choose the correct answer.

a schools (b) houses c space stations

B **Skim the article.** Underline the things that 3D printers can make.

C **Talk with a partner.** How is a 3D printer different from a regular printer? A regular printer prints things on paper. A 3D printer makes things in 3D.

PRINTING THE FUTURE

A 9.6 There's an emergency on the International Space Station! The astronauts are **repairing** a **machine**, but they need a special tool. Engineers on Earth send **instructions** to a 3D printer on the Space Station, and it makes the tool quickly. Thanks to the 3D printer, the emergency is over.

What are 3D printers?

B To make objects, 3D printers use different **materials**, such as plastic. They can make tools, jewelry, toys, and sunglasses! They're becoming very popular because they can make almost everything. Some designers are even using 3D printers to print food and houses!

How do 3D printers work?

C There are three main steps in 3D printing. First, a person uses a computer **program** or a scanner to **plan** the design of an object. Then, the printer checks the object's shape and size. Finally, the printer prints the object.

Unit 9 109

Tell students that they will try this brainstorming technique by drawing a circle in the middle of a piece of paper and writing *3D Printing* in the center. Explain that they should write words related to 3D printing in the circles radiating from *3D Printing*. Tell them they will then write words related to these new words.

Briefly demonstrate the process on the board.

Emphasize that the goal is to write many words (i.e., ideas).

Point out that each idea is related to the previous idea even though it may not be connected to ideas several steps (i.e., circles) away.

Give students several minutes to brainstorm.

Have students get into pairs and discuss their ideas.

Additional Discussion Questions

1 *What do you think of food made by a 3D printer? Would you like to try it? Why or why not?*

2 *Would you prefer to wear jewelry made by hand, or beautiful jewelry that was made by a 3D printer? Why?*

Headings

Draw students' attention to the two bold questions in the text. Point out that they are in bold and on a line by themselves.

Tell students that these are called *headings*. Explain that headings help us understand what we are going to read about next. Tell them that the headings divide the text into groups of topics.

Explain to students that headings are also useful when you are searching for information, because you can use them to decide if the information is probably in that section.

Have students look at the headings again. Ask, *Why did the writer use questions?* Have students give their ideas before explaining that these questions are specific but also make the reader more interested in the content that will follow. You may also want to explain that we can use questions to help the reader start thinking about the content even before they begin reading.

Critical Thinking

Ask, *How could 3D printing change our view of things in the future?* Have students brainstorm ideas in pairs or small groups.

Question Construction

Have students get into pairs and take turns asking and answering factual questions about the reading. For example: *Are people making food with 3D printers?* (*Yes, they are!*)

COMPREHENSION

A Have students read the questions to themselves and circle the correct answers. Check answers.

IDIOM

Read the idiom and answer choices aloud, as students follow along. Have students raise their hands to show whether they think the answer is *a* or *b* (b). Explain that we use *It's not rocket science* when we want to emphasize that something is not difficult. We can use it when we think someone is making a situation too complicated; in this case, it may be said out of frustration.

B EXAM PRACTICE

A flowchart is a kind of graphic organizer that provides a visual representation of a series of actions or events. These types of question items appear on standardized tests such as the Listening and Reading Modules of the IELTS exam.

Flowcharts have arrows that indicate the direction of the steps. Students must understand how different parts of the text relate to each other.

On standardized exams, the flowchart structure gives hints about the general order of events. In addition, some actions/events are also provided. When completing the exam items, students must note how many key words are required for each blank. It is not necessary to spend time thinking of synonyms; instead, students should use the exact words from the passage to complete the chart.

Remind students that flowcharts can help us better understand the steps involved in making something. Ask one student to read the title of the flowchart aloud, as the other students follow along. Tell students that the flowchart expands on the **READING** content.

COMPREHENSION

A Answer the questions about *Printing the Future*.

1 PURPOSE What's the purpose of paragraph A?
 (a) to show how 3D printers can be useful
 b to describe the world's first 3D printer
 c to explain why 3D printers are popular

2 REFERENCE The word *They* in the second sentence of paragraph B refers to ____.
 a materials (b) 3D printers c 3D objects

3 COHESION What's the best place for this sentence?
 "3D printers look like regular printers, but they make 3D objects."
 a paragraph A (b) paragraph B c paragraph C

4 DETAIL The instructions to a 3D printer give information about ____.
 a the object's material b how to use the object (c) the object's shape and size

5 DETAIL Which of the following advantages of 3D printers does the article describe?
 a They're easy to use. b They're cheap to build. (c) They make all kinds of things.

IDIOM

"It's not rocket science" means ____.
a it isn't exciting
(b) it isn't difficult

B Complete the flowchart. Use the words in the box.

material design prints checks instructions

How a 3D Printer Works

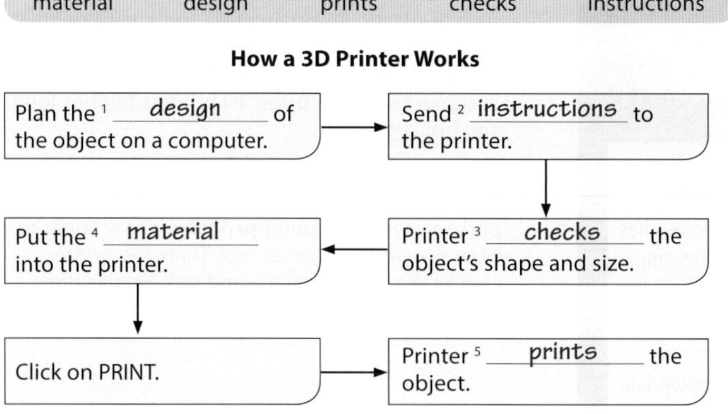

Plan the 1 design of the object on a computer.
Send 2 instructions to the printer.
Printer 3 checks the object's shape and size.
Put the 4 material into the printer.
Click on PRINT.
Printer 5 prints the object.

C CRITICAL THINKING Applying **Talk with a partner.** Make a list of things that 3D printers can make to improve our lives. Answers will vary.

Ask students how many steps there are in the flowchart (six).

As students follow along, read the words in the box and each of the flowchart steps aloud.

Have students write the correct words to complete the flowchart. Check answers.

C CRITICAL THINKING

Have students get into pairs and make a list of things they think 3D printers could make to improve their lives.

VOCABULARY

A As students follow along in their books, read the words in the box. Have students find the words in the **READING** passage.

Have students write the correct words to complete the sentences. Check answers.

DO YOU KNOW?

Read the sentence and answer choices aloud, as students follow along. Have a few students give their answers before providing it (b).

VOCABULARY

A **Find the words below in the article.** Then complete the sentences.

repair	machines	instructions
materials	program	plan

1 My phone's not working. Can you ___repair___ it?

2 To make this toy robot, follow the ___instructions___ in the video.

3 Let's have a meeting to ___plan___ the school party.

4 Plastic and wood are common ___materials___ for making tables and chairs.

5 Many people today use ___machines___ such as computers to help them in their jobs.

6 This computer ___program___ allows people to check and organize their email.

DO YOU KNOW?

You can use VR technology to ____.
a listen to music
(b) play video games

B **Read the information below.** Then circle the correct answers.

We add *every* to some words to talk about all the things in a group.
everyone: all people
everything: all things
everywhere: all places

1 I like **everywhere** / **(everything)** in that store.

2 **(Everyone)** / **Everything** likes that movie. It's great!

3 I take my backpack with me **everything** / **(everywhere)**.

WRITING

A **Look at the photo.** Read the beginning of a description of the photo.

B **Make notes about the photo.** What are the people doing?

C **Write a description of the photo.** Say what the people are doing. Answers will vary.

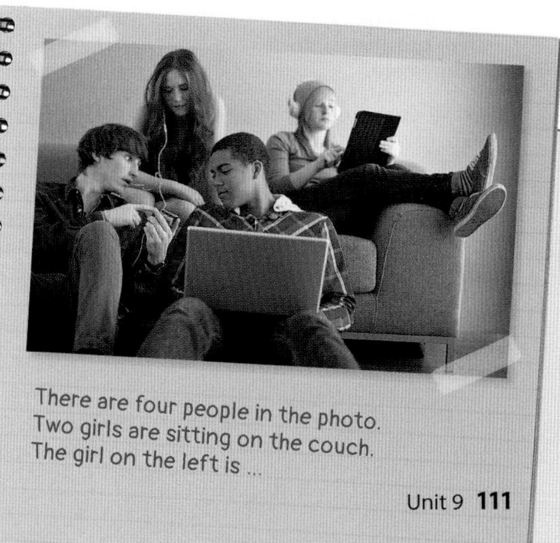

There are four people in the photo. Two girls are sitting on the couch. The girl on the left is ...

CONTENT NOTE: VR TECHNOLOGY

Virtual reality (VR) utilizes computer-generated graphics to allow us to feel like we are in a different place. For instance, if we put on a VR headset, we may feel like we are standing on the rocky cliffs of Ireland even though we are still sitting in our living room.

VR technology will continue to change our world as more realistic technology is created. For example, scientists are currently developing a "skin" that would allow parents to hug their children virtually.

B As students follow along, read the information in the box aloud. Point out that although these words are made from two different words (e.g., *every* + *one*), the combination is one word, not two.

Have students circle the correct words to complete the sentences. Check answers.

CHALLENGE Tell students we add *every* to many nouns when we want to emphasize that all are included or an act is done consistently. Explain that in most cases, the two words remain distinct. On the board, write, *I watch TV every day.* Point out that the two words did not become one.

Have students brainstorm other combinations with *every* (e.g., *every time*, *every year*) and write sentences.

Collect their papers and correct grammatical mistakes. When you return the papers to the students, discuss any mistakes that many students made.

WRITING

Tell students they are going to describe a photo, saying what the people are doing.

A Have students look at the photo. Then, as students follow along, read the example aloud.

B Have students make notes about what the people in the photo are doing.

C Have students use their notes from **B**, along with other observations, and write a description of the photo. Emphasize they should talk about what all four people are doing. Encourage them to also describe the people's clothes, hair, and other aspects of the photo. Set a minimum number of sentences students must write (e.g., seven).

VIDEO

CONTENT NOTE: e-NABLE

The *e-* in e-NABLE is important not only because the name mimics *enable* (i.e., make possible), but also because of the nature of the work that the organization does. First, it's an online community. Second, it utilizes free (open source) online designs. Third, the first project the founder of the organization did was to design fingers for a man in South Africa, using online communication tools to overcome the 16,000-kilometer distance between them. Fourth, as the two men on the original project worked to create the fingers, a blog was created and more people started asking for help. The beginning of the community was born!

As students follow along in their books, read the title, the sentence about the video, and the photo caption aloud. Explain to students that a *prosthetic* is a man-made body part, such as an arm or leg.

OPTIONAL Have students find South Africa on a world map.

BEFORE YOU WATCH

As students follow along, read the sentence and questions aloud. Have students get into pairs and talk about their ideas.

OPTIONAL Have students get into small groups and talk about what else they know about prosthetics.

WHILE YOU WATCH

A Tell students they will watch a video and they should circle **T** if the sentence is true and **F** if it is false. As students follow along in their books, read the statements aloud.

▶ 9.2 Play Video 9.2. Don't check answers yet.

VIDEO **ABOUT THE VIDEO** An organization is helping people by making prosthetics.

A **Helping Hand**

Before You Watch

Talk with a partner. The person in the photo has a prosthetic hand. Who uses prosthetics? Do you think prosthetics are expensive? *Answers will vary.*

While You Watch

A ▶ 9.2 **Watch the video.** Circle **T** for true or **F** for false.

1 e-NABLE makes prosthetics using 3D printers. (T) F

2 e-NABLE sells prosthetics to people. T (F)

3 e-NABLE's prosthetics are cheap to make. (T) F

B ▶ 9.2 **Watch again.** Circle the correct answers.

1 Kieran's hand is made of **metal** / (**plastic**).

2 e-NABLE's prosthetics are for **children** / (**children and adults**).

3 The video shows people (**doing sports**) / **carrying hot things** with their 3D-printed hands.

4 Kieran wants **to make 3D-printed hands** / (**more kids to have 3D-printed hands**) in the future.

After You Watch

Read the problems below. Match them to the ways e-NABLE's prosthetics can help.

1 Kids grow quickly, so their prosthetics don't fit anymore. — It's easy to redesign and make prosthetics with 3D printers.

2 Prosthetics are expensive. — The prosthetics from e-NABLE are free.

3 It's difficult for people in some places to get prosthetics. — e-NABLE has volunteers around the world.

An Australian teenager tests her prosthetic hand from e-NABLE.

CHALLENGE Have students make theories about why the organization uses *e-* in its name before providing an explanation. (See **CONTENT NOTE.**)

B Explain to students that they will watch the video again. Tell them they should circle the correct words to complete the sentences. As students follow along, read the sentences aloud.

▶ 9.2 Play Video 9.2. Play the video again, if necessary.

Check answers as a class for **A** and **B**.

OPTIONAL Tell students they will listen to the last part of the video again and should deduce what *gonna* means.

▶ 9.2 Play the last part of Video 9.2. Have students answer (*going to*). Tell students that in informal English, we often blend *going to* so it is said *gonna*. Explain that we do not write *gonna*, particularly in formal writing. Have students get into pairs and practice using *gonna* in sentences.

REVIEW

ABOUT THE PHOTO

This photo shows Hailey Wright, an Australian teenager, trialing a 3D prosthetic hand made from recycled hair salon waste. Born without her left hand, the prosthetic hand would aid her in simple everyday tasks like tying her hair. Bernie Craven, founder of Waste Free Systems, created the prosthetic hand as part of a collaboration with e-NABLE in which he is creating prosthetic limbs from recycled shampoo and conditioner bottles. Craven estimates that hair salons in Australia produce between 40,000 to 50,000 tons of waste per year.

A Complete the phrases. Circle the correct answers.

1 (call) / **play** your family
2 (text) / **check** a friend
3 **chat** / (play) a game
4 (check) / **take** email
5 (chat) / **text** with a friend
6 **call** / (take) a photo

B Write sentences and questions. Use the present progressive (*-ing*).

1 he / read a book
He's reading a book.
2 she / text a friend?
Is she texting a friend?
3 I / write an email
I'm writing an email.
4 you / play a game?
Are you playing a game?
5 they / not / listen to music
They aren't listening to music.

C Complete the sentences. Circle the correct answers.

1 I'm texting **everywhere** / (everyone) to tell them about the party.
2 This restaurant is great. (Everything) / **Everyone** here is delicious.
3 Please clean your room. Your clothes are (everywhere) / **everyone**.

SELF CHECK Now I can ...

- ☐ describe my activities
- ☐ use language for talking about actions in progress
- ☐ talk about how technology helps improve lives

REVIEW

Explain to students that they are going to review the material from the unit and this will help them remember what they have studied.

A Explain that activity **A** reviews vocabulary from the unit. Have students circle the correct words.

Check answers.

B Explain that activity **B** reviews the grammar from the unit. Have students use the words to write questions and sentences. Have students get into pairs and check answers, before you randomly call on students to give the answers.

OPTIONAL Have students write questions that would result in responses 1, 3, and 5. Have students make the responses for numbers 2 and 4.

Check answers. Have students get into pairs and take turns asking and answering the questions.

C Tell students that the activity reviews words from **VOCABULARY** activity **B**. Have them circle the correct words to complete the sentences.

Check answers.

SELF CHECK

These *I can* statements provide vital feedback on students' perceived ability to use the language from the unit. If you find students are reluctant to check that they can do the skills, consider asking them to rate themselves from 1 (not very confident) to 3 (very confident).

AFTER YOU WATCH

As students follow along in their books, read the problems aloud. Tell them e-NABLE is working to overcome these problems.

Have them match the problems with the solutions. Check answers.

CHALLENGE Give students additional questions to discuss.

1 *Would you like to do volunteer work with e-NABLE? Why or why not?*
2 *Why do you think e-NABLE helps both children and adults?*
3 *Why do you think the organization gives the prosthetics away rather than asking the people who get them to pay the cost (often less than $100)?*
4 *If prosthetics can be made very cheaply with a 3D printer, why are usual prosthetics so expensive? (How are normal prosthetics similar to and different than the ones made with a 3D printer?)*

UNIT 10

WHAT'S THE WEATHER LIKE?

CONTENT AREA: SCIENCE AND TECHNOLOGY

Topic: weather

Vocabulary: weather: rainy, sunny, windy, stormy, hot, warm, cool, cold, snowy, icy, dry; **seasons:** summer, winter; **other words:** weather balloon, record, temperature, project, launch, upload, view

Grammar: talking about weather

Extra material: a short weather clip from the TV or the internet, a world map

Other useful vocabulary:
seasons: spring, autumn/fall; **weather:** hazy, foggy, clear, mild, drizzling, humid, thunderstorm, thunder, lightning, mist, freezing, hail, sleet, dreary; **extreme weather:** tornado, heat wave, typhoon, hurricane, snowstorm, sandstorm

10

WHAT'S THE *WEATHER* LIKE?

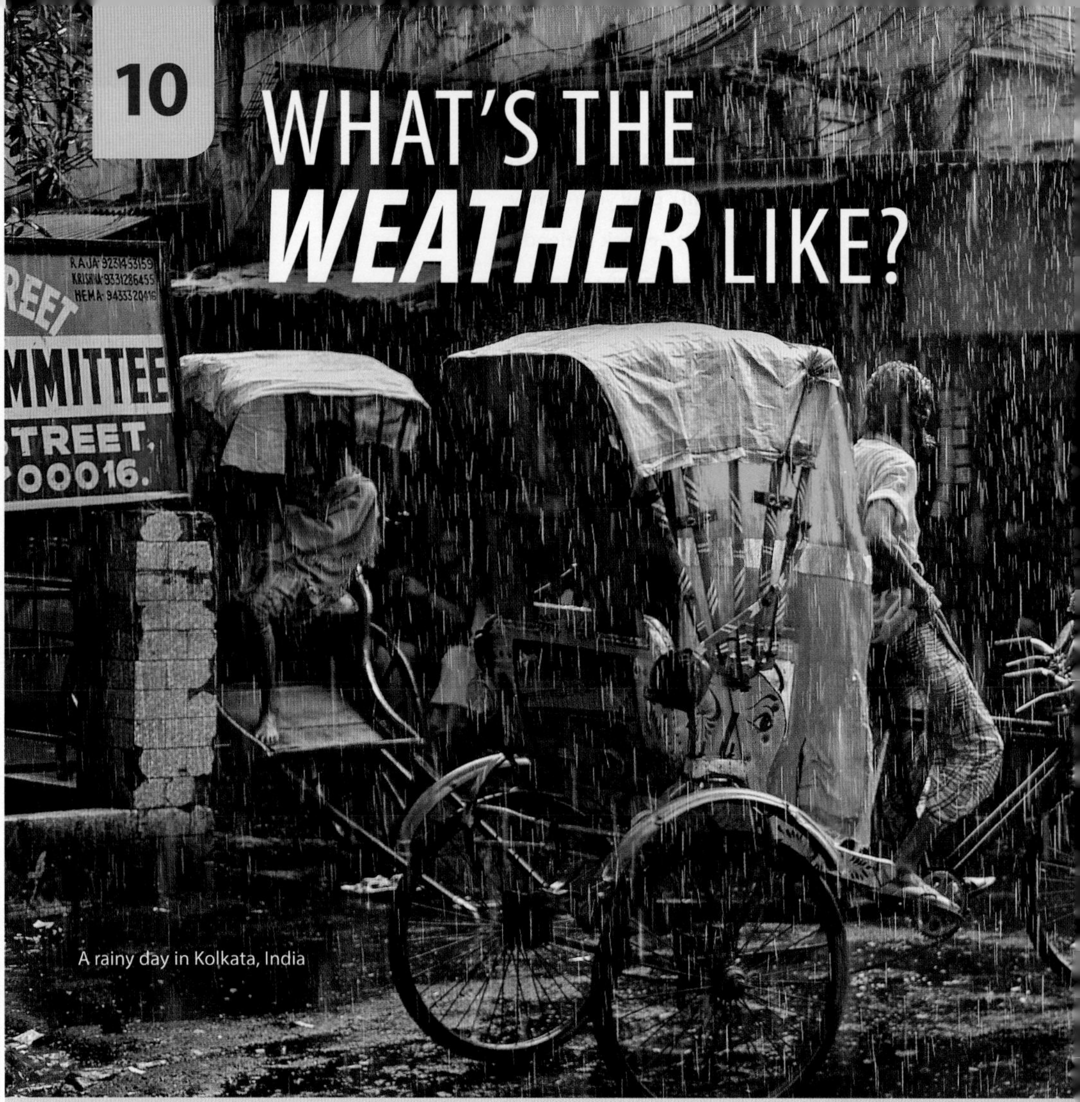

A rainy day in Kolkata, India

PREVIEW

A 10.1 **Listen.** Number the weather conditions in the order you hear them (**1–4**).

rainy 4

sunny 1

windy 3

stormy 2

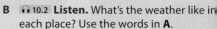

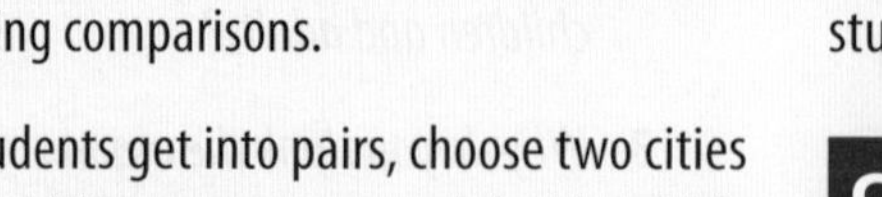

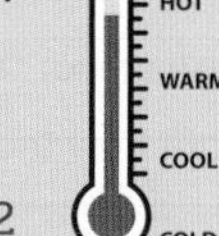

B 10.2 **Listen.** What's the weather like in each place? Use the words in **A**.

1 Shanghai cold, windy
2 Rio de Janeiro warm, rainy
3 Cape Town hot, windy
4 Stockholm cold, stormy

114

END OF UNIT PROJECT Have students make a graph about a city's temperature.

Tell students they are each going to do research about a city's temperatures. Ask students to look at the weather chart with average monthly temperatures on page 117.

Explain that after they do their research, they will combine their information with a partner's information.

As students look at the weather chart, ask students why the temperatures in the two countries are so different. (One city is in the Northern Hemisphere while the other is in the Southern Hemisphere. If necessary, explain that the Northern Hemisphere and the Southern Hemisphere have opposite seasons.) Point out that choosing two cities that aren't geographically near each other makes more interesting comparisons.

Have students get into pairs, choose two cities they would like to compare, and decide which city each will research.

Have students do the research and make their charts. (This can be assigned as homework.)

When students have finished making their charts, have students get into pairs and take turns discussing their city's information. Explain that they should use a pen that is a different color to draw their partner's information on their chart.

Collect completed graphs to check students' work.

CONTENT NOTE: STUDYING WEATHER

The study of weather is called meteorology. Meteorologists measure and look at the causes of weather conditions. They also forecast the weather by recording and putting together information about temperature, rainfall, wind speed and direction, air pressure, and humidity.

ABOUT THE PHOTO

This photo shows rain pouring down on a street in Kolkata, India. Kolkata has an average rainfall of 1,800 millimeters per year. India experiences two monsoon seasons annually—the summer monsoon, and the winter monsoon. India depends on the summer monsoon, which usually occurs from June to September. The summer monsoon is essential for agriculture, and helps dairy farms to keep their cows healthy. The rain brought by the monsoon also provides water for wells and aquifers. However, severe summer monsoons can result in floods and mudslides, causing great damage and loss of lives.

C **Talk with a partner.** What kind of weather do you like? *Answers will vary.*

What kind of weather do you like?

I like warm, sunny weather.

SCIENCE AND TECHNOLOGY

UNIT GOALS

- describe the weather in different places
- use language for talking about the weather
- learn how scientists study the weather

115

PREVIEW

Have students read the unit title to themselves as you read it aloud. Explain that in this unit they will learn to talk about the weather. Point to the word *weather* as you say it. As students follow along, read the photo caption aloud and point to the rain in the photo.

OPTIONAL Ask, *Do you like this weather? Do we often have weather like this?*

Have students find Kolkata, India, on a world map. Ask students what continent it is in (Asia).

A Explain to students that they will hear four sentences about the weather and they should number the weather conditions in the order they hear them, from one to four.

As they follow along in their books, read the types of weather aloud.

10.1 Play Audio Track 10.1. Play it again, if necessary. Check answers.

As students follow along, read the words on the right side of the thermometer aloud. Ask, *Is it hot today?* Have a student answer.

CHALLENGE Have students say what temperatures they think are *cold*, *cool*, *warm*, and *hot*. Have them compare ideas with a partner.

B Explain to students that they will hear a weather report about cities around the world and they should use the words in **A** to describe the weather in each city.

As students follow along, read the names of the cities aloud.

10.2 Play Audio Track 10.2. Play it again, if necessary. Check answers.

SUPPORT Ask students additional questions about where they are from using the vocabulary. For example: *Is it stormy at Christmas? Is it cold in July?*

C Tell students they will get into pairs and talk about the kind of weather they like. Model the conversation with a student.

Have students do the task.

OPTIONAL When pairs have finished discussing their ideas, take a poll (by having students raise their hands) to find out what kind of weather students like the most.

CHALLENGE Before students start the task, have them brainstorm other kinds of weather. (See **Other useful vocabulary**.)

UNIT GOALS

Direct students' attention to the **UNIT GOALS** box. Explain that these are some of the things students will learn in this unit. Point out that this unit is about science and technology. As students follow along, read each of the unit goals to the class. Remind students that at the end of the unit there is a self check.

LANGUAGE FOCUS

A Tell students they will listen to a conversation between Stig and Nadine.

🎧 10.3 Play Audio Track 10.3 as students listen and follow along in their books. If necessary, play the conversation again, pausing after each speaker so students can repeat.

As students follow along, read the question, *Are Stig and Nadine in the same country?* Have students provide evidence for their answer. (e.g., Nadine asks if Stig is enjoying his vacation in Sweden, which suggests she is not there. In Stig's question, he mentions Nadine is in South Africa, suggesting he is not there.) Explain that in natural English, we would not say the location if we were also there.

Have students work in pairs and practice the conversation once. Point out the bold words and read them aloud as students follow along in their books.

Tell students they will practice the conversation two more times, changing the bold words each time and swapping roles after the first time.

REAL ENGLISH

Direct students' attention to the expression in the **REAL ENGLISH** box. Explain that *What's up?* is an informal way of asking *How are you?* or *What have you been up to recently?* Point out that Nadine doesn't actually answer the question, and tell students this is acceptable. Tell students that another natural response is *Not much*. (Meaning nothing particularly special has happened recently.)

A: Hey. What's up?
B: Not much. You?

LANGUAGE FOCUS

A 🎧 10.3 **Listen and read.** Are Stig and Nadine in the same country? Then repeat the conversation and replace the words in **bold**. *No, they aren't.*

REAL ENGLISH What's up?

Stig: Hey, Nadine. What's up?

Nadine: Hi, Stig. Are you **enjoying your vacation** in Sweden? (**having a good time / having fun**)

Stig: Yes, I am. In fact, I'm **playing video games** with my cousins now. (**having lunch / chatting**)

Nadine: What's the weather like there?

Stig: It's minus 5 degrees and it's **snowy**. It's always **snowy** here in winter. (**icy / freezing**)

Nadine: That sounds cold!

Stig: Yeah, it is. So how's your vacation in South Africa?

Nadine: Not so good. It's too **hot** here! (**warm / sunny**)

B 🎧 10.4 **Look at the chart.** Then circle **T** for true or **F** for false.

TALKING ABOUT WEATHER	
What's the weather **like** today? **What's** the weather **like** in the summer? **What's** the weather **like** in April?	**It's** cold. **It's** always hot and dry. **It's** usually warm, but sometimes it's rainy.
Is it usually cold in the winter?	Yes, **it is**. / No, **it isn't**.
How hot **is** it? **How** cold **is** it?	**It's** (about) 30 degrees. **It's** (about) minus 12 degrees.

1 We use a *be* verb before weather adjectives like *rainy*. **T** (circled) **F**
2 We use *how* + adjective + *is it* to ask for detailed information. **T** (circled) **F**
3 We use time expressions at the beginning of questions. **T** **F** (circled)

B Ask students to look at the chart. Tell them that the chart teaches the language needed to talk about the weather.

🎧 10.4 Have students follow along as they listen to Audio Track 10.4.

SUPPORT Ask students to look at the board. Write, *What's = What is, It's = It is.* Point out that both the questions and the answers in the chart include the word *is*.

Read the first question aloud. Have one student answer by describing the real weather.

Read the second question aloud, as students follow along in their books. If necessary, explain that *summer* is a season.

CHALLENGE Tell students that many countries have four seasons. Have students name the seasons, telling them, if necessary (*spring*, *summer*, *autumn/fall*, *winter*).

C 10.5 **Look at the weather chart.** Complete the conversation. Then listen and check your answers.

Jake: What's the weather [1] **is** / (**like**) in Perth?

Leah: Well, it's always [2] **cool** / (**hot**) in January and February.

Jake: [3] **What is** / (**Is it**) always hot in the summer?

Leah: Yes, it is.

Jake: [4] (**How**) / **What** hot is it?

Leah: About 28 degrees at noon. [5] **Is** / (**What's**) the weather like in Ottawa in January and February?

Jake: Well, it's [6] **summer** / (**winter**) so it's always [7] (**cold and snowy**) / **warm and sunny**.

D **What's the weather like where you live?** Answer the questions. Talk about your answers with a partner. Answers will vary.

1 What's the weather like in March? __________

2 What's the weather like in October? __________

3 How hot is it in the summer? __________

4 Is it usually warm and sunny in August? __________

E **Choose three cities.** Write their weather conditions in the chart. Take turns asking about the weather with a partner. Answers will vary.

CITY	WEATHER	TEMPERATURE
London	warm and sunny	23°C

What's the weather like in London now?
It's warm and sunny.
Is it hot?
No, it isn't. It's 23 degrees.

Read the next two questions aloud, having students provide answers for the place they live.

Draw students' attention to the last two questions and answers. Explain how to say temperatures by telling students that temperatures are read as *(number) degrees*.

Explain that temperatures below zero are said *minus (number) degrees*. Tell students we normally do not say Fahrenheit or Celsius because it is usually obvious by the context and local customs. Ask students which they usually use. You might want to explain that Celsius is also called *Centigrade* in some countries.

SUPPORT Practice saying numbers. For example, emphasize the difference between *13* and *30*. Write some temperatures on the board and have students practice as a class until they are all comfortable saying temperatures.

Draw students' attention to the three statements under the chart.

Have students circle the correct answers. Check answers. Have students correct the last statement. (We use time expressions at the end of questions.)

C Ask students to study the weather chart for a moment. Ask, *What does the red line mean?* (the average temperature each month in Perth, Australia) Ask, *What does the blue line represent?* (the average temperature each month in Ottawa, Canada) Ask, *Which city has higher temperatures most of the year?* (Perth)

Have students use the information in the chart to help them choose the correct words to complete the conversation.

Tell students they will listen to the conversation and check their answers.

10.5 Play Audio Track 10.5. Check answers.

D Tell students they will think about the weather where they live. Have students read the questions and write answers.

Have students get into pairs and discuss their answers. If necessary, check answers as a class.

E Tell students they are going to play a game in pairs. Explain that they will ask and answer questions to find out about the weather and temperatures in different cities. Have students choose three different cities, writing them in the chart.

Have students complete the chart by writing the weather and temperature for each city. You may need to allow students to do some research (e.g., with their electronic devices).

Model the conversation with a student.

Have students get into pairs and take turns asking and answering questions about their cities.

THE REAL WORLD

As students follow along in their books, read the title and photo caption aloud. Ask, *What is a shearwater?* (It is a kind of bird.)

A Tell students they will watch a video about scientists who study the weather by using birds. Tell students to circle **T** if the statement is true and **F** if it is false. As students follow along, read the statements aloud.

▶ 10.1 Play Video 10.1. Check answers.

B Have students look at the photos.

As students follow along in their books, read the sentences aloud. Tell students they will watch the video again and should write words to complete the descriptions of the photos.

▶ 10.1 Play Video 10.1. Check answers.

OPTIONAL Ask students the following True/False questions.

1 *Shearwaters fly thousands of kilometers every spring.* (False. They fly thousands of kilometers every year.)

2 *Katsufumi Sato is a scientist.* (True.)

3 *Shearwaters lay their eggs in holes in the ground.* (True.)

C Tell students they must decide if each sentence presents an advantage or a disadvantage of using birds to collect weather data, writing **A** or **D**, respectively. As students follow along in their books, read the sentences aloud.

Have students do the task. Check answers.

D CRITICAL THINKING

As students follow along, read the questions aloud. Have students get into pairs and discuss their ideas.

THE REAL WORLD

WEATHER BIRDS

ABOUT THE PHOTO

This photo shows Dr. Katsufumi Sato holding a streaked shearwater. Shearwater birds live most of their lives out at sea in flocks, feeding on fish that come close to the surface of the sea. These birds only return to land to mate, and Dr. Sato and his team use this opportunity to put data recorders on the birds before they go out to sea again. It is anticipated that in the future, the data collected from seabirds like the shearwater can make weather forecasting more accurate.

Katsufumi Sato holding a shearwater

A ▶ 10.1 **Watch the video.** Circle **T** for true or **F** for false.

1 Katsufumi and his team study birds that spend a long time at sea. (T) F
2 In the winter, shearwaters fly to East Asia to sleep. T (F)
3 Data recorders on the birds collect information about the weather. (T) F

B ▶ 10.1 **Watch again.** Complete the descriptions of the photos.

1 Scientists are looking for a(n) adult bird.

2 Scientists put a data recorder on the bird's leg.

3 The birds help collect information such as wind speed and surface current.

118 Unit 10

PROJECT As students follow along, read the project instructions aloud. Tell students they should make notes about the weather forecast so it is easier to check the accuracy the next day. Have students notice the weather the next day and make notes, deciding if the forecast was accurate.

Set a deadline by which students must bring their details to class. In the next lesson, have students discuss their findings.

CHALLENGE Tell students that scientists try to predict extreme weather so that people will be prepared and stay safe. Have students name some types of extreme weather. (See **Other useful vocabulary**.) Have students say whether they have experienced these types of weather before.

PRONUNCIATION

Tell students that when they talk about weather, they need to pronounce the final *-y* sound so that the listener understands which word they are saying. Explain that they will practice this.

C **Read the sentences below.** Is each one an advantage (A) or a disadvantage (D) of using birds to collect weather data?

1 Data recorders can fall off the birds when they fly. D
2 The data recorders on the birds don't cost a lot to make. A
3 Scientists can't control where the birds travel. D
4 Birds can travel to parts of the ocean that are difficult to reach. A

D CRITICAL THINKING Evaluating **Talk with a partner.** Do you think it's OK to use birds this way? What are the possible problems for the birds? Answers will vary.

PROJECT Check tomorrow's weather forecast. The next day, record details of the weather in your notebook. Was the forecast accurate?

PRONUNCIATION final *-y* sound

10.6 **Listen.** Circle the words you hear. Then listen again and repeat the sentences.

1 (snow) snowy   3 rain (rainy)
2 (storm) stormy   4 cloud (cloudy)

COMMUNICATION

Work with a partner. Student A: Look at the weather map below. **Student B:** Turn to page 153. Ask and answer questions to complete the temperatures and weather conditions on your map.

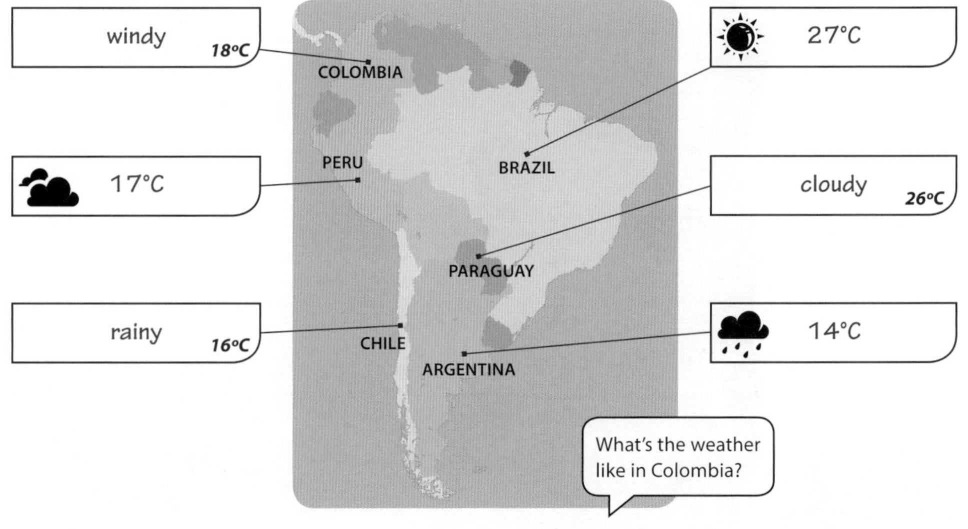

As students follow along, read the names of the countries aloud.

Model the example. Have students do the task, taking turns asking and answering questions. Check answers.

OPTIONAL Tell students they are going to get into pairs and take turns reporting the weather in the countries on the map.

Show students a short weather clip from TV or the internet. Ask students to describe a typical weather report, providing assistance as needed. (A newscaster in the studio often asks the weather reporter about the weather. The weather reporter then talks about the weather while using a large weather map behind him or her, or gives the report while standing outside—particularly in major storms.)

Have students get into pairs and do the task.

CHALLENGE Direct students' attention to the temperatures. Tell students that although most countries now use the Celsius scale, the Fahrenheit scale is still used in the United States, Belize, and several other countries.

Explain that normal body temperature is 37°C. Tell them that water freezes at 0°C and boils at 100°C. Have students convert these temperatures to Fahrenheit. Give them the following formula for converting Celsius to Fahrenheit: Multiply the Celsius temperature by 9/5. Add 32 to that number.

Have students look at the words and identify the differences (with and without the final *-y* sound). Tell students they will listen to four short sentences, and for each sentence they need to decide which word the speaker uses and circle it.

10.6 Play Audio Track 10.6. Play it again, if necessary. Check answers.

10.6 Play Audio Track 10.6, pausing after each sentence so students can repeat.

COMMUNICATION

Tell students to get into pairs and decide who will be Student A and who will be Student B. Have the Student Bs turn to page 153.

Explain that they have the same weather map but with different information missing. Tell students they need to ask and answer questions about the temperatures and weather conditions in the countries on the maps to complete their weather maps.

CONTENT NOTE: FAHRENHEIT AND CELSIUS

The Fahrenheit scale was created in 1724. It was used until the 1960s and 1970s, when most countries started to use the Celsius scale. The same degree symbol (°) is used for Celsius and Fahrenheit, and, when necessary, a capital *C* or capital *F* is added.

READING

A Ask students to look at the photo and read the caption. As students follow along, read the question and answer choices aloud. Have students circle their answer but don't check answers yet.

B Ask students to read the title. Ask, *What do you think a weather balloon does?* Have students answer.

C Tell students that they will skim the text and find out what happens to the balloon.

Have students do the task. Check answers.

Ask students if their answers for **A** and **B** were correct.

Give students the opportunity to read the article in more detail so they can more fully comprehend it and answer the **COMPREHENSION** questions.

OPTIONAL The text can also be used as a listening activity. Have students close their books. Tell students they will listen to the passage.

10.7 Play Audio Track 10.7. Ask students to get into pairs and discuss what information they heard. Then have them read the article more carefully.

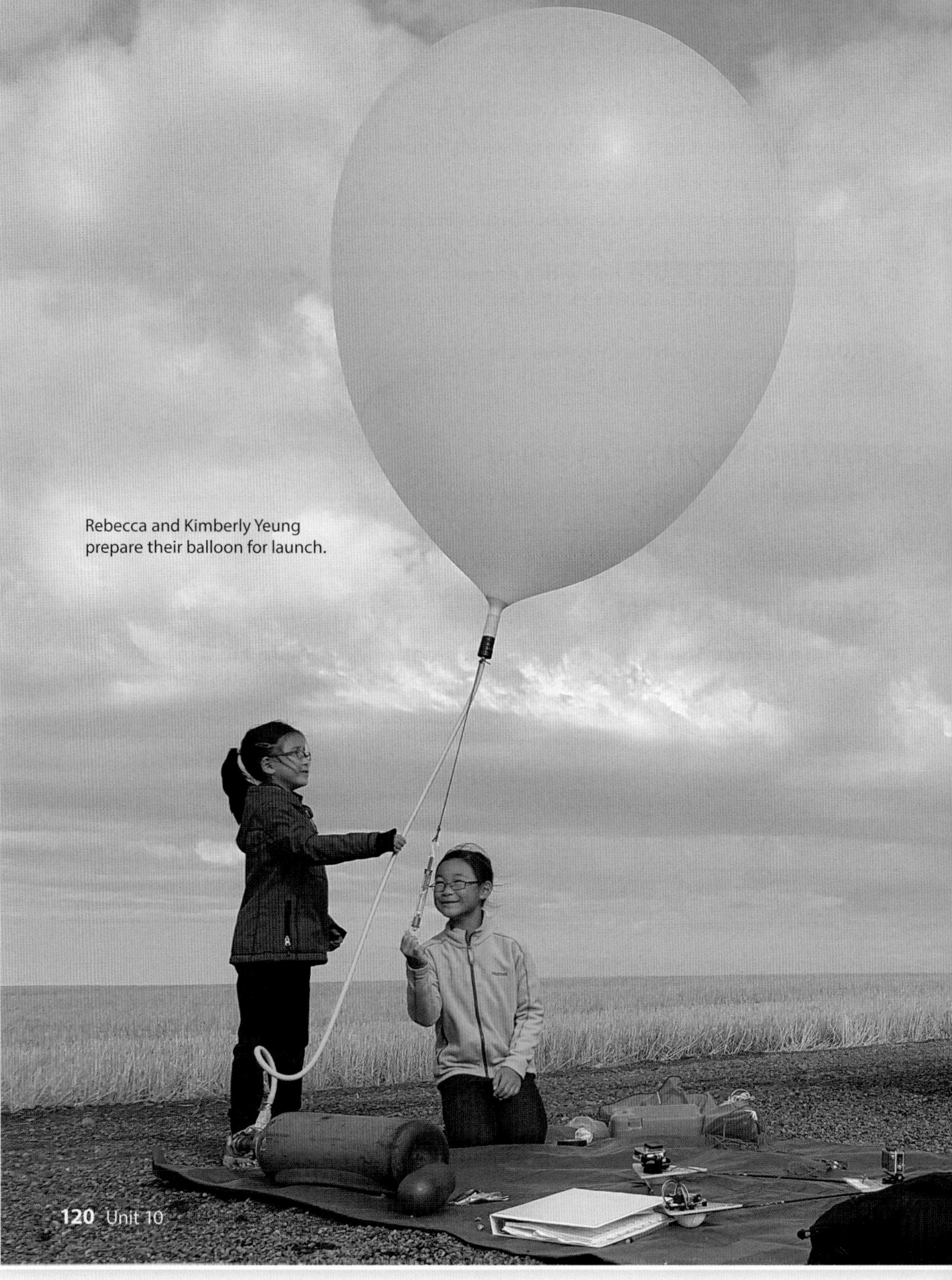

Rebecca and Kimberly Yeung prepare their balloon for launch.

120 Unit 10

CONTENT NOTE: WEATHER BALLOONS

In order to collect information that is used in computer algorithms to predict weather (e.g., temperature, humidity, wind information) around the world, weather balloons are launched twice a day from about 900 locations.

Additional Activities to Use with the Reading

Inference

Tell students sometimes they must infer a meaning. Explain that when we infer we understand a point even if the information is not said directly. Have students read the first sentence in paragraph C. Ask, *Have they launched a balloon before?* (No. This is their first time.)

Pronunciation (Focused)

If necessary, review the pronunciation of *-y*. Tell students to listen to the first paragraph and notice the pronunciation of *windy*.

10.7 Play Audio Track 10.7. Play it again, having students repeat.

Avoiding Repetition

Tell students that using the same words several times in sentences near each other makes a passage sound less developed. Explain that instead we usually use other words that are good substitutes.

ABOUT THE PHOTO

This photo shows sisters Rebecca and Kimberly Yeung preparing their first Loki Lego Launcher for launch in 2015. The sisters created the Loki Lego Launcher with the goal of getting as close to space as possible. The launcher was made with bent archery arrows and plywood to make it as light as possible. Sensors and two action cameras were attached to the launcher, and the sisters placed a photo of their cat Loki and a miniature R2-D2 Lego figure in front of one of the cameras.

READING

A **Look at the photo.** What do you think the two girls are doing?

- a taking a photo of the area
- ⓑ working on a science project
- c looking for animals

B **Read the title.** What do you think a weather balloon does? It collects weather data such as wind speed and temperature.

C **Skim the article.** What happens to the balloon? It travels up to 23,000 meters.

A WEATHER BALLOON PROJECT

A 10.7 What's the weather like today? Is it hot or windy? Weather balloons can help scientists find out. Every day, thousands of weather balloons fly high above the clouds. The balloons **record** wind speed and **temperature**. They send information to scientists.

B Rebecca and Kimberly Yeung are two sisters from the United States. Their favorite school subject is science, and they like to do **projects**. One of their projects is making a weather balloon. They call it the Loki Lego Launcher—Loki is the name of their cat!

C Today, the Yeung sisters are **launching** their balloon for the first time. It travels up to 23,000 meters! The girls are very excited. The balloon records information for them to study.

D Rebecca and Kimberly **upload** a video of their balloon launch on their YouTube channel. It gets more than 300,000 **views**—they're famous! Now, they're planning their next launch.

Ask students to find the word *information* in the last sentence of the first paragraph of the text. Tell students that this has been explained earlier in the paragraph. Have students identify what information this represents (wind speed and temperature).

Tell students that the author used many different words to refer to *Rebecca and Kimberly Yeung*. Ask students to identify another word (*girls* in paragraph C), phrase (*the Yeung sisters* in paragraph C, *Rebecca and Kimberly* without *Yeung* in paragraph D), and pronouns (*they, them*).

Emphasize that this variety makes the article more interesting and succinct. To demonstrate this, read paragraph C. Then read it again without all of the substitutions. (*Today, Rebecca and Kimberly Yeung are launching their balloon for the first time. The balloon travels up to 23,000 meters! Rebecca and Kimberly Yeung are very excited. The balloon records information for Rebecca and Kimberly Yeung to study.*) Ask which version is easier to read and understand.

Tell students that as they read they need to look for words that are being used as substitutes for similar words. Also encourage them to remember this example when they are writing.

Paragraph Construction

Tell students that each paragraph has a new idea in it. Ask students to identify the gist (main idea) of each paragraph.
(A: Introduction—purpose of weather balloons. B: Introducing the sisters and their project. C: Information about the launch.
D: What happens after the launch.)

Weather and Climate

Explain to students that the question *What's the weather like today?* asks about the weather conditions outdoors in a given place at a given time.

Tell them that when we want to ask what the weather is like in a country or place in general we ask about *climate* instead of *weather*. Tell students that the climate of a place describes the general weather conditions occurring over a period of years.

Ask students to think about the weather and climate of their area.

Skills for Meeting New People

Explain to students that weather is a nonthreatening topic that people who do not know each other well can easily discuss. Give them the following example: When we get into an elevator with someone we don't know well, we may say *Wow! It's really hot!* The other person will agree.

This short discussion establishes a common bond without exchanging any personal information.

Have students think of other weather-related comments and questions that they could use to talk with people they don't really know.

COMPREHENSION

A EXAM PRACTICE

There are many kinds of multiple-choice test items, and students must practice and become proficient in each type.

In order to answer **reference** items, students must understand who or what is being replaced. Test items usually have:

- a personal pronoun, such as *I*, *you*, *it*, and *they*.
- a possessive pronoun, including *my*, *its*, and *their*.
- a demonstrative pronoun like *these*, *that*, and *such*.
- an interrogative pronoun, for example *who*, *what*, and *which*.
- an indefinite pronoun, for instance *a few*, *some*, *all*, and *anything*.

Students must not assume that the correct answer is the noun nearest the pronoun.

Have students read the questions to themselves and circle the correct answers. Check answers.

DO YOU KNOW?

Read the statement and answer options aloud, as students follow along. Have students guess before providing the answer (a).

CONTENT NOTE: CLOUD WEIGHT

Although many people may think of clouds as weightless, they are made of water, which has weight. Clouds float over our heads, however, because the air below them is even heavier than the clouds.

B Tell students that when they take tests, it is important to think about where the information is so they can find it quickly. Remind them that on tests, they cannot reread the entire article each time they need to answer a question.

Explain that they should write the letter of the paragraph, **A–D**, indicating where the information is.

As students follow along, read the four items of information aloud.

Have students do the task. Check answers as a class.

OPTIONAL Ask students additional *True/False* comprehension questions.

1 *Weather balloons can fly over clouds.* (True.)
2 *Rebecca and Kimberly live in Singapore.* (False. They are from the United States.)
3 *The sisters take a video when they launch their balloon.* (True.)
4 *The girls want to launch more weather balloons.* (True.)

COMPREHENSION

A Answer the questions about *A Weather Balloon Project*.

1 DETAIL Which of the following things does the weather balloon NOT record?
   a wind speed   b air temperature   (c) water temperature

2 PURPOSE What's the purpose of paragraph B?
   a to describe the Yeung sisters' family
   (b) to introduce the Yeung sisters and their project
   c to describe how the Yeung sisters make their weather balloon

3 DETAIL The girls name their weather balloon after their _____.
   (a) pet   b father   c favorite movie character

4 REFERENCE The word *It* in the second sentence of paragraph C refers to _____.
   (a) the balloon   b their cat   c the weather

5 INFERENCE Which of the following can you infer from the article?
   a The girls live outside the city.
   (b) The girls put data recorders on the weather balloon.
   c The girls' weather balloon project is not successful.

DO YOU KNOW?

Clouds can weigh as much as 100 elephants.
(a) True
b False

B Read the article again. Which paragraph (**A–D**) has the following information?

1 the distance the balloon travels ___C___
2 the number of weather balloons in the sky ___A___
3 the number of times people watch the girls' video ___D___
4 why the balloon is called the Loki Lego Launcher ___B___

C CRITICAL THINKING Applying

Talk with a partner. Who uses the information from the weather balloons? What do you think they use it for?
Answers will vary.

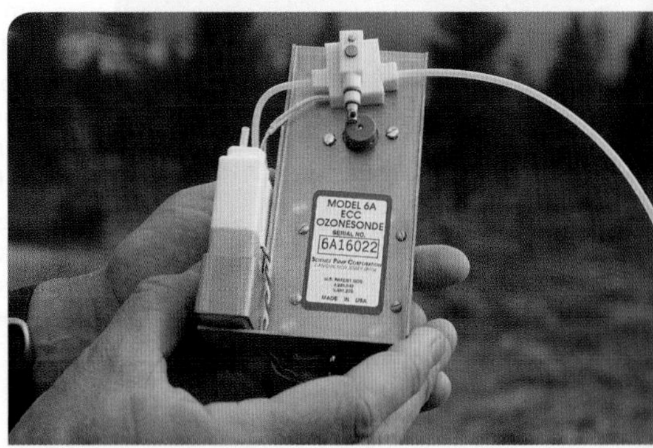

One of the data recorders from a weather balloon

VOCABULARY

A **Find the words below in the article.** Then complete the sentences.

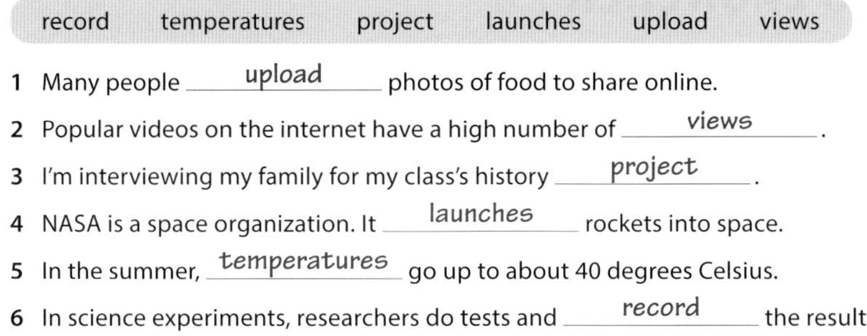

record | temperatures | project | launches | upload | views

1 Many people ___upload___ photos of food to share online.

2 Popular videos on the internet have a high number of ___views___.

3 I'm interviewing my family for my class's history ___project___.

4 NASA is a space organization. It ___launches___ rockets into space.

5 In the summer, ___temperatures___ go up to about 40 degrees Celsius.

6 In science experiments, researchers do tests and ___record___ the results.

B **Read the information below.** Then circle the correct answers.

We can add *out* to some verbs to make phrasal verbs.
look out: be careful
find out: discover
hang out: spend time with your friends
go out: go to a place outside the house

1 **Go** / **(Look)** out! There's a car coming.

2 My parents always **(go)** / **find** out on Friday evenings.

3 You can **(find)** / **look** out lots of information on the internet.

4 I often **go** / **(hang)** out with my best friend at his house.

IDIOM

"I'm under the weather" means ____.
(a) I feel sick
b I feel happy

WRITING

A **Read the beginning of an email about the weather in someone's country.**

B **Imagine your friend wants to visit your country.** Make notes about the weather and suitable clothes to wear.

C **Write an email to your friend.**
Answers will vary.

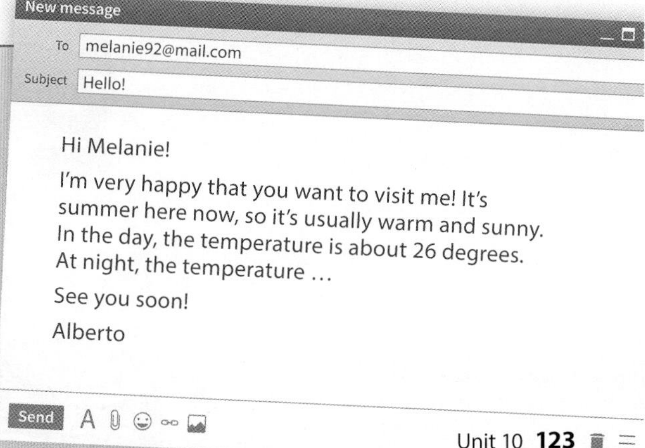

New message
To melanie92@mail.com
Subject Hello!
Hi Melanie!
I'm very happy that you want to visit me! It's summer here now, so it's usually warm and sunny. In the day, the temperature is about 26 degrees. At night, the temperature …
See you soon!
Alberto
Send

Unit 10 **123**

C CRITICAL THINKING

As students follow along, read the questions. Have students get into pairs and discuss it.

VOCABULARY

A As students follow along, read the words in the box aloud. Have students find them in the **READING** passage.

Have students write the correct words to complete the sentences. Check answers.

B As students follow along, read the information in the box aloud. Have students circle the correct words to complete the sentences. Check answers as a class.

CHALLENGE Have students do research about other phrasal verbs with *out* (e.g., *figure out*, *turn out*, *phase out*, *work out*) and make sentences with them.

IDIOM

As students follow along in their books, read the statement and answer options aloud. Ask several students to guess the answer before providing it (a). Give students another example: *He has a really bad cold. He feels under the weather*.

WRITING

Tell students that they are going to write an email.

A As students follow along, read the example email aloud. If necessary, remind students about important elements of an email (e.g., the greeting, closing, when to start on a new line). Ask, *What did Alberto say first?* (He showed his excitement about her request to visit his country.)

B Tell students to imagine their friend wants to visit their country. Have them make notes about what the weather is like and what kind of clothes their friend should bring.

C Have students use their notes from **B** to write an email.

Give students a time limit for finishing the email, and set a minimum number of sentences students must write (e.g., five).

OPTIONAL After students have completed their emails, have them take turns reading them with a partner. Encourage them to ask their partner questions about their suggestions for clothes.

VIDEO

CONTENT NOTE: THE YEUNG SISTERS

The Yeung sisters' projects started after their father encouraged them to find something they could do that would require both setting goals and working toward solutions. In April 2016, their project was part of a White House Science Fair, and the girls met then-President Obama. In addition to their cat, the Loki Lego Launcher is named after the Lego figures that the girls attach to their balloons.

Tell students they are going to watch a video about the second version of the weather balloon that they read about in the **READING** passage. As students follow along in their books, read the title, the sentence about the video, and the photo caption aloud.

OPTIONAL Have students discuss what they remember about the Yeung sisters and their weather balloon from the **READING** section.

BEFORE YOU WATCH

Ask students to read the question and circle their guess.

WHILE YOU WATCH

A Tell students they will watch the video and they should circle **T** if the statement is true and **F** if it is false. As students follow along, read the sentences aloud.

▶ 10.2 Play Video 10.2. If necessary, play the video again. Check answers.

B Explain to students that they will watch the video again and should complete each sentence by writing a word or number. As students follow along in their books, read the sentences aloud.

▶ 10.2 Play Video 10.2. If necessary, play the video again. Check answers.

Discuss students' answers from **BEFORE YOU WATCH**.

VIDEO **ABOUT THE VIDEO** Rebecca and Kimberly Yeung build a weather balloon.

LOKI LEGO LAUNCHER 2.0

Before You Watch

Guess. Where is the best place to launch a weather balloon?

a near an airport b in the middle of a lake (c) in a field with no buildings

While You Watch

A ▶ 10.2 **Watch the video.** Circle **T** for true or **F** for false.

1 The weather is good on the day of the balloon launch. (T) F
2 The camera on the weather balloon stops working halfway. T (F)
3 The weather balloon goes above 30,000 meters. (T) F

B ▶ 10.2 **Watch again.** Complete each sentence with a word or a number.

1 The girls want their weather balloon to go up to 27,000 meters.
2 The girls' father helps them put gas into the balloon.
3 The data recorders collect information about height, wind speed, and temperature.
4 The camera takes photos and videos of the Earth.
5 The weather balloon goes up to 31,000 meters.

After You Watch

Talk with a partner. The weather balloon is called the Loki Lego Launcher 2.0. Why do the girls call it "2.0"? It's the second version of their weather balloon.

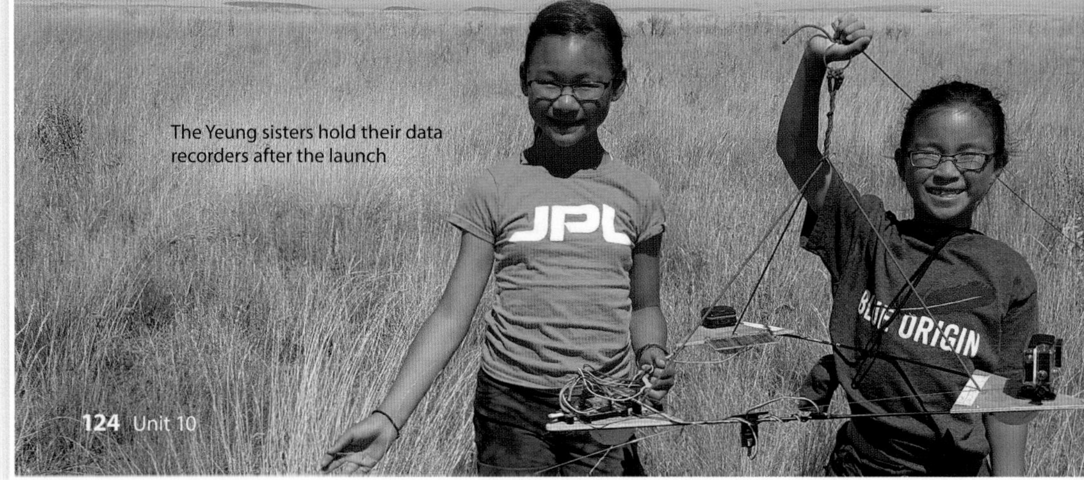

The Yeung sisters hold their data recorders after the launch

OPTIONAL Ask students additional comprehension questions.

1 *In what month do they launch Loki Lego Launcher 2.0?* (August)

2 *What does* takeoff *mean?* (the beginning of the launch)

3 *Do they have good results from the balloon?* (Yes. It goes higher than the first one, and they get lots of information from the data recorders and camera.)

CHALLENGE Ask, *Why do you think they add a photo of their cat, Loki?* Have students get into pairs and discuss their ideas.

AFTER YOU WATCH

Tell students they are going to get into pairs and talk about the video. As students follow along in their books, read the question aloud.

Have students get into pairs and discuss their ideas. Then have students share their ideas with the class.

ABOUT THE PHOTO

This photo shows Rebecca and Kimberly Yeung holding the data recorders for the second Loki Lego Launcher after the launch. After their previous success with the first Loki Lego Launcher, the sisters created Loki Lego Launcher 2.0, an improved version of the first launcher. Their aim was to reach a higher altitude and test if solar panels worked better if they were closer to the sun. To reach a higher altitude, they used a larger balloon than the balloon used in the first version of the launcher.

REVIEW

A Read the descriptions. Match them to the most suitable words.

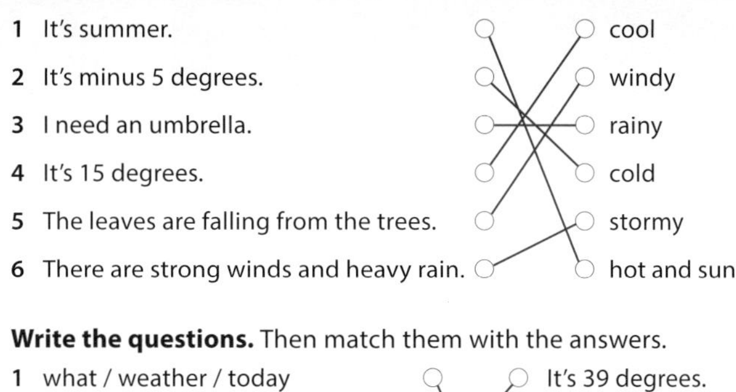

1 It's summer. — cool
2 It's minus 5 degrees. — windy
3 I need an umbrella. — rainy
4 It's 15 degrees. — cold
5 The leaves are falling from the trees. — stormy
6 There are strong winds and heavy rain. — hot and sunny

B Write the questions. Then match them with the answers.

1 what / weather / today
What's the weather like today? — It's 39 degrees.

2 how / hot / it
How hot is it? — Yes, it is.

3 is / very cold / the winter
Is it very cold in the winter? — It's warm and sunny.

C Complete the sentences. Use the words in the box.

look	go	find	hang

1 I usually stay home on the weekends. I don't ___go___ out.
2 My friends and I always ___hang___ out at the café near our school.
3 There are holes in the ground, so ___look___ out for them when you walk.
4 Visit the store's website to ___find___ out more about the things they sell.

SELF CHECK Now I can ...

- [ ] describe the weather in different places
- [ ] use language for talking about the weather
- [ ] talk about how scientists study the weather

REVIEW

Explain to students that they are going to review the material from the unit and this will help them remember what they have studied.

A Explain that activity **A** reviews vocabulary from the unit. Have students match the descriptions to the correct words. Check answers as a class.

CHALLENGE Point out that the answer to **1** is *hot and sunny*. Explain that this may not be true in all countries. Explain seasons in different areas of the world. (See **TEACHING NOTE.**)

TEACHING NOTE: SEASONS

Countries located near the equator generally have two seasons while countries farther away have four. However, some countries may have more—it is sometimes said that Japan has six seasons—winter, spring, rainy, summer, typhoon, and autumn.

B Explain that activity **B** reviews the grammar from the unit. Tell students they have to do two things. First, have them write questions using the words provided. Next, have students match the questions with the answers. Have students get into pairs and check their answers, before you randomly call on students to give the answers.

C Remind students that they studied phrasal verbs with *out* in **VOCABULARY** activity **B**. Have them use the words in the box to complete the sentences.

Check answers.

SELF CHECK

These *I can* statements provide vital feedback on students' perceived ability to use the language from the unit. If you find students are reluctant to check that they can do the skills, consider asking them to rate themselves from 1 (not very confident) to 3 (very confident).

SUPPORT If students lack confidence to put a check next to each statement, have them get into pairs. Tell them they will make quiz questions for another pair, focusing on the three **SELF CHECK** points.

Give an example: *What is the weather like in the summer?*

Have students make their quiz questions, including answers.

Have two pairs get together and take turns asking and answering their questions.

After students have finished reviewing, confirm they have confidence with the material, providing additional review in class as necessary.

UNIT 11

I WENT TO AUSTRALIA!

CONTENT AREA: PEOPLE AND PLACES

Topic: vacations, vacation activities

Vocabulary: activities: go sightseeing, visit a museum, stay at a hotel, go camping, go cycling, go hiking; **past tense verbs:** was, went, visited, stayed, were, did, climbed, got, saw, had, walked, took, played, enjoyed; **other words:** vacation, adventure, trip, arrive, journey, celebrate, desert, tired, finally

Grammar: simple past

Extra material: a map of Australia, a world map

Other useful vocabulary: past tense verbs: boarded, rode, got on, got off, reserved, checked in, landed, took off, camped, cruised

A group of campers in Gawler Ranges, Australia

END OF UNIT PROJECT Have students do a presentation about an imaginary trip. Tell students they have to imagine they went on a trip with their family, friends, or classmates. Explain that they will have to give a group presentation about this trip.

Tell students they must do research and decide:

- when they went (what season).
- how long they stayed.
- what they saw.

Explain that during their presentation, they should tell the class all of these details. Tell them they should have photos of the places they visited and say one or two things about each place. Also tell students that they should show the class a map and talk about the order in which they visited the various places.

Have students get into groups and decide where they are going to imagine they visited.

Have the groups make their plan, do the research, and prepare their presentations.

In class, have groups take turns giving their presentations.

When all the presentations are finished, have the class decide which trip sounds the most interesting.

CONTENT NOTE: AUSTRALIA

The Commonwealth of Australia, more often just called Australia, is the only country in the world that is its own continent. It is the sixth largest country in the world, and the largest country without land borders. Australia has an abundance of natural resources and good land for growing food.

The capital of Australia is Canberra. English is widely used, although there are many other languages that are also used. The Australian dollar is the country's currency.

ABOUT THE PHOTO

This photo shows a group of campers under the Milky Way at Gawler Ranges National Park, South Australia. Away from the light pollution of the city, the Milky Way can be seen clearly at Gawler Ranges. The national park is home to rare and threatened plants and animals, such as the crimson mallee and the yellow-footed rock-wallaby. Visitors who want to camp in the national park have six different campgrounds to choose from. A famous spot in the national park is the Organ Pipes, where visitors can climb to the top of rock formations that were formed over 1,500 million years ago as a result of volcanic eruptions.

PREVIEW

A 11.1 **Listen.** Check (✓) the activities that Koji did.

☑ went sightseeing

☑ visited a museum

☐ stayed at a hotel

☑ went camping

☐ went cycling

☑ went hiking

B 11.1 **Listen again.** Write the activities Koji did. Use the activities in **A**.

In the city:
went sightseeing, visited a museum

Outside the city:
went camping, went hiking

C **Talk with a partner.** What activities do you like to do on vacation?

I like to go sightseeing.

I like to go camping.

Answers will vary.

PEOPLE AND PLACES

UNIT GOALS

- describe your travel activities
- use language for talking about events in the past
- learn about different adventures

127

A Tell students they will hear a short conversation about Koji's vacation and they should check the activities Koji did. As they follow along, read the activities aloud. Have students look at the verbs. Explain that we use these verbs to talk about things that have already happened.

11.1 Play Audio Track 11.1. Play it again, if necessary. Check answers.

SUPPORT Ask students to look at the verb *went* and explain that the present tense verb is *go*.

B Tell students they will listen again and should classify the activities Koji did according to whether he did them in or outside the city.

11.1 Play Audio Track 11.1. Play it again, if necessary. Check answers.

C As students follow along, read the question aloud.

Model the conversation with a student.

Have students get into pairs and discuss the question.

CHALLENGE Have students brainstorm other vocabulary they might use when talking about a trip they took. (See **Other useful vocabulary**.)

PREVIEW

Have students read the unit title to themselves as you read it aloud. Explain that in this unit they will learn to talk about vacations and vacation activities.

Ask students what time of the year people often take vacations in their country.

OPTIONAL As students follow along in their books, read the photo caption aloud. Have students find Australia on a world map. Also have students study a map of Australia to learn more about the country.

Then have students use adjectives to describe the photo (e.g., *beautiful, exciting, fun, amazing*).

UNIT GOALS

Direct students' attention to the **UNIT GOALS** box. Explain that these are some of the things students will learn in this unit. Point out that this unit is about people and places. As students follow along, read each of the unit goals to the class. Explain any words students do not know. Explain to students that at the end of the unit there is a self check that allows them to see if they have accomplished each goal.

LANGUAGE FOCUS

A Tell students they will listen to a conversation in which Ming tells Maya about his vacation.

11.2 Play Audio Track 11.2 as students listen and follow along in their books. If necessary, play the conversation again, pausing after each speaker so students can repeat.

As students follow along, read the question, *Where did Ming go for his vacation?* Have students answer.

OPTIONAL Ask students to find *well* in Ming's first and second utterances. Tell students we often use *well* to think for a minute before answering a question. We also use it to start or continue a story rather than starting it abruptly. In this case, it is used as a softener.

Have students work in pairs and practice the conversation once. Point out the bold words and read them aloud as students follow along in their books. You might want to have students repeat the words after you say them.

Tell students they will practice the conversation two more times, changing the bold words each time and swapping roles after the first time.

LANGUAGE FOCUS

A 11.2 **Listen and read.** Where did Ming go for his vacation? Then repeat the conversation and replace the words in **bold**. *He went to Sydney, Canada.*

REAL ENGLISH That sounds great!

Maya: How was your **vacation**, Ming? (**adventure** / **trip**)
Ming: Well, it was good and bad.
Maya: Why's that?
Ming: Well, my **dad** got us air tickets to Sydney. My family loves Australia. (**brother** / **grandfather**)
Maya: OK … so what did you do?
Ming: We went to a **museum**. We saw the harbor. We had fun. (**restaurant** / **mall**)
Maya: That sounds **great**! So what was the problem? (**amazing** / **good**)
Ming: He got air tickets to Sydney, Canada, not Sydney, Australia! We went to the wrong country!

B 11.3 **Look at the chart.** Then match the rules of the simple past with the examples below.

TALKING ABOUT PAST EVENTS (USING SIMPLE PAST)	
How **was** your vacation? How **were** the beaches?	It **was** amazing! They **were** beautiful!
What **did** you **do**?	I **stayed** at home. I **swam** in a river. I **ate** a lot of good food.
Did you **go** camping?	Yes, I **did**. / No, I **didn't**.
When **did** you **go**?	I went **last summer** / **last week** / **last year**.

1 Add *-ed* or *-d* to regular verbs to make the simple past.
2 The spelling of some regular verbs changes a little.
3 Irregular verbs have different simple past forms.

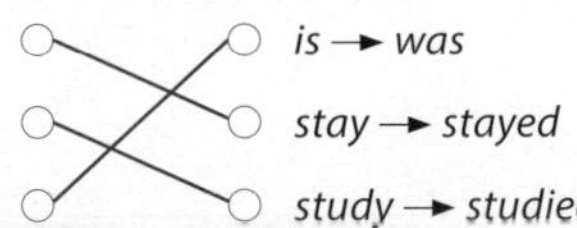

REAL ENGLISH

Direct students' attention to the expression in the **REAL ENGLISH** box. Explain that *That sounds great!* is used to positively react to something you were told. It can also be used to say *yes* to a suggestion or offer.
For example:

A: What are you doing? Do you want to go shopping?
B: That sounds great! Let's go!

B Ask students to look at the chart. Explain that they are going to study how to talk about something that happened in the past. On a calendar, point to the current date and say *today*. Point to the day before as you say *in the past*.

11.3 Have students follow along as they listen to Audio Track 11.3.

As students follow along in their books, read the first three questions and answers aloud, as well as the last question and answer. Explain that *How*, *What*, and *When* questions ask for specific information about a time or experience, and the answer cannot be *Yes/No*.

Read the fourth question and answer aloud as students follow along in their books. Point out that the answer is *Yes/No*. Tell students that *did* is the past tense of *do*.

C Write the past forms of the verbs. Use the words in the box.

~~liked~~ got went climbed saw had did walked

1 like → liked
2 go → went
3 have → had
4 do → did
5 walk → walked
6 see → saw
7 climb → climbed
8 get → got

D 11.4 **Complete the conversation.** Write the past forms of the verbs. Then listen and check your answers.

Jasmine: How [1] was (**be**) your weekend, Tiago?

Tiago: Great, thanks! I [2] went (**go**) to the beach with my cousins.

Jasmine: Really? What [3] did you do (**do**) there?

Tiago: Well, we [4] played (**play**) volleyball. We also [5] had (**have**) a barbecue!

Jasmine: That sounds great!

Tiago: Yeah, we really [6] enjoyed (**enjoy**) ourselves!

E Play a game. Work in small groups. Take turns to add a sentence and make a story.

Yesterday I went to the park …
It was hot and sunny …
… I saw many people exercising.

Answers will vary.

Explain that when we ask about the past, we only use one past tense verb in the question. Have students find the past tense verb in each question (*was*, *were*, *did*).

Ask students to look at the responses on the right side of the chart. Explain that there are two kinds of past tense verbs. The first, regular verbs, are made by adding *-ed* to the basic verb. Have students look at the responses and identify this verb (*stay–stayed*).

Tell students that the second kind of verb is called an irregular verb. Explain that for these verbs the entire word changes. Have students identify the irregular verbs in the chart (*was*, *were*, *swam*, *ate*, *did*, *went*) and the basic verb for each (*is*, *are*, *swim*, *eat*, *do*, *go*). Tell them that they need to memorize these verb forms. (See **TEACHING NOTE**.)

Draw students' attention to the three statements under the chart.

Have students match the rules with the examples. Check answers.

TEACHING NOTE: IRREGULAR VERBS

If students are frustrated by the irregular verbs, give them some encouragement by reminding them that they don't have to worry about the verb changing with the subject.

C As students follow along, read the words in the box aloud. Point out that these are the simple past forms of the verbs. Have them write the correct words next to the present tense verbs.

Check answers.

D Point to the words in parentheses. Tell students that they should use the past forms of these verbs to complete the conversation.

Tell students they will listen to the conversation and check answers.

11.4 Play Audio Track 11.4. Check answers by calling on individual students and writing the answers on the board.

E Tell students they are going to get into groups and play a game in which they make a story about what happened yesterday. Tell them that the story can be fictional (not true).

Explain that they will take turns adding a new sentence to the story so it gets longer.

Model the example with two students.

Have students get into small groups and do the task. You might want to have a few groups share their stories after the game is finished.

THE REAL WORLD

CONTENT NOTE: ALASTAIR HUMPHREYS

Alastair Humphreys, who was a National Geographic Adventurer of the Year, started his adventures when he was nine years old, and his adventures have continued since—teaching in South Africa, running a marathon in a rhino costume, cycling around the world for four years, racing a yacht across the Atlantic Ocean. Humphreys made the term *microadventure* popular, and he believes that everyone can have these adventures if they have this attitude.

Ask students to look at the photo. As students follow along in their books, read the title and photo caption aloud.

OPTIONAL Have students find the United Kingdom on a world map. Tell them that the United Kingdom is made up of England, Wales, Scotland, and Northern Ireland.

A As students follow along, read the definition of *adventure* aloud. Have students get into pairs and make a list of things they consider to be an adventure. You may want to have some pairs share their ideas when everyone is finished.

B Tell students they are going to watch a video about Alastair Humphreys and his adventures. Tell them they should check the things that are special about his adventures. As students follow along, read the choices aloud.

▶ 11.1 Play Video 11.1. If necessary, play the video again. Check answers.

C Tell students they are going to watch the video again and they should circle the correct answers to complete the sentences. As students follow along, read the sentences aloud.

▶ 11.1 Play Video 11.1. If necessary, play the video again. Check answers.

THE REAL WORLD

MICROADVENTURES

ABOUT THE PHOTO

This photo shows Alastair Humphreys having a microadventure in the Shetland Islands in the United Kingdom. The Shetland Islands are located in the northernmost part of the United Kingdom. On this particular microadventure, Humphreys's plan was to travel from the south of the island to the north using only a foldable bicycle and foldable boat. (See **CONTENT NOTE** for more information.)

Alastair Humphreys on an adventure in the Shetland Islands, United Kingdom

A Read the definition below. What is your idea of an adventure? Make a list of examples with a partner. *Answers will vary.*

adventure *noun* an exciting experience or trip

B ▶ 11.1 **Watch the video.** What's special about Alastair's adventures?

- ☑ They're small.
- ☑ They're easy to do.
- ☐ They take a lot of time to plan.
- ☐ They help people make new friends.

130 Unit 11

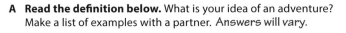

D CRITICAL THINKING

As students follow along, read the statement and questions aloud. Point out that they should *justify* their opinion by including reasons. Have students get into pairs and discuss their opinions.

PROJECT As students follow along, read the project instructions aloud. Have students make their lists. Then have students get into pairs and share ideas.

CHALLENGE Tell students that one of Alastair's main ideas is that a microadventure does not need to be expensive. Encourage students to have a microadventure, even if it is only for one or two hours. Afterward, have them report back to the class about what they did, how they felt, and how much money it cost. Have students discuss whether they would like to have more microadventures, giving reasons for their answers.

C ▶ 11.1 **Watch again.** Circle the correct answers.

1 Alastair's microadventure was to walk along a **highway** / **river**. (circled: highway)

2 Alastair chose an adventure he thought was **interesting** / **not interesting**. (circled: not interesting)

3 Alastair and his friend walked through some **towns** / **farms**. (circled: towns)

4 Alastair showed that people can have an adventure in **different countries** / **ordinary places**. (circled: ordinary places)

D CRITICAL THINKING Justifying **Talk with a partner.** Alastair says it's possible to have an adventure anywhere. Do you agree? Why or why not? Answers will vary.

PROJECT Plan a microadventure in your town. Make a list of places you can go and activities you can do. Share your ideas with a partner.

PRONUNCIATION *-ed* sounds

A 11.5 **Listen and repeat.**

1 *d*, stay<u>ed</u> 2 *t*, check<u>ed</u> 3 *id*, visit<u>ed</u>

B 11.6 **Listen.** Write the sound (*d*, *t*, *id*) of the past forms.

1 play<u>ed</u> d 2 want<u>ed</u> id 3 invit<u>ed</u> id

4 lik<u>ed</u> t 5 shar<u>ed</u> d 6 hik<u>ed</u> t

COMMUNICATION

Complete an adventure calendar with activities you did. Student A: Write your own ideas in the calendar on this page. Ask your partner about their activities. **Student B:** Turn to page 154.

My Adventure Calendar						
Monday	Tuesday	Wednesday	Thursday	Friday	Saturday	Sunday
cycled in the park						

Answers will vary.

What did you do on Monday?

I visited a museum.

PRONUNCIATION

Tell students they will practice their pronunciation of regular past tense verbs ending with *-ed*.

A Explain that there are three different sounds for the *-ed* in past tense verbs: the /*d*/ sound, the /*t*/ sound, and the /*id*/ sound. Tell them it is important to know which sound each verb makes. Have students look at the examples and then follow along as you play the audio.

11.5 Play Audio Track 11.5.

Tell students you will play the audio again and they should repeat the words.

11.5 Play Audio Track 11.5, pausing after each word so students can repeat.

B Tell students to listen and write the sounds they hear.

11.6 Play Audio Track 11.6. Play it again, if necessary.

Check answers by randomly calling on students. Write the answers on the board as they are given.

11.6 Play Audio Track 11.6 a final time, if necessary, so students who made mistakes can identify the correct pronunciation.

SUPPORT Have students look through the unit up until this point and find regular past tense verbs that end in *-ed*. Write them on the board as they are given (*visited, stayed, liked, walked, climbed, played, enjoyed, studied, showed*).

Have students close their books so they can practice the words they have already studied.

Say the words slowly and have students decide the correct *-ed* sound for each.

/d/: stayed, climbed, played, enjoyed, studied, showed

/t/: liked, walked

/id/: visited

Have students make sentences with the words. Then have them get into pairs and take turns reading the sentences.

COMMUNICATION

Tell students they are going to complete an adventure calendar with activities they did.

Have students get into pairs. Have Student As use the calendar on page 131 and Student Bs use the calendar on page 154.

Have them fill in their activities.

Model the conversation with a student.

Have students take turns asking and answering questions about their activities.

READING

CONTENT NOTE: ANDREW EVANS

Andrew Evans shares his experiences with the world at the same time he has them. For example, he was the first person to make a live tweet while climbing Mount Kilimanjaro, and people around the world followed his 12,000-mile (over 19,000-kilometer) trip from Washington, D.C., to Antarctica, during which he traveled by bus and other public transportation. He has also reported live from more than 100 countries.

Ask a student to read the title aloud as the others follow along in their books.

Ask students to look at the photo. Read the photo caption aloud as students follow along.

A Tell students they are going to take a quiz to see how much they know about Jordan. As students follow along, read the sentences aloud. Have students circle their answers.

Check answers. Have students find Jordan on a world map.

OPTIONAL Ask students what facts, if any, surprised them. Also have them talk about what else they know about Jordan and the area around it.

B As students follow along in their books, read the question aloud. Have students scan the article for the answer.

Check answers.

C Have students get into pairs and talk about where people hike in their country.

After completing the task, give students the opportunity to read the article in more detail so they can more fully comprehend it and answer the **COMPREHENSION** questions.

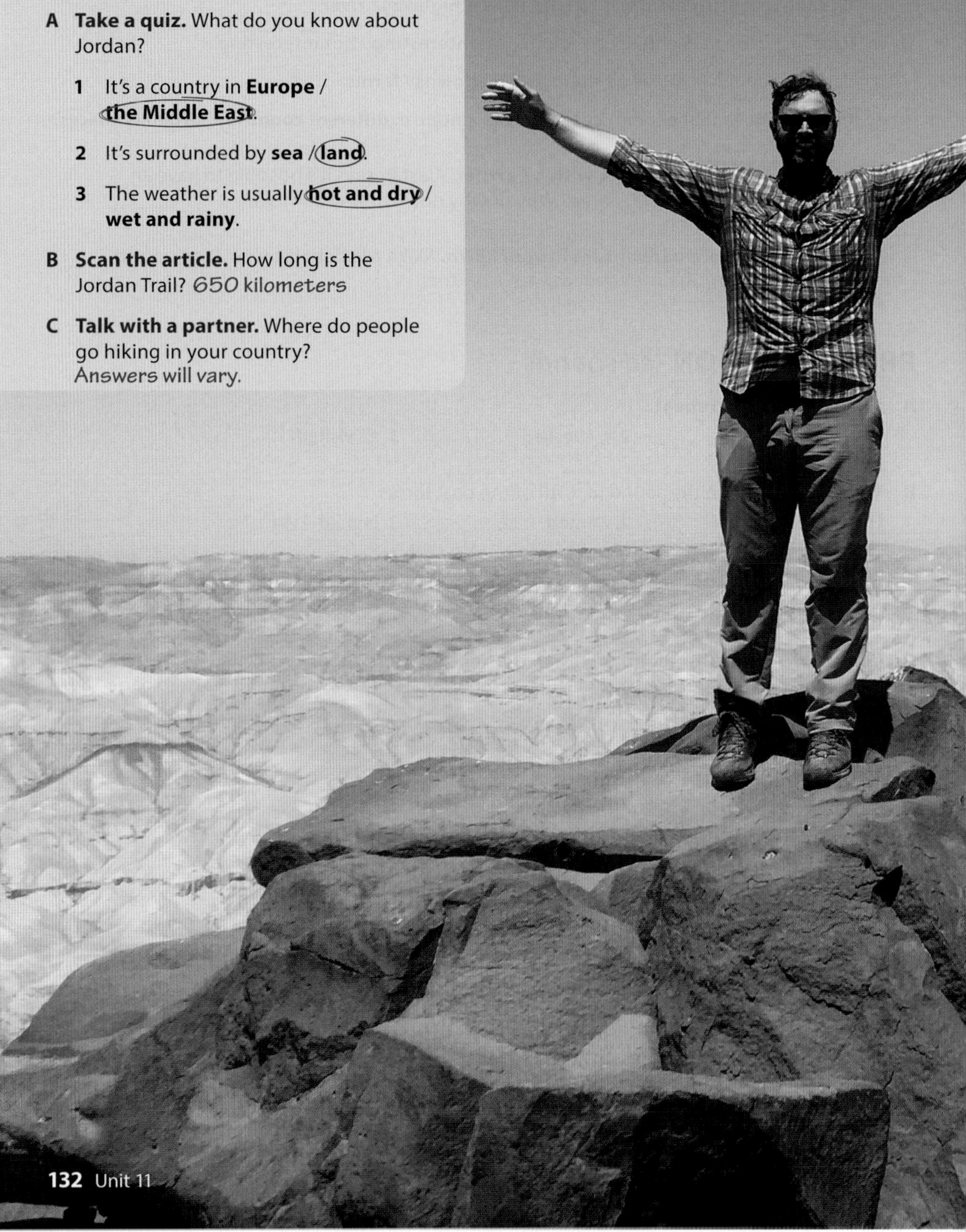

READING

A Take a quiz. What do you know about Jordan?

1. It's a country in **Europe** / **the Middle East**.
2. It's surrounded by **sea** / **land**.
3. The weather is usually **hot and dry** / **wet and rainy**.

B Scan the article. How long is the Jordan Trail? *650 kilometers*

C Talk with a partner. Where do people go hiking in your country? *Answers will vary.*

OPTIONAL The text can also be used as a listening activity. Have students close their books. Tell students they will listen to the passage.

11.7 Play Audio Track 11.7. Ask students to get into pairs and discuss what information they heard. Then have them read the article more carefully.

Additional Activities to Use with the Reading

Pronunciation (Focused)

Have students look through the reading text and find regular past tense verbs that end in *-ed*, writing them on the board as they are given (*passed, arrived, explored, continued, climbed, walked*).

WALKING THROUGH JORDAN

11.7 On March 31, 2017, explorer Andrew Evans and a group of hikers met in Um Qais in northern Jordan. They were ready to start their adventure on the Jordan Trail, a 650-kilometer-long hiking trail.

Andrew began his hike walking through beautiful green fields. There were many colorful flowers. Village children said "hello" as he passed.

After a few weeks of walking, Andrew **arrived** at the city of Karak—the halfway point of his **journey**. He ate some ice cream to **celebrate**. He also explored the 800-year-old Karak Castle.

The hikers continued their walk down south. They climbed mountains and saw the amazing ruins of Petra. Then they walked across a **desert**. There were many snakes. This was a difficult part of the walk. Andrew often felt **tired** because it was very hot.

Finally, after 44 days, Andrew arrived at Aqaba. Many people came to cheer the group on. Together, the hikers walked the last steps of the journey toward the Red Sea.

Andrew Evans on a mountain in Wadi Mujib, Jordan

ABOUT THE PHOTO

This photo shows adventurer Andrew Evans standing on a mountain in Wadi Mujib on the way to Karak. The Jordan Trail is a long-distance hiking trail. Spanning a length of 650 kilometers, the trail crosses the country of Jordan, connecting Um Qais in the north to Aqaba in the south. People who hike the full trail from Um Qais to Aqaba will travel through 52 villages and towns. Along the trail, hikers get to experience the diverse landscapes of the country, from wooded hills in the north to cliffs overlooking the Jordan Rift Valley to the waters of the Red Sea.

11.7 Play Audio Track 11.7 so students can determine the correct sound for each.

/d/: arrived, explored, continued, climbed

/t/: passed, walked

Ask students to draw some conclusions. (e.g., When saying regular past tense verbs, the /d/ sound is more frequent than the other two sounds.)

11.7 Play Audio Track 11.7 again, pausing after each sentence with a regular past tense verb so students can repeat.

Question Construction

Have students get into pairs and take turns asking and answering factual questions about the reading. For example: *Did they climb a mountain?* (Yes, they did.)

Developing Reading Fluency

11.7 Play Audio Track 11.7 and have students read along. Play it again, pausing after each sentence, so students can repeat. Have them practice reading it several times. Play the audio a final time so they can check any pronunciation and intonation.

Understanding Names

Tell students that in English, *last name* is also called the *surname* or *family name*. Ask students what the man's surname is (Evans).

Tell students that, unlike some languages, in English we write our personal, or given, name first, so it is called our *first name*. Ask students what his first name is (Andrew).

Explain to students that many Westerners also have a middle name, but we usually don't write it.

Research

Ask students what months Andrew was walking in the desert (April and May). Have students research the average monthly temperatures in Petra and Aqaba for these months and compare these temperatures to average temperatures in their city.

Rephrasing

On the board, write, *On March 31, 2017, explorer Andrew Evans and a group of hikers met in Um Qais in northern Jordan.* Have students get into pairs and reword the sentence at least two different ways. Emphasize that because they are rephrasing, they may not use all of the words or may need to use additional words. Emphasize that the important point is that all of the information is included. (e.g., *Explorer Andrew Evans and a group of hikers met in Um Qais in northern Jordan on March 31, 2017. / Andrew Evans went to Um Qais, Jordan, and met a group of hikers on March 31, 2017. / Andrew Evans, an explorer, met a group of hikers in Um Qais, Jordan, on March 31, 2017.*)

COMPREHENSION

A Have students read the questions to themselves and circle the correct answers. Check answers.

IDIOM

Read the question, sentence, and answer choices aloud, as students follow along. Have students raise their hands to show whether they think the answer is *a* or *b* (a). Explain that a *bug* can refer to an illness or disease, so *getting bitten by the travel bug/having the travel bug* is used to refer to someone who is (not literally) *infected with the travel virus* (i.e., crazy about traveling).

B **EXAM PRACTICE**

The ability to understand graphic information, including maps, is an important twenty-first century skill. Exams such as IELTS ask students to label maps, particularly in the listening section. Practicing with reading passages gives students knowledge, vocabulary, and confidence to progress to listening.

To complete this task, students must use the information in the passage to label the map. Students should study the map carefully before writing any answers because an error in one location will affect at least one more answer. Because students are looking for place names that start with capital letters, encourage them to use skimming, which is an important technique to use with standardized tests.

Explain to students that maps help us understand a journey.

Have students write the names of the places on the map.

Check answers.

COMPREHENSION

A Answer the questions about *Walking Through Jordan*.

1 PURPOSE The purpose of the article is to _____.
- a explain why hiking is popular in Jordan
- (b) describe a hike through Jordan
- c list the best places to hike in Jordan

2 DETAIL Andrew was happy to reach Karak because _____.
- a he had friends there
- b there was ice cream to eat
- (c) it was the halfway point of the walk

3 REFERENCE The word *This* in line 11 refers to _____.
- a climbing mountains   b seeing Petra   (c) walking in the desert

4 DETAIL Which of the following landscapes did Andrew NOT see on his walk?
- a mountains   (b) snowy fields   c the sea

5 INFERENCE The Red Sea is in the _____ of Jordan.
- (a) south   b north   c east

IDIOM

Do you like to travel a lot? That means you have the _____.
(a) travel bug
b visit worm

B Label the map. Write the names of the places Andrew visited.

Petra   Um Qais   Aqaba   Karak

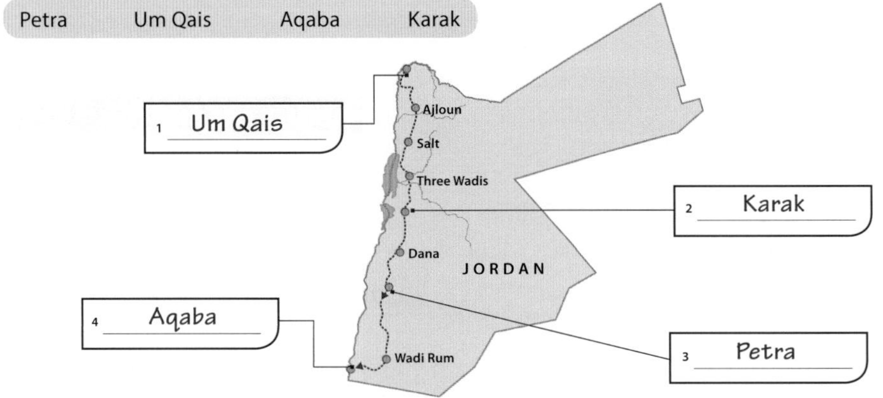

C CRITICAL THINKING Evaluating **Talk with a partner.** Andrew hiked with a group of people. What are the advantages of hiking in a group? Answers will vary.

OPTIONAL Have students name locations that are about 650 kilometers from their school. Then ask them to consider walking to those places in 44 days. Have students calculate how many kilometers, on average, Andrew walked each day (between 14 and 15 kilometers each day). Ask them if they think this pace is too fast, too slow, or just right. Encourage them to provide reasons for their answers.

C CRITICAL THINKING

As students follow along, read the statement and question aloud. Have students get into pairs and discuss their ideas.

CHALLENGE Ask students to discuss these additional questions. Encourage them to give reasons for their answers.

1 *The children said* hello *to Andrew as he passed. Would the children in your city say* hello?

VOCABULARY

A Find the words below in the article. Then complete the sentences.

arrived	journey	celebrate	deserts	tired	finally

1 I'm really tired because I exercised a lot today.
2 I traveled for 10 hours by bus. It was a very long journey.
3 Not many plants can grow in deserts because there's very little rain.
4 My friends and I had a party to celebrate the end of our school year.
5 After much discussion, we finally decided on a place to go for vacation.
6 The plane left Beijing at 8 p.m. and arrived in Los Angeles 12 hours later.

B Read the information below. Then circle the correct answers.

We can make adjectives by adding *-ful* to some nouns. The meaning of the adjective *-ful* is "full of something." For example, *colorful* means "full of color."

1 There were many **colorful** / **useful** clothes in the store.
2 Thanks for lending me your book. It was really **useful** / **careful**.
3 The salesperson was friendly and **colorful** / **helpful**.
4 She always checks her work before she hands it in. She's a very **helpful** / **careful** person.

DO YOU KNOW?

Which country has the most tourists every year?
(a) France
b The United States

WRITING

A Read the beginning of a description of someone's day.

B Think about a fun day you had. Make notes about things you did and people you were with.

C Write about the fun day you had. Answers will vary.

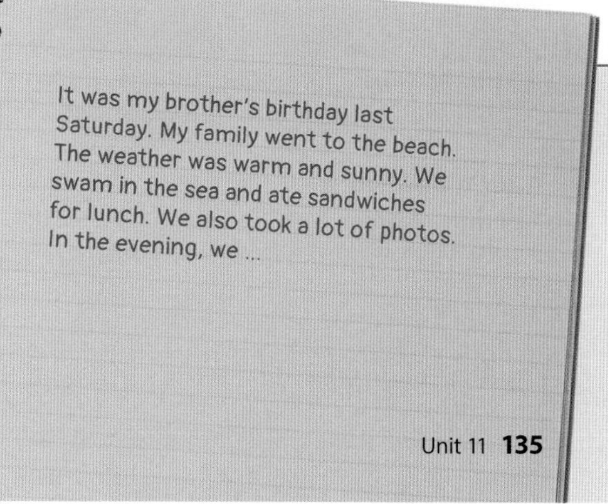

It was my brother's birthday last Saturday. My family went to the beach. The weather was warm and sunny. We swam in the sea and ate sandwiches for lunch. We also took a lot of photos. In the evening, we ...

Unit 11 135

2 *Why do people like to complete difficult challenges like the hike Andrew did?*
3 *Why would ice cream probably be a good way to celebrate the halfway point of the journey?*
4 *If you were going to do this hike, what would be the most difficult part for you?*
5 *If you were going to do this hike, who would you like to go with?*
6 *Which part of the adventure sounds like the most fun?*

VOCABULARY

A As students follow along in their books, read the words in the box aloud. Have students find the words in the **READING** passage.

Have students write the correct words to complete the sentences. Check answers.

B As students follow along, read the information in the box aloud. Have students circle the correct adjectives to complete the sentences. Check answers as a class.

DO YOU KNOW?

Read the question and answer choices aloud, as students follow along in their books. Ask a few students to give their answer before providing it (a).

OPTIONAL Have students brainstorm reasons why France, which is much smaller than the United States, might have the most tourists every year. Then give them more information. (See **CONTENT NOTE**.)

CONTENT NOTE: TOURISM

With 89 million visitors in 2018, France had the most international tourists arrive in their country. Spain was second (83 million visitors), while the United States and China were third and fourth, respectively, with 80 and 63 million guests.

WRITING

Tell students they are going to write about a fun day they had.

A As students follow along in their books, read the example aloud. If necessary, remind students that we don't start each sentence on a new line.

Point out that the author says when the fun day was, who it was with, what they did, and how the weather was.

B Have students think about a fun day they had and make notes.

C Have students write about their fun day. Encourage them to include lots of details, not just *we went, we did*. Give students a time limit for finishing, and set a minimum number of sentences they must write (e.g., eight).

Collect their papers and correct any grammar or spelling errors.

VIDEO

Tell students they are going to watch a video about Andrew Evans.

As students follow along in their books, read the title, the sentence about the video, and the photo caption aloud.

CHALLENGE Ask students to guess what a salt flat is before explaining that it's a flat area that has a salt crust because of the evaporation of water.

BEFORE YOU WATCH

As students follow along, read the names of the types of transportation aloud. Ask them to guess which Andrew used and circle their answers.

OPTIONAL Before watching the video, ask students to predict things they might see (e.g., an island, a temple, animals). After watching the video, ask students how many of their predictions were correct.

WHILE YOU WATCH

A As students follow along, read the names of the countries and the activities aloud. Tell students they will watch the video and they should match the countries with the activities Andrew did.

▶ 11.2 Play Video 11.2. Check answers.

Discuss the students' answers from **BEFORE YOU WATCH**. You might also mention that the last country he visited before returning to England was Spain.

B Explain to students that they will watch the video again and they should connect the dots on the map to show Andrew's path. As students follow along, read the names of all the countries aloud. Explain that he is talking about his journey from London. Point out that the first line, from England to Oman, has been drawn. Explain that they will connect the other countries, starting from Oman, so they will draw seven more lines.

An *Amazing Journey*

Before You Watch

Guess. Circle the types of transportation Andrew Evans took on his trip.

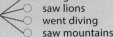

(a boat)

a train

(a plane)

a bike

(a car)

While You Watch

A ▶ 11.2 **Watch the video.** Match the places to the activities.

1 Nepal
2 Maldives
3 Botswana
4 Rwanda

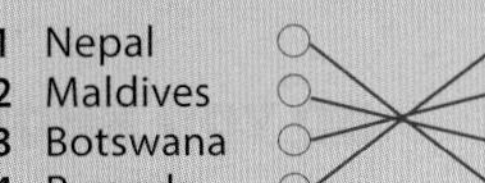

saw gorillas
saw lions
went diving
saw mountains

B ▶ 11.2 **Watch again.** Draw Andrew's journey on the map below.

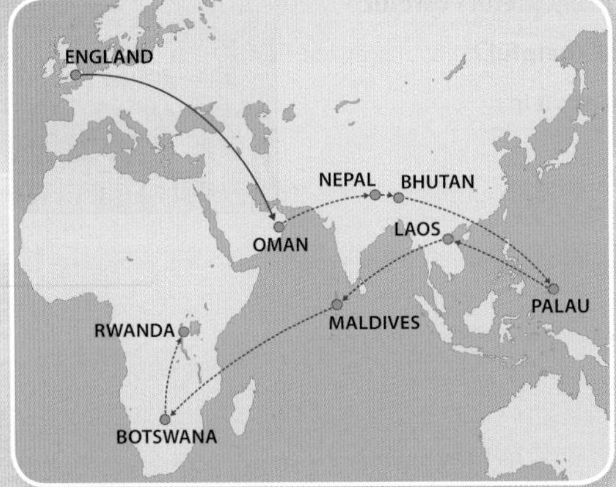

After You Watch

Talk with a partner. Which country in the video do you want to visit? Why?
Answers will vary.

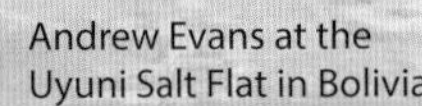
Andrew Evans at the Uyuni Salt Flat in Bolivia

▶ 11.2 Play Video 11.2. Play the video again, if necessary. Check answers.

CHALLENGE Ask students to get into small groups and brainstorm discussion questions about the video. Emphasize that because they are not content questions there are no wrong answers. (e.g., *Andrew went to many countries in a short amount of time. Do you think it is better to visit a few countries for a longer period of time in each country or go to many countries but only stay in each one for a short time?*)

Have students discuss the questions.

After students have discussed the questions, have them work in their groups and rank the questions from *we had the most discussion* to *we had the least discussion*.

As a class, have students talk about why some questions allowed for more discussion.

AFTER YOU WATCH

Tell students they are going to get into pairs and talk about what country they would like to visit.

REVIEW

ABOUT THE PHOTO

This photo shows Andrew Evans at the Uyuni Salt Flat in Bolivia. The Uyuni Salt Flat is the biggest salt flat in the world. Salt flats are formed when desert lakes dry up and leave behind salt that was once in the water. When a nearby lake overflows, it spills over into the salt flat, creating a thin layer of water. When this thin layer of water covers the salt flat entirely, it becomes a mirror. During the drier seasons, the salt flats crack, forming hexagonal shapes on the ground. There is so much salt in the Uyuni Salt Flat that the locals have used the salt to build a salt hotel for tourists to visit and enjoy their stay in.

A **Complete the Venn diagram.** Use the phrases in the box.

go cycling	go hiking	stay at a hotel
visit a museum	go camping	go sightseeing

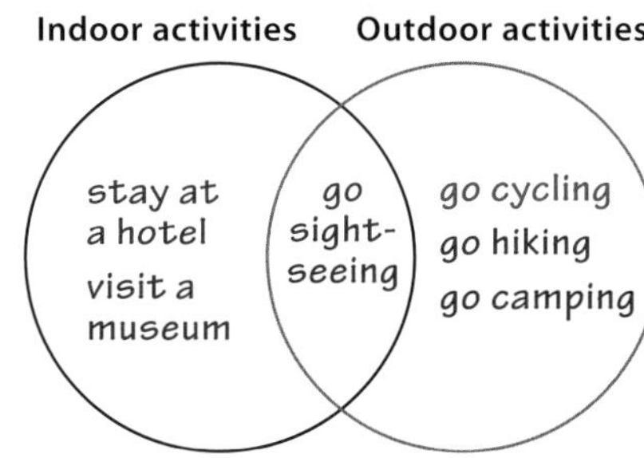

B **Write sentences and questions in the simple past.** Use the words below.

1 He / swim / in the sea
He swam in the sea.

2 I / not / go camping
I didn't go camping.

3 They / go sightseeing
They went sightseeing.

4 She / stay / at a hotel?
Did she stay at a hotel?

C **Complete the sentences.** Circle the correct answers.

1 The paintings in the museum are **helpful** / **colorful**.
2 The ground is wet, so be **useful** / **careful** when you walk.
3 This travel app is very **useful** / **careful** for planning trips.
4 The tourist map has **colorful** / **helpful** information about the area.

SELF CHECK Now I can ...

- ☐ describe my travel activities
- ☐ use language for talking about events in the past
- ☐ talk about different adventures

As students follow along in their books, read the two questions aloud. Point out that they need to include reasons for their choices.

Have students do the task.

REVIEW

Explain to students that they are going to review the material from the unit and this will help them remember what they have studied.

A Explain that activity **A** reviews vocabulary from the unit. Remind students that a Venn diagram creates a visual representation of how ideas are related. Have students identify the two ideas that are being compared (indoor activities and outdoor activities).

Have students use the activities in the box to complete the diagram. Check answers.

B Explain that activity **B** reviews the grammar from the unit. Have students use the words to write sentences and questions in the simple past tense. Have students get into pairs and check answers, before you randomly call on students to give the answers, writing them on the board as they are given.

C Remind students that they studied adjectives with *-ful* in **VOCABULARY** activity **B**. Have them circle the correct words to complete the sentences.

Check answers.

SELF CHECK

These *I can* statements provide vital feedback on students' perceived ability to use the language from the unit. Have students check the statements.

SUPPORT If students lack confidence to put a check next to each statement, have them get into pairs. Tell them they will make quiz questions for another pair, focusing on the three **SELF CHECK** points. Tell them each question/answer set should have one mistake (grammar or vocabulary), and the other pair must correct it.

Give an example: *What did you do yesterday? I goes to school.* (The other pair must say, *I went to school.*)

Have students make their quiz questions and answers.

Have two pairs get together and take turns saying their questions and answers, with the other pair correcting the mistake.

After students have finished reviewing, confirm they have more confidence with the material, providing additional review in class as necessary.

UNIT 12

WHAT DID YOU DO FOR NEW YEAR'S?

CONTENT AREA: HISTORY AND CULTURE

Topic: festivals

Vocabulary: festival words: fireworks, decorations, gift, meal, parade, festival, occasion, birthday, vacation, celebrate, celebration, costume, skeleton, grave, skull, barbecue, party;
other words: competition, last, hard, huge, sculpture, bright

Grammar: prepositions of time—*in, on, during, for*

Extra material: a calendar, a world map

Other useful vocabulary:
festival words: float, clown, juggler, marching band, candles, dress up, makeup

12

WHAT DID YOU DO FOR **NEW YEAR'S?**

138

END OF UNIT PROJECT Have students do a group project about a winter festival.

Explain to students that they are going to do a group research project about a winter festival, and later they are going to tell their classmates what they learned. Encourage students to bring in photos to show their classmates.

Divide students into groups and assign each group one of the following winter festivals—the Quebec Winter Carnival in Canada; the Holmenkollen Ski Festival in Norway; the Madison Winter Festival in Wisconsin, USA; or the Sapporo Snow Festival in Japan.

If necessary, as a class, brainstorm information they could give in their presentation. For example: when the festival started, when it is held each year, the length of the festival, what kind of activities there are, average temperature during the festival.

Have students use the internet and/or other resources to research their respective festivals.

Create a chart with the information students brainstormed in class. Include several blank spaces at the bottom of the chart for additional information. This chart can be used to promote active listening during the in-class group activity. Make copies for all the students.

In class, pass out the chart. Tell students they will get into groups, one student from each festival, and they should take turns asking and answering questions to share their information with their group members. Explain that students who are listening should complete their charts with the information about the other festivals.

Have students get into groups and do the task.

When students have finished, ask them to talk about how the festivals are similar and different, and which they would like to visit the most.

ABOUT THE PHOTO

This photo shows New Year fireworks over Marina Bay, Singapore. Many cities around the world welcome a New Year with a countdown on New Year's Eve. At the stroke of midnight, fireworks can be seen in major cities worldwide. London celebrated the start of the new decade of the 2020s using 12,000 fireworks for a 15-minute show. An iconic New Year's Eve celebration is the ball drop held every year at Times Square in New York City. At 11:59 p.m., the ball, a sphere covered with a total of 2,688 Waterford Crystal triangles, starts its descent as people count down the final seconds of the year and usher in the new year. (See **CONTENT NOTE** for more information.)

New Year fireworks over Marina Bay, Singapore

PREVIEW

A 12.1 **Listen.** Number the items you hear in order (**1–5**).

decorations 4 — parade 1

fireworks 2 — gift 5

meal 3

B 12.2 **Listen.** Complete the activities with the words in **A**.

1 Maria received gifts.
2 Yang prepared a meal.
3 Philippe watched the parade.
4 Christie watched the fireworks.
5 Sanjay put up decorations.

C **Talk with a partner.** How do you celebrate your favorite festival? Answers will vary.

What's your favorite festival? How do you celebrate it?

I always watch the fireworks on New Year's Eve.

HISTORY AND CULTURE

UNIT GOALS

- describe festivals you celebrate
- use language for talking about when things happened
- learn about famous festivals around the world

139

Have students hand in their charts so you can grade students on their work.

CONTENT NOTE: NEW YEAR'S EVE COUNTDOWN

In countries around the world, people gather to count down the end of the old year and ring in the new year. In Singapore, people do a variety of things, including attending countdown concerts, enjoying outdoor light art exhibitions, and watching fireworks in locations across the city.

PREVIEW

Have students read the unit title to themselves as you read it aloud. Explain that in this unit they will learn to talk about festivals.

A As students follow along, read the words aloud. Tell students they should number the words in the order they hear them, from one to five.

12.1 Play Audio Track 12.1. Play it again, if necessary. Check answers.

B Explain that students will hear five short conversations and they should use the words in **A** to complete the sentences. As students follow along in their books, read the sentences aloud.

12.2 Play Audio Track 12.2. Play it again, if necessary. Check answers.

OPTIONAL Ask students extra comprehension questions.

1 *Who did Maria have the party with?* (her friends)

2 *Who did Yang prepare the meal with?* (his family)

3 *When did Philippe watch the parade?* (during summer vacation)

4 *Who did Christie watch the fireworks with?* (her family)

5 *Where did Sanjay put up decorations?* (in his house)

C As students follow along, read the question aloud. Model the conversation with a student. Have students do the task.

CHALLENGE Ask students to say some other words they associate with festivals. (See **Other useful vocabulary**.)

UNIT GOALS

Direct students' attention to the **UNIT GOALS** box. Explain that these are some of the things students will learn in this unit. Point out that this unit is about history and culture. As students follow along, read each of the unit goals to the class. Explain any words students do not know. Remind students that at the end of the unit there is a self check that allows them to see if they have accomplished each goal.

LANGUAGE FOCUS

A Tell students they will listen to a conversation between Maya and Nadine.

12.3 Play Audio Track 12.3 as students listen and follow along in their books. If necessary, play the conversation again, pausing after each speaker so students can repeat.

As students follow along, read the question, *Why is Nadine sleeping?* Have students answer.

Have students work in pairs and practice the conversation once. Point out the bold words and read them aloud as students follow along in their books. You might want to have students repeat the words after you say them.

Tell students they will practice the conversation two more times, changing the bold words each time and swapping roles after the first time.

REAL ENGLISH

Direct students' attention to the expression in the **REAL ENGLISH** box. Explain that *That's nice!* is commonly used in conversation. It means *neat*, *great*, or *cool*. For example:

A: I had a really fun time on the weekend.

B: That's nice! Tell me all about it!

B Ask students to look at the chart. Tell them that the chart teaches prepositions. Tell students that prepositions help explain time, place, and directions. Explain that prepositions are words (or phrases) that come before a noun, pronoun, or the *-ing* form of a verb (a gerund).

12.4 Have students follow along as they listen to Audio Track 12.4.

Point out that the statements, questions, and answers are about things that have already happened. If necessary, remind them to use the past tense verbs they studied in **UNIT 11**.

LANGUAGE FOCUS

A 12.3 **Listen and read.** Why is Nadine sleeping? Then repeat the conversation and replace the words in **bold**. *She's tired because she went to a night festival yesterday.*

REAL ENGLISH That's nice!

Maya: Hi, Nadine! How was your weekend?

Nadine: It was **good**, thanks. (**OK** / **great**)

Maya: What did you do on Saturday?

Nadine: Um, I visited my **aunt and uncle**. (**grandparents** / **cousins**)

Maya: That's nice! What about yesterday? Did you do anything fun?

Nadine: Yesterday … I went to a **night festival**. (**barbecue** / **party**)

Maya: That sounds great! And what are you doing now?

Nadine: **Taking a nap** … you woke me up! (**Sleeping** / **Napping**)

B 12.4 **Look at the chart.** Then circle **T** for true or **F** for false.

TALKING ABOUT SPECIAL OCCASIONS (USING PREPOSITIONS OF TIME)	
There was a big festival **during** the winter / the holidays.	
What did you do **on** Friday / July 1st? Where did you go **in** August / 2019 / the summer?	We went to a party. I traveled to the Philippines.
Did you go on vacation **for** two weeks / the New Year?	Yes, I did. No, I didn't. I stayed at home.

1 We use *on* with days and dates. (T) F

2 We use *in* with months and seasons. (T) F

3 We use *during* with years. T (F)

4 We use *for* with lengths of time. (T) F

Point out the words in bold. Tell students we use these words to make our questions and answers more specific. On the board, write, *What did you do?* Also write, *What did you do on New Year's Eve?* Ask students how they are different, providing the answer if necessary. (We don't know *when* the first question is asking about—it's vague. The second question is much more specific.)

Explain that *during* is used when the time frame is broad, and not a specific day. For example: *We light lanterns during Diwali.* (Diwali is a five-day celebration.)

Explain that *on* is used for specific dates and days. Point to various days on a calendar as you say *on (day)*. Do the same for dates. For example: *on Friday, on December 31st.*

C 🎧 12.5 **Complete the conversation.** Some words can be used more than once. Then listen and check your answers.

in on during for

David: When's your birthday, Elisa?

Elisa: It was last month. It was [1] ___on___ July 10th.

David: Great! What did you do?

Elisa: Well, it was [2] ___during___ summer vacation, so I went to Spain. I was there [3] ___for___ a week. When's your birthday?

David: Well, my birthday is [4] ___in___ December. It's [5] ___during___ the holidays!

Elisa: Oh, I remember! It's [6] ___on___ December 23rd. I went to your birthday party last year!

DO YOU KNOW?

Diwali, a big festival in India, is also called "the festival of ___."

a colors

(b) lights

D Complete the sentences. Use the correct form of the words in parentheses.

1 **Hugh:** How was your weekend? [1] ___Did___ you ___do___ (**do**) anything interesting?

Patti: I [2] ___saw___ (**see**) fireworks at a festival.

2 **Ling:** What [3] ___did___ you ___get___ (**get**) Lucy for her birthday yesterday?

Carlos: I [4] ___got___ (**get**) her a watch.

3 **Juan:** Happy New Year, Rosa! [5] ___Did___ you ___go___ (**go**) anywhere for Christmas?

Rosa: Happy New Year, Juan. No, I [6] ___stayed___ (**stay**) home with my family. We put up decorations and [7] ___prepared___ (**prepare**) a big meal.

E Work in groups of four. Play a memory game. Take turns saying one activity you did.

Answers will vary.

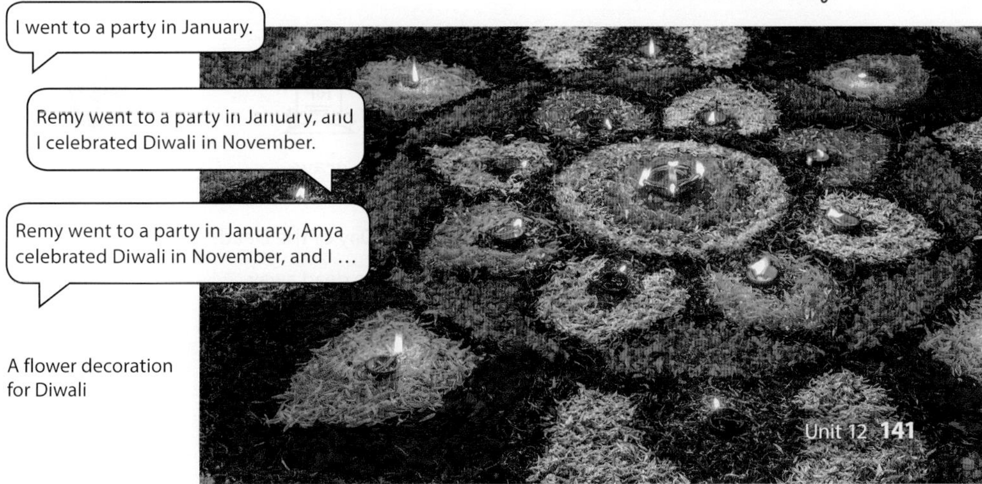

I went to a party in January.
Remy went to a party in January, and I celebrated Diwali in November.
Remy went to a party in January, Anya celebrated Diwali in November, and I …

A flower decoration for Diwali

Unit 12 141

DO YOU KNOW?

Have students guess the answer before providing it (b).

CONTENT NOTE: DIWALI

Diwali, which was traditionally celebrated in India but has now spread to countries around the world, is one of the major Hindu festivals. It lasts for five days. Because it follows the lunar calendar, it is usually celebrated in late October or November.

D Have students complete the conversations by using the correct form of the words in parentheses.

Check answers.

CONTENT NOTE: NEW YEAR'S CELEBRATIONS

New Year's Eve is December 31, and New Year's Day is January 1. In Japan during the holiday, family and friends gather, people visit a shrine, and some people wake up early to witness the first sunrise of the new year.

In contrast, Chinese New Year celebration dates are based on the lunar calendar (i.e., the calendar based on the phases of the moon), with the celebration occurring sometime between late January and mid-February.

E Tell students they are going to play a game in groups of four.

Explain that Student A will say a sentence. Student B will repeat what Student A said before adding another sentence. The game will continue with the amount each person must repeat getting increasingly longer.

Model the conversation with two students. Have students do the task.

Tell students that we use *in* with the months, years, and seasons. Point out that we are not told the specific day or date, just the month or the season within that time period. On a calendar, point to January. Say, *It (snows/rains/etc.) in January.*

Tell students that we use *for* with a period of time. For example: *I stayed with my grandmother for a month.*

Draw students' attention to the four statements under the chart. Have students circle the correct answers. Check answers.

C As students follow along, read the words in the box aloud. Tell students they should use the words to complete the conversation and they may use some words more than once.

Tell students they will listen and check their answers.

🎧 12.5 Play Audio Track 12.5. Check answers.

THE REAL WORLD

CONTENT NOTE: DAY OF THE DEAD

The origins of the Day of the Dead, which is celebrated for two days, go back thousands of years to the Aztec and Toltec peoples, as well as other Native American cultures in the Mesoamerican area. In 2008, UNESCO (the United Nations Educational, Scientific and Cultural Organization) included it on its list of Intangible Cultural Heritage of Humanity.

Ask students to look at the photo. As students follow along in their books, read the title and the photo caption aloud.

A As students follow along in their books, read the words in the box aloud. Have students write the words under the correct pictures.

Check answers.

B Tell students they are going to watch a video about the Day of the Dead and they should notice what people do. As students follow along in their books, read the sentences aloud.

▶ 12.1 Play Video 12.1. Tell students that they can confirm their answer as they watch the video again in **C**.

C Explain to students that they will watch the video again and they should check the activities they see.

▶ 12.1 Play Video 12.1. If necessary, play the video again.

Check answers. Then check answers for **B**.

D CRITICAL THINKING

As students follow along, read the questions aloud. Have students get into pairs and talk about their ideas. Emphasize that they should *justify* their ideas by answering the question *Why or why not?*

THE ***DAY OF THE DEAD***

A girl in a costume at the Catrina Parade in Mexico City

ABOUT THE PHOTO

This photo shows a girl in a Catrina costume taking part in the Catrina Parade in Mexico City. Catrina—a female skeleton that wore a big, fancy hat—was a character created by Mexican artist José Guadalupe Posada. The character grew in popularity with Mexicans and became a symbol associated with the Day of the Dead. The Day of the Dead is a celebration of life and death. During the holiday, people honor deceased family members by cleaning and decorating their gravesites, and enjoy food, drinks, and activities that their deceased loved ones enjoyed in life. (See **CONTENT NOTE** for more information.)

A Match the words with the pictures.

grave skull costume skeleton

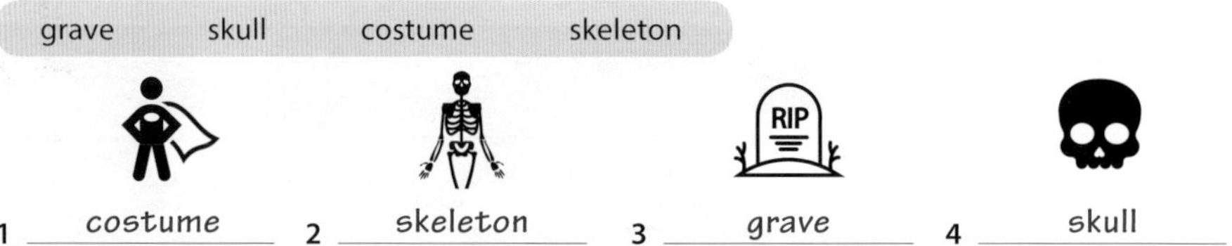

1 costume 2 skeleton 3 grave 4 skull

B ▶ 12.1 **Watch the video.** What do people do on the Day of the Dead?

a They wear costumes and play lively music to send the dead away.

b They wish for good luck from their family members who have died.

ⓒ They celebrate the lives of their family members who have died.

142 Unit 12

PROJECT As students follow along, read the project instructions aloud. Set a deadline by which students must do their research. In the next lesson, have students get into pairs and take turns sharing their research.

PRONUNCIATION

Explain to students that syllable stress (which part of the word is said more strongly) is important in spoken English. If necessary, teach students more about syllables. (See **TEACHING NOTE**.)

Slowly say, *fes-ti-val*, clapping as you say each of the three syllables. Do the same with *va-ca-tion* (three syllables).

Have students look at the words.

Explain that they will listen to the words and they should underline the stressed syllable in each word.

🎧 12.6 Play Audio Track 12.6. If necessary, play it again. Check answers.

🎧 12.6 Play Audio Track 12.6 again, pausing after each word so students can repeat.

C ▶ 12.1 **Watch again.** Check (✓) the activities you see.

- [x] visiting the graves
- [x] decorating the graves
- [ ] writing letters to the dead
- [x] playing music for the dead
- [ ] taking family photos at the graves
- [x] putting out food and drink for the dead

D CRITICAL THINKING Justifying **Talk with a partner.** Is it good to remember the dead with a celebration? Do you think it's OK to have fun on that day? Why or why not? *Answers will vary.*

PROJECT Go online. Find one other celebration similar to the Day of the Dead. What do people do? Share with a partner.

PRONUNCIATION syllable stress

12.6 **Listen and underline the stressed syllable.** Then listen again and repeat.

1 festival 2 vacation 3 party 4 celebrate
5 around 6 summer 7 amazing 8 winter

COMMUNICATION

Work in a group. Find someone who did the following activities recently. Ask for more information about their activities. *Answers will vary.*

Find someone who ...	Name	More information
hung out with friends.		
spent time with their family.		
prepared a meal.		
went somewhere interesting.		
had a party.		
received a gift.		

Did you hang out with friends recently?
Yes, I did.
What did you do?

Unit 12 143

Students may have difficulty hearing which syllable to stress, so if necessary, play the audio a last time.

SUPPORT Before doing the activity, have students get into pairs. Slowly say the words. Have students decide how many syllables are in each word. Say each word again, having students make a note of where each syllable starts and stops.

Have students write their answers on the board. Check as a class.

1	fes-ti-val	**2**	va-ca-tion
3	par-ty	**4**	cel-e-brate
5	a-round	**6**	sum-mer
7	a-ma-zing	**8**	win-ter

TEACHING NOTE: SYLLABLES

Syllables are distinct units of sounds in each word. They are larger than the sounds of individual letters. Words that are made up of one or more syllables have only one syllable with primary stress, but other syllables can have secondary stress. In dictionaries, syllables are separated by dots or hyphens (e.g., syl-la-ble).

Some words have the same pronunciation but the syllable stress changes the meaning and form. For example, for the word *subject*, stress on the first syllable (sub-) makes it a noun, and stress on the second syllable (-ject) makes it a verb.

COMMUNICATION

Tell students they are going to get into a group and find classmates who did specific activities, and then ask those classmates for more information about the activities.

As students follow along in their books, read the items in the first column aloud.

Point out that they should write the students' names in the second column. Tell them to talk to different students for each item.

Point to the final column in the chart and tell students they should ask for additional information, writing it here.

Model the conversation with a student. Explain that *What did you do?* asks for more information.

Have students do the task.

READING

CONTENT NOTE: THE HARBIN ICE AND SNOW FESTIVAL

The Harbin Ice and Snow Sculpture Festival is the world's largest ice and snow festival. It takes place annually in Harbin, in northeast China. The temperatures there drop as low as –38°C, often because of the cold winds blowing in from Siberia.

The sculptures are often huge. For instance, the Flamenco Ice Tower, which took two years to build and was displayed in 2018, reached 31 meters. This is even more amazing when you consider that most of the ice used for the sculptures comes from the nearby Songhua River.

A Ask students to look at the photo. Read the caption aloud, as they follow along. Then read the title.

Ask the two questions. Allow students to share their ideas.

B Tell students that they will scan the article and find out where Harbin is.

Have students do the task. When all the students have finished, check answers.

OPTIONAL Have students find China on a world map. Have them find Harbin, if it is marked.

C Have students skim the article and find four different season and weather words.

Check answers.

After completing the task, give students the opportunity to read the article in more detail so they can more fully comprehend it and answer the **COMPREHENSION** questions.

READING

A Look at the photo and read the title. What season do you think this festival takes place in? What do you think the weather is like? It takes place in winter. It's probably very cold.

B Scan the article. Where is Harbin? It's in northeast China.

C Skim the article. Find four different season and weather words.

The Harbin Ice and Snow Festival

OPTIONAL The text can also be used as a listening activity. Have students close their books. Tell students they will listen to the passage.

12.7 Play Audio Track 12.7. Ask students to get into pairs and discuss what information they heard. Then have them read the article more carefully.

CHALLENGE Ask students to find the word *wonderland* in line 3. Ask students to get into pairs and talk about the images this word creates. (It can refer to a marvelous imaginary place or a real-world place that has beautiful dreamlike qualities.) Then tell students the term became well known after Lewis Carroll used it in the book *Alice's Adventures in Wonderland*, which was published in 1865.

THE HARBIN ICE AND SNOW FESTIVAL

12.7 Every year, on January 5th, the city of Harbin in northeast China changes into a winter wonderland. Tourists from around the world come to visit this amazing ice and snow festival.

The festival started in 1963. It began as a winter party. The festival usually **lasts** for one month. The weather is very cold—temperatures can go down to –35°C.

Artists use different tools to make shapes from the **hard** ice and snow. The artists show their work in two main areas. "Sun Island" has **huge** snow **sculptures** of people and animals. "Ice and Snow World" has ice sculptures of buildings. At night, these buildings light up with **bright**, colorful lights.

Visitors can do many activities, such as skating and playing on the slides. For those who really like the cold, there's also a swimming **competition** in the Songhua River!

ABOUT THE PHOTO

This photo shows the Harbin Ice and Snow festival in Harbin, China. This winter event attracts tourists and locals alike to see the intricately sculpted structures. During the night, these structures are illuminated, making them look like crystal palaces. With a different theme each year, competitors transform the location into a completely different world every year. In 2007, the festival was awarded the Guinness World Record for Largest Snow Sculpture and is currently still the record-holder. The sculpture, entitled *Romantic Feelings*, was 35 meters tall and 200 meters long. It took a team of 600 sculptors from 40 different countries to create the sculpture. (See **CONTENT NOTE** for more information.)

Additional Activities to Use with the Reading

Additional Comprehension Questions

1 *How many kinds of sculptures are there?* (three—people, animals, and buildings)

2 *Which sculptures have colorful lights?* (the buildings)

3 *Was the festival held in 1964?* (Yes. It started in 1963.)

Grammar (Focused)

Have students look at the article and find the word *on* that is used in the same way as in the chart on page 140 (*on January 5th*).

Have students find uses of *for* with a period of time (*for one month*).

You might want to have students find *for* in the last paragraph and explain that rather than specifying time, this preposition identifies people who are participating in the festival.

Have students find the uses of *in* related to time (*in 1963*).

Then ask them to find the other instances of *in* (*in northeast China, in two main areas, in the Songhua River*). Have them decide how these are different than *in 1963* (*in* shows location in these cases).

Vocabulary Building

Tell students that when we meet people who don't speak the same languages as us, we must use gestures and other creative ways to communicate.

Tell students they are going to play a game guessing words from the article. Explain that they will get into small groups and they will take turns using gestures, but no words. Tell students that the rest of the group must guess what the activity is. Explain that group members should call out possible answers freely, but the person doing the gestures should not stop until the correct activity is guessed.

You might want to have students go through the article and decide which words can be used (e.g., *tourist*, *snow*, *party*, *cold*, *artist*, *tool*, *sculpture*, *people*, *animal*, *building*, *skate*, *swim*).

Provide an example by telling students you will do gestures and they must guess the activity. For example, use your hands to outline the shape of a building. Continue until students guess *building*.

Have students get into small groups and play the game. Then, ask students which words were the easiest and the most difficult to guess and why.

COMPREHENSION

A EXAM PRACTICE

The focus of multiple-choice questions varies.

Both **main idea** and **purpose** items require students to think about the entire passage. As a global question, students need to think about what the author (speaker) wants to emphasize. One way to do this is to ask for an alternative title or the main topic. Students can usually eliminate any distractor that is only applicable to one part of the passage.

Detail items test students' understanding of the information in the reading (or listening) passage. Although the passage and question may use the same words, synonyms are also used. These items are generally more straightforward and less complex than other types of multiple-choice questions.

Have students read the questions to themselves and circle the correct answers.

Check answers.

B If necessary, remind students that the main idea is in the center of a word web, and the further the information is from the center, the more detailed it is.

Have students complete the word web.

Have students write their answers on the board to check answers.

C CRITICAL THINKING

As students follow along, read the statements aloud.

Have students get into pairs and make comparisons. Encourage pairs that finish quickly to find more differences.

Have pairs share their ideas with the class, encouraging students to present ideas that have not yet been given.

COMPREHENSION

A Answer the questions about *The Harbin Ice and Snow Festival*.

1 PURPOSE Which of the following does the article NOT do?

ⓐ compare different winter festivals

b describe the attractions at a winter festival

c give background information about a winter festival

2 INFERENCE Most people at the festival are likely to wear ______.

a costumes ⓑ warm clothes c swimwear

3 REFERENCE The word *It* in line 6 refers to ______.

a Harbin b China ⓒ the festival

4 INFERENCE Which of these sculptures is likely to be in "Ice and Snow World"?

a a woman ⓑ a bridge c a bird

5 DETAIL Which activity is NOT mentioned in the article?

ⓐ skiing b skating c swimming

B Complete the word web. Use information from the article.

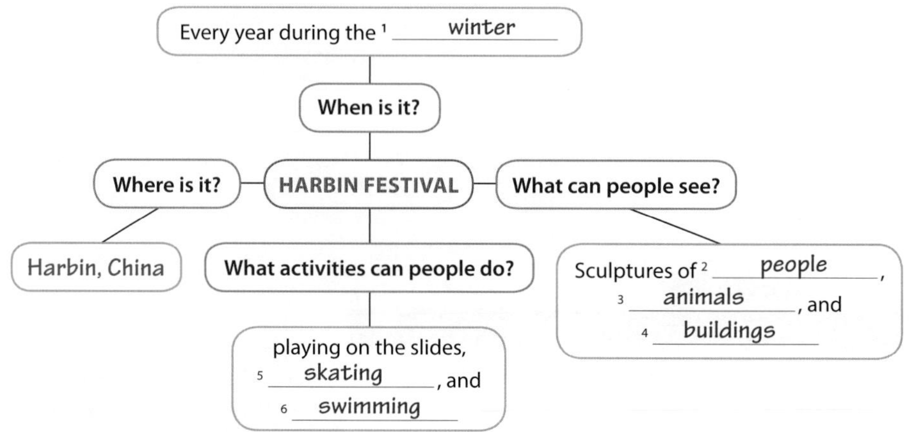

C CRITICAL THINKING Synthesizing **Talk with a partner.** Compare the Harbin Festival with the Day of the Dead. Name three differences. *Answers will vary.*

VOCABULARY

A As students follow along in their books, read the bold words aloud. Have students find the words in the **READING** passage. (Note that *starts* appears as *started* in the passage.)

Have students circle the correct words to complete the sentences.

Check answers.

IDIOM

Read the sentence and answer choices aloud, as students follow along. Have students guess whether the answer is *a* or *b* (a). Explain that the idiom is often used in informal English when someone (suddenly) doesn't have the courage to do something. Tell students it is often used to talk about weddings, but it can also be used when discussing other big events. Give the following example:

VOCABULARY

A Find the words below in the article. Then circle the correct answers.

1 The song **lasts** / **starts** for three minutes.
2 I can't eat this bread—it's really **hard** / **bright**.
3 London is a **hard** / **huge** city of more than 8 million people.
4 There is a soccer **sculpture** / **competition** in my school every year.
5 It's a good day to go to the beach. It's **bright** / **huge** and sunny outside.
6 The statue of David is a famous **sculpture** / **competition** in Italy.

IDIOM

If you get cold feet, you feel ______.
a afraid
b tired

B Read the information below. Then complete the sentences.

We can make phrasal verbs with *go*.
go over: look again
go back: return
go through: experience something
go down: become smaller in number

1 I left my wallet at home. I need to *go back* and get it.
2 I always *go over* my notes before a test.
3 It's hot during the day, but temperatures *go down* at night.
4 All workers in the company *go through* one week of training before they start work.

WRITING

A Read the beginning of a description of a festival.

B Choose a festival you celebrated recently. Make notes about it. What kind of festival is it? When was it? What did you do?

C Write a postcard. Tell your friend about the festival.
Answers will vary.

POSTCARD

Hi Sergio,

I celebrated Chinese New Year last month. Chinese New Year is a national holiday in my country. I ate a lot of good food and I spent time with my family and friends. I also watched a parade on TV ...

Unit 12 147

The night before the big competition she was so worried. She was getting cold feet and wanted to give up. Her coach reminded her of all her training, and she decided to run the race. She got first place!

B As students follow along, read the information in the box aloud. Have students write the correct phrasal verbs to complete the sentences.

Check answers as a class.

WRITING

Tell students they are going to write a postcard to a friend about a festival. Ask them if they have ever sent a postcard, and if so, where they sent it from and who they sent it to.

A As students follow along, read the example postcard aloud. Point out that it starts with *Hi Sergio*. Remind them this is called a greeting.

Point out that the next paragraph starts on a new line. Have students identify the information the author gives (what festival, when the festival was, why the festival is important, what the person did).

B As students follow along in their books, read the questions aloud.

Have students choose a festival they (recently) celebrated and make notes about it.

SUPPORT Tell students that a word web can help them generate ideas so that it is easier to write information clearly. Have students make a word web for the example postcard.

Center circle: *Chinese New Year*

Circles from center circle: *last month*, *national holiday*, *things I did*

Circle from things did: *ate*, *spent time with family and friends*, *watched parade on TV*

Have students make a word web to brainstorm ideas about their festival.

C Have students use their notes from **B**, and other ideas, to write their postcards.

Give them a time limit for finishing the postcard, and set a minimum number of sentences they must write (e.g., six).

SUPPORT Have students use the word webs they made in **B** as they do the writing task. Explain that they don't have to use all of the ideas from their word web. Emphasize they should choose the ones that will make their postcard interesting.

CONTENT NOTE: CHINESE NEW YEAR

Chinese New Year (the Lunar New Year) is also called the Spring Festival, and it is celebrated across China, Southeast Asia, and in countries with large Chinese populations. Red, which is a symbol of prosperity and happiness, is used for decorations and is also a popular clothing color during the Chinese New Year.

VIDEO

As students follow along, read the title aloud. Tell students they are going to watch a video about the Harbin Ice and Snow Festival.

BEFORE YOU WATCH

Ask students what they remember about the festival from the **READING**. Have them circle their ideas.

Check answers.

OPTIONAL Ask students to brainstorm words they think they will hear during the video. After watching the video, check their predictions.

WHILE YOU WATCH

A Tell students they will watch the video and they should circle **T** if the statement is true and **F** if it is false. As they follow along, read the statements aloud.

▶ 12.2 Play Video 12.2. Play the video again, if necessary.

Check answers.

B Explain to students that they will watch the video again, and they should match the photos of the sculptures to the names. As students follow along, read the names of the sculptures aloud.

▶ 12.2 Play Video 12.2. Play the video again, if necessary.

Check answers.

OPTIONAL Explain shadowing to students. (See **TEACHING NOTE.**) Because students may have focused on the content as they watched the video, have students watch the video again and pay attention to the delivery.

▶ 12.2 Play the video again, as necessary, until students feel comfortable attempting to shadow it. Emphasize that they may not be able to mimic the video perfectly but they are developing fluency through the activity.

VIDEO **ABOUT THE VIDEO** Thousands of tourists go to the Harbin Ice and Snow Festival.

WINTER ***WONDERLAND***

Before You Watch

Complete the sentences. What do you remember about the Harbin Ice and Snow Festival?

1 It's in **northeast** / **southeast** China. (northeast circled)
2 It takes place every **year** / **two years.** (year circled)
3 It lasts for a **week** / **month** in the winter. (month circled)

While You Watch

A ▶ 12.2 **Watch the video.** Circle **T** for true or **F** for false.

1 The Harbin Ice and Snow Festival is the world's biggest ice festival. **(T)** F
2 Workers get ice from another city to build the sculptures. T **(F)**
3 Visitors pay money to go into the theme park. **(T)** F

B ▶ 12.2 **Watch again.** Match the photos of the sculptures to their names (**a–d**).

a Colosseum **b** Temple of Heaven **c** Forbidden City **d** snowmen

1 a

2 d

3 c

4 b

After You Watch

Talk with a partner. Do you want to go to this festival? Why or why not? *Answers will vary.*

Visitors ride bumper cars at the Harbin Festival.

TEACHING NOTE: SHADOWING

Shadowing is a technique that helps students practice their pronunciation, rhythm, and intonation. With shadowing, students listen to a passage at least once. Students then listen again and try to simultaneously mimic (repeat) what they are hearing. They sometimes look at a script while doing this.

AFTER YOU WATCH

Tell students they are going to get into pairs and talk about the video.

As students follow along in their books, read the questions aloud.

Have them get into pairs and do the task.

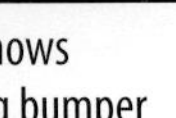

ABOUT THE PHOTO

This photo shows visitors riding bumper cars on the frozen Songhua River at the Harbin Ice and Snow Festival in Harbin, China. The river is the fifth largest river in China. During winter, cold temperatures as low as –35°C allow for the river to freeze and turn into 1-meter-thick ice. This allows visitors to ride bumper cars, ice skate, and even ride dog sleds on the river. Horse-drawn carriages can also be seen transporting people across the slippery ice.

EW

A Match the phrases.

1 put up	a gift
2 watch	a meal
3 receive	time
4 prepare	a festival
5 spend	fireworks
6 celebrate	decorations

B Complete the sentences. Circle the correct answers.

1 I don't go to school **on** / **during** the summer.
2 I went to the United States **on** / **in** June.
3 My friend's party is **for** / **on** Saturday.
4 I was at my friend's house **for** / **during** three hours.
5 My sister's birthday is **in** / **on** March 22nd.
6 My friend always goes to his grandmother's house **for** / **in** Christmas.

C Complete the sentences. Circle the correct answers.

1 The number of car accidents went **down** / **over** last year.
2 I forgot the details of the plan. Can we go **back** / **over** it again?
3 I go **back** / **down** to my hometown every year to visit my family.
4 He's going **down** / **through** a difficult time because he can't find a job.

SELF CHECK Now I can ...

- ☐ describe festivals I celebrate
- ☐ use language for talking about when things happened
- ☐ talk about famous festivals around the world

REVIEW

Explain to students that they are going to review the material from the unit and this will help them remember what they have studied.

A Explain that activity **A** reviews vocabulary from the unit. Have students match the words to make phrases about festival activities.

Check answers as a class.

B Explain that activity **B** reviews the grammar from the unit. Have students circle the correct words to complete the sentences. Have students get into pairs and check answers, before you randomly call on students to give the answers.

C Remind students that they studied phrasal verbs in **VOCABULARY** activity **B**. Have them circle the correct words to complete the sentences.

Check answers.

SELF CHECK

These *I can* statements provide vital feedback on students' perceived ability to use the language from the unit. If you find students are reluctant to check that they can do the skills, consider asking them to rate themselves from 1 (not very confident) to 3 (very confident).

SUPPORT If students lack confidence to put a check next to each statement, have them get into pairs. Tell them they will make a board game that reviews the material in the unit.

Have students get into pairs, take out a large piece of paper, and draw a series of boxes that make a "path" from the beginning to the end of the game. Explain that they will write questions inside these boxes. Encourage students to be creative and make the game board any shape. Tell them they can add *go back* and *lose a turn* squares if they want.

Give an example on the board: *What did you do ______ New Year's Eve?* (answer: *on*)

Have students review the unit as they make content, discussion, grammar, and vocabulary questions, one in each box. Point out that they also need to make an answer key on another piece of paper. You might want to explain that discussion questions have no correct answer, so an answer is not required.

When pairs have made their game boards, demonstrate flipping a coin to determine whether to move one or two spaces on the game board.

Have pairs trade game boards and play the game they receive. Encourage students to use their books as they play the game and review anything that they do not have confidence about.

UNIT 3 COMMUNICATION

Draw your partner's picture below. Compare the pictures.

UNIT 4 LANGUAGE FOCUS E

Work with a partner. Ask and answer questions to make your partner's family tree. Look at Lisa's family tree below to help you.

Lisa's Family Tree

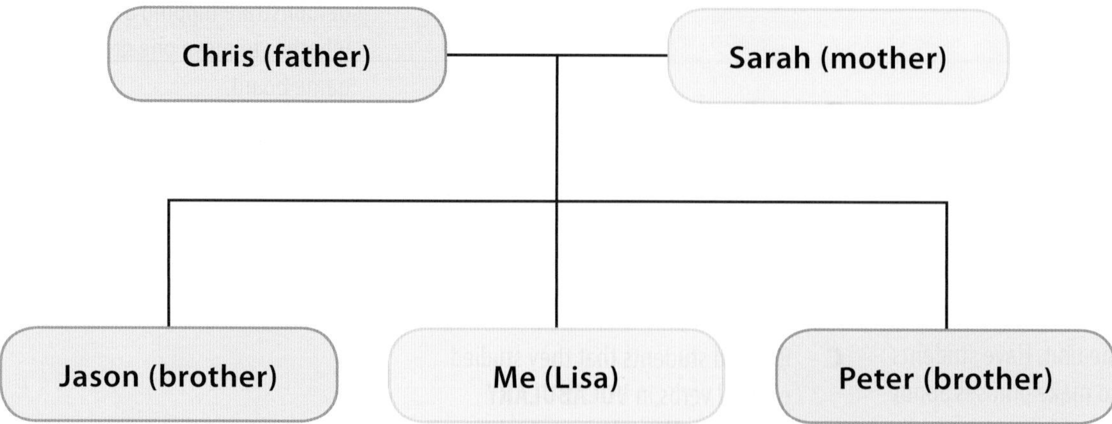

UNIT 5 LANGUAGE FOCUS E

A **Work with a partner.** Ask them what foods they like and don't like. Remember your partner's answers.

B **Play tic-tac-toe.** One student is **X**, and the other is **O**. Take turns to make sentences. Say what your partner likes or doesn't like. When you make a true sentence, draw your letter on a square.

You don't like milk.
That's right. I don't like milk.

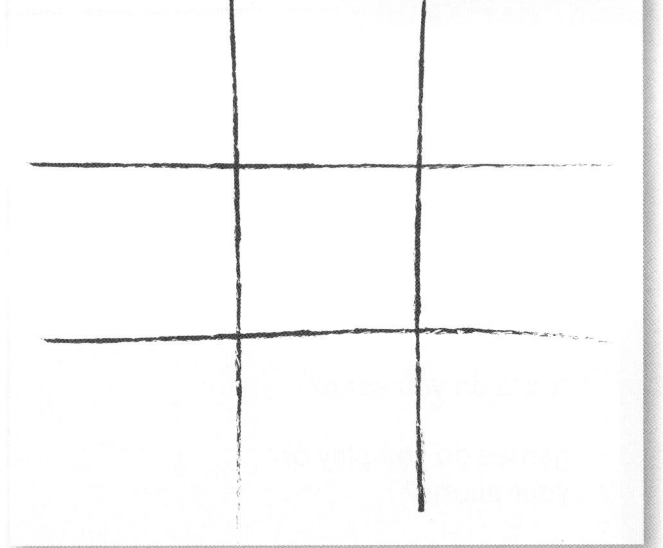

UNIT 5 COMMUNICATION

Work in a group. Create a meal plan. Use food that everyone in your group likes.

What do you like for breakfast?
I like bread.

UNIT 9 PREVIEW

Complete the survey below. Then count your points and see your results.

SURVEY

IN ONE DAY HOW MANY ...	0–2	3–6	7 or more
texts do you send?	☐	☐	☐
games do you play on your phone?	☐	☐	☐
hours do you spend on your computer?	☐	☐	☐
times do you check messages on your phone?	☐	☐	☐
friends do you chat with online?	☐	☐	☐
phone calls do you make?	☐	☐	☐

Points	0–2 = 1 point 3–6 = 2 points 7 or more = 3 points

SURVEY RESULTS

1–7 points: You don't spend much time using technology. You like to spend more time with people around you.

8–14 points: You balance your time well between the online world and the real world.

≥ 15 points: You find it very hard to live without technology, even for a few hours!

UNIT 9 COMMUNICATION

Look at the picture below. Ask and answer questions about the pictures.

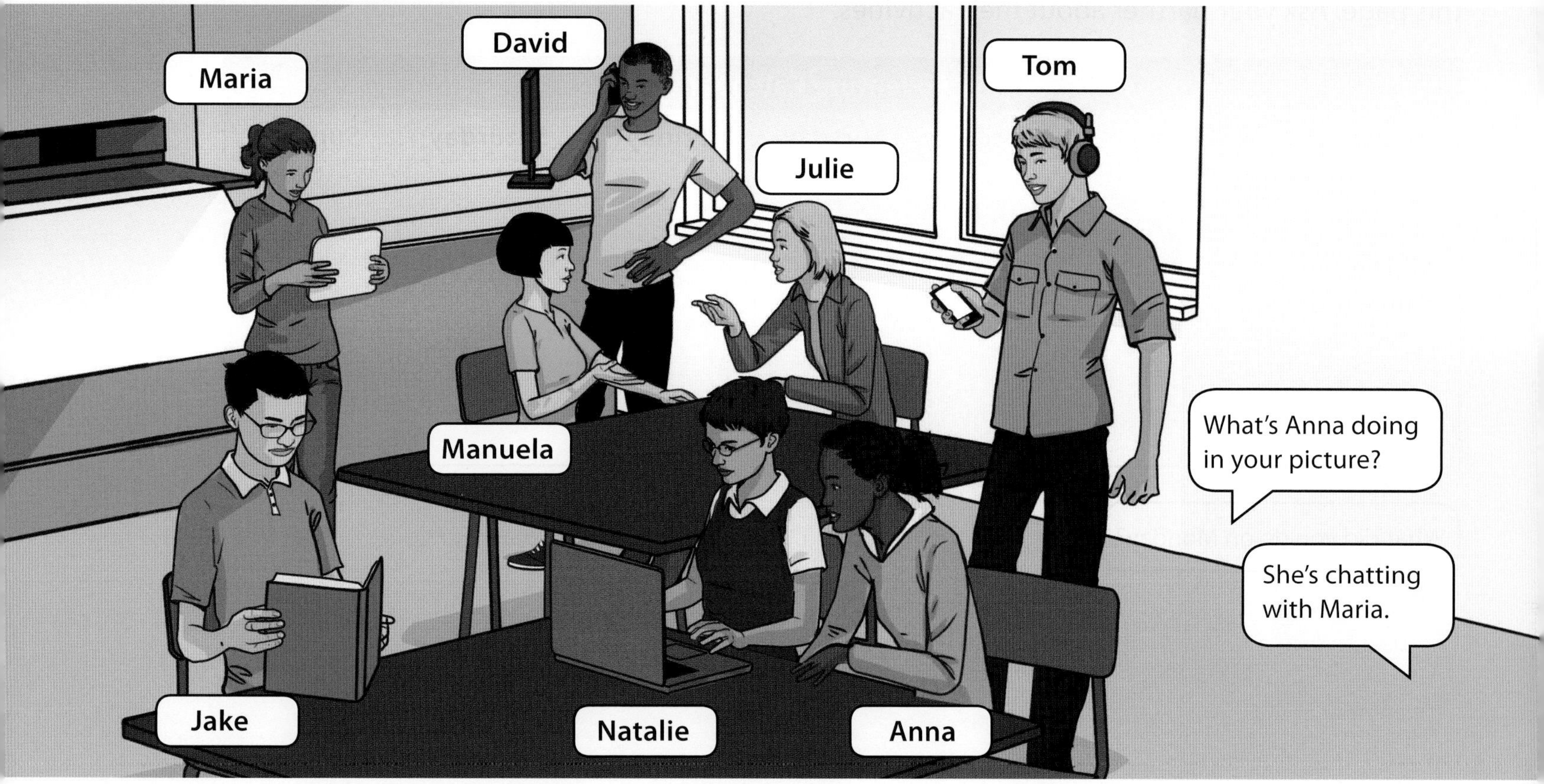

Maria
David
Tom
Julie
Manuela
What's Anna doing in your picture?
She's chatting with Maria.
Jake
Natalie
Anna

UNIT 10 COMMUNICATION

Complete the map. Ask and answer questions about the temperatures and weather conditions.

18°C
COLOMBIA
sunny 27°C
PERU
BRAZIL
cloudy 17°C
26°C
PARAGUAY
16°C
CHILE
ARGENTINA
rainy 14°C
What's the temperature like in Colombia?

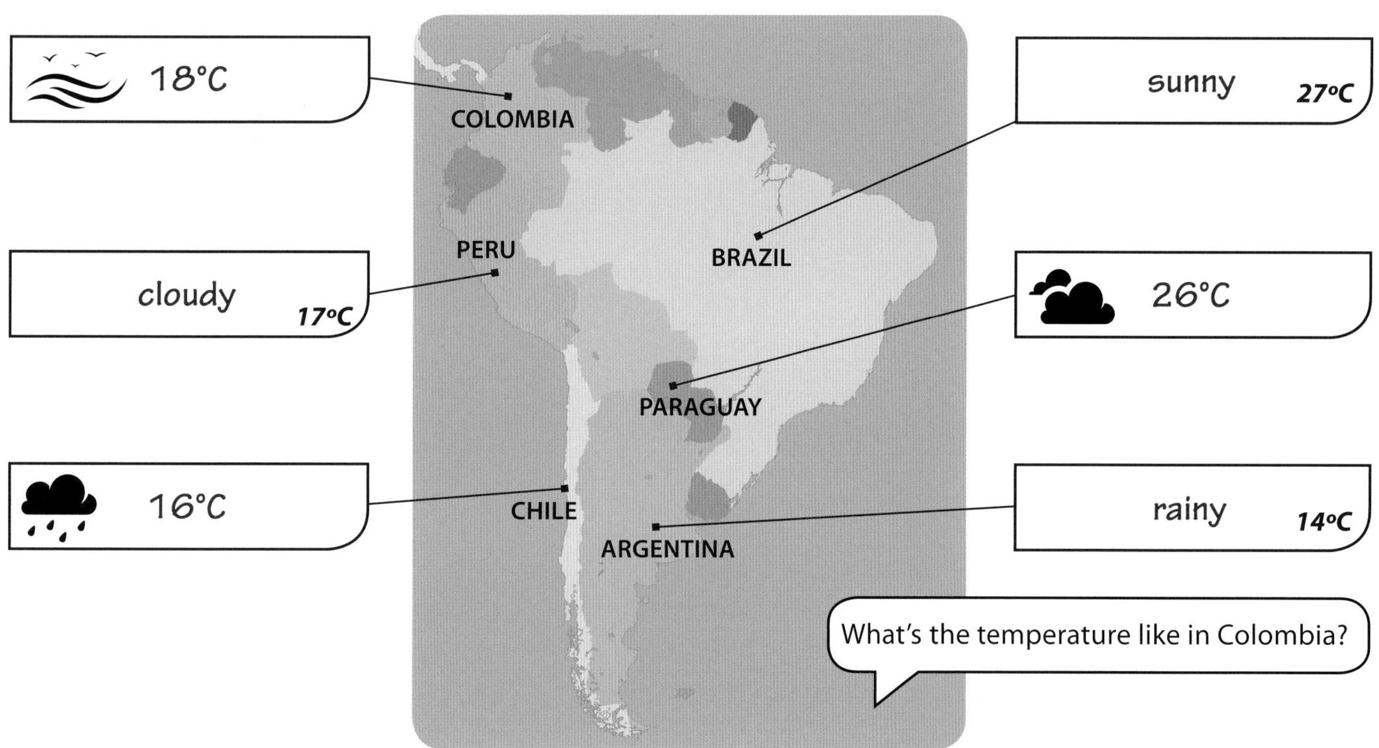

UNIT 11 COMMUNICATION

Complete an adventure calendar with activities you did. Write your own ideas in the calendar on this page. Ask your partner about their activities.

My Adventure Calendar						
Monday	**Tuesday**	**Wednesday**	**Thursday**	**Friday**	**Saturday**	**Sunday**
visited a museum						

What did you do on Monday?

I cycled in the park.

WORKBOOK ANSWER KEY

UNIT 1

Preview

A

1 writer
2 movie
3 video game
4 singer
5 app
6 TV show

B

1 app
2 movie
3 singer
4 TV show
5 video game
6 writer

C

Person: writer, singer

Thing: app, movie, video game, TV show

Language Focus

A

1 your
2 His
3 Who's
4 My
5 her
6 What's

B

1 Her favorite color is green.
2 Her favorite movie is *Aladdin*.
3 Her favorite singer is Bruno Mars.
4 His favorite video game is *World of Warcraft*.
5 His favorite color is white.
6 His favorite movie is *Star Wars*.

C

1 c
2 d
3 a
4 b

The Real World

A

1 baseball
2 table tennis
3 soccer
4 basketball

B

Asia: Japan, China

North America: the United States

South America: Brazil

C

1 F
2 T
3 T

Reading

A Francisco

B

1 b
2 a
3 a
4 c
5 b

C

1 São Paulo / Brazil
2 Real Madrid
3 favorite singer

Vocabulary

A

1 love
2 travel
3 watch
4 difficult
5 easy
6 interesting

B

Nouns: app, table tennis, China

Verbs: travel, is, are

Adjectives: exciting, difficult, interesting

Writing

B Answers will vary.

C Answers will vary.

UNIT 2

Preview

A

1 sea
2 beach
3 building
4 street
5 store
6 city

B

1 sea
2 store
3 city
4 building
5 beach
6 street

C

1 Answers will vary.
2 Answers will vary.

Language Focus

A

1 is
2 aren't
3 are
4 They're
5 streets
6 're not

B

1 Is your house new?
No, it's not.

2 Is Polihale Beach in Hawaii amazing?
Yes, it is.

3 Is your city clean?
Yes, it is.

4 Is the store famous?
No, it isn't.

5 Are these streets popular?
Yes, they are. Tourists love them!

6 Is the design of the Louvre Museum interesting?
Yes, it is.

C

1 It's not very clean.
2 The style isn't popular.
3 The designs aren't new.
4 It isn't very famous.
5 They're very colorful.

The Real World

A

1 c
2 a
3 b

B

1 El Castillo; Christ the Redeemer; the Colosseum

2 the Colosseum; El Castillo; Christ the Redeemer

Reading

A b

B

1 German
2 Switzerland
3 hotel
4 Tourists
5 amazing

C Answers will vary.

Vocabulary

A

1 town
2 restaurant
3 island
4 tourists
5 hotel
6 boat

B

1 and
2 and
3 but
4 and
5 but

Writing

B Answers will vary.

C Answers will vary.

UNIT 3

Preview

A

1 frog
2 shark
3 hippo
4 giraffe
5 elephant
6 lion
7 fish
8 dolphin
9 bear
10 monkey

B

Animals on land: giraffe, monkey, elephant, lion, bear

Animals in the water: shark, fish, dolphin

Animals on land and in the water: hippo, frog

Language Focus

A

1 F
2 T
3 T
4 F
5 T
6 F

B

1 Where
2 How
3 is / 's
4 Is
5 Are

C

1 They're on the rock.
2 There are two (frogs).
3 It's next to the tree. / It's under the tree.
4 Yes, it is.
5 No, they aren't. / No, they are not.

The Real World

A

1 leopard seal
2 leopard seal
3 gentoo penguin
4 penguins
5 fish

B Answers will vary.

Reading

A b

B

cuttlefish: c, f

mimic octopus: b, e

both: a, d

C

1 an octopus
2 cuttlefish
3 mimic octopus

Vocabulary

A

1 hide
2 body
3 the same as
4 seaweed
5 branches
6 leaves

B

1 in the middle
2 on the right
3 on the left

Writing

B

1 an
2 a
3 a
4 an

C

1 There is a giraffe.
2 There is an octopus.
3 There is a lion.
4 There is a hippo.
5 There is an owl.

UNIT 4

Preview

A

1 me

2 brother

3 father

4 mother

5 sister

B

female: mother, sister, niece, daughter, aunt

male: father, brother, nephew, son, uncle

both: cousin, grandparents, parents

C

1 aunt

2 uncle

Language Focus

A

1 has

2 doesn't have

3 does

4 Do

5 have

6 don't have

7 have

B

1 They are Jenny and Ann's parents.

2 No, she doesn't.

3 Does Ann have any brothers?

4 Do Ruth and Peter have any daughters?

5 Yes, she does.

C

1 b

2 d

3 a

4 e

5 c

The Real World

A

1 Beth

2 Andre and Rebecca

3 Paola

4 Matteo and Massimo

5 Rebecca

6 Andre

B

1 have three

2 has two

3 have four

4 doesn't have any / has no

Reading

A b

B

1 c

2 b

3 b

4 a

5 c

C

1 Answers will vary.

2 Answers will vary.

3 Answers will vary.

Vocabulary

1 d

2 f

3 b

4 c

5 a

6 e

B

1 great-uncle

2 great-grandfather

3 great-grandmother

4 great-aunt

Writing

B

grandfather: Bob

grandmother: Sue

uncle: Steve

mother: Ruth

father: Jack

me: Jessie

sister: Leah

C Answers will vary.

UNIT 5

Preview

A

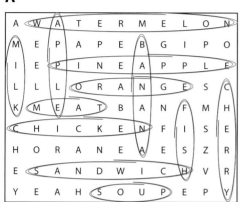

A	W	A	T	E	R	M	E	L	O	N
M	E	P	A	P	E	B	G	I	P	O
I	E	P	I	N	E	A	P	P	L	E
L	L	L	O	R	A	N	G	E	S	C
K	M	E	A	T	B	A	N	F	M	H
C	H	I	C	K	E	N	F	I	S	E
H	O	R	A	N	E	A	E	S	Z	R
E	S	A	N	D	W	I	C	H	V	R
Y	E	A	H	S	O	U	P	E	P	Y

B

Countable Nouns: apple, banana, watermelon, pineapple, cherry, orange, sandwich

Uncountable Nouns: meat, milk, fish, chicken, soup

C

apple, banana, cherry, orange, pineapple, watermelon

Language Focus

A

1 like

2 likes

3 doesn't like

4 don't like

5 like

6 don't like; like

B

1 like

2 don't

3 Does

4 does

5 Do

6 do

C

1 I'm hungry! Let's have lunch.

2 Do you like meat?

3 No, I don't, but I like vegetables.

4 Do you like rice?

5 Yes, I do. I really like it.

6 Let's have rice and vegetables.

The Real World

A

1 France

2 South Korea

3 India

B

	South Korea	France	India
bread		✓	✓
curry			✓
meat	✓	✓	
rice	✓		✓
soup	✓		
vegetables	✓	✓	
cheese		✓	

Reading

A b

B

1 a

2 a

3 c

4 b

5 c

C

1 Answers will vary.

2 Answers will vary.

Vocabulary

A

1 real

2 made of

3 builds

4 fresh

5 landscape

B

1 c

2 a

3 b

C

1 fresh

2 homemade

3 fast

Writing

B a

C Answers will vary.

UNIT 6

Preview

A

1 b

2 c

3 a

4 e

5 f

6 d

B

1 8:15

2 7:00

3 11:30

4 1:30

5 12:15

6 5:45

C

1 never

2 sometimes

3 often

4 usually

5 always

Language Focus

1 does

2 do

3 eat

4 go

5 start

6 have

B

1 gets up

2 goes home

3 has

4 does homework

5 goes to bed

C Answers will vary.

The Real World

A b

B

Name of organization: Experience Aviation

Founder of organization: Barrington Irving

Purpose of project: Build a car

Number of students: More than 50

Amount of materials used: 1,000 car pieces

Time taken: 18 weeks

Reading

A school subjects; after school activities

B

1 a

2 b

3 c

4 c

5 a

C

8:30 a.m., Mon-Fri: goes to school

9:00 a.m., Sat-Sun: gets up

12 p.m., Mon-Fri: has lunch

12:45 p.m., Mon: studies geography

12:45 p.m., Tue: studies art

12:45 p.m., Wed: studies science

3:30 p.m., Mon-Fri: finishes school / goes home

Vocabulary

A

1 finish

2 enough

3 get married

4 dream

5 history

6 early

B Answers will vary.

Writing

B Answers will vary.

C Answers will vary.

UNIT 7

Preview

A

1 swim
2 climb
3 jump
4 dance
5 tool
6 fly
7 drums
8 piano

B

Actions: swim, climb, jump, dance, fly
Things: tool, drums, piano

C

1 a mountain
2 a tool
3 in the sky
4 the drums

Language Focus

A

1 can
2 Can
3 can't
4 can
5 can
6 play
7 can

B

1 Yes, he can.
2 No, she can't.
3 They can sing.
4 Can Paula
5 (Answers will vary.); Yes, I can. / No, I can't.
6 can you do; (Answers will vary.)

C

1 b
2 c
3 a
4 d

The Real World

A Answers will vary.

B

1 b
2 c
3 a
4 b

Reading

A a

B

1 NG
2 F
3 NG
4 T

C

Tigers: d
Orangutans: c, f
Both: a, b, e

Vocabulary

A

1 points
2 zoo
3 hot
4 smart
5 communicate
6 understand

B

1 c
2 d
3 a
4 b

C

1 fire
2 plans
3 dinner
4 call

Writing

B Answers will vary.

C Answers will vary.

UNIT 8

Preview

A

1 hat
2 shirt
3 shoe
4 T-shirt
5 wallet
6 backpack

B

1 hat
2 T-shirt
3 shoe
4 wallet
5 shirt
6 backpack

Language Focus

A

1 I'd like
2 like to see
3 to see; I'd
4 much; It's

B

1 like
2 I'd
3 is
4 It's
5 are
6 They're
7 How
8 Would

C

1 They're $8.
2 How much is the T-shirt?
3 It's red.
4 How much are the sneakers?
5 Would you like to; sweatshirts

The Real World

A

1 a buyer and a seller
2 cheap
3 after discussing more than one price

B

1 $20
2 $10
3 $17
4 $15

Reading

A

Possible answers: watch a movie, go ice skating, eat, shop, visit the aquarium, swim, play in the waterpark (any three)

B

1 a
2 b
3 b
4 c
5 c

C

1 Answers will vary.
2 Answers will vary.

Vocabulary

A

1 instead
2 creative
3 Customers
4 common
5 try
6 pay

B

1 wake up
2 give up
3 look up

Writing

B Answers will vary.

C Answers will vary.

UNIT 9

Preview

A

1 b

2 e

3 d

4 f

5 c

6 a

B

1 check

2 chat

3 text

4 play

5 call

6 take

Language Focus

A

1 doing; I'm

2 playing; are

3 are; texting

B

1 Who are you texting, Manuela?
I'm texting my mom.

2 Hey, Mark. What are you doing?
I'm playing games with my friend in Singapore.

3 Natalie, is Dana listening to music.
Yes, she is.

4 Are your brothers watching a movie now?
No, they aren't. They're playing basketball.

C

1 Yes, they are.

2 What is / What's Jake doing?

3 No, she isn't.

4 What's Tom doing?

5 She's chatting (with Anna).

The Real World

A c

B

1 science

2 math

3 subjects

4 questions

5 pictures

Reading

A b

B

1 b

2 a

3 c

4 c

5 a

C

1 F

2 T

3 F

4 T

5 T

Vocabulary

A

1 repair

2 plan

3 machine

4 instructions

5 programs

6 materials

B

1 everywhere

2 everyone

3 everything

Writing

B Answers will vary.

C Answers will vary.

UNIT 10

Preview

A

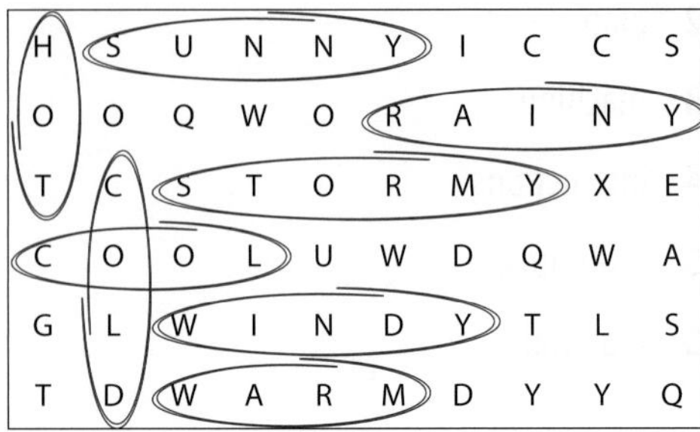

B

Weather: rainy, sunny, stormy, windy

Temperature: cool, cold, warm, hot

C Answers will vary.

Language Focus

A

1 What's
2 It's
3 How
4 It's
5 is
6 is

B

1 No, it isn't.
2 It's rainy.
3 It's stormy.
4 It's 14 degrees.

C

1 What's the weather like in May?
2 What's the weather like today?
3 How hot is it in the summer?

The Real World

A b

B

1 bio-logging
2 green turtles
3 study what turtles do in the ocean

Reading

A b

B

1 cyclone
2 typhoon
3 strong winds
4 storms
5 heavy rain
6 often calm
7 no rain sometimes
8 can sometimes see the sky

C

1 warm
2 ice
3 the opposite direction to

Vocabulary

A

1 projects
2 temperature
3 views
4 upload
5 launch
6 record

B

1 I like to hang out with my friends on the weekend.
2 My family usually goes out to the beach on Sundays.
3 Look out! That's dangerous.
4 I don't know, so I want to find out the answer.

Writing

B Answers will vary.

C

1 Thanks. OK. I'm in London. It's sunny but very cold today.
2 I'm in Sydney. It's hot and cloudy today.
3 Answers will vary.
4 What's the temperature like today? Here, it's 2 degrees, but usually it's 9 degrees.
5 Really? Here, it's 30 degrees, but usually it's 24 degrees.
6 Answers will vary.

UNIT 11

Preview

A

1 camping

2 cycling

3 museum

4 sightseeing

5 hotel

6 hiking

B

Places: museum, hotel

Activities: camping, cycling, sightseeing, hiking

Language Focus

A

1 was

2 went

3 was

4 did

5 walked

6 ate

7 Did

8 were

B

1 I went to New Zealand

2 When did you go

3 I went to the beach

4 I went hiking

5 No, I didn't

C

1 He visited an art museum.

2 No, he didn't.

3 He went home on August 12th.

The Real World

A He went camping.

B

1 T

2 F

3 T

4 T

Reading

A a

B

1 c

2 b

3 b

4 a

5 c

C

1 Answers will vary.

2 Answers will vary.

Vocabulary

A

1 d

2 c

3 f

4 e

5 b

6 a

B

1 useful

2 colorful

3 careful

4 helpful

Writing

B Answers will vary.

C Answers will vary.

UNIT 12

Preview

A

1 festival
2 decorations
3 meal
4 fireworks
5 parade
6 gift

B

1 prepared
2 watched
3 put
4 received
5 watched
6 went

Language Focus

A

1 during
2 on
3 on
4 in
5 for
6 on
7 in

B

1 spent
2 had
3 put
4 ate
5 swam

C

1 What did you do for Chinese New Year?
2 When is your mom's birthday?
3 Where did you go on February 5th?

The Real World

A

1 1st
2 small faces
3 eight

B

1 c
2 b
3 a

Reading

A c

B b; c; a; d; e

C

1 a
2 b
3 a
4 b
5 c

Vocabulary

A

1 hard
2 sculptures
3 last
4 competition
5 bright
6 huge

B

1 back
2 over
3 down
4 through

Writing

B Hi! I'm from Munich, Germany. This is a photo from Oktoberfest. We celebrate this festival every year in September or October. Tourists from around the world come to celebrate, too. It's an amazing festival.

The festival started over 200 years ago. It lasts for about 16 days. During the festival, people sometimes wear beautiful costumes. It's an old tradition. They meet friends, family, and relatives. They eat special food. It's a fun day!

C Answers will vary.

CREDITS

Photo Credits

Cover Achim Meurer, **iv** (from top to bottom) AP Images/Tony Avelar; marchello74/iStock/Getty Images; Richard Du Toit/Minden Pictures; Jekaterina Nikitina/DigitalVision/Getty Images; Prisma by Dukas/Universal Images Group/Getty Images; Robert Daemmrich Photography Inc/Corbis Historical/ Getty Images, **v** (from top to bottom) National News/Zuma Press/London/Great Britain; Catherine Karnow/National Geographic Image Collection; Mike Theiss/National Geographic Image Collection; Julie Mayfeng/National Geographic Image Collection; Robert Lang Photography/Moment/Getty Images; Kjersti Joergensen/Alamy Stock Photo, **xix** 24Novembers/Shutterstock.com, **xxvii** SDI Productions/Getty Images, **6–7** AP Images/Tony Avelar, **7** (tl) (tc) (tr) (cl) WonderfulPixel/Shutterstock.com; (c) VoodooDot/Shutterstock.com, **9** NightAndDayImages/E+/Getty Images, **10** (t) Johannes Simon/Getty Images Sport/Getty Images; (bl1) (bl2) (bl3) (bl4) Bioraven/Shutterstock.com; (br) encikAn/Shutterstock.com, **12–13** Susan Seubert, **13** Susan Seubert, **15** Dragan Milovanovic/Shutterstock.com, **16–17** Sompop Srinophan/Moment/Getty Images, **18–19** marchello74/iStock/Getty Images, **18** (bl1) anthonycz/Shutterstock.com; (bl2) Lenin Graphics/Shutterstock.com; (bc1) Kittichai/Shutterstock. com; (bc2) Indayani/Shutterstock.com; (br1) bioraven/Shutterstock.com; (br2) jehsomwang/Shutterstock.com, **21** John Coletti/Photolibrary/Getty Images, **22** zorazhuang/E+/Getty Images, **23** efired/iStock/Getty Images, **24–25** lulejt/Shutterstock.com, **25** John W Banagan/Lonely Planet Images/Getty Images, **26** Matyas Rehak/Shutterstock.com, **27** Ian Dagnall/Alamy Stock Photo, **28** OldCatPhoto/iStock/Getty Images, **30–31** Richard Du Toit/Minden Pictures, **31** (tl) (tc) hippo/Shutterstock.com; (tr) Voropaev Vasiliy/Shutterstock.com; (cl) Helga Potter/Shutterstock.com; (c) Azar Shikhaliyev/Shutterstock.com; (cr) hippo/ Shutterstock.com, **33** George Grall/National Geographic Image Collection, **34** Paul Nicklen/National Geographic Image Collection, **35** Radmila/Shutterstock. com, **36–37** Michael Patrick O'Neill/Alamy Stock Photo, **37** Alan Murphy/BIA/Minden Pictures, **38** James Urbach/SuperStock/Alamy Stock Photo, **39** (cr) cynoclub/Shutterstock.com; (br1) Damocean/iStock/Getty Images; (br2) Dragan Milovanovic/Shutterstock.com, **40–41** Robert Harding Picture Library/ National Geographic Image Collection, **41** (cl1) M.Leheda/Shutterstock.com; (cl2) veronchick_84/Shutterstock.com; Puckung/Shutterstock.com; (cl3) Puckung/Shutterstock.com; Cristopher Orange/Shutterstock.com; (cl4) veronchick_84/Shutterstock.com; Puckung/Shutterstock.com, **42–43** Jekaterina Nikitina/DigitalVision/Getty Images, **45** Juanmonino/E+/Getty Images, **46** Annie Griffiths/National Geographic Image Collection, **48–49** David Croxford, **49** James Rubio, **50** Jacopo Ventura/iStock/Getty Images, **51** YummyBuum/Shutterstock.com, **52–53** ITV Archive, **54–55** Prisma by Dukas/Universal Images Group/Getty Images, **55** (tl) Skarida/Shutterstock.com; (tr) nilamsari/Shutterstock.com; (cl) premium design/Shutterstock.com; (cr) nikolae/Shutterstock. com; (bl) drvector/Shutterstock.com; (br) pambudi/Shutterstock.com, **57** (from left to right, top to bottom) jocic /Shutterstock.com; MaraZe/Shutterstock. com; Drozhzhina Elena/Shutterstock.com; M. Unal Ozmen/Shutterstock.com; © Cengage; jocic / Shutterstock.com; Nipaporn Panyacharoen/Shutterstock. com; New Africa/Shutterstock.com; Danny Smythe/Shutterstock.com; Nataly Studio/Shutterstock.com; Somchai Som/Shutterstock.com; Donald Erickson/ iStock/Getty Images; (b) Maximilian Stock Ltd./Photolibrary/Getty Images, **58** (t) Michael Gottschalk/Photothek/Getty Images; (bl1) Douglas Perkins; (bl2) (br1) ©"What's for Lunch" - Andrea Curtis Photographs courtesy of Yvonne Duivenvoorden Inc.; (br2) DebbiSmirnoff/E+/Getty Images, **59** Dragan Milovanovic/Shutterstock.com, **60–61** Carl Warner, **61** Carl Warner, **62** Maxim Komissarov/Shutterstock.com, **63** Charles Brutlag/Shutterstock.com; nitrub/ iStock/Getty Images, **64–65** Paulo Vilela/Shutterstock.com, **66–67** Robert Daemmrich Photography Inc/Corbis Historical/Getty Images, **67** (tl) VectorV/ Shutterstock.com; (tr) SalimCreative/Shutterstock.com; (cl) Djent/Shutterstock.com; (cr) Vector Stall/Shutterstock.com; (bl) Birdiegirl/Shutterstock.com; (br) Illizium/Shutterstock.com, **69** Katharina Hesse/laif/Redux, **70** Barrington Irving/National Geographic Image Collection, **71** ChristianChan/Shutterstock.com, **72** (tl) Nikiteev_Konstantin/Shutterstock.com, **72–73** Kate Cummings/National Geographic Image Collection, **74** Jonas Gratzer/LightRocket/Getty Images, **75** YummyBuum/Shutterstock.com, **76–77** Kakenya's Dream, **78–79** National News/ZUMA Press/London/Great Britain, **79** (tl) (tc) Kapreski/Shutterstock.com; (tr) Leremy/Shutterstock.com; (bl) RedKoala/Shutterstock.com; (bc) Hein Nouwens/Shutterstock.com; (br) Tanya Leanovich/Shutterstock.com, **81** (c) NOVICA, (bl1) RedKoala/Shutterstock.com; (bl2) masata/Shutterstock.com; (bl3) (bl4) (bl5) Leremy/Shutterstock.com, **82** Sebastien Salom Gomis/AFP/Getty Images, **83** philia/Shutterstock.com, **84–85** Laurentiu Garofeanu/Barcroft Media/Getty Images, **85** AF archive/Alamy Stock Photo, **87** (cr) Manoj Shah/Photolibrary/ Getty Images; (br) Dragan Milovanovic/Shutterstock.com, **88–89** Brian J. Skerry/National Geographic Image Collection, **90–91** Catherine Karnow/National Geographic Image Collection, **91** (tl) pnDl/Shutterstock.com; (tc) Hein Nouwens/Shutterstock.com; (tr) Aliya Salsabila/Shutterstock.com; (bl) (bc) Hein Nouwens/Shutterstock.com, **93** Africa Studio/Shutterstock.com, **94** Ira Block/National Geographic Image Collection, **95** Jarva Jar/Shutterstock.com, **96–97** Gary Burke/Moment/Getty Images, **98** Jasni/Shutterstock.com, **100** Qilai Shen/Getty Images, **102–103** Mike Theiss/National Geographic Image Collection, **103** (tl) iconspro/Shutterstock.com, (tr) (cl) (cr) Epsicons/Shutterstock.com, (bl) iconspro/Shutterstock.com, (br) Epsicons/Shutterstock.com, **106** Chris Millbern/National Geographic Image Collection, **108–109** Christian Hartmann/REUTERS, **111** (tr) fotoinfot/Shutterstock.com, (br1) sturti/E+/ Getty Images, (br2) Dragan Milovanovic/Shutterstock.com, **112–113** Lisa Maree Williams/Getty Images News/Getty Images, **114–115** Julie Mayfeng/ National Geographic Image Collection, **114** (bl1) (bl2) (bl3) (bl4) Kapreski/Shutterstock.com; (bl5) jkcDesign/Shutterstock.com, **118** (t) Yusuke Goto/ National Geographic Image Collection; (b) National Geographic Image Collection; (br) Katsufumi Sato/National Geographic Image Collection, **119** (graphic icons) Kapreski/Shutterstock.com, **120–121** Winston Yeung, **122** (t) rayisa/Shutterstock.com; (b) David Hay Jones/Science Source, **123** YummyBuum/ Shutterstock.com, **124–125** Winston Yeung, **126–127** Robert Lang Photography/Moment/Getty Images, **127** (tl) Igor Shikov/Shutterstock.com; (tc) (tr) lana rinck/Shutterstock.com; (bl) ekler/Shutterstock.com; (bc) Leremy/Shutterstock.com; (br) ekler/Shutterstock.com, **129** (b) Jeff Greenberg/Universal Images Group/Getty Images, **130** Joe Sheffer, **132–133** Andrew Evans/National Geographic Image Collection, **135** (c) Christian Bertrand/Shutterstock.com; (b) Dragan Milovanovic/Shutterstock.com, **136–137** Andrew Evans/National Geographic Image Collection, **136** (t) IhorZigor/Shutterstock.com, (c) BigBigbb1/ Shutterstock.com, **138–139** Kjersti Joergensen/Alamy Stock Photo, **139** (tl) (tr) (cl) (cr) MuchMania/Shutterstock.com; (bl) Gembuls/Shutterstock.com, **141** yodamclaren/Shutterstock.com, **142** (t) Ronaldo Schemidt/AFP/Getty Images; (b1) popicon/Shutterstock.com; (b2) REVector/Shutterstock.com; (b3) Secon/Shutterstock.com; (b4) Maksim M/Shutterstock.com, **143** (b) Tang Chhin Sothy/AFP/Getty Images, **144–145** Gavin Hellier/robertharding/Alamy Stock Photo, **147** Oleksii Arseniuk/Shutterstock.com; Saigoneer/Shutterstock.com, **148–149** aphotostory/iStock Editorial/Getty Images, **148** (cl1) (cl2) Tao Zhang/ Getty Images News/Getty Images; (cr1) Christian Kober/John Warburton-Lee Photography/Alamy Stock Photo; (cr2) Dashu Xinganling/Shutterstock.com, **151** (b) DwaFotografy/Shutterstock.com, **152** Joel_420/Shutterstock.com, **153** (graphic icons) Kapreski/Shutterstock.com

Art Credits

8, **20**, **32**, **44**, **56**, **68**, **80**, **92**, **104**, **107**, **116**, **128**, **140**, **153** (t) Ed Hammond/Deborah Wolfe Ltd, **33**, **107**, **119**, **134**, **150**, **153** (b) Peter Bull Art Studio

Text Credits

83 Adapted from "We Knew Ravens Are Smart. But Not This Smart," by Shaena Montanari: National Geographic News, July 13, 2017